Drawing for Paintings

Donald S. Vogel

Valley House Dallas, Texas

Drawing for Paintings by Donald S. Vogel
Library of Congress Number: 51-65519
ISBN 1-879154-05-6 (hardcover)
ISBN 1-879154-06-4 (softcover)
Produced by Valley House Gallery
Design: Donald S. Vogel
Typography: Eric S. Vogel
Editing: Peggy Goad
Produced by Pacific Offset Ltd, Printed in Hong Kong
 Published in the
United States by Valley House Gallery Press,
6616 Spring Valley Road,
Dallas, Texas, 75240
Phone: 214/239-2441, Facsimile: 214/239-1462

Contents

It seems to me that there are too many words about art. They flow continually, flooding the art world in an effort to explain what constitutes a work of art, to explain the why, when, and how of what the artist intended. This verbiage has become an end in itself, in competition with its subject.

This book deals with a single phase of art, and perhaps the most personal one: the drawings produced by the artist as he seeks ideas to use for a composition in another medium. These drawings express the first thoughts of the artist. They are not inhibited by the possibility that others might see them, or that they might be exhibited publicly.

I share these drawings with you, along with the resulting paintings and a minimum of words, to induce you to discover for yourself the pleasures of drawing and to learn to understand the secrets hidden in a simple line. I hope you derive pleasure from each page, for that, too, is the reason I offer them to you.

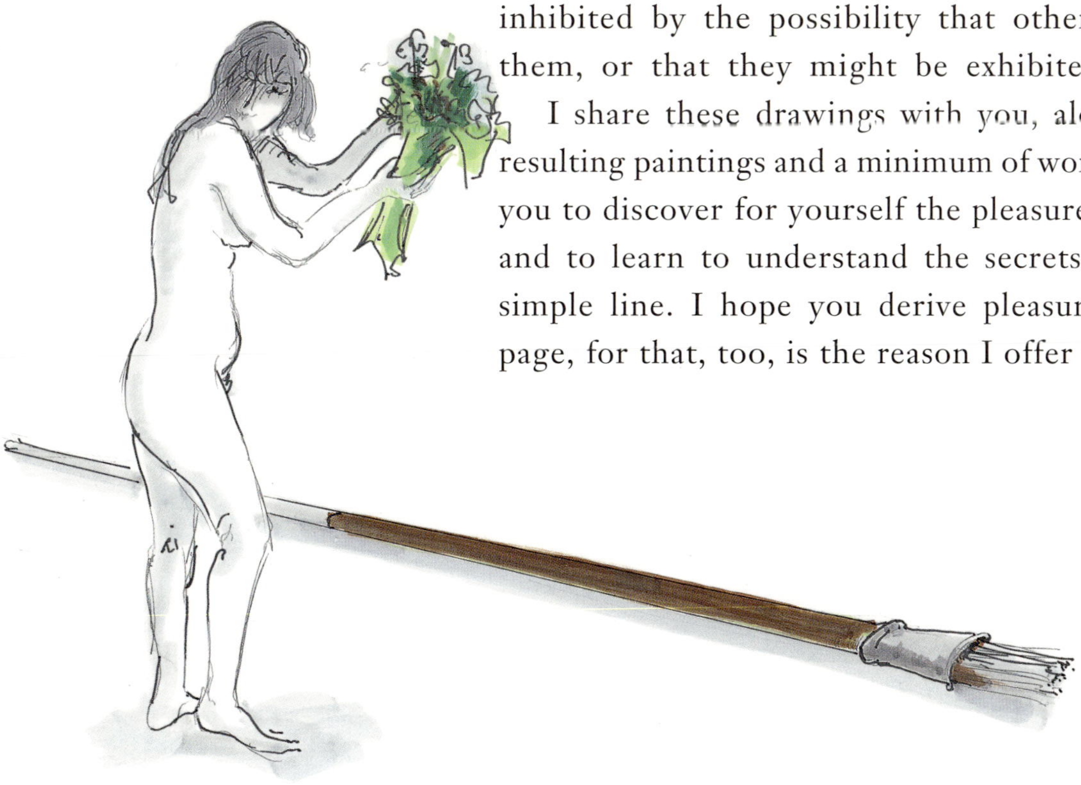

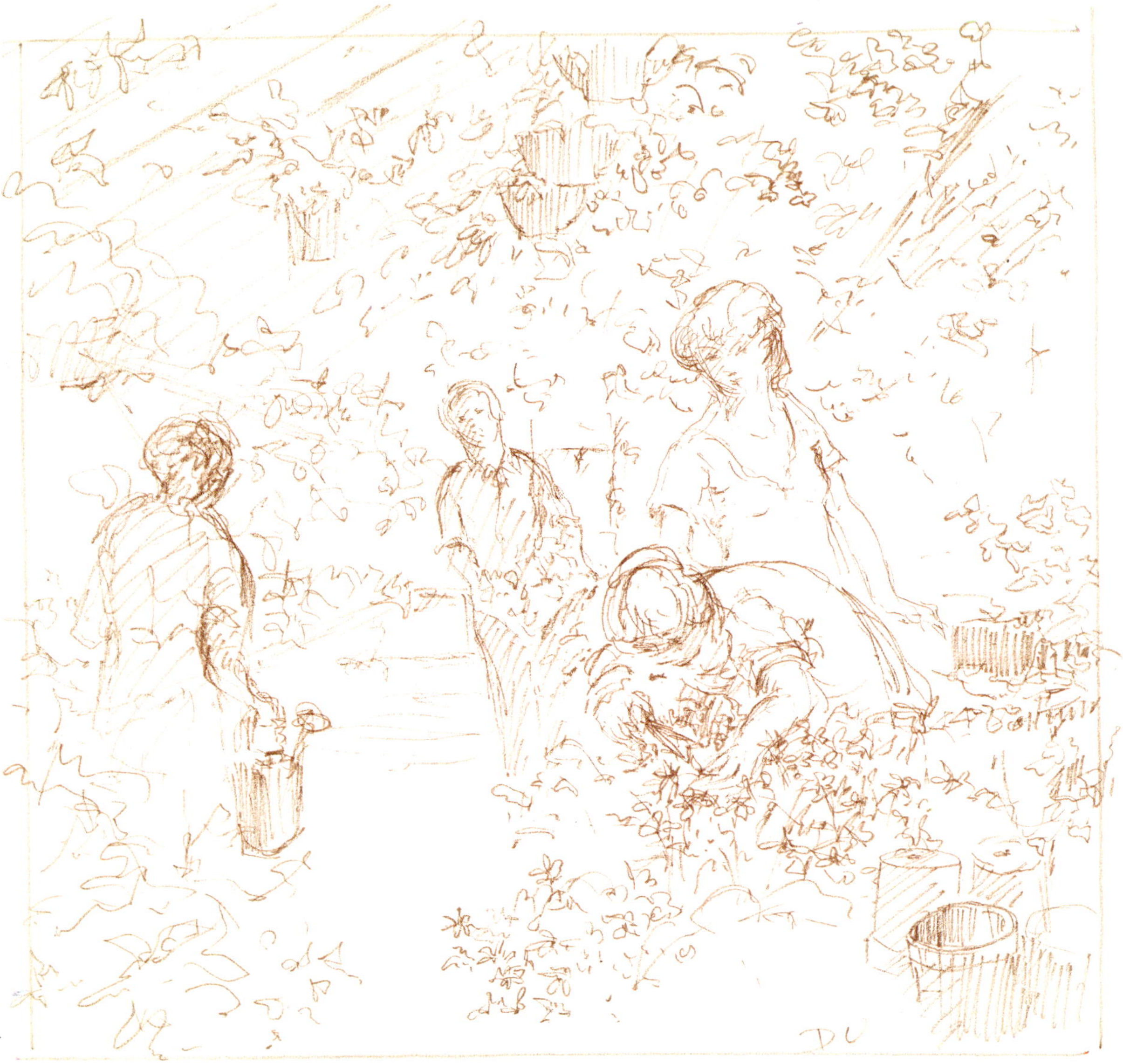

Foreword

There are hidden pleasures to be found in drawings, especially in one's own. For those who have wondered where the source of inspiration begins for the painter, this may, in part, give some insight. The painter often accepts without question the impressions his pen has left on paper. For him, the drawings hold promise of adventures to come, for from them, new paintings will emerge from blank surfaces. The paintings may deviate from the sketches, but they will hold to the essence and spirit of their source.

Drawings are often set aside to be called upon in the future, as new ideas take hold. They will be revisited from time to time to inspire paintings.

There are times when the painter's needs do not require the drawing, for when a picture is firmly established in his mind's eye then the drawing is quickly accomplished directly with the brush. In drawing, each line suggests the next to complete the thought. In painting, each brush stroke responds to the same demands. The process soon becomes automatic. The secret to this is so simple that few can believe it: It is just to fully relax and trust your feelings. There is no formula. The drawing you do is right for you, as it can express what and how only you feel. The criteria that one sets make the difference, and there lies the greatest challenge.

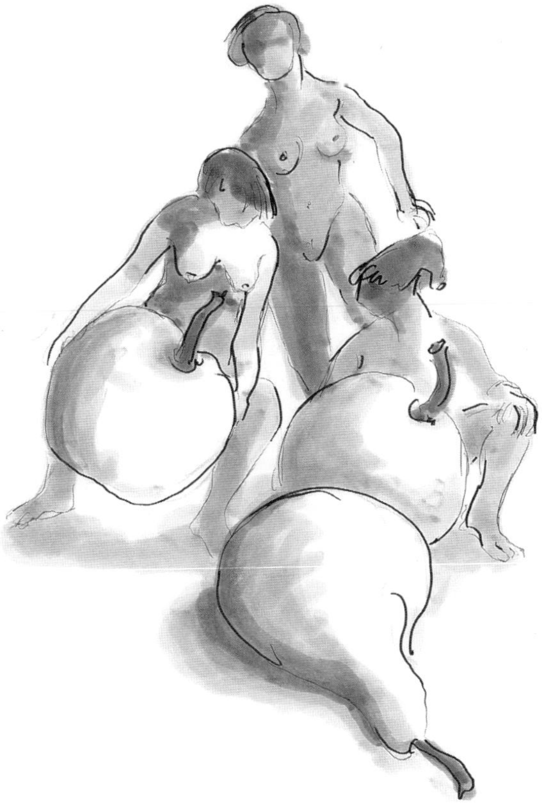

Introduction

The drawings presented here are not intended to be finished works in themselves. They are, for the most part, the result of a search for ideas for future paintings. They came into being on days too dark to paint or on evenings while this artist watched television, listened to music or traveled on a cruise ship. Such times produced hundreds of ideas that have served well and will continue to do so.

A few multi-figured drawings were the source of ideas that were employed in two or three different paintings. At times, parts of separate sketches gave inspiration for a single composition. A particular movement or gesture of a figure from a drawing can be found in more than one picture. A drawing done several years ago retains its idea and may later produce an entirely new response, a still different interpretation.

Drawing is like a love affair. It is a joy that ripens into a fulfillment that becomes a painting. I liken it to a good marriage: The first stirrings are the most exciting, but over time, it ripens and matures, fulfilling all it promises.

Drawings are very personal. When they are shared, it should be with sensitive, responsive people who will understand the privilege you offer them. If their response is a flicker of a smile, a moment of enjoyment, you have succeeded.

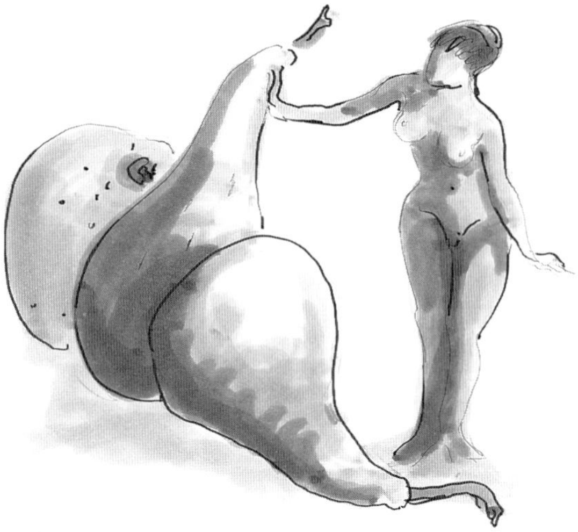

Drawing gives such pleasure that I can only suggest that you draw, draw, and then draw some more. Don't be concerned about producing bad drawings, for from them new ideas may spring forth. Recognize their faults and make improvements. Only time and work are required — and, of course, desire.

The tools to draw with are numerous. Anything that leaves a mark should do. What counts is what you do with it. Try several things, for you will find pleasure in them all. Charcoal, Conté, pastel, pen or pencil — each has its own response, as does the surface you will work on.

There is magic in the simplest of lines. Lines can express weight, volume, texture, sensitivity, boldness, movement, and emotion. They can become anything you might conjure up. Only the depth of your imagination limits the possibilities. It is even possible to express air, light, and atmosphere.

A student asked how he could possibley draw a horse when none were available to look at.

"Have you seen a horse?" the instructor asked.

"Yes, of course, many of them," the student responded.

"Well then, close your eyes. Now think of the last horse you saw. Can you see it? Think only of the horse. When you do, study it. Now draw a line around it," the instructor suggested.

Does that sound impossible? Well try it. You don't need to have an apple before you to draw one. A single, continuous line should be enough to express its weight, volume, size, and texture. Perhaps even its color. If you can feel "apple," your drawing will respond.

A line itself is always right. It will suggest something to you. Look again, then ask yourself about it. Understand all it offers. When the line connects with others, inviting the eye to move with it, you are on the way to enjoying an exciting adventure. When the drawing is successful, you will know and begin to understand its pleasures. This is most personal, depending on taste.

We tend to classify paintings into schools, relating styles and techniques. Drawings more often than not transcend such labels, for, as with handwriting, they are very exclusive to the individual. When viewing a letter written by a friend or loved one, you need only glance at it to recognize its author. The writing will also reveal the emotion of the writer. It may express tenderness, anger, authority, or other feelings. The "drawing" of each word will reveal itself unknowingly. In drawing you reveal knowingly, intentionally. Through drawings you reach the soul of the artist.

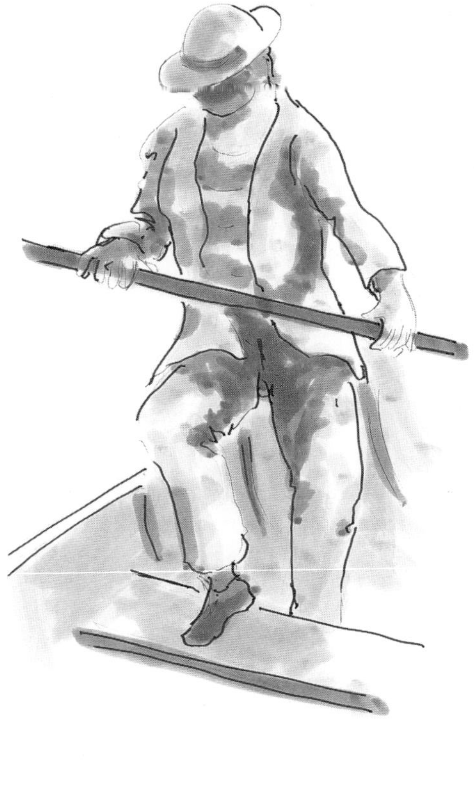

The drawings presented here are personal notes to be shared with you. They are unpretentious, involving the simple moments-- the ones we seek that make life pleasant, cherished time remembered. Enjoy.

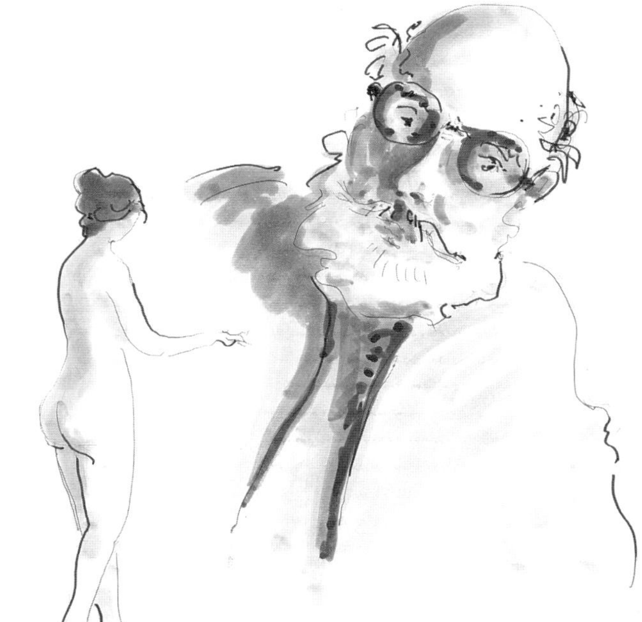

Part One - Gardens

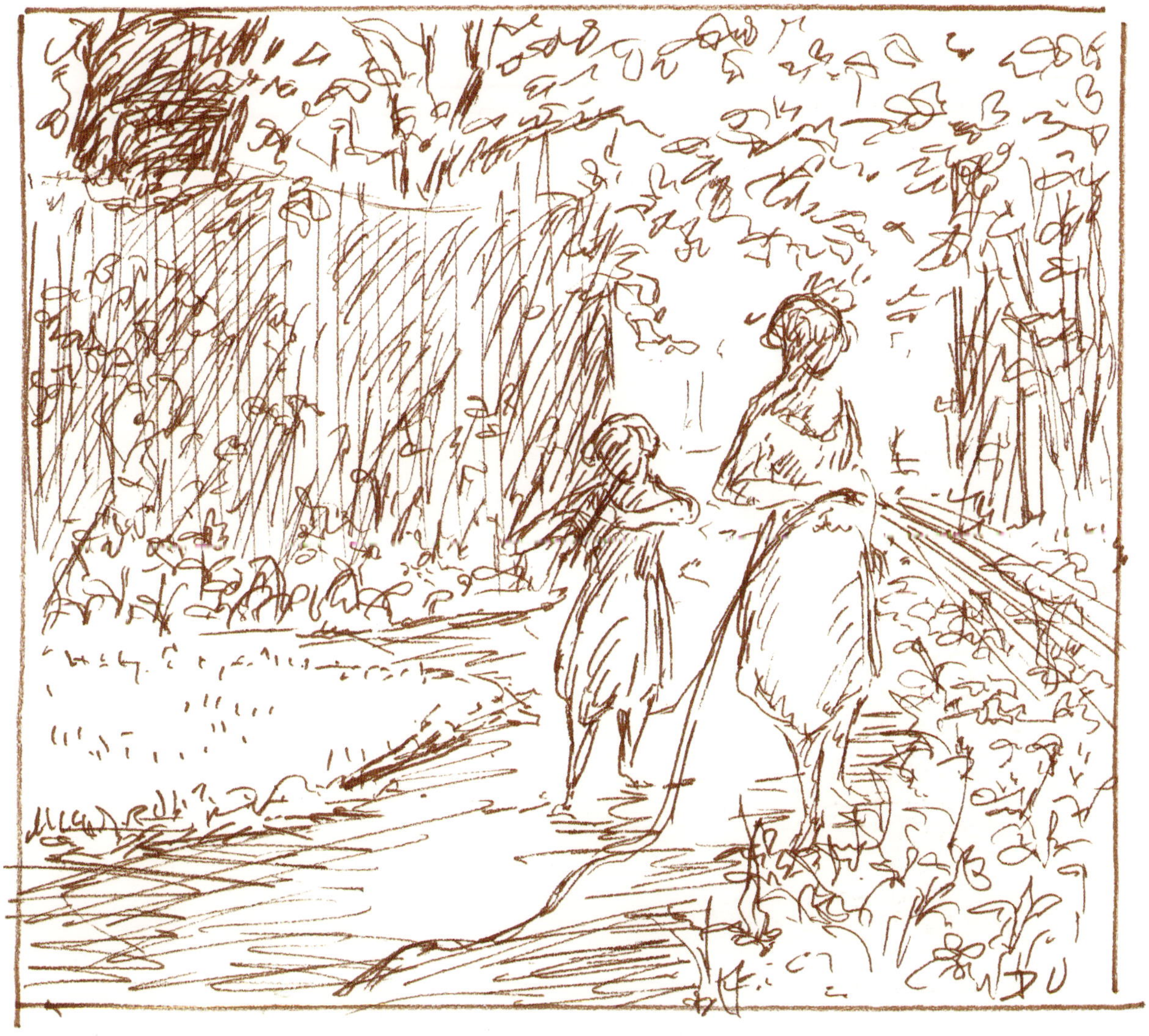

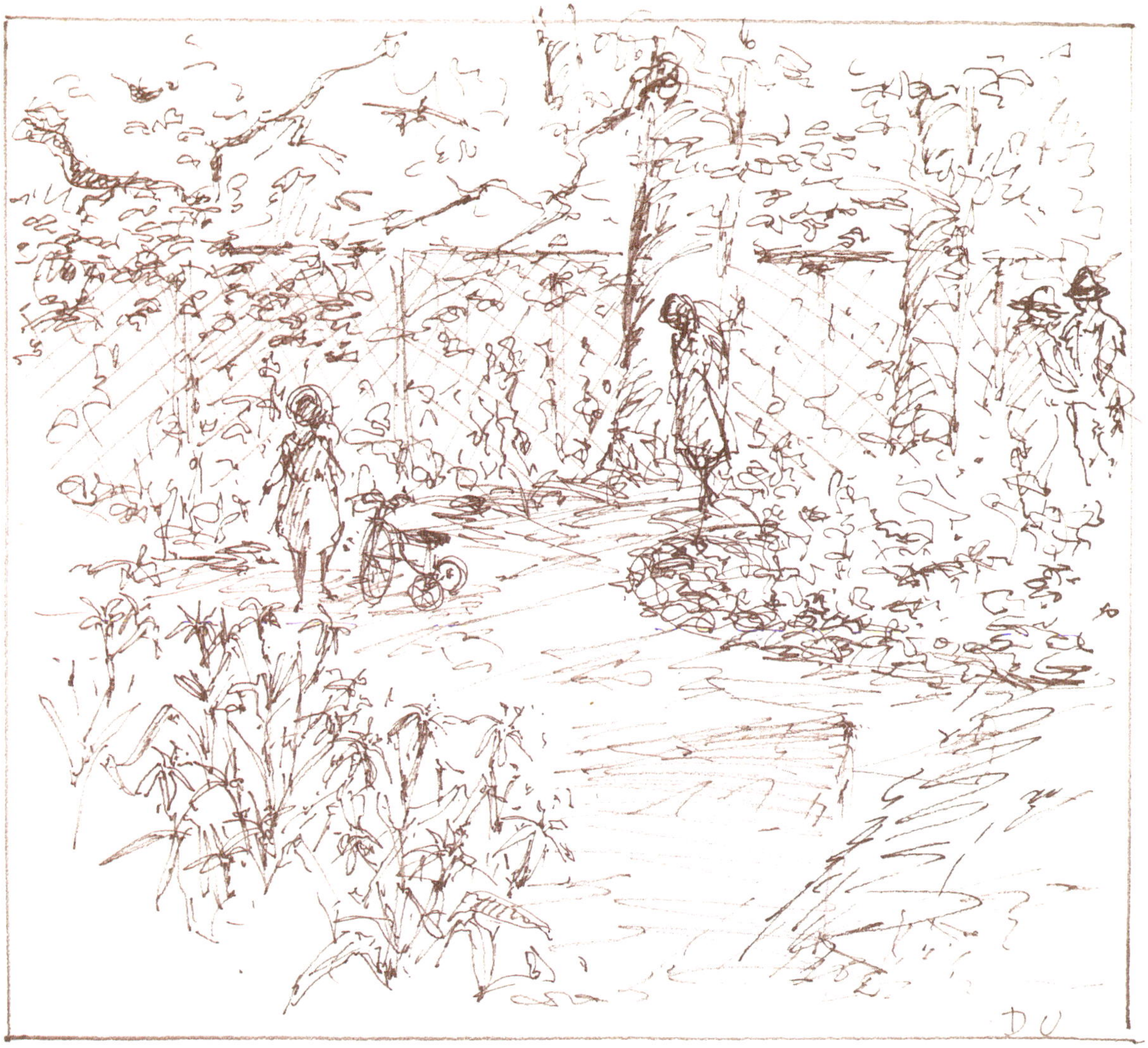
DU

As a young boy, I was privileged to live for a couple of years with an aunt and uncle in a small village in the northern part of Illinois. There, as I mowed the grass, I learned to revel in its sweet fragrance. Pulling weeds in the vegetable garden also gave forth a special odor from the fertile soil. There was a special, new awareness of the wondrous shapes and textures of plants and their fruits in the warmth of clear, fresh, summer air for this city-bred boy. It was the beginning of my ongoing love for gardens.

Some years later, I spent many hours drawing in various gardens in several countries about the world. Some were quite small, informal flower gardens, and others were stately. Each possessed a quality unique to itself and left an impression that has been called upon from time to time throughout the years. My gardens are mostly invented to provide pleasant surroundings for the figures that inhabit them. The fun of drawing is making your own world to fill your needs and desires.

More important than reproducing exactly the outward appearance and form of a subject is to capture its inner nature.

My drawn gardens are full of wondrous flowers without specific identity. They are presented with a few rapid strokes, a shorthand note indicating mass, form, density, texture, and volume to be related to surrounding areas. Often, when such lines are established, the color and fragrance of the flowers are felt. It is the magic of a line.

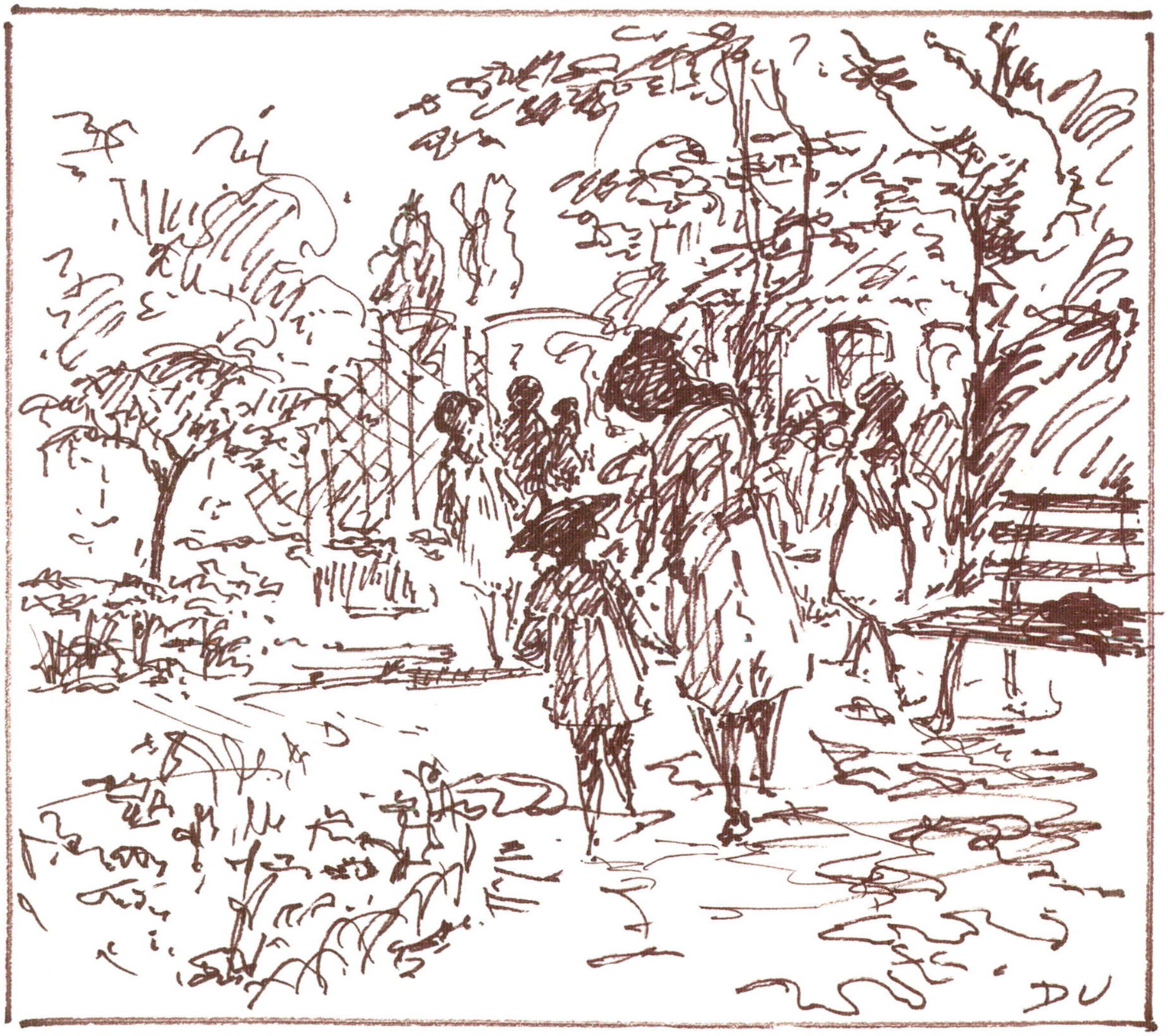

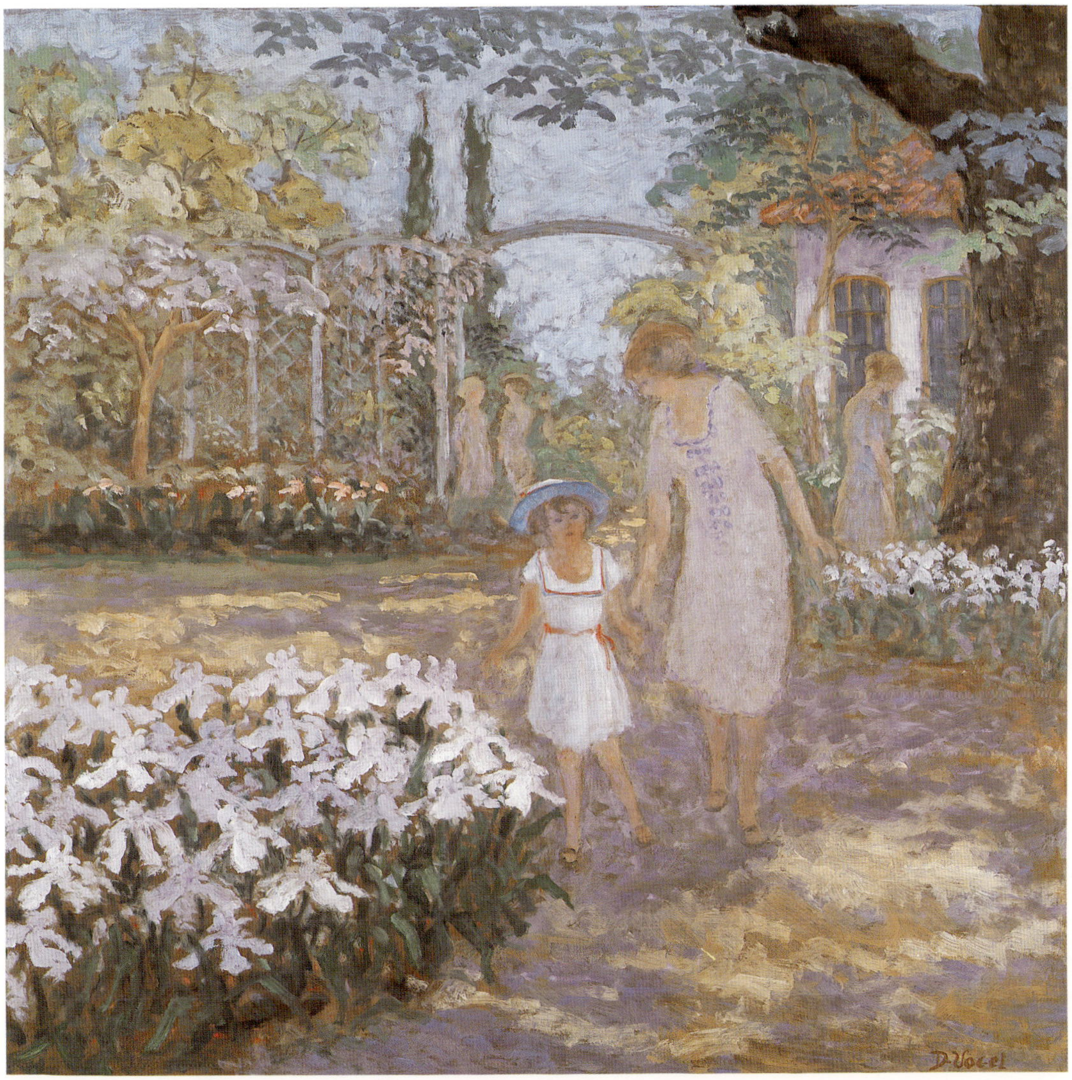

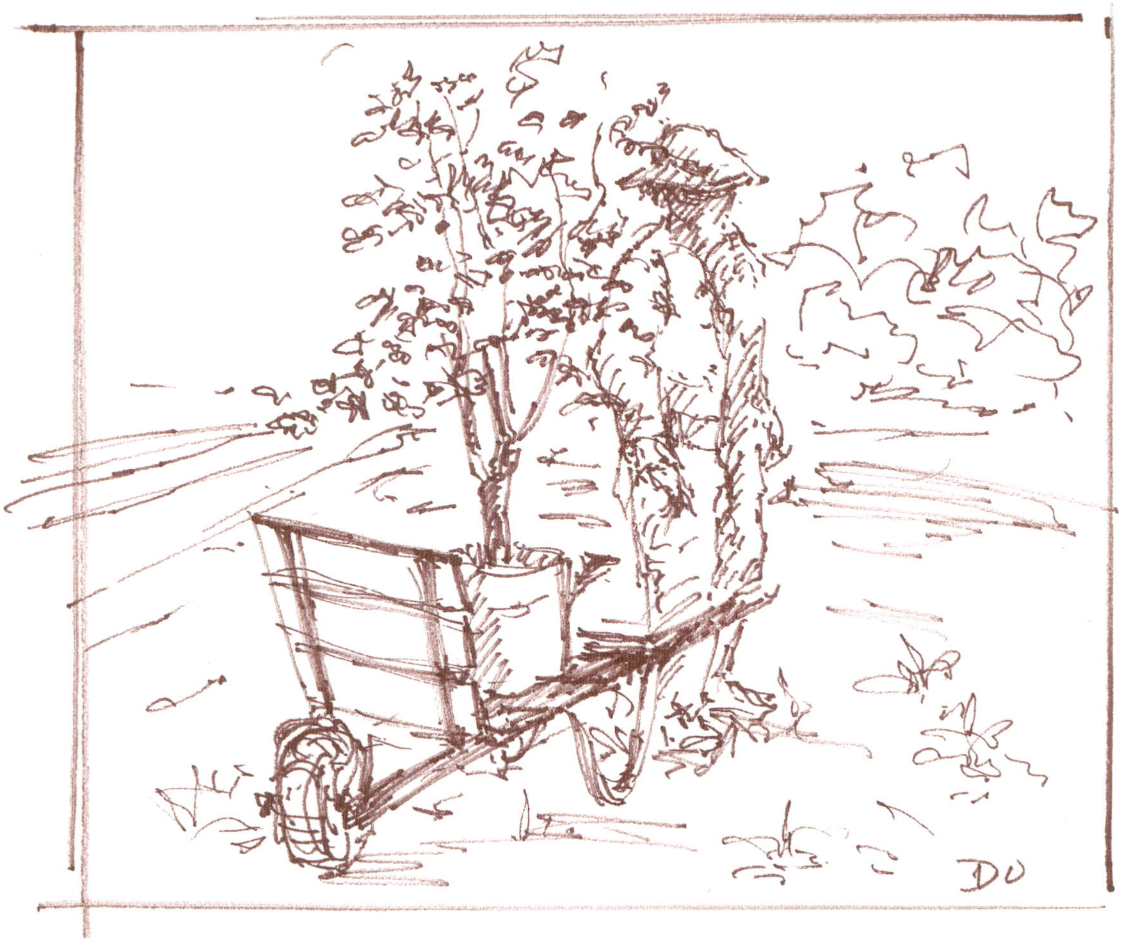

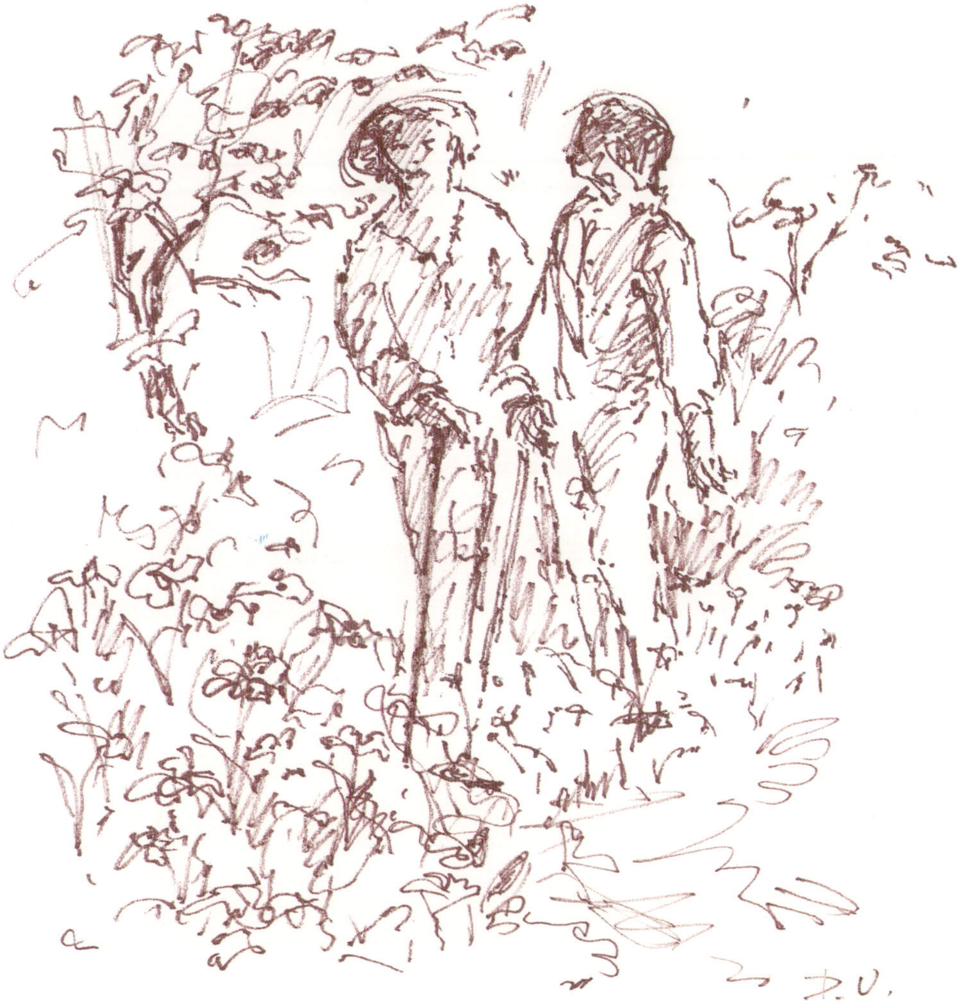

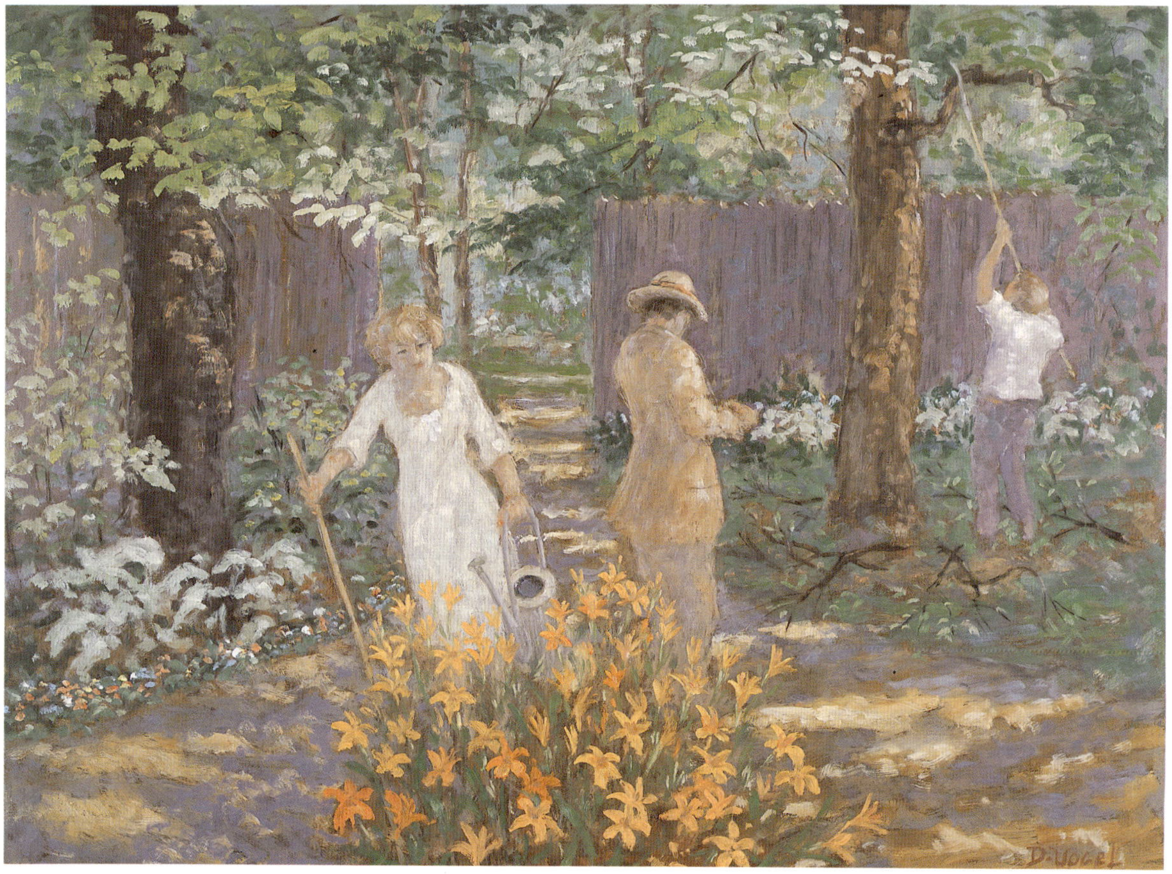

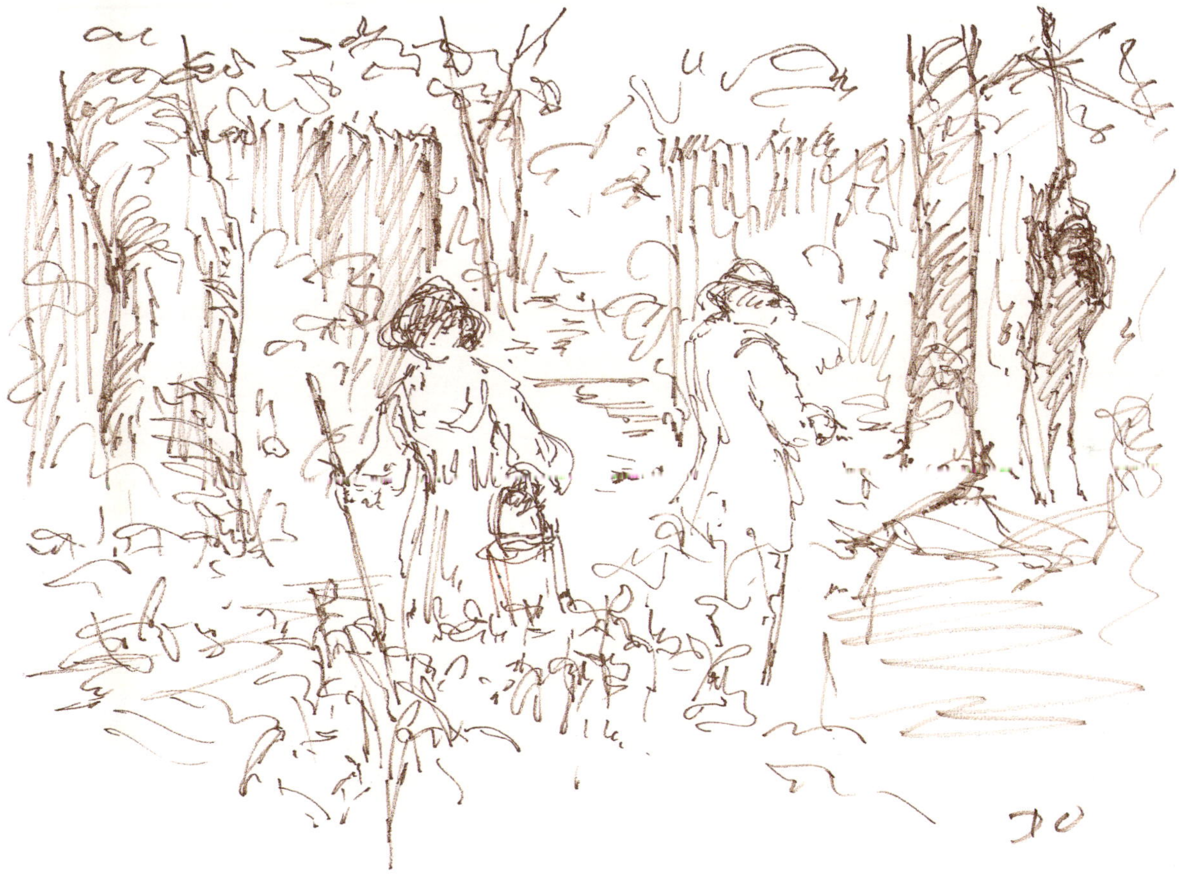

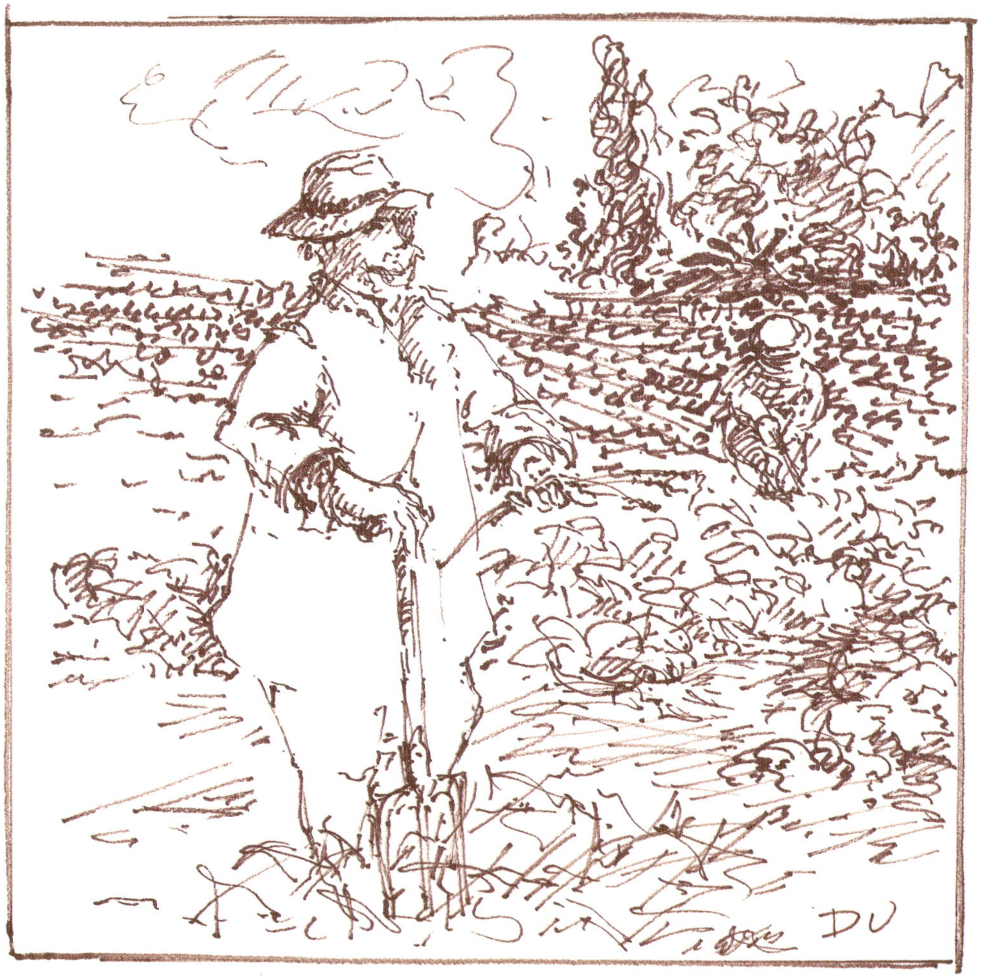
DU

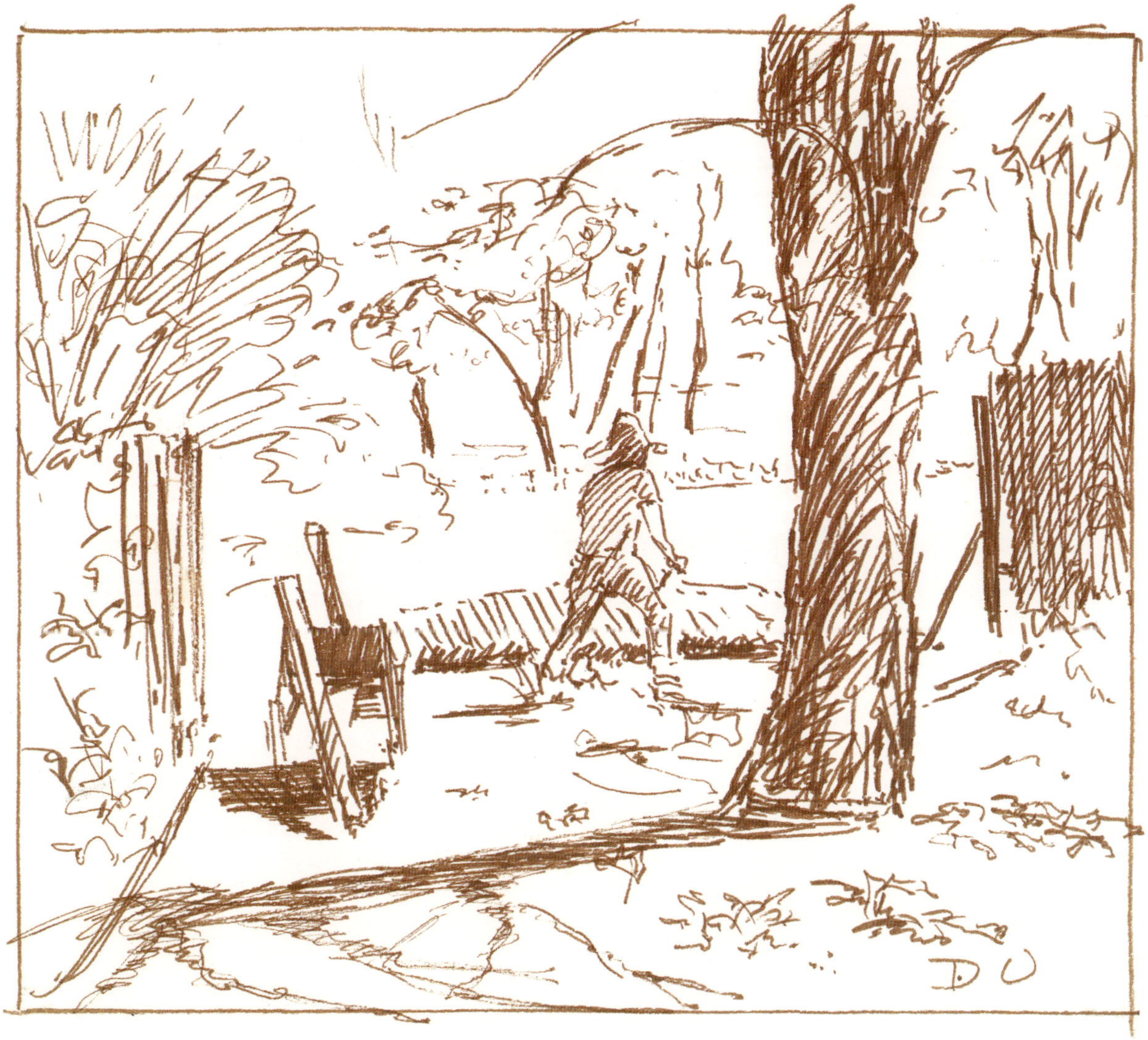

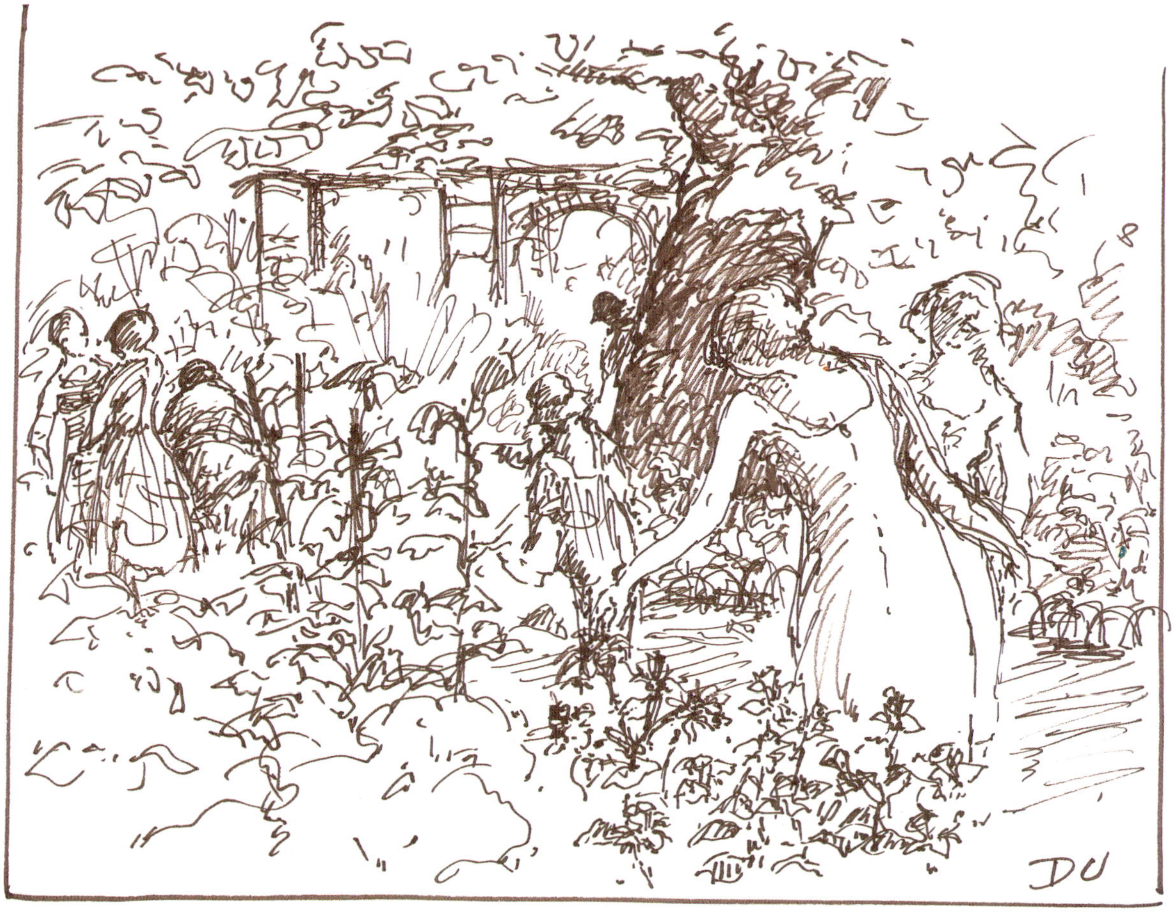
DU

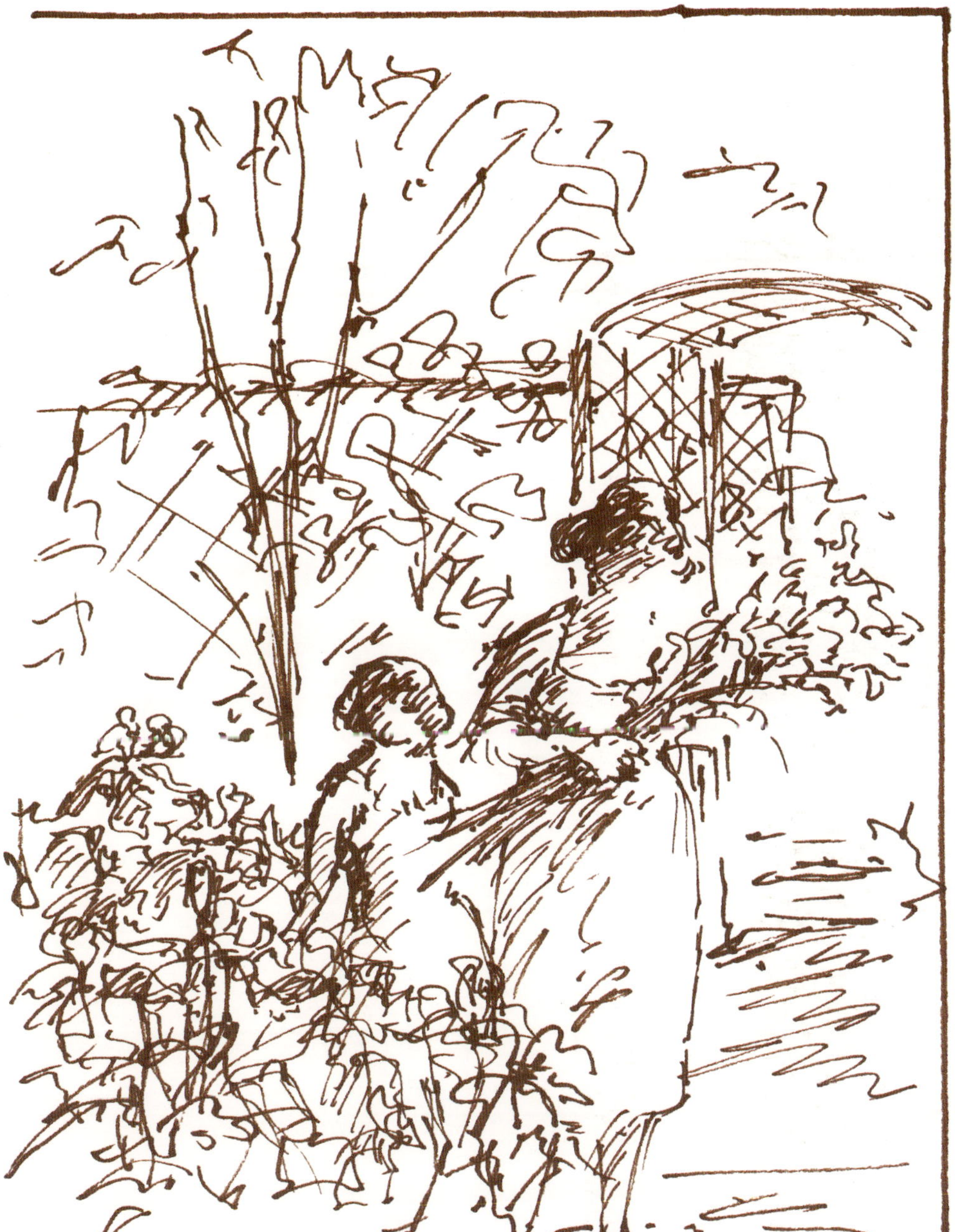
DU

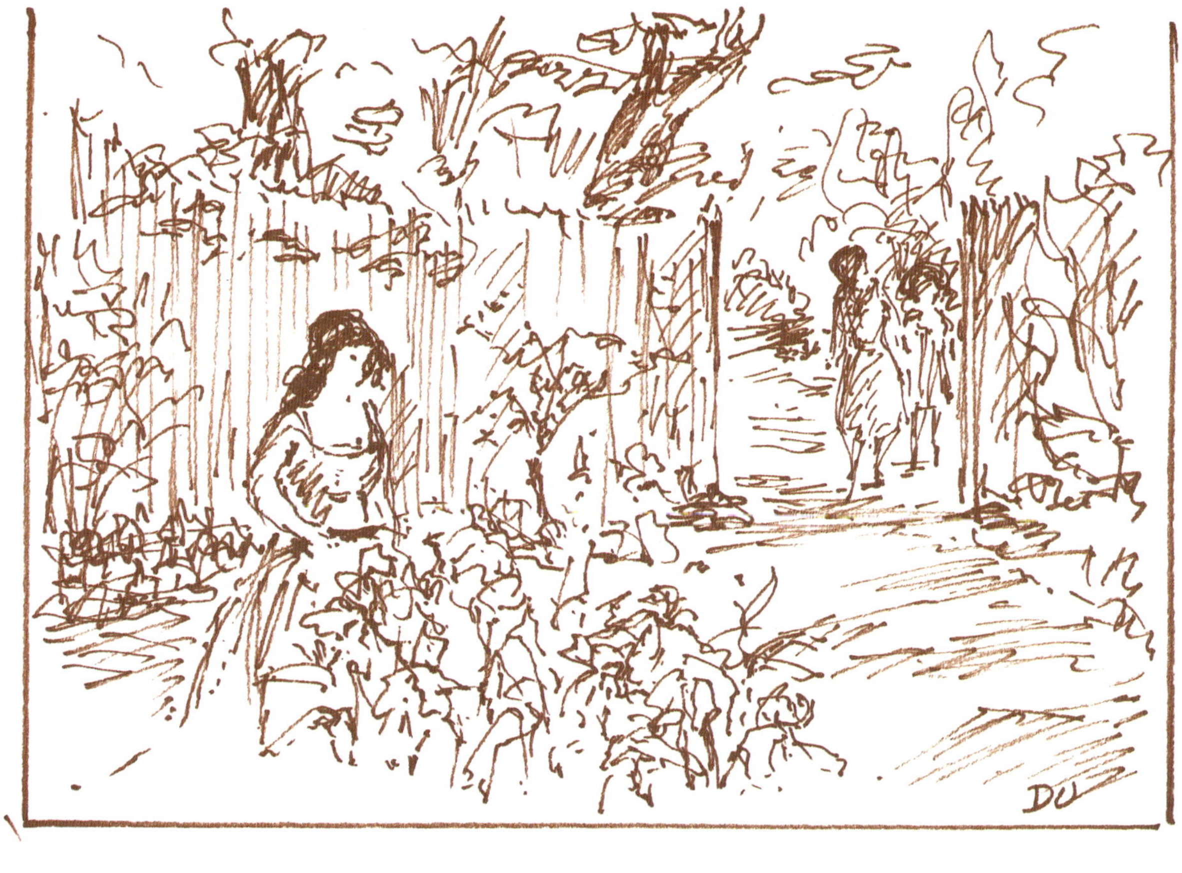
DU

Amsterdam Aug 15-85

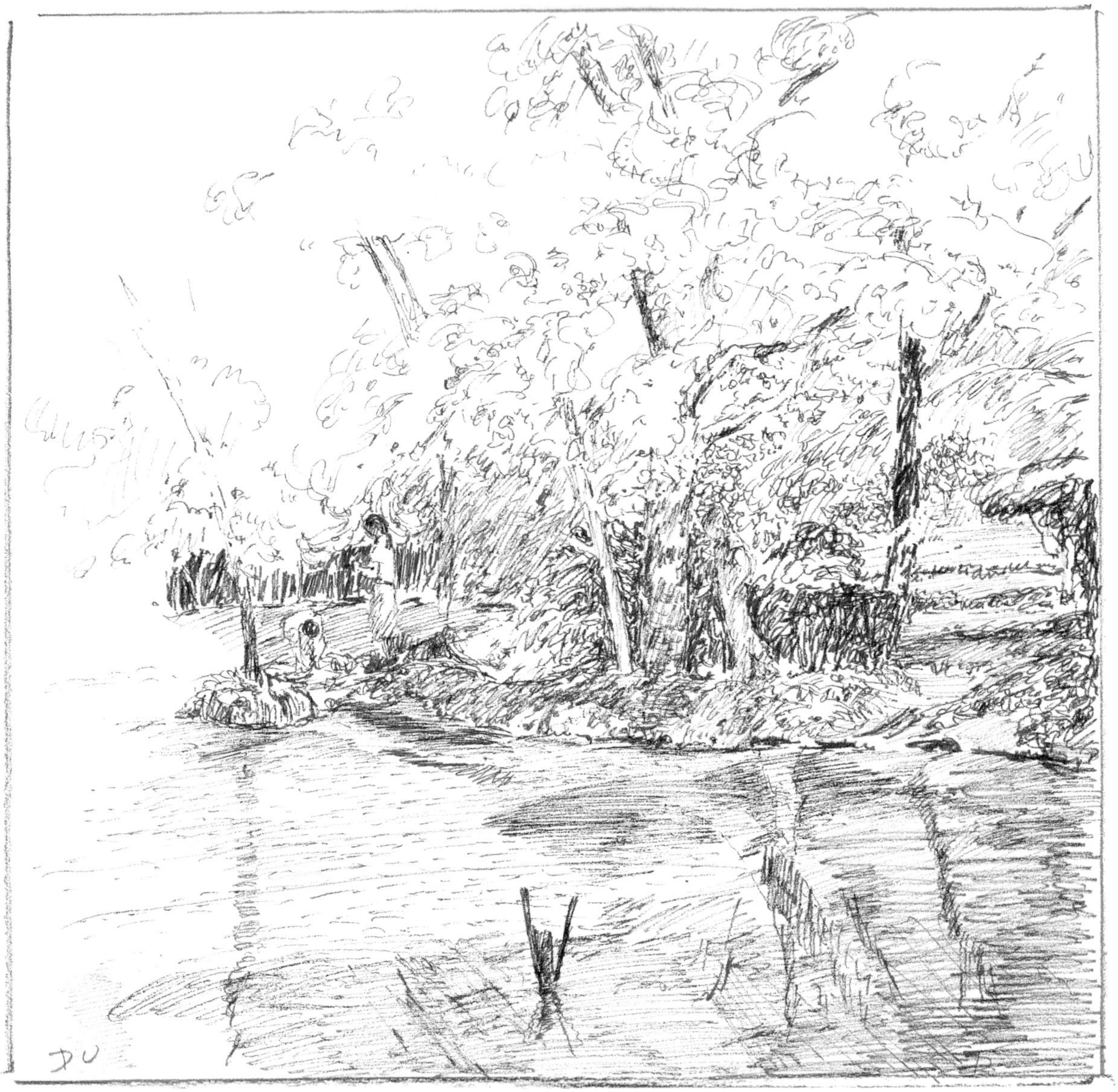
DU

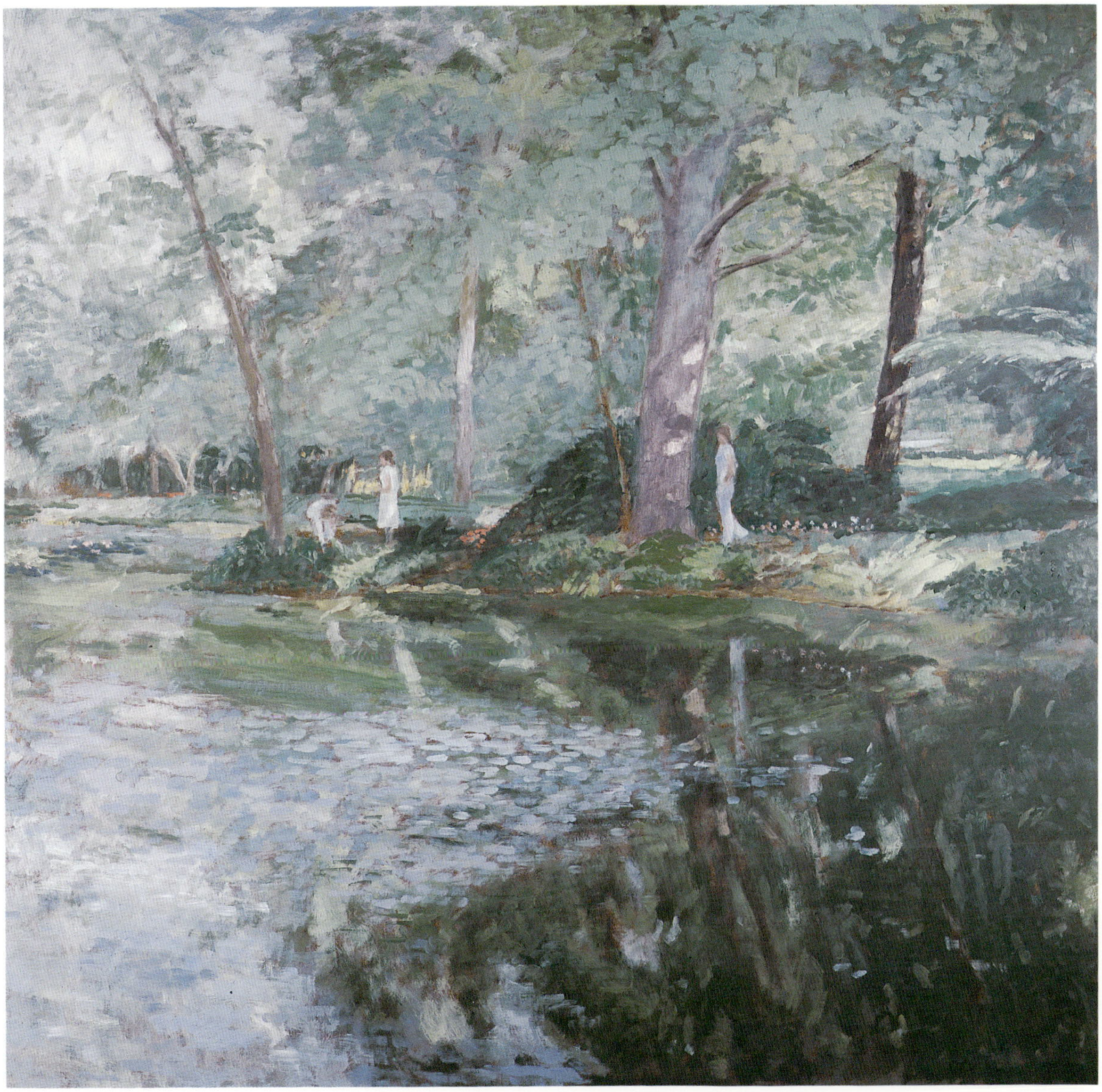

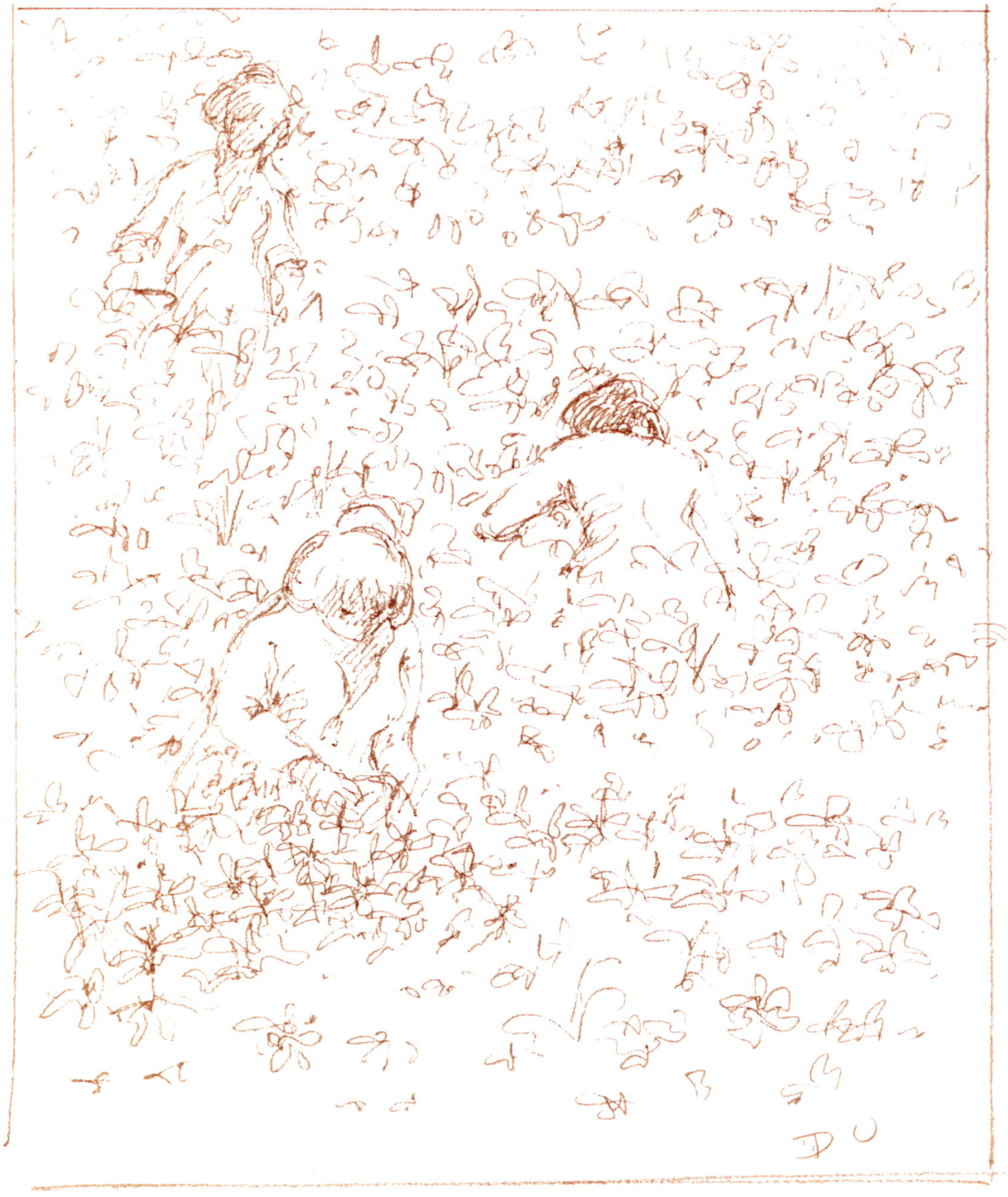

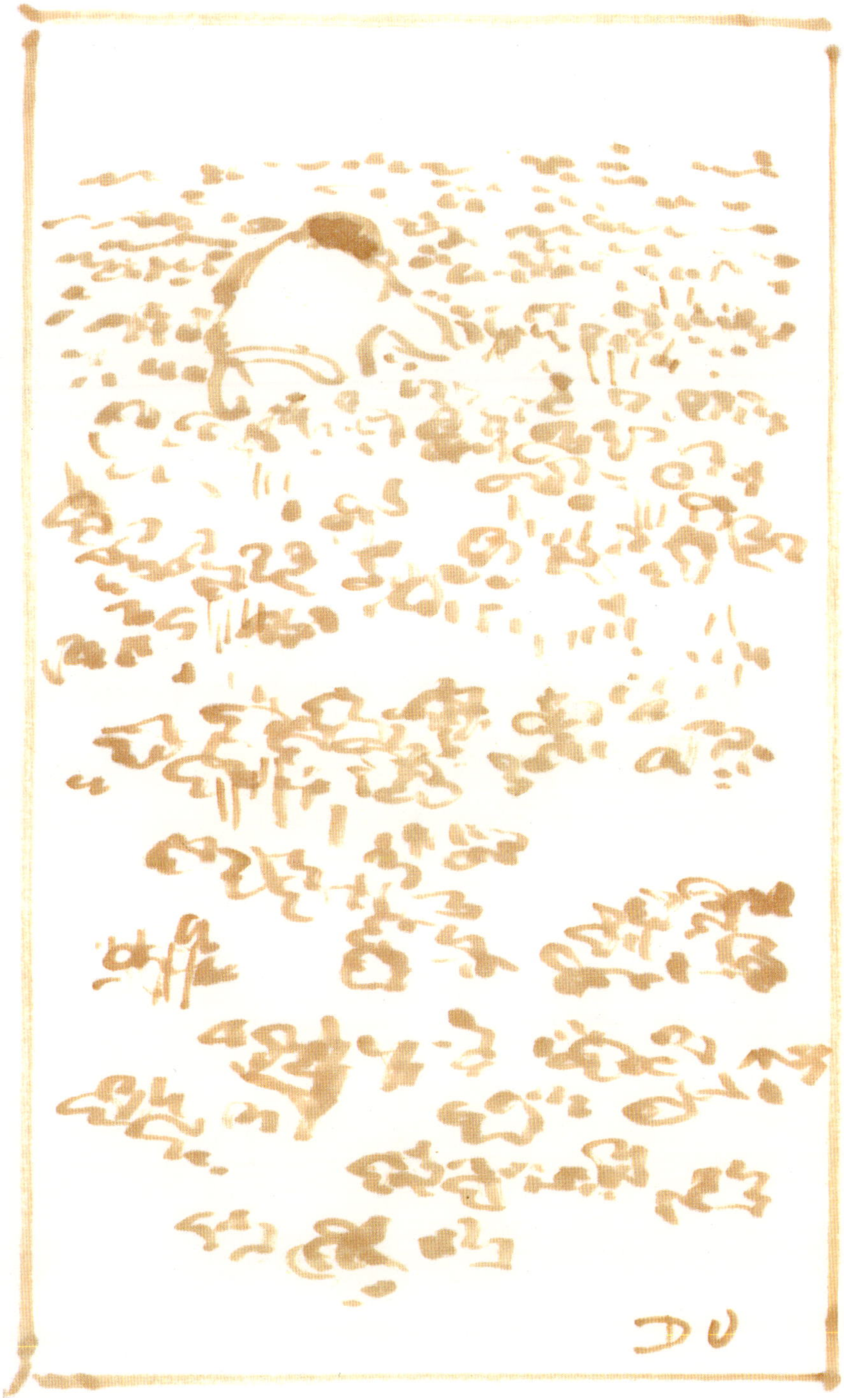
DU

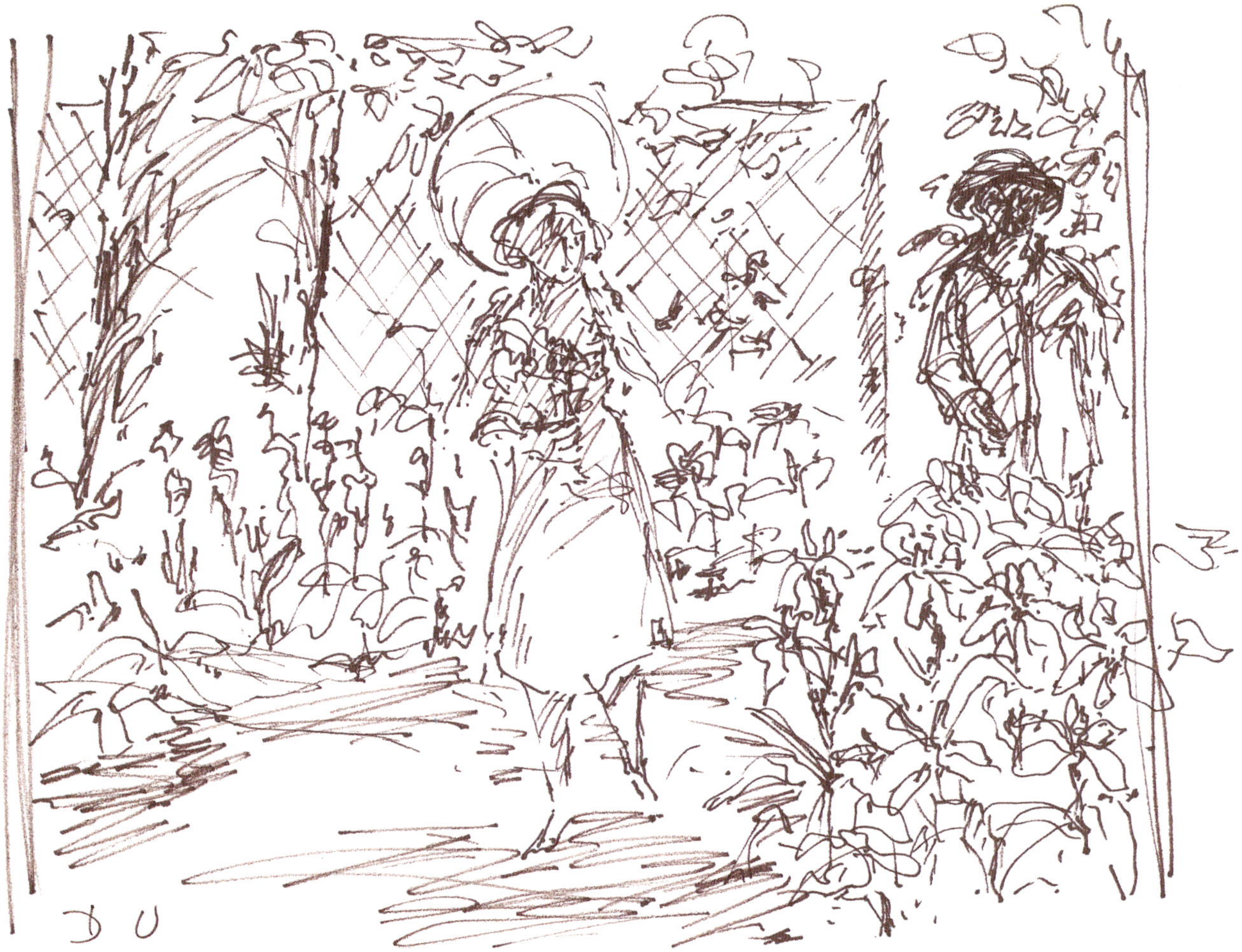
D U

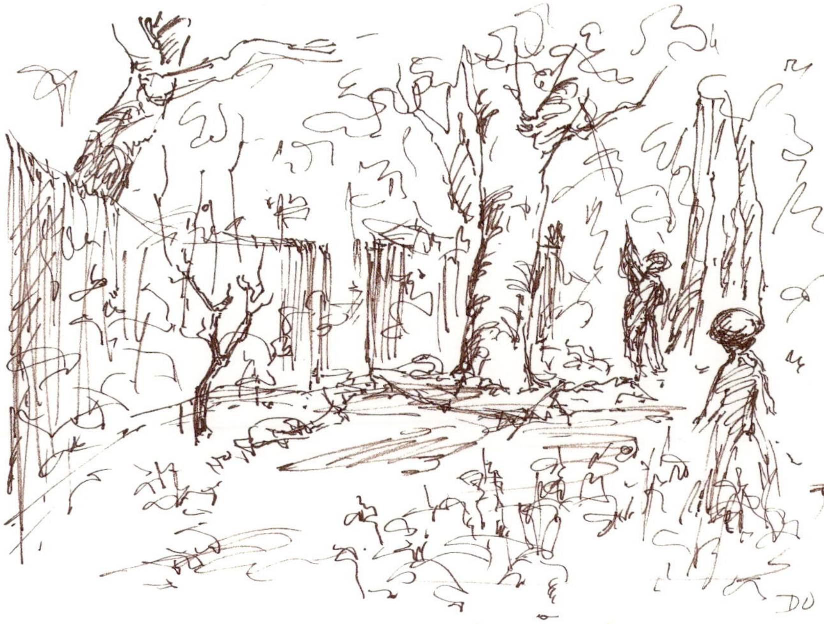
DU

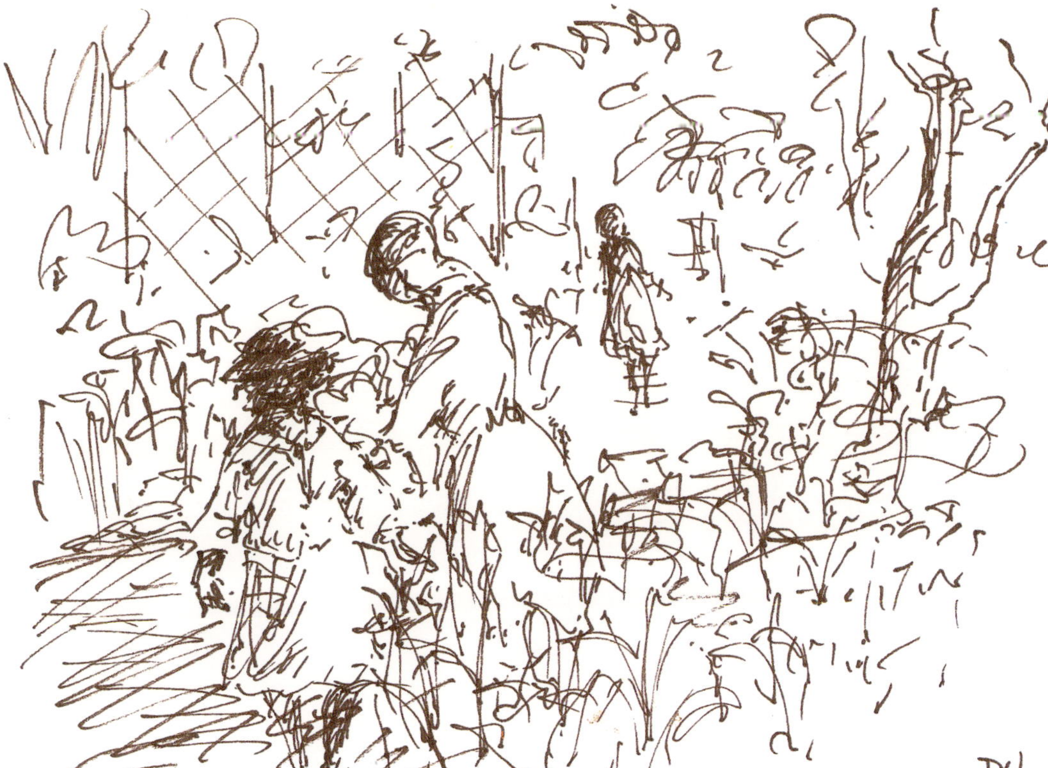
DU

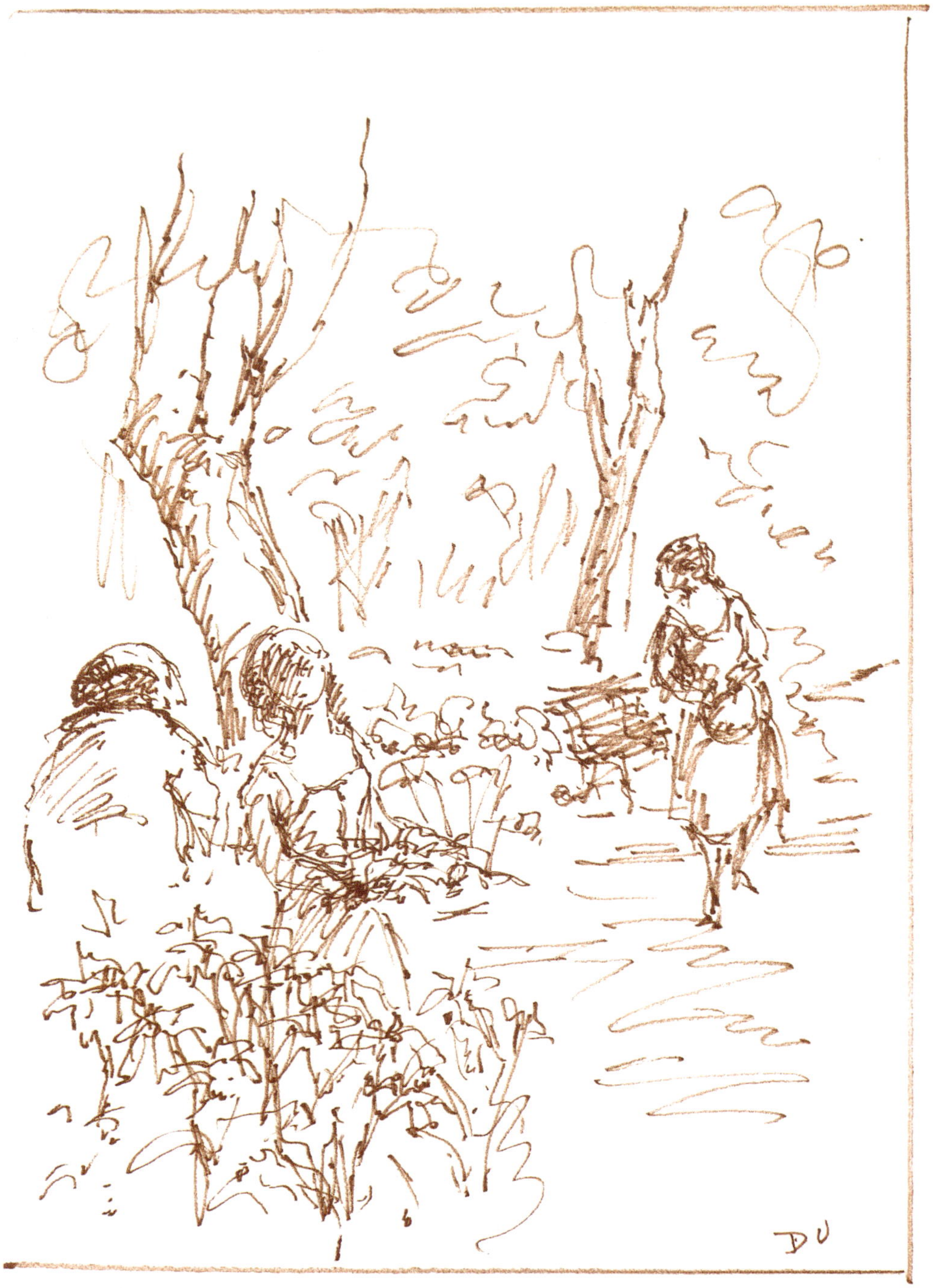

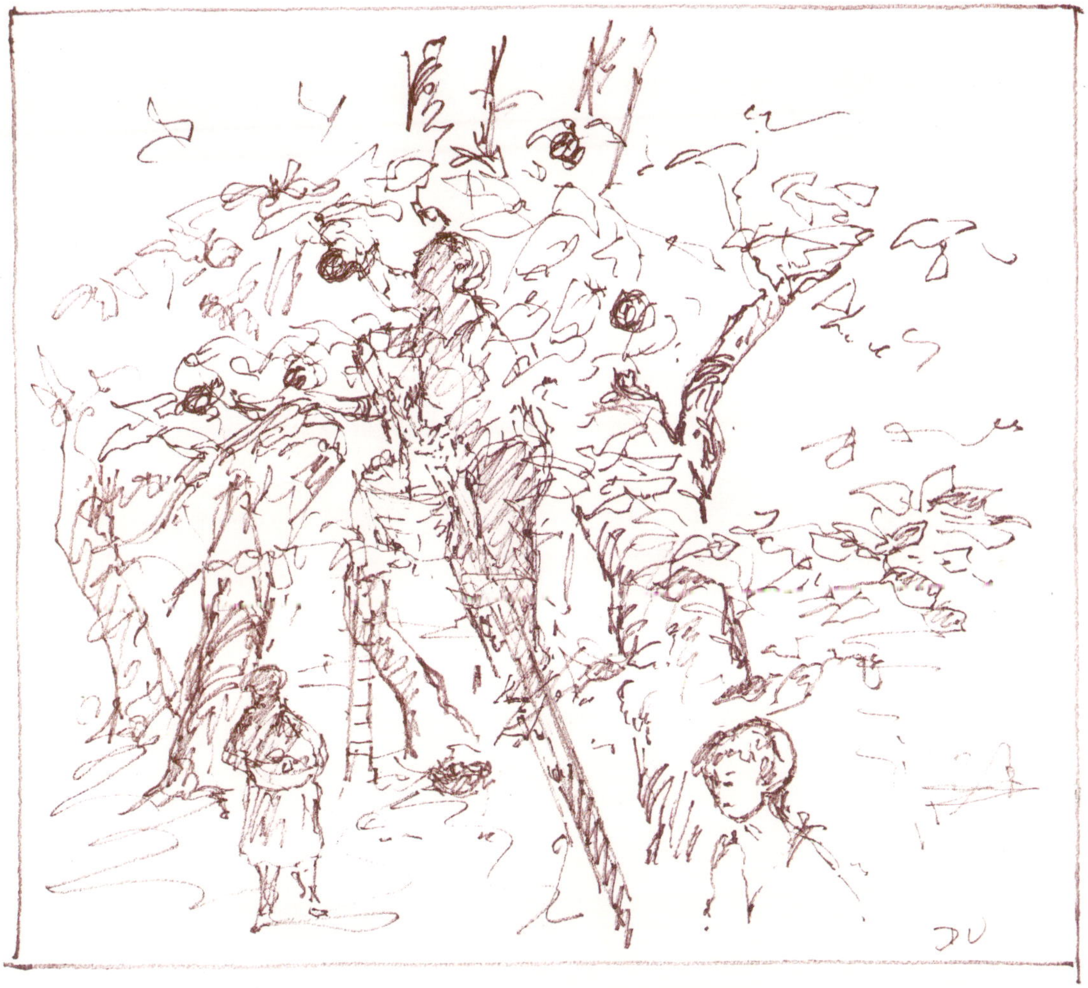

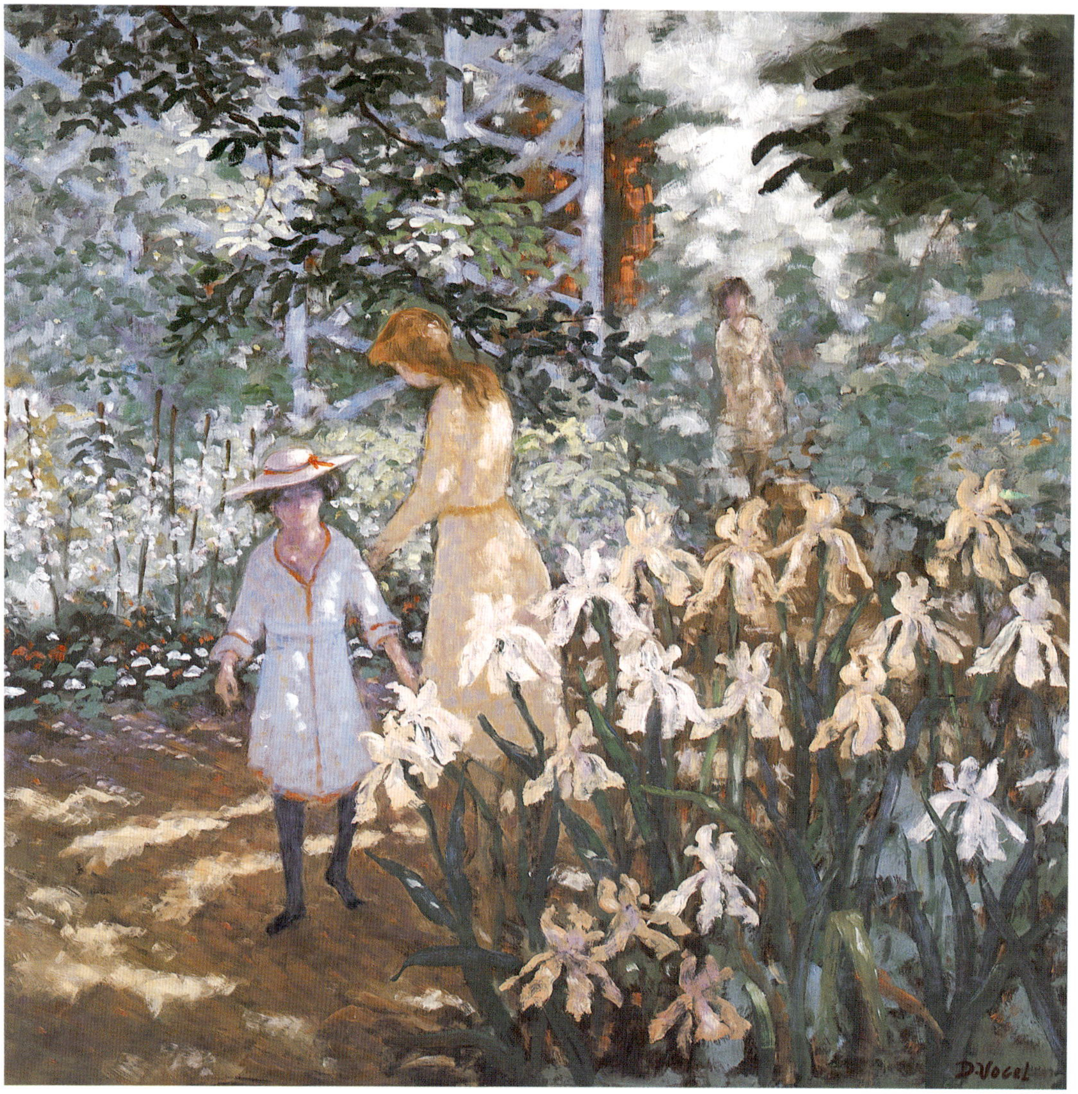
D.VOGEL

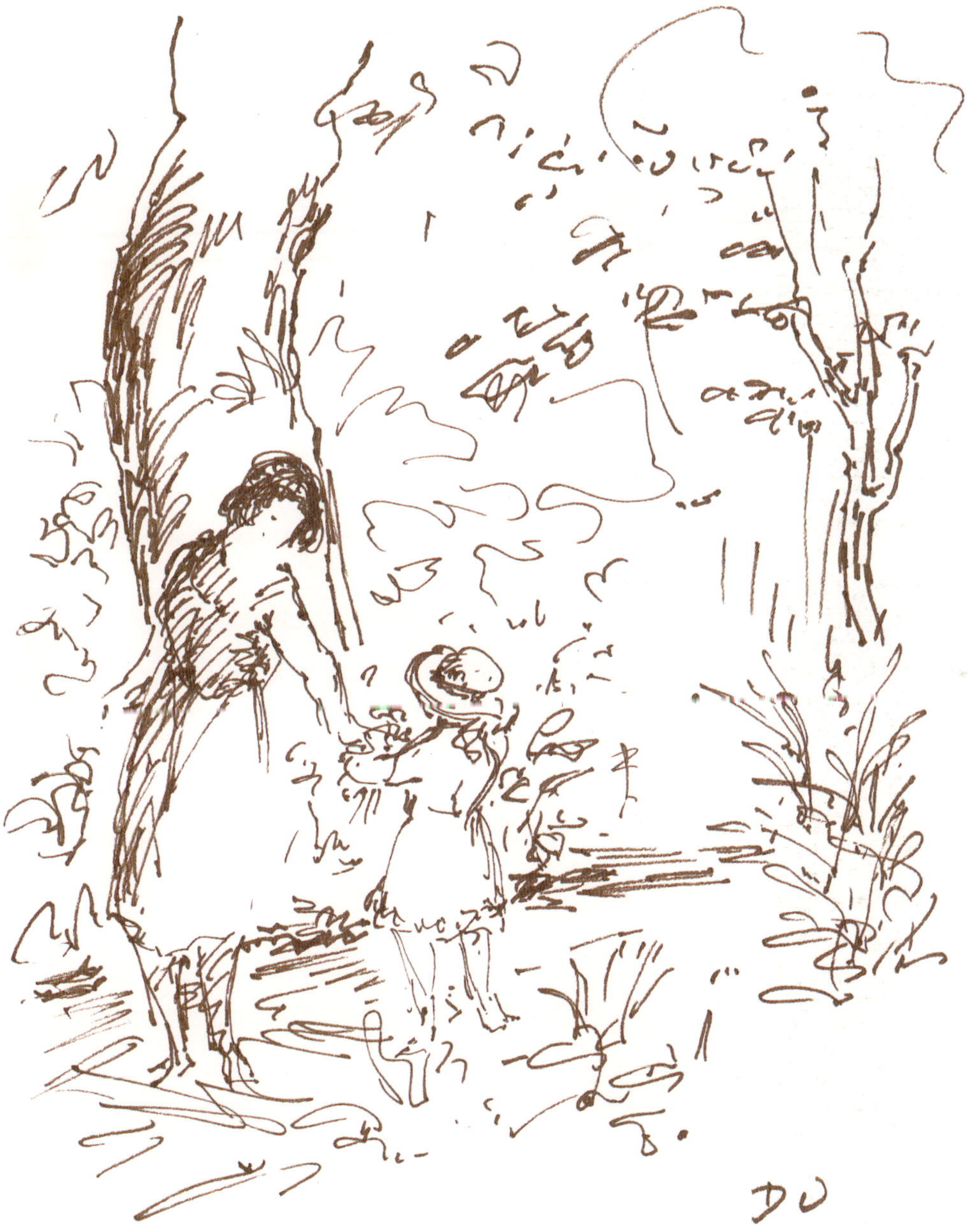
DO

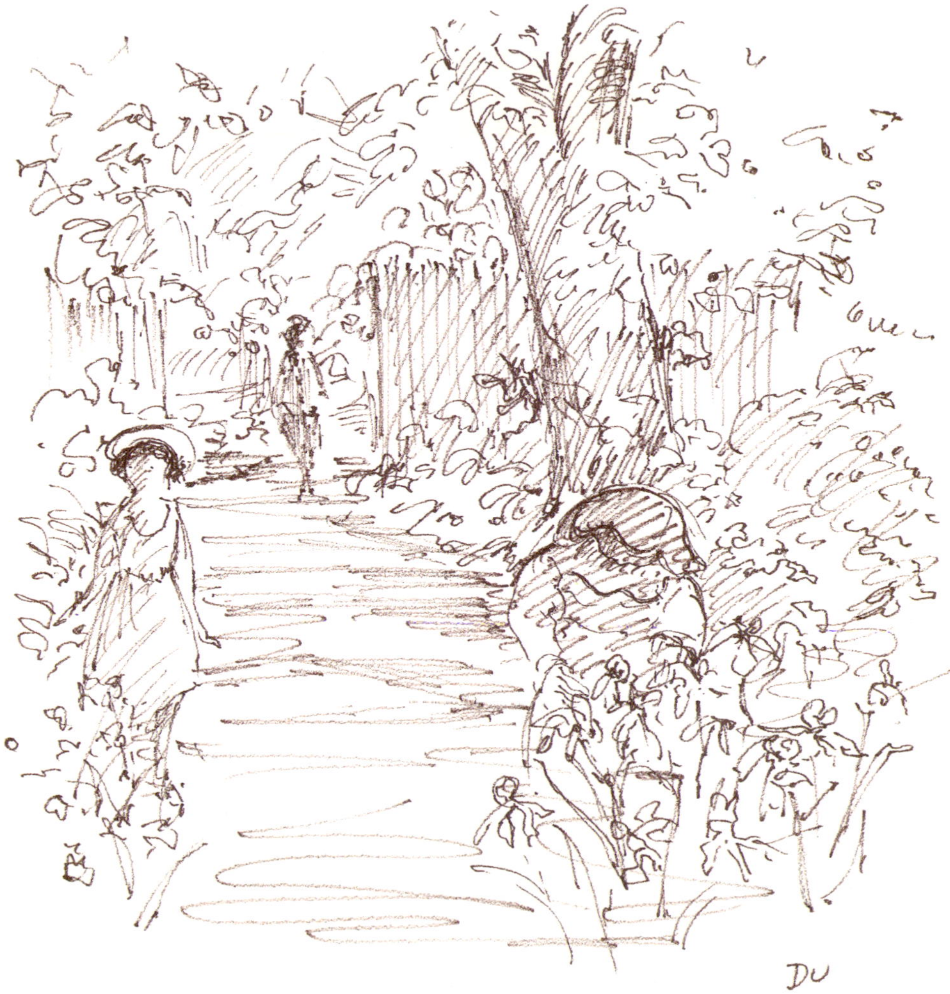
DU

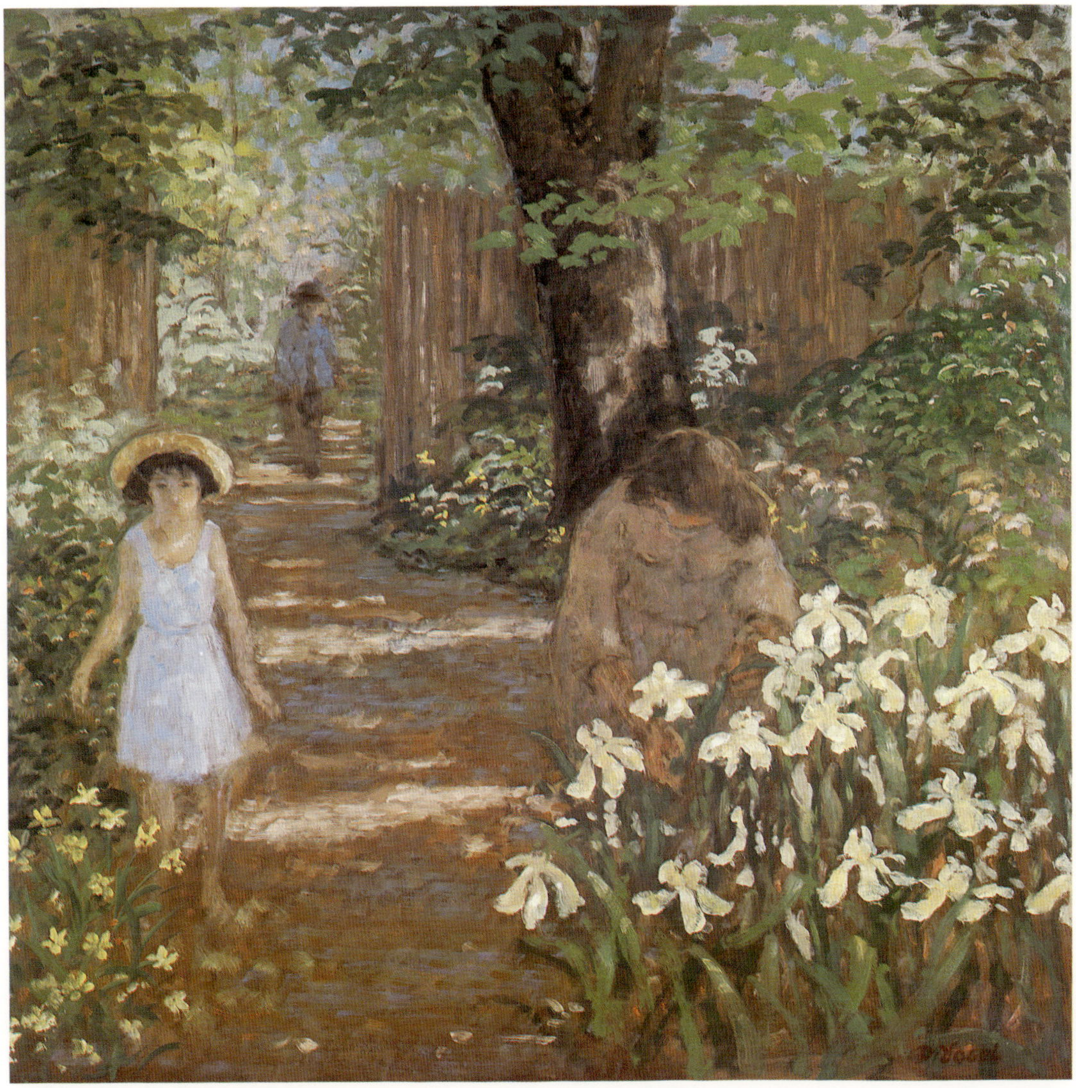

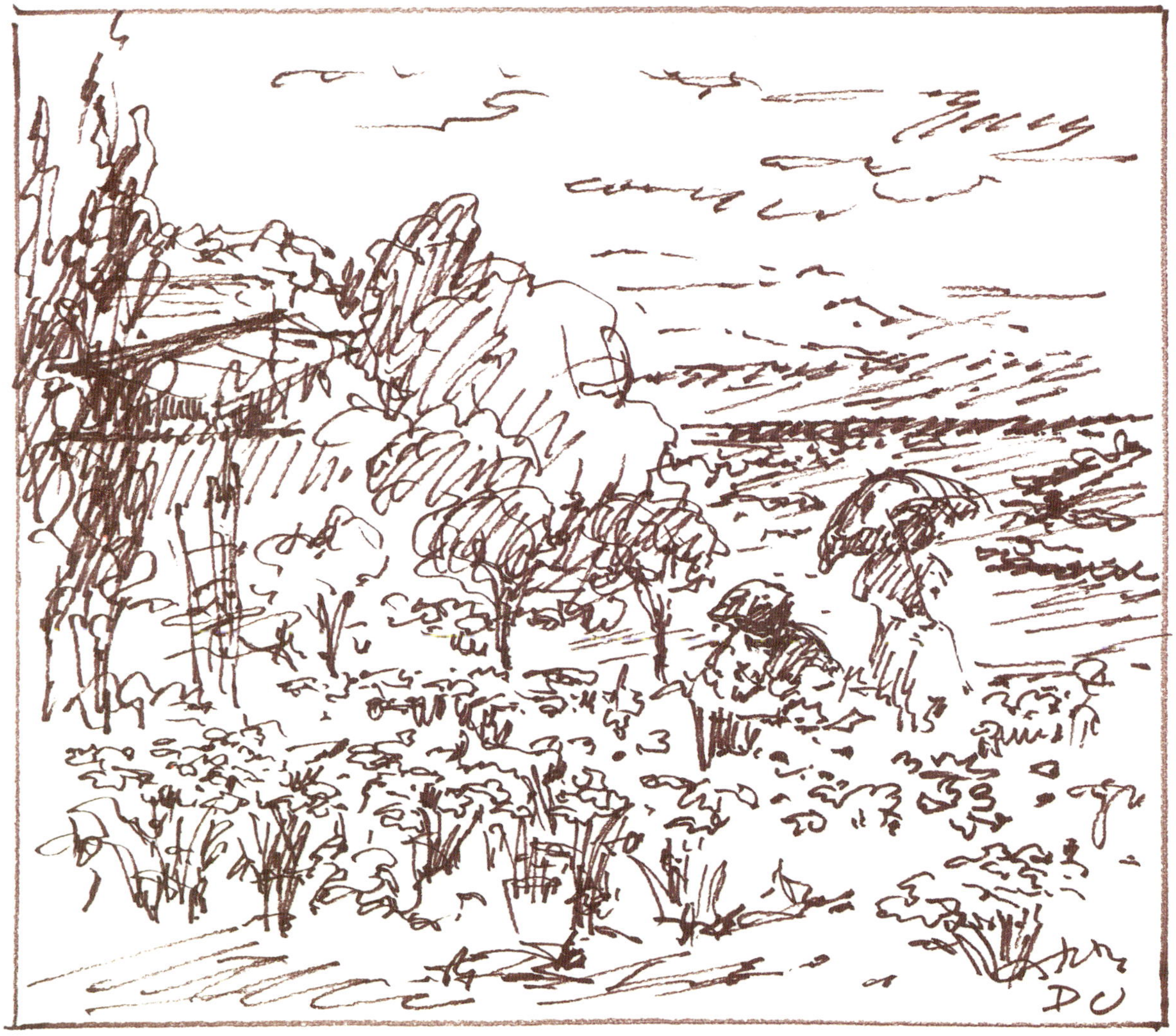
DC

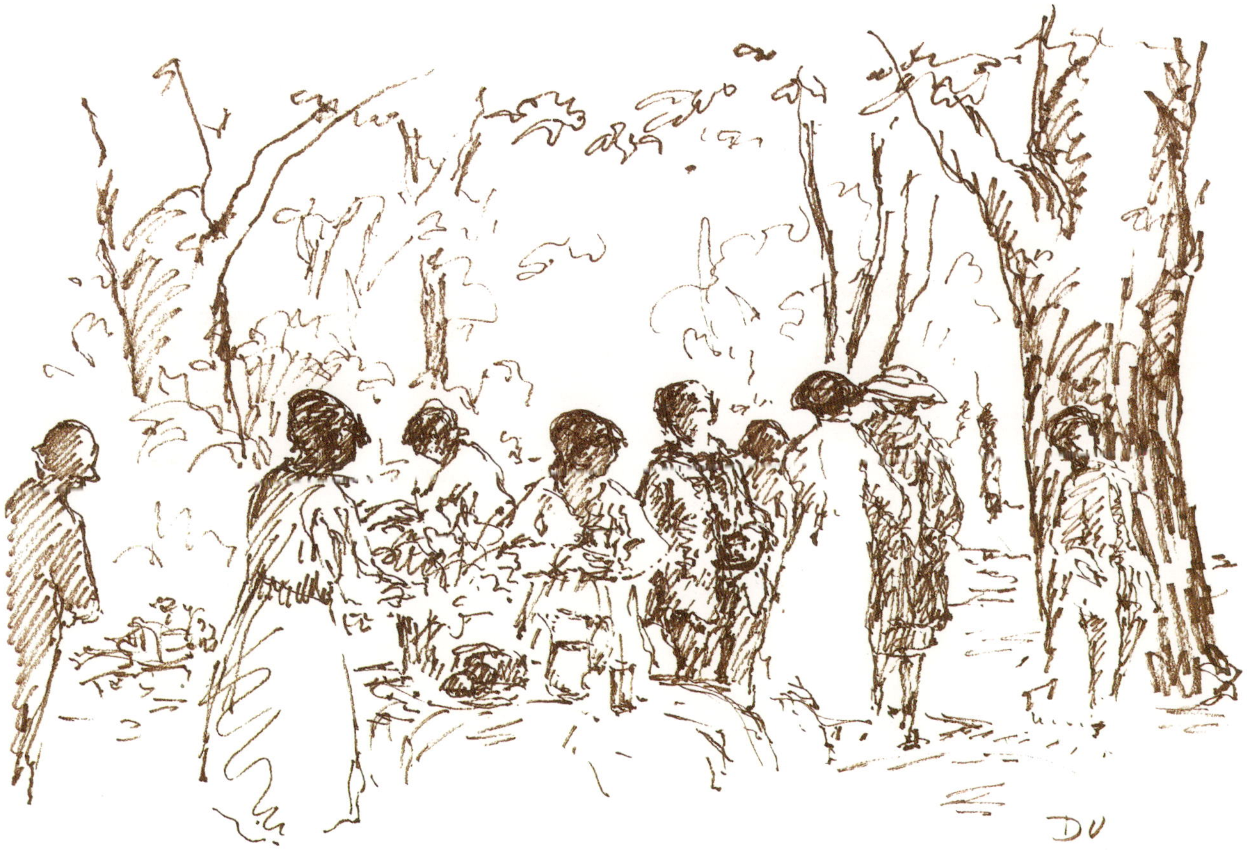

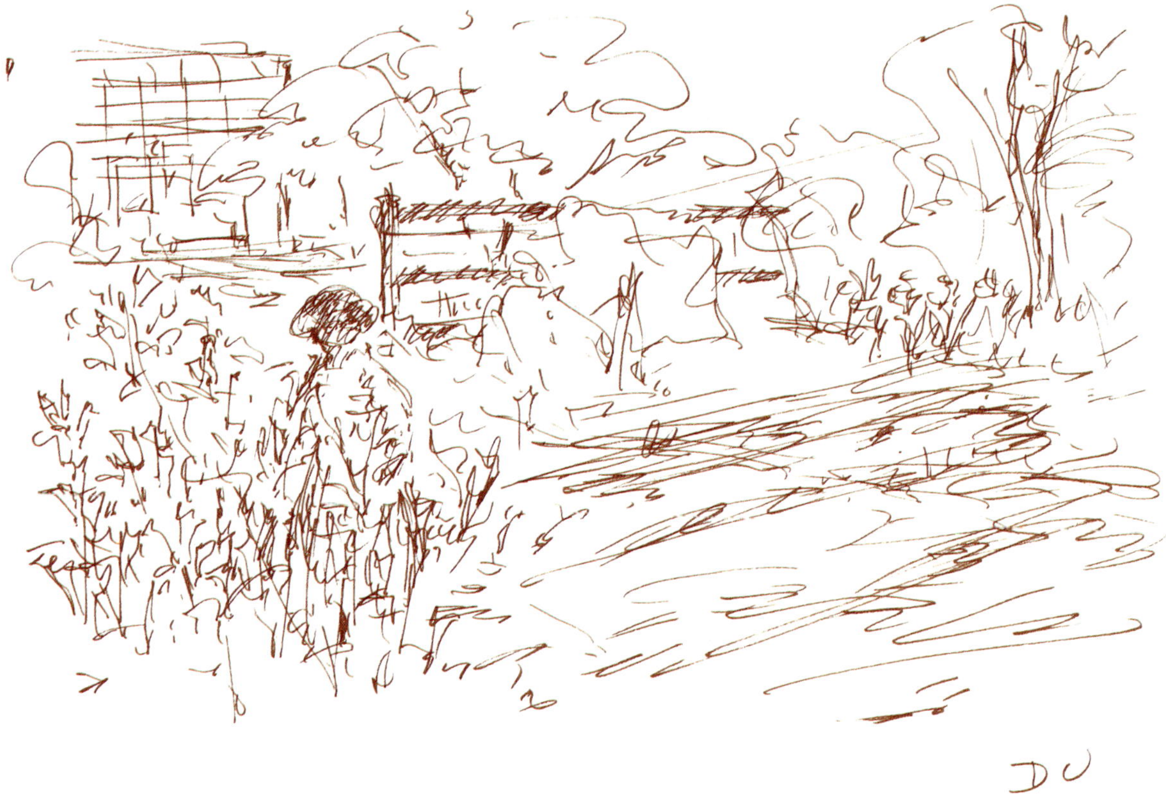

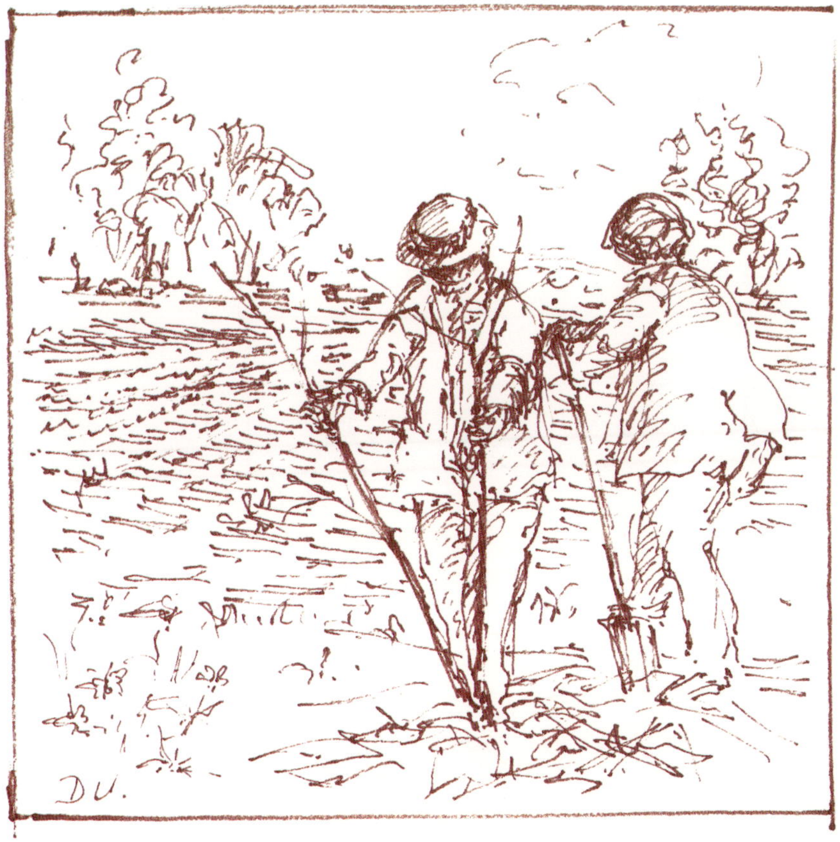
DV.

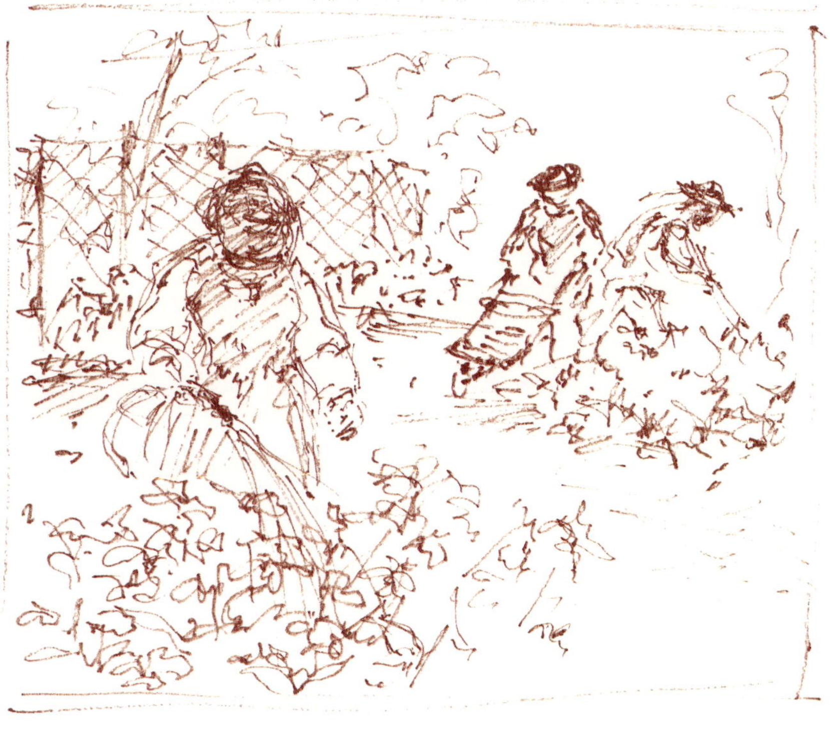

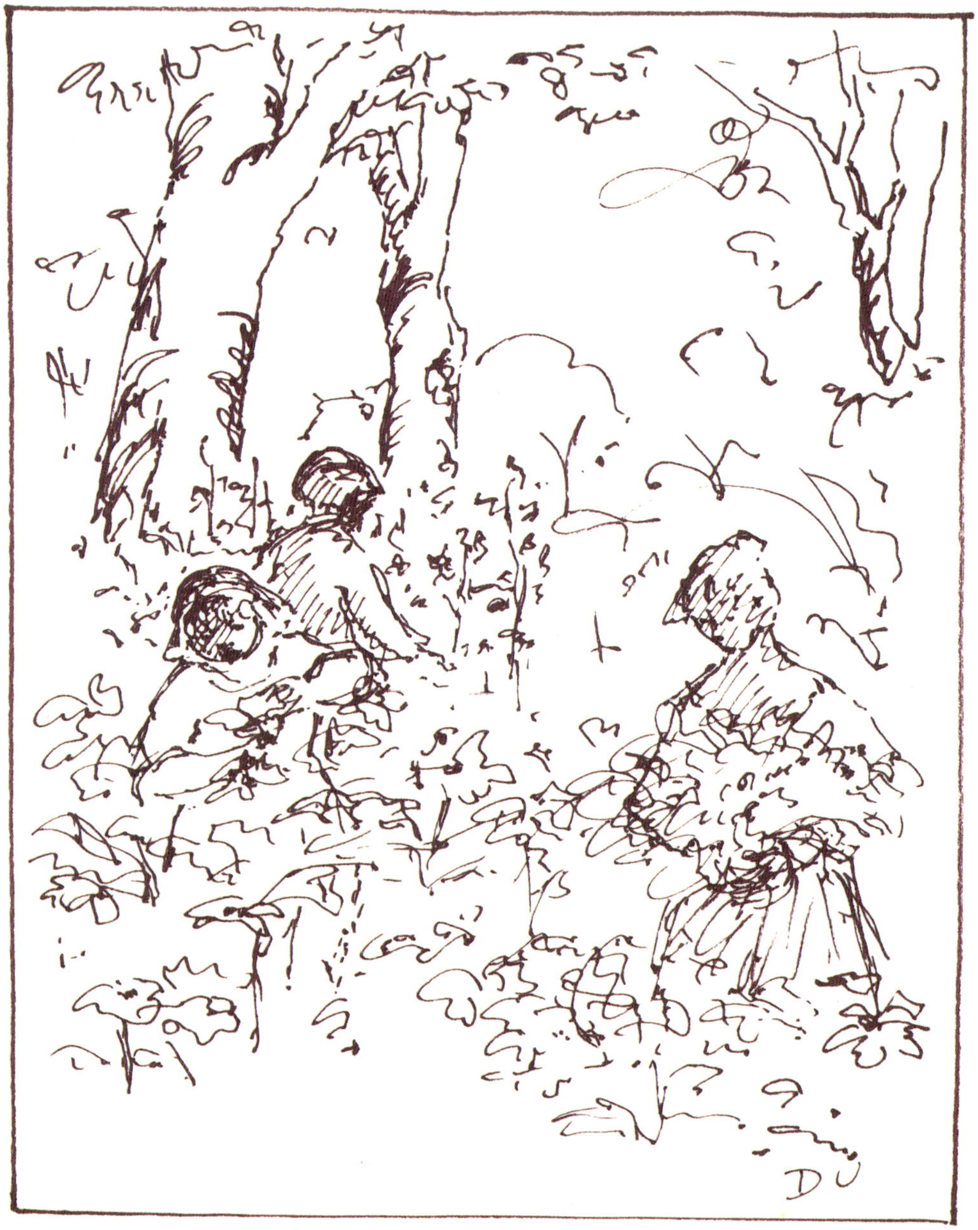

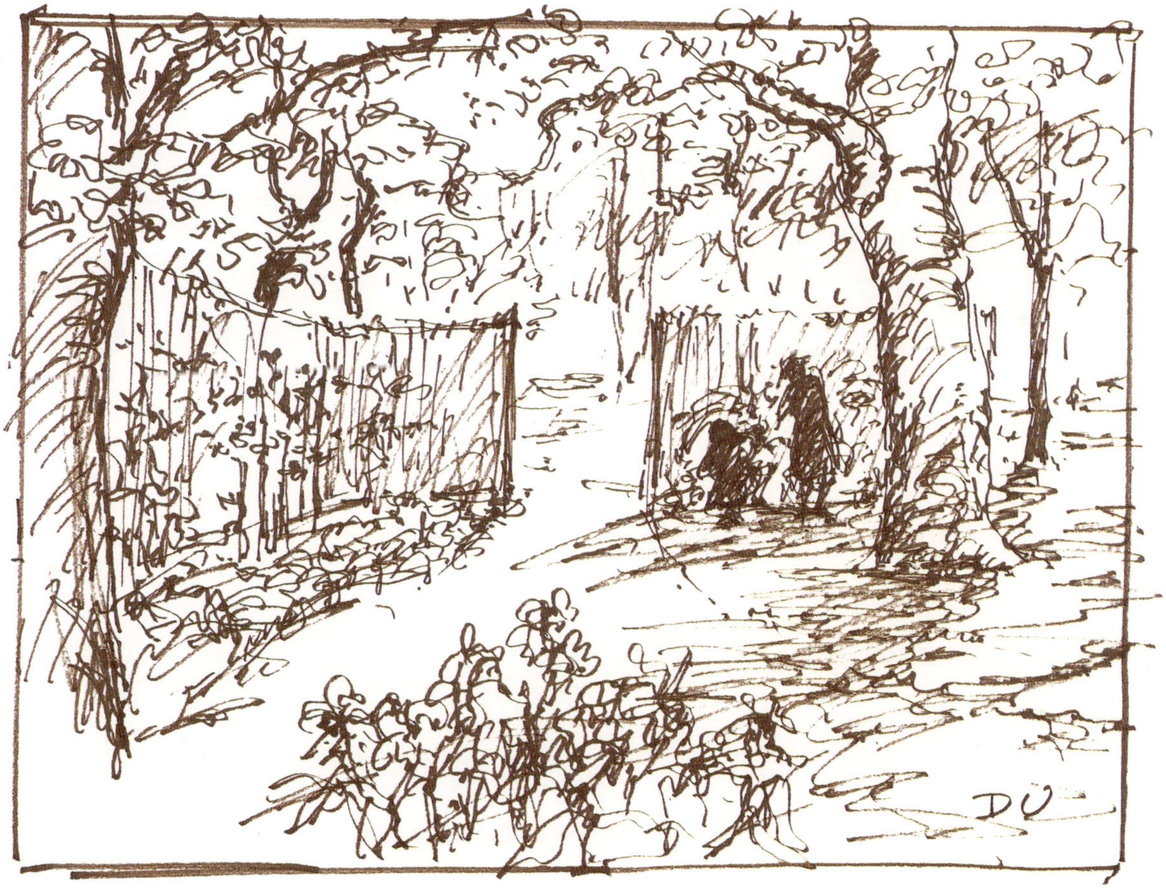
DU

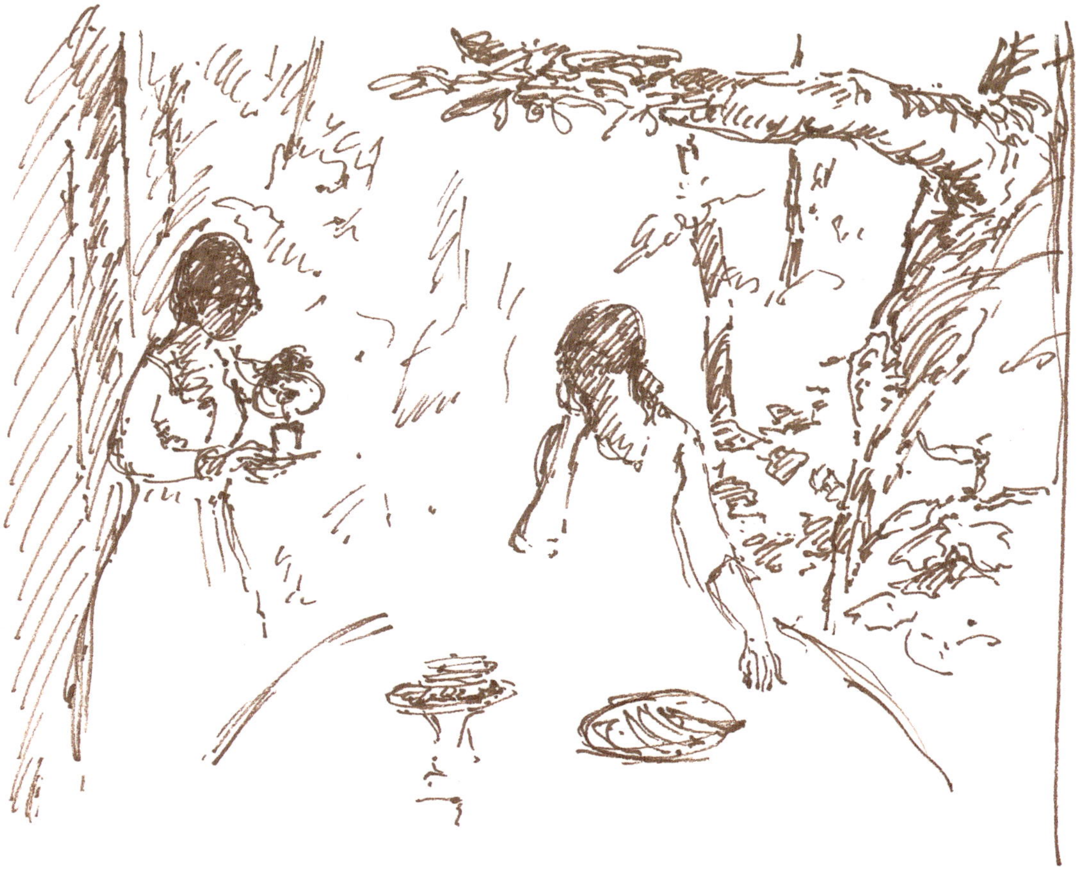

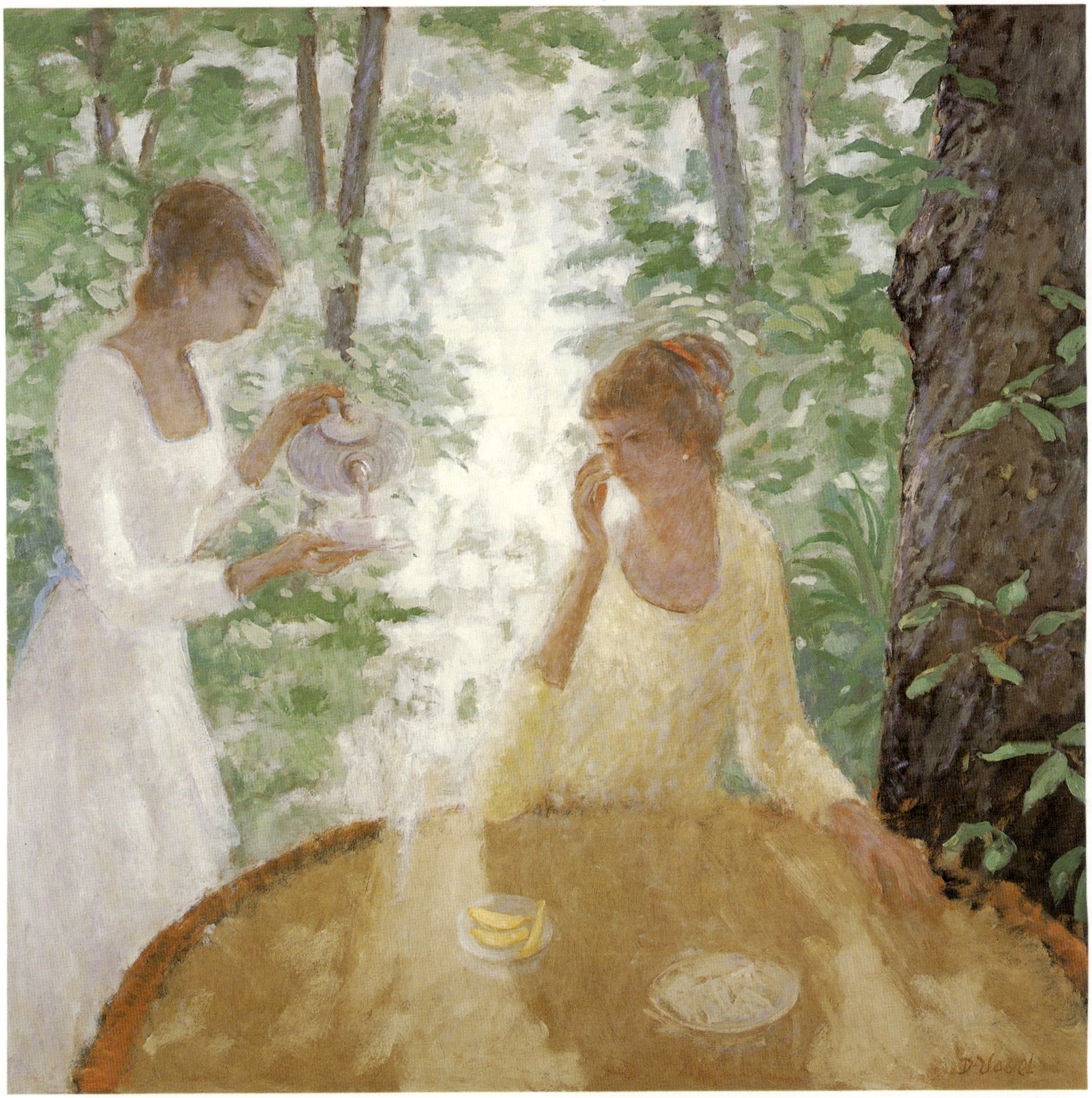

Part Two - The Country Dance and River Houses

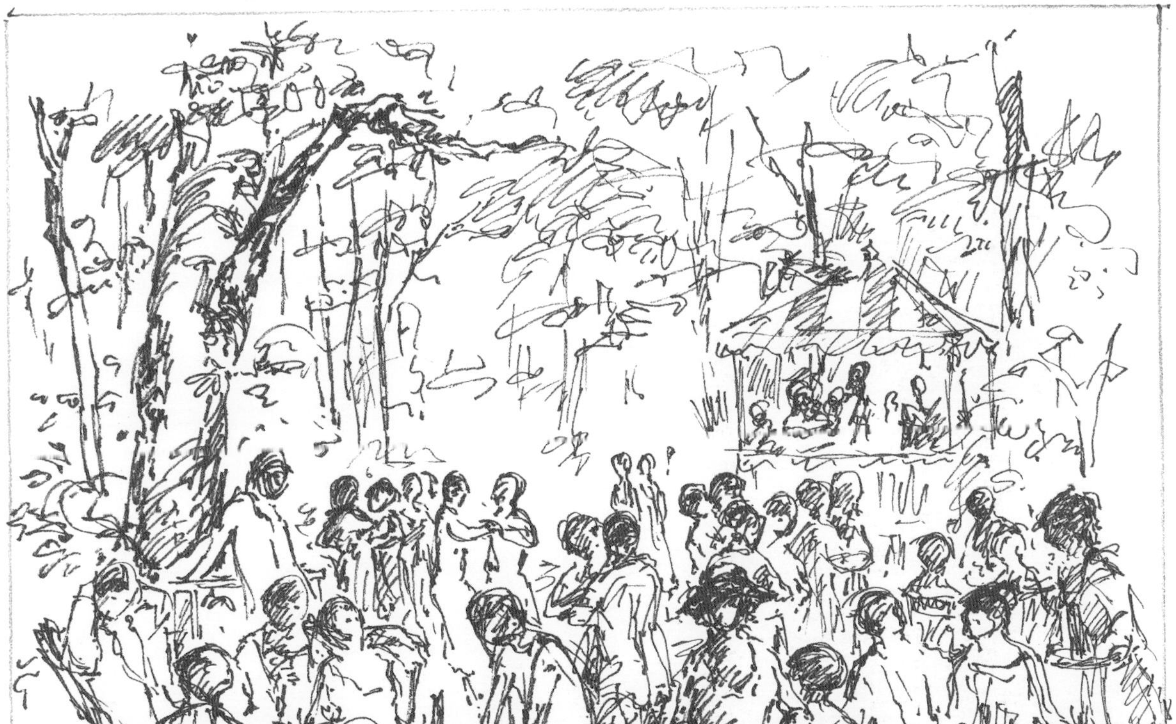

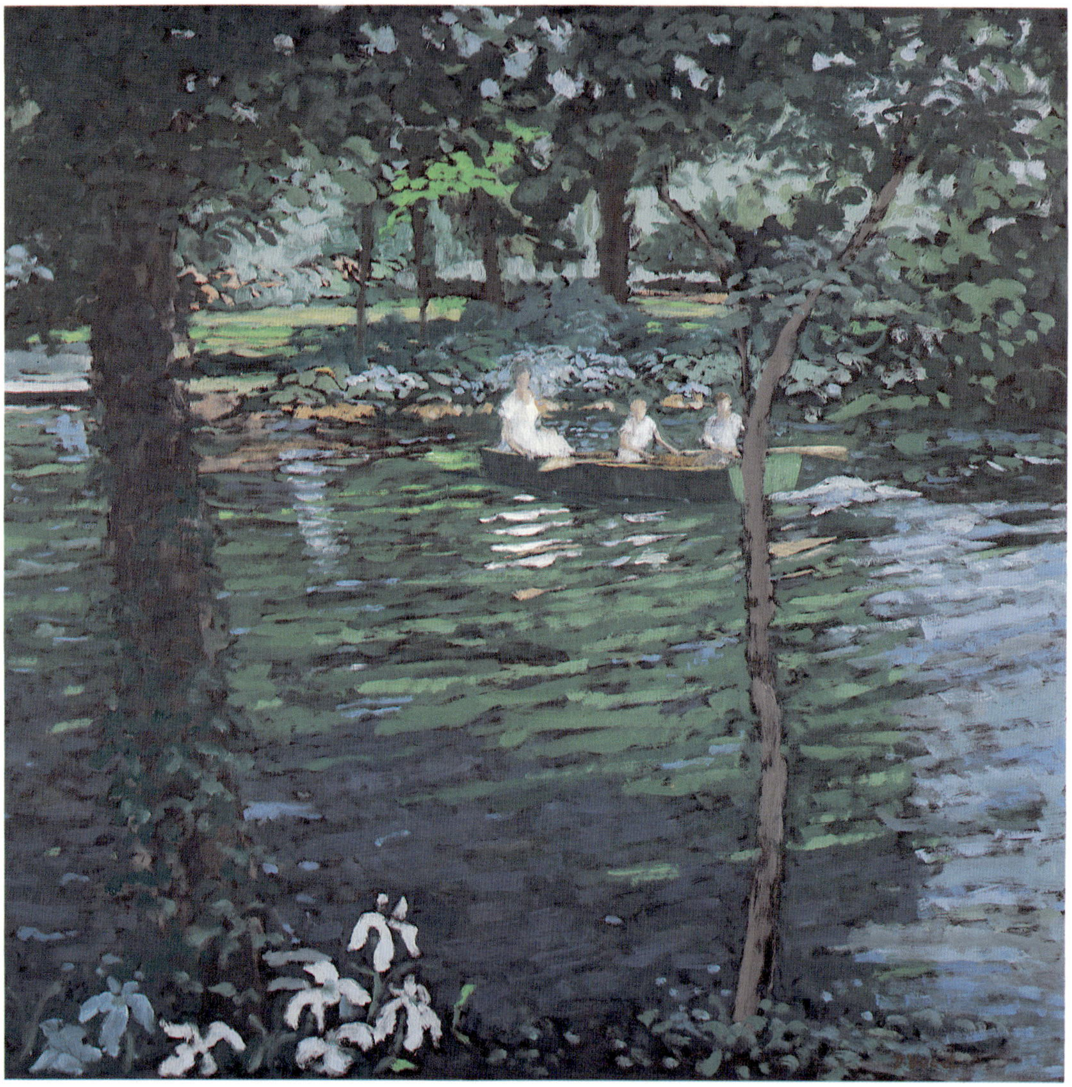

The village in Illinois that introduced me to the pleasures of nature's gifts acquainted me also with the simple joys of the villagers. In close proximity to this small population was a river that supported many boats with summer homes along its banks.

The men of the village on special occasions would fish from early morning through mid-day, while the women set up a kitchen and tables in a clearing surrounded by tall trees. Early evening brought most of the village people together to eat, drink, and dance.

To find and depict the essentials, it is necessary to achieve harmony with nature and a oneness with the subject.

The drawings selected are from memories of such events. While drawing them, I often find myself smiling. I hope that all who see them will respond to the pleasures they recall.

It is a fascinating challenge to establish a group of figures juxtaposed to one another, in movement, in a happy, light hearted atmosphere. Such drawing puts a line around a pleasant memory, keeping it ever alive.

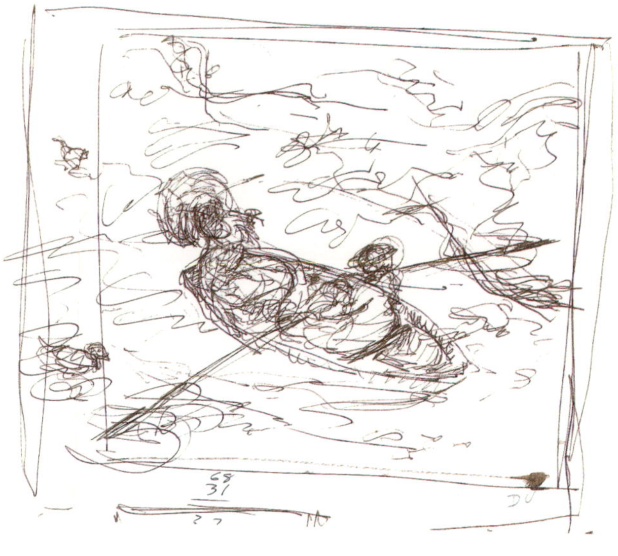

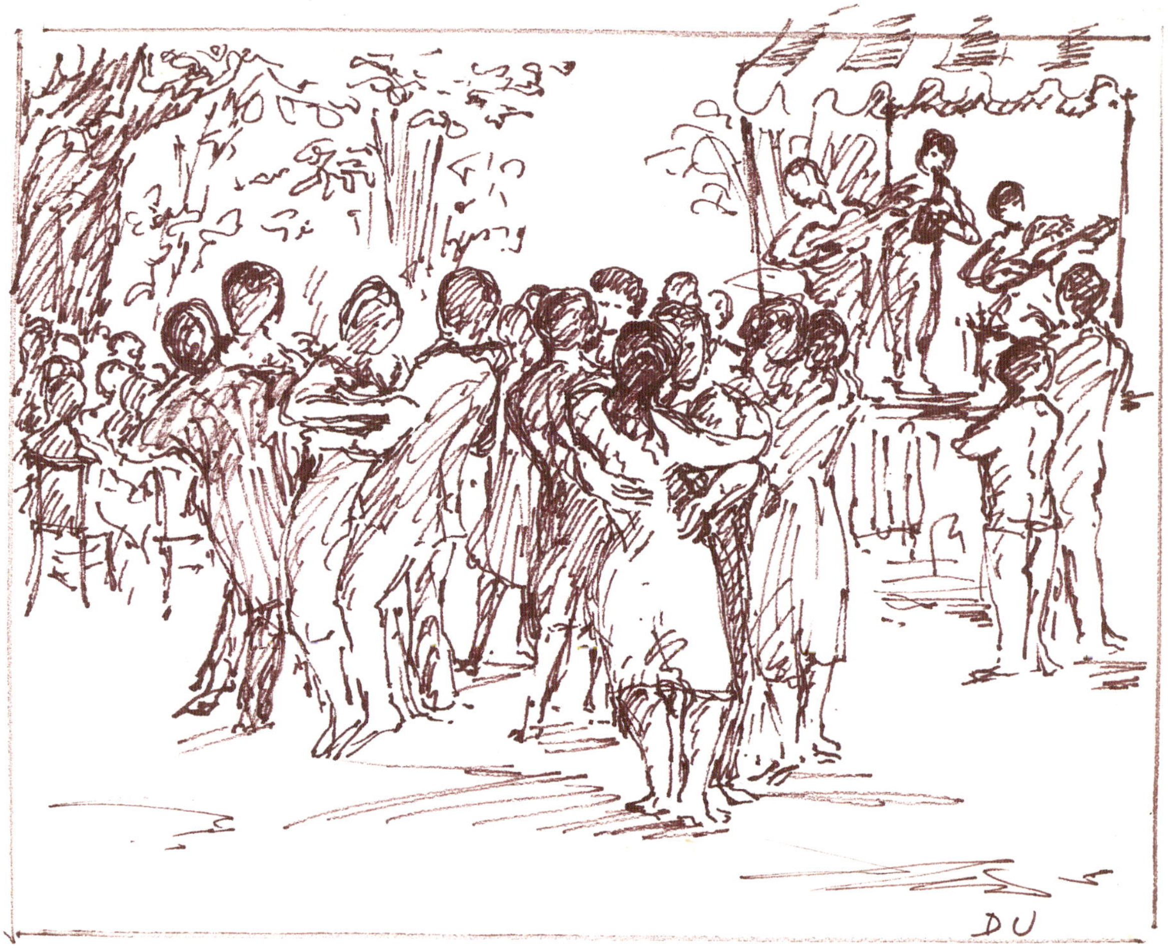
DU

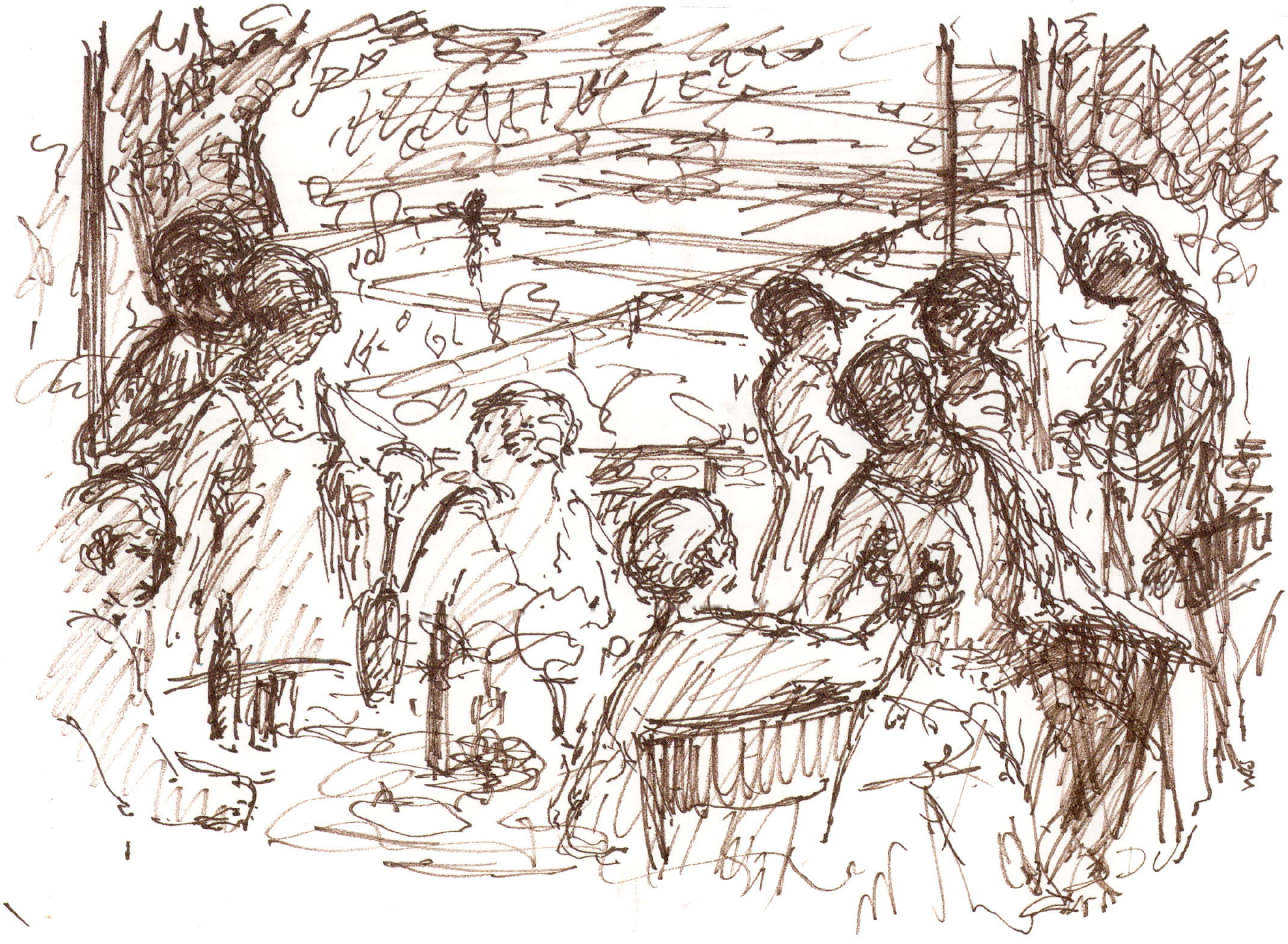

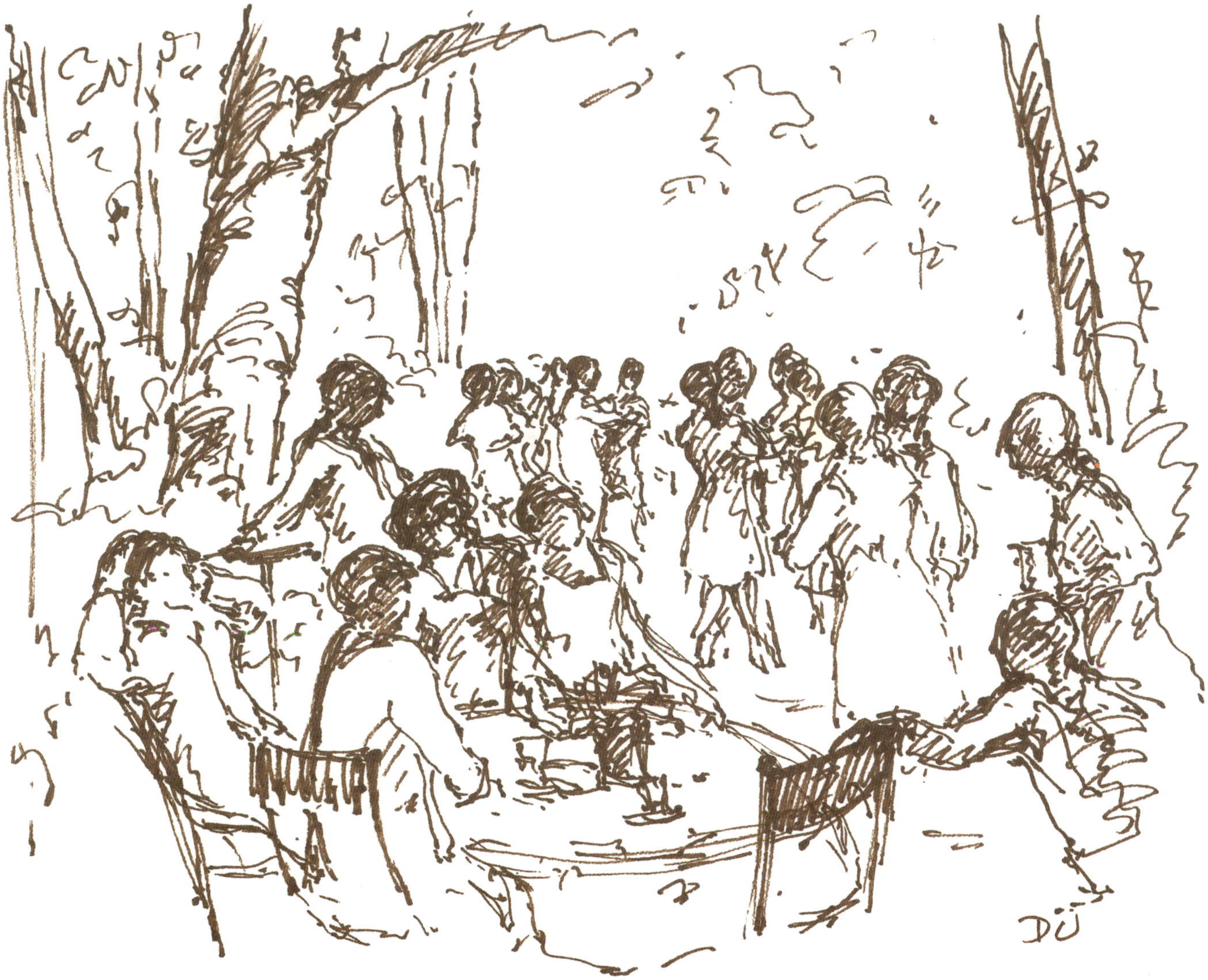
DÜ

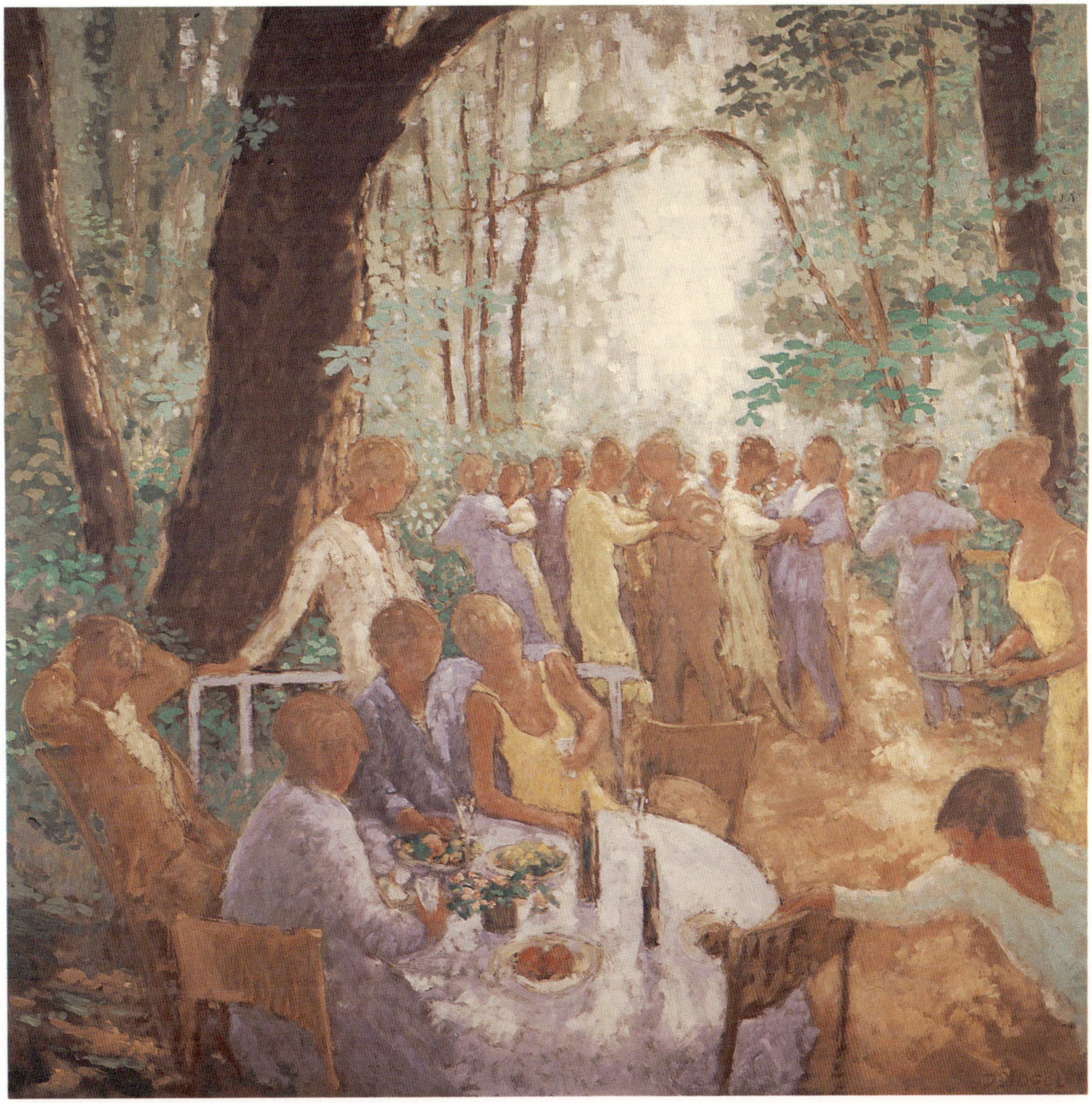

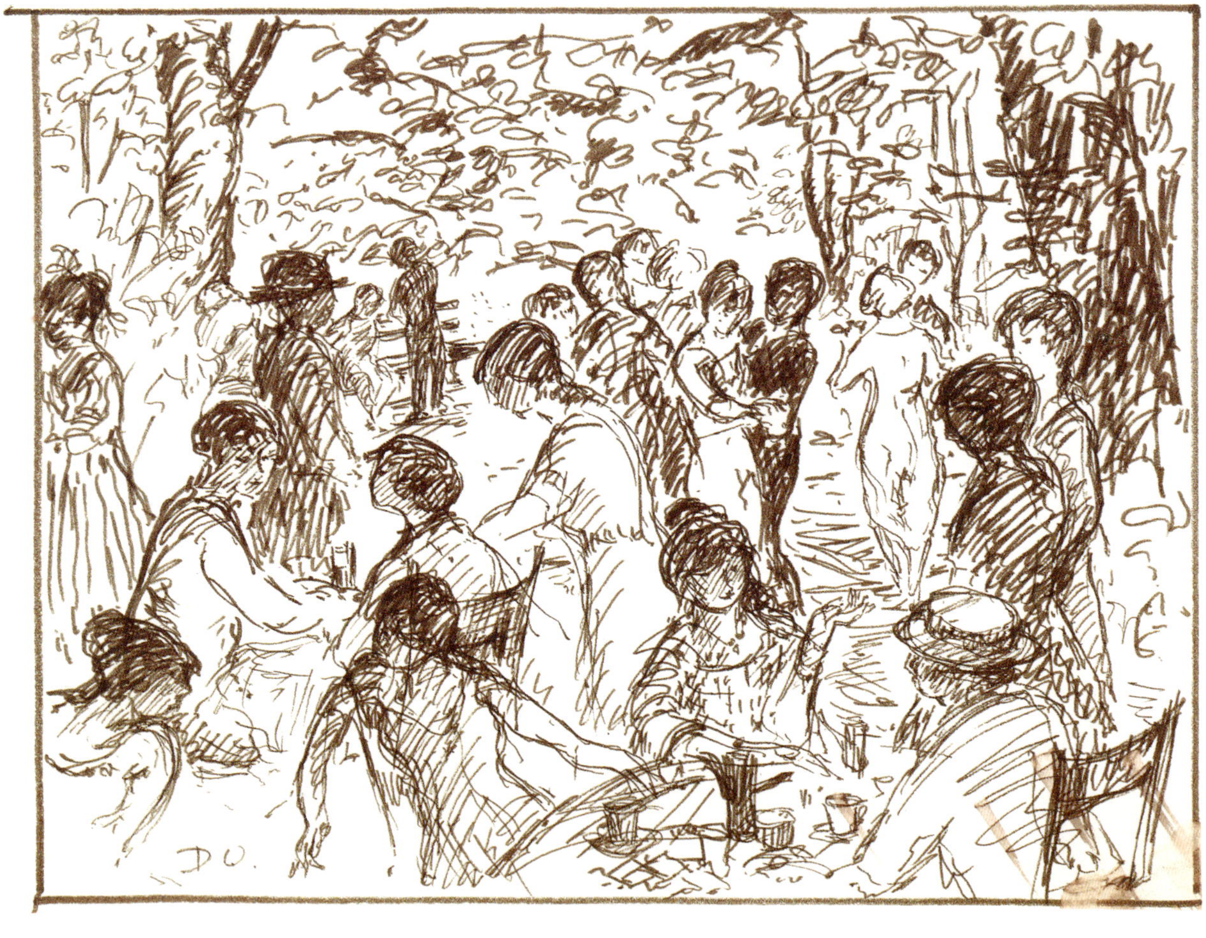

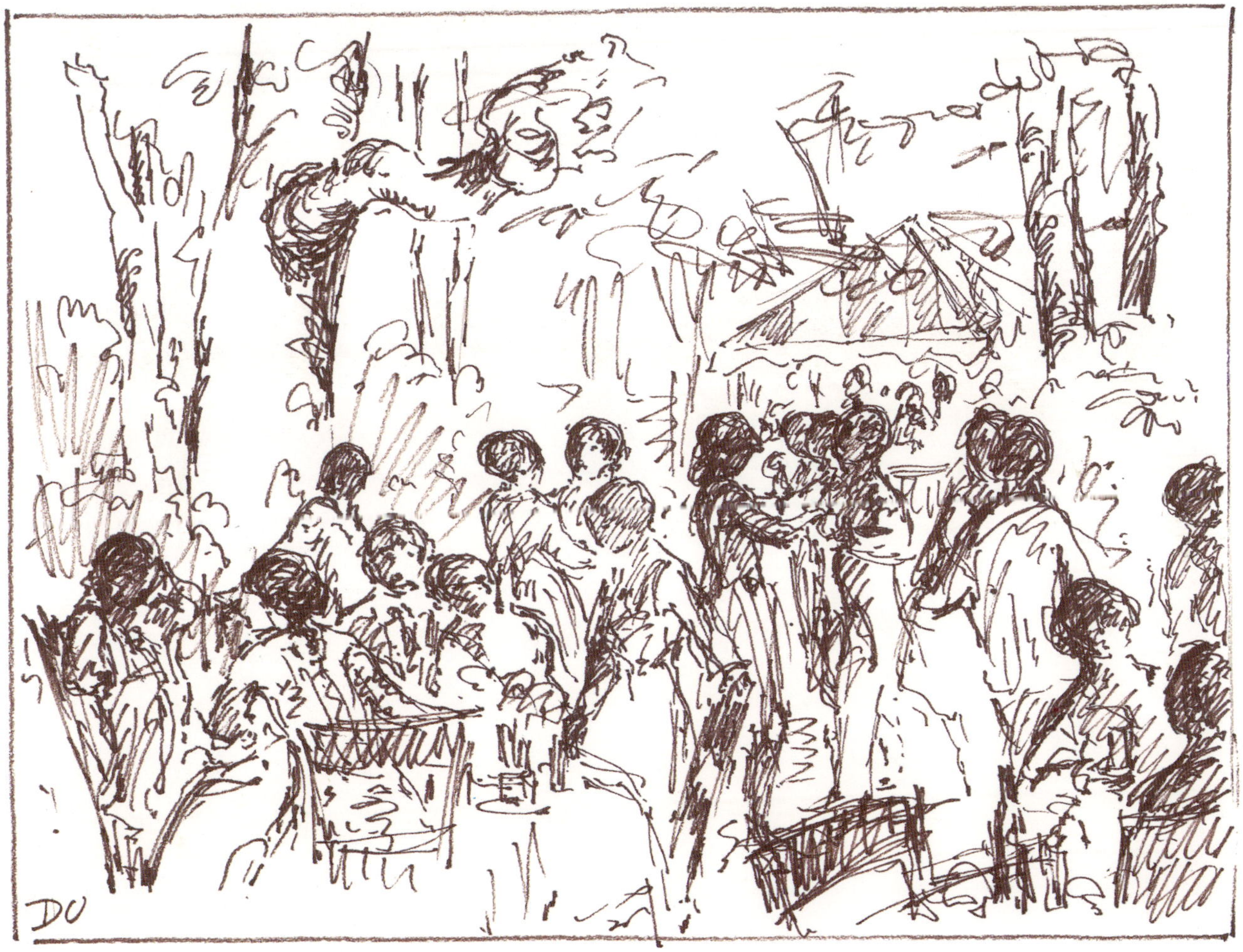
DO

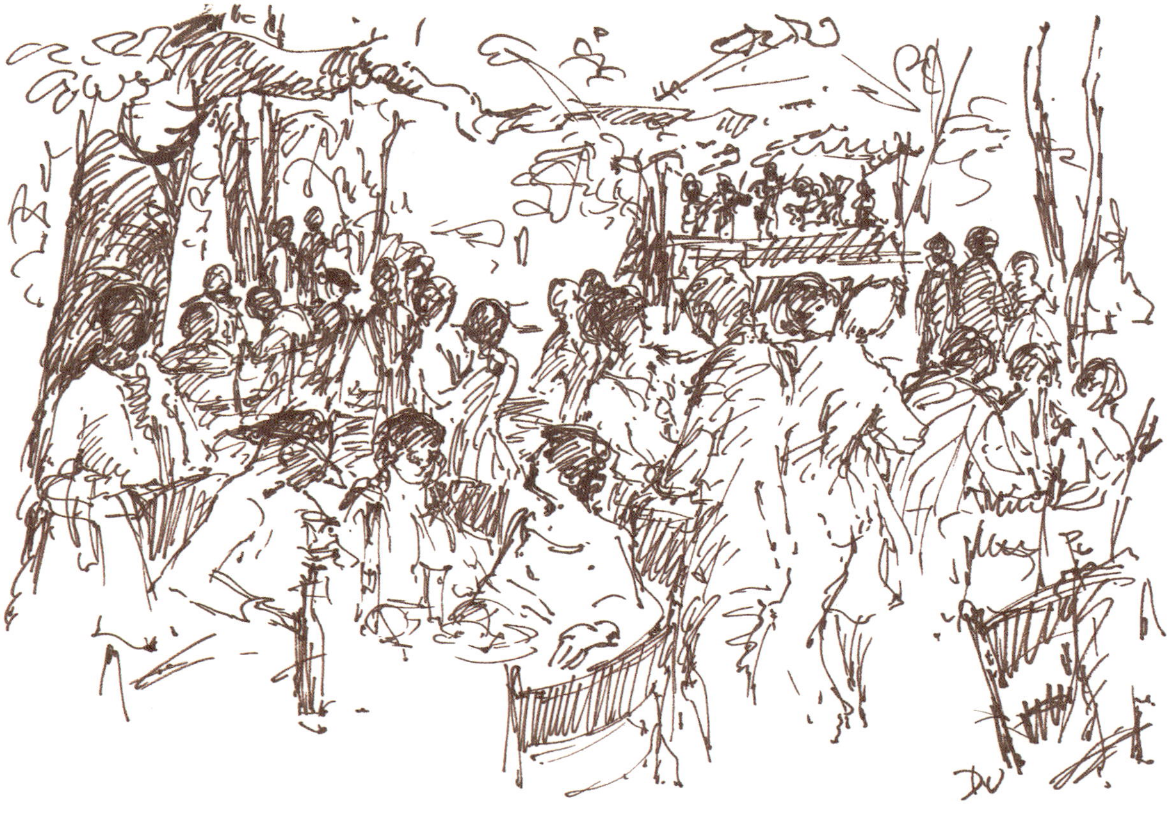

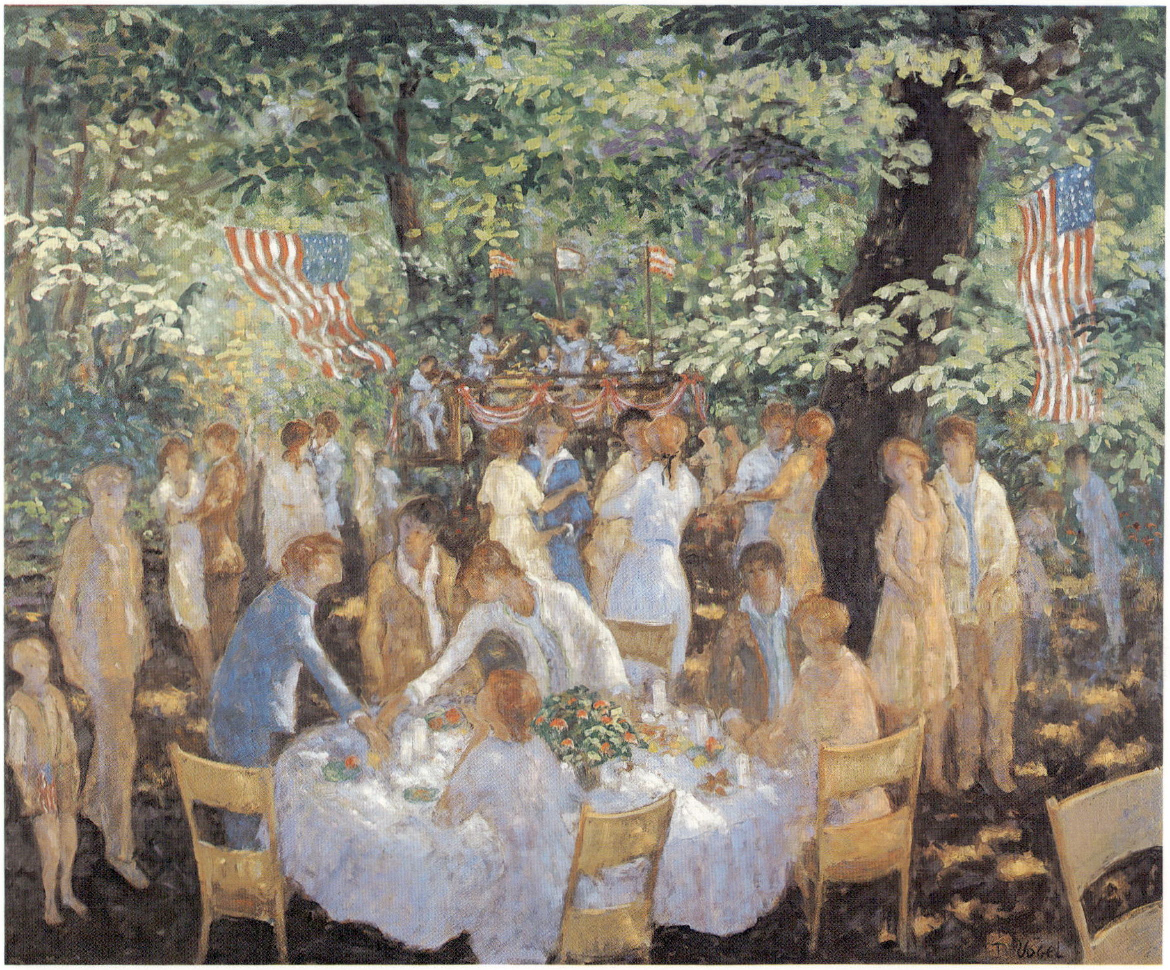
T. VOGEL

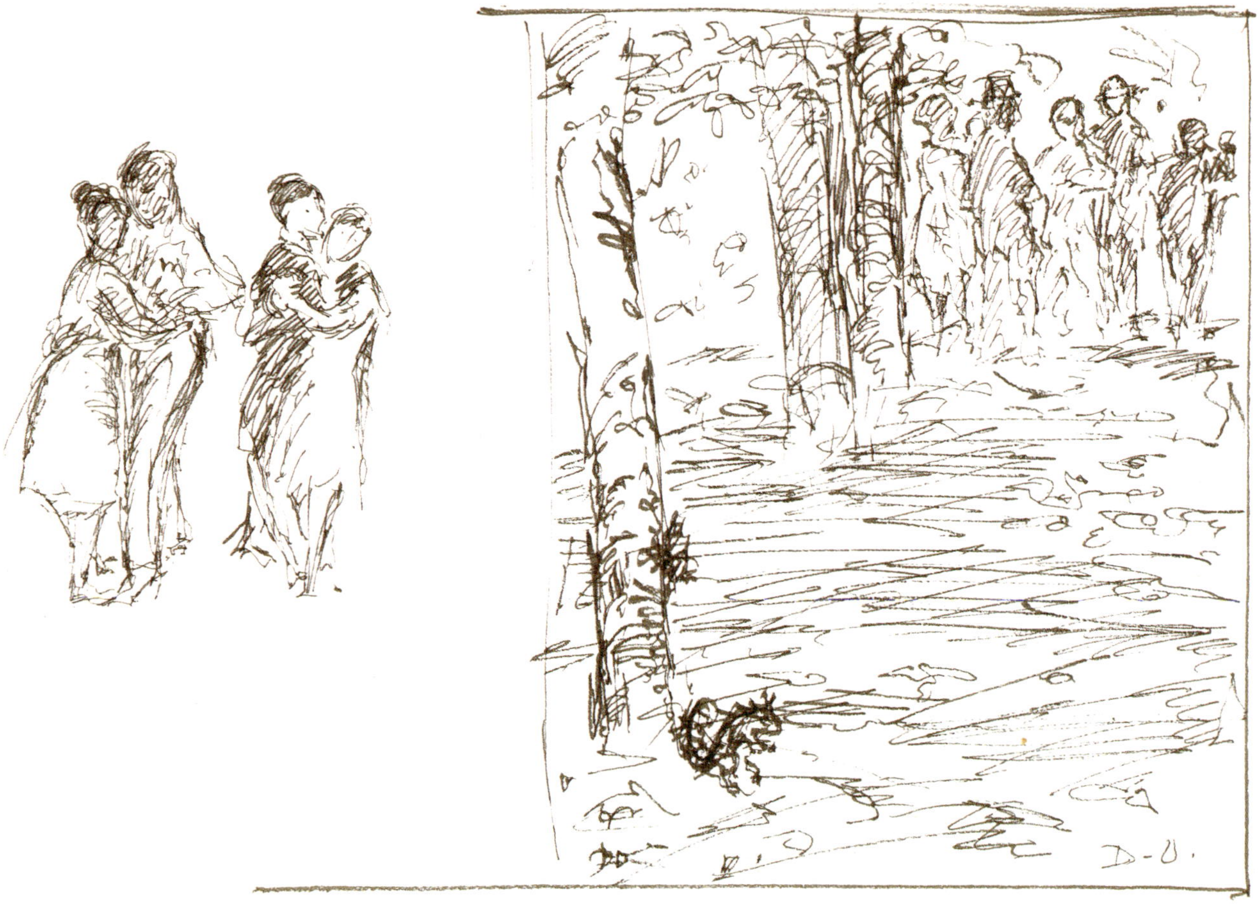
D-U.

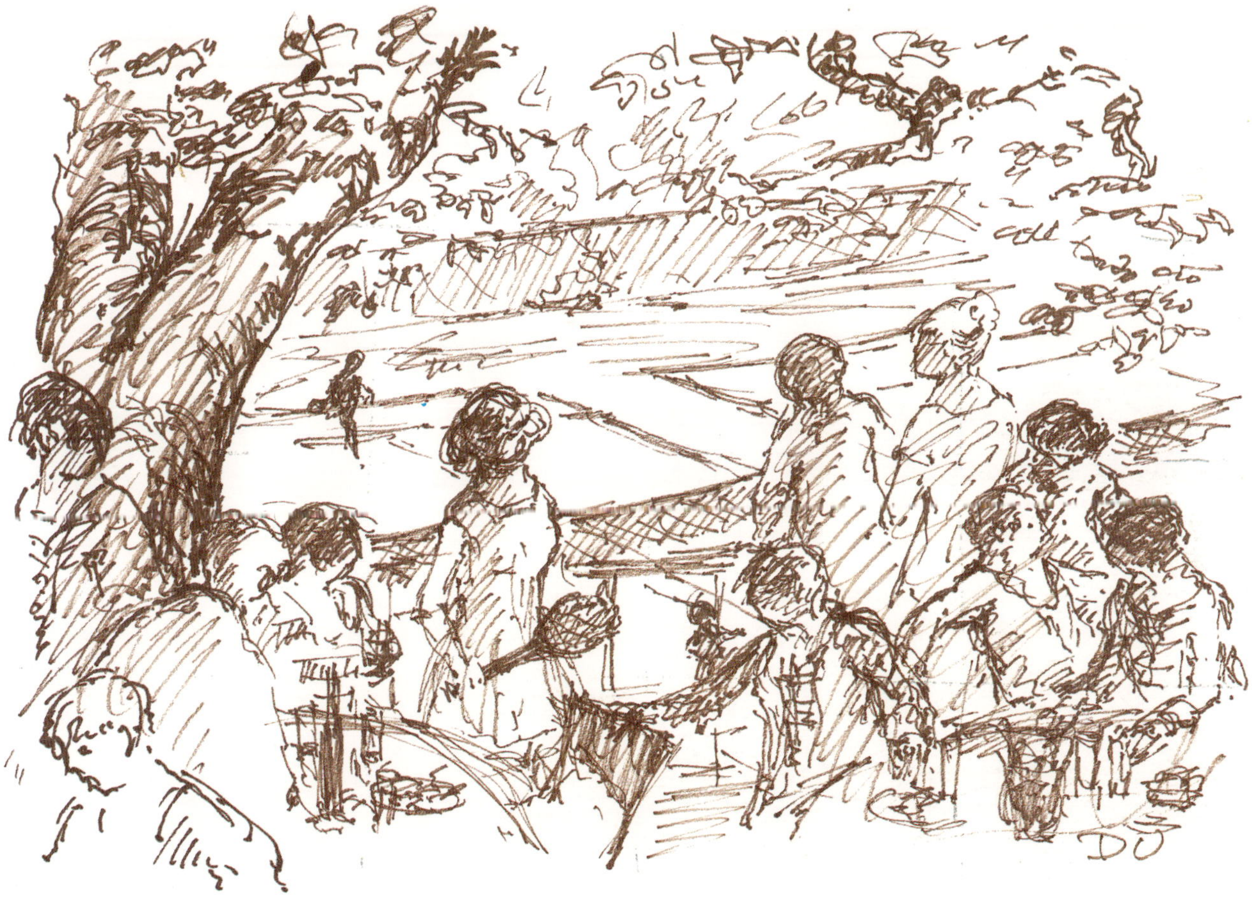

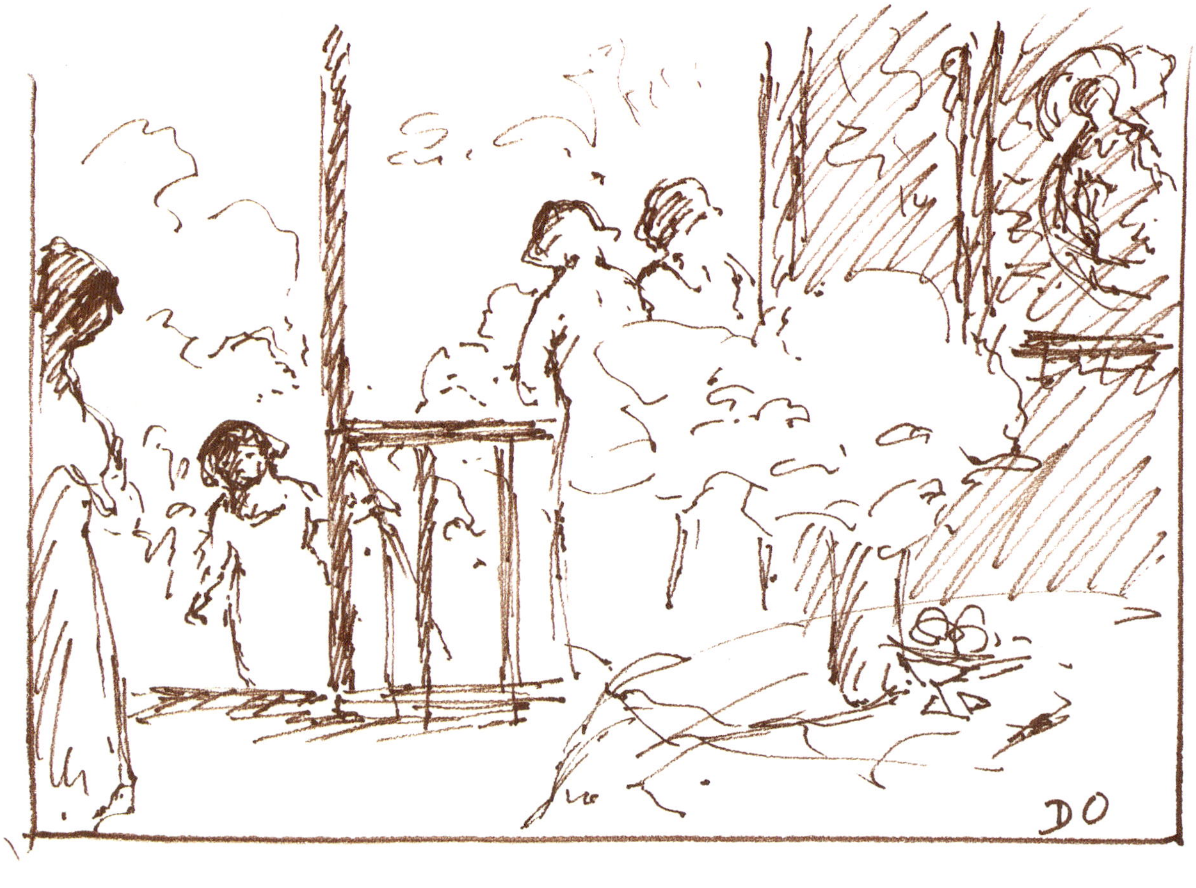

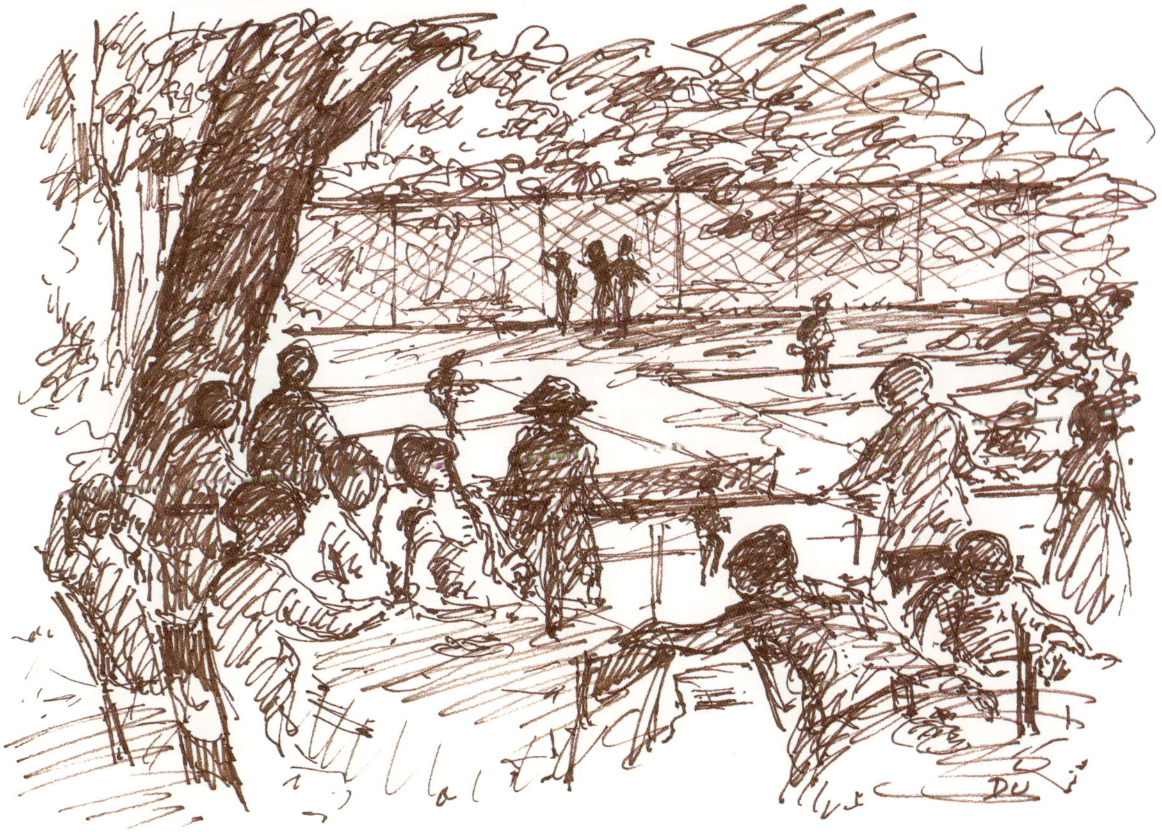

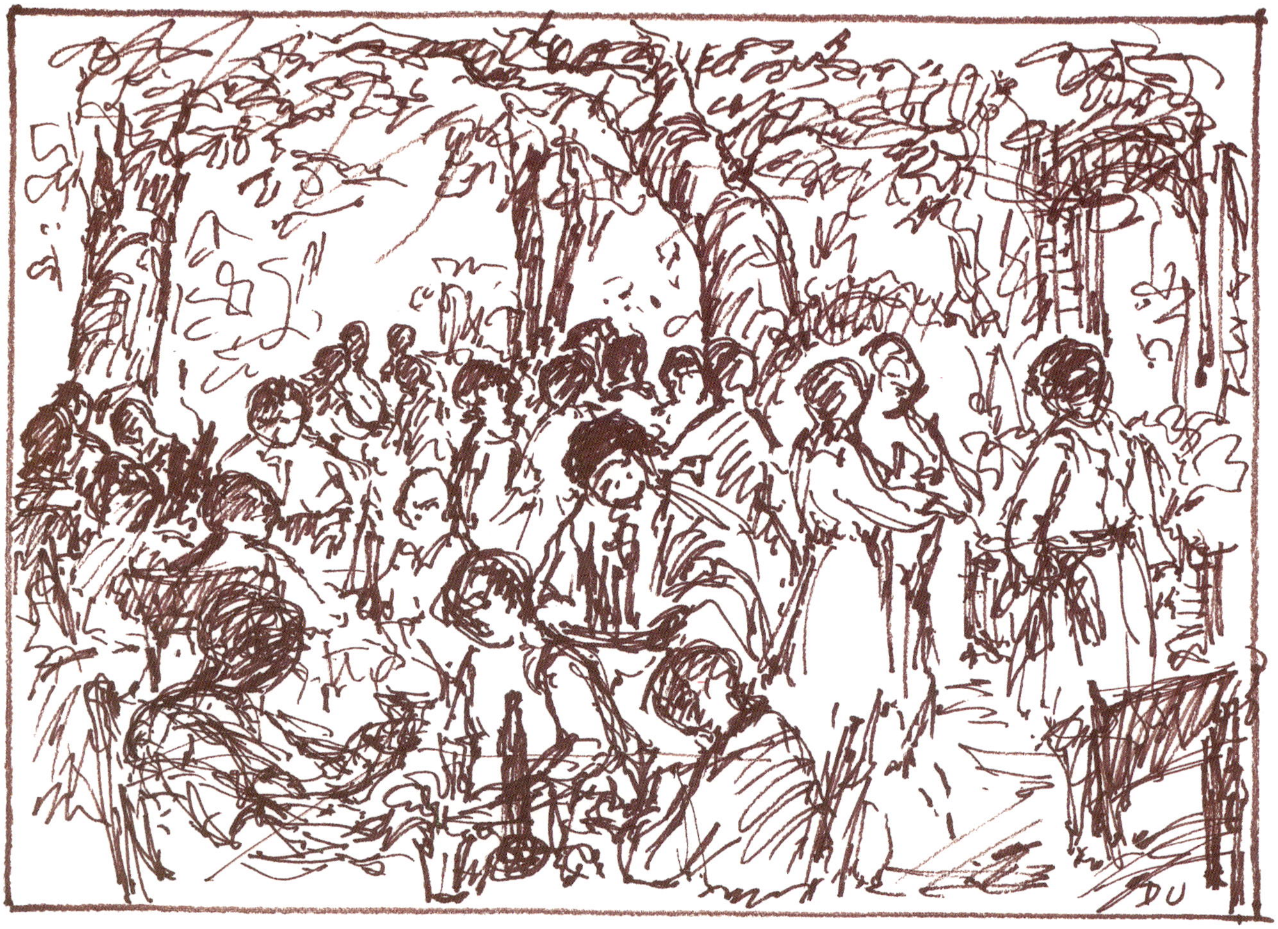

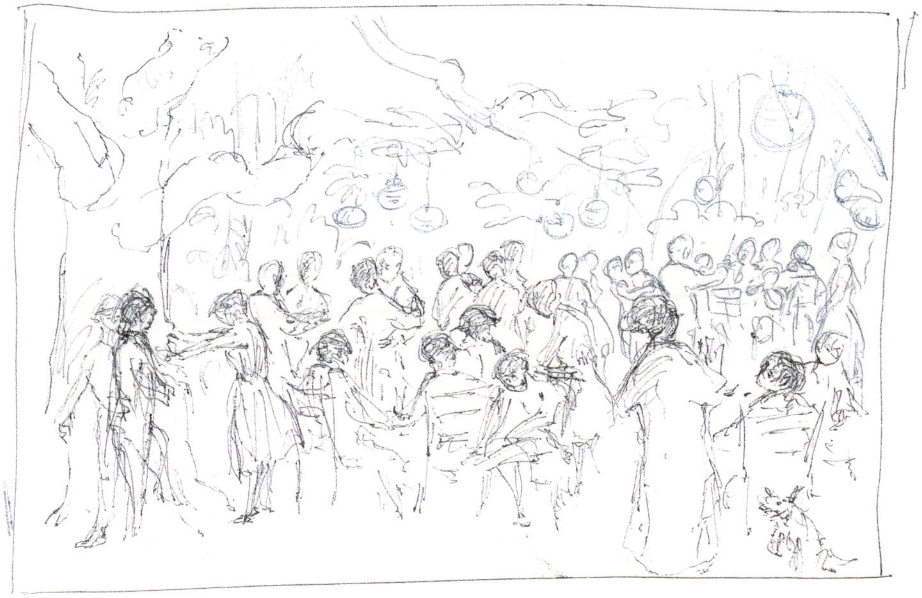

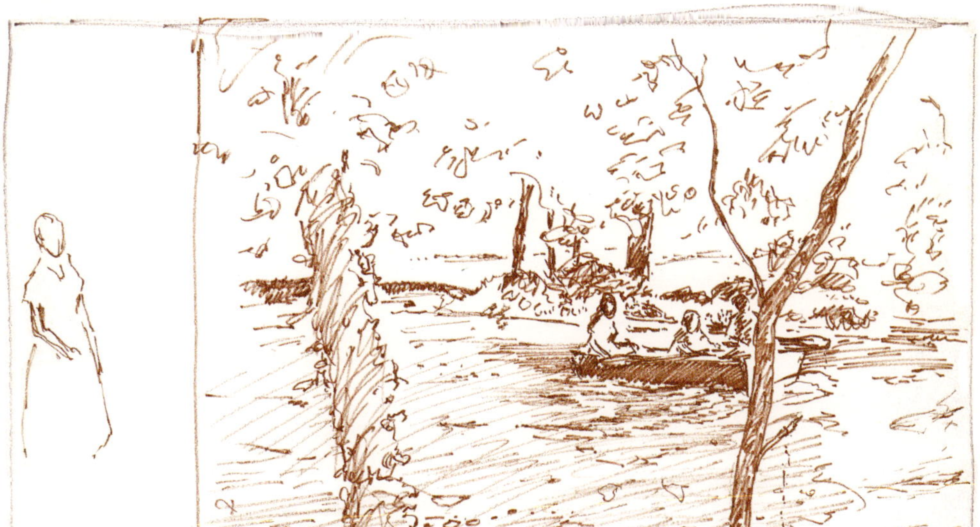

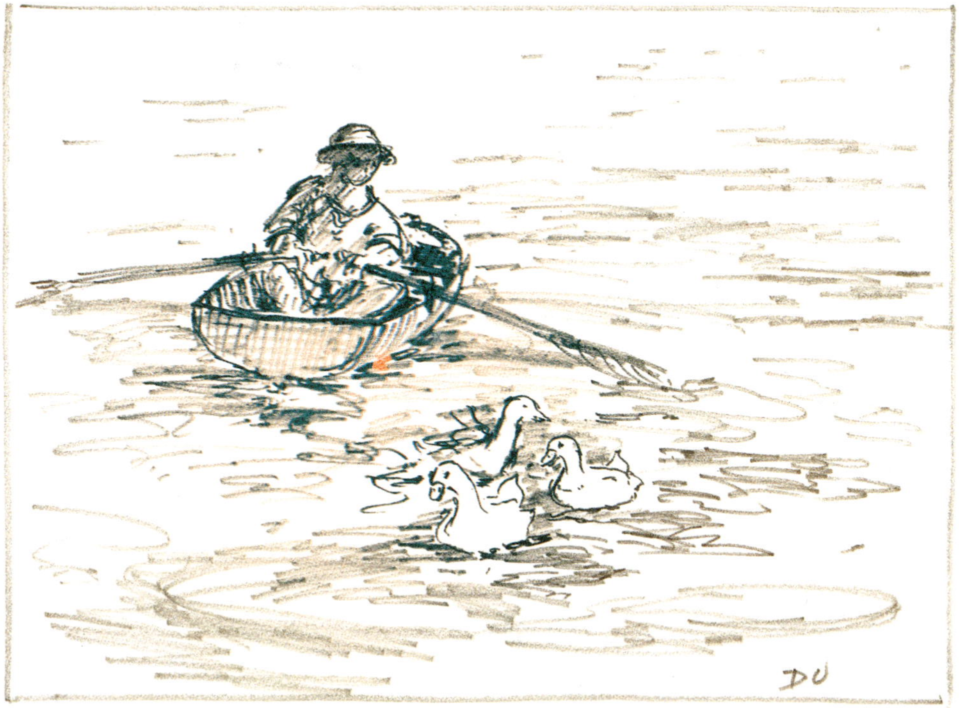
DU

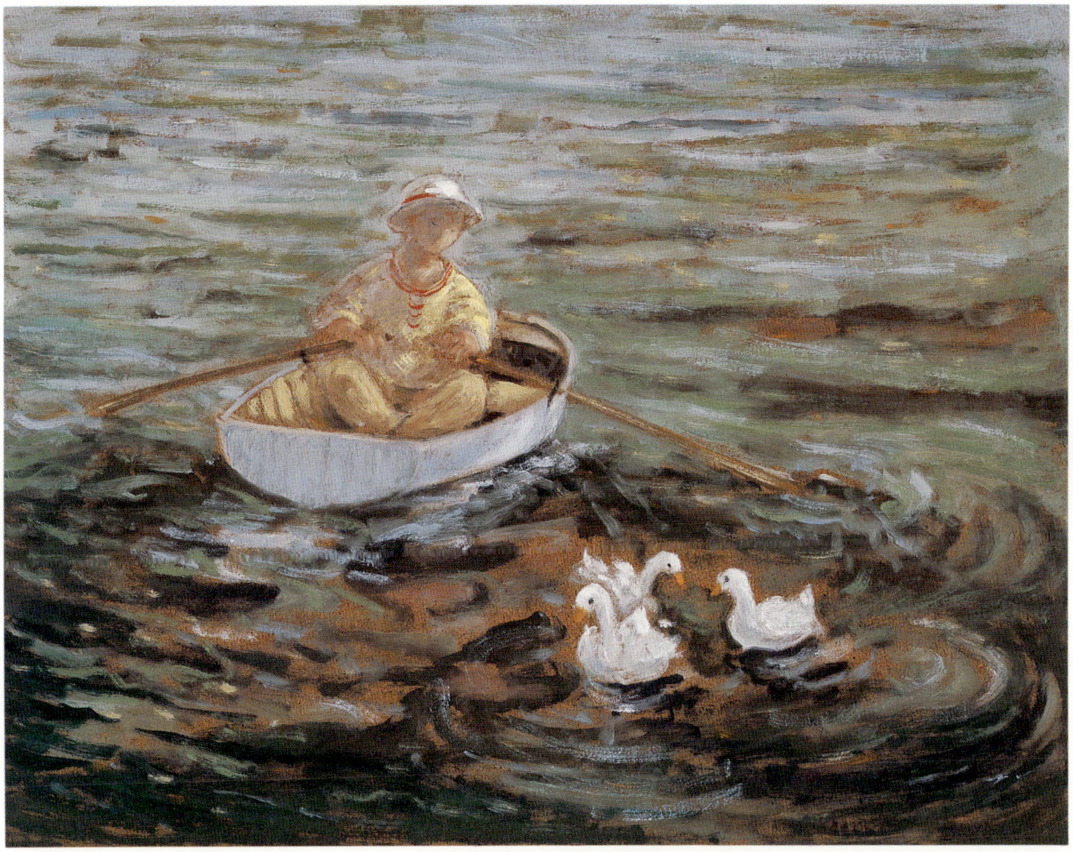

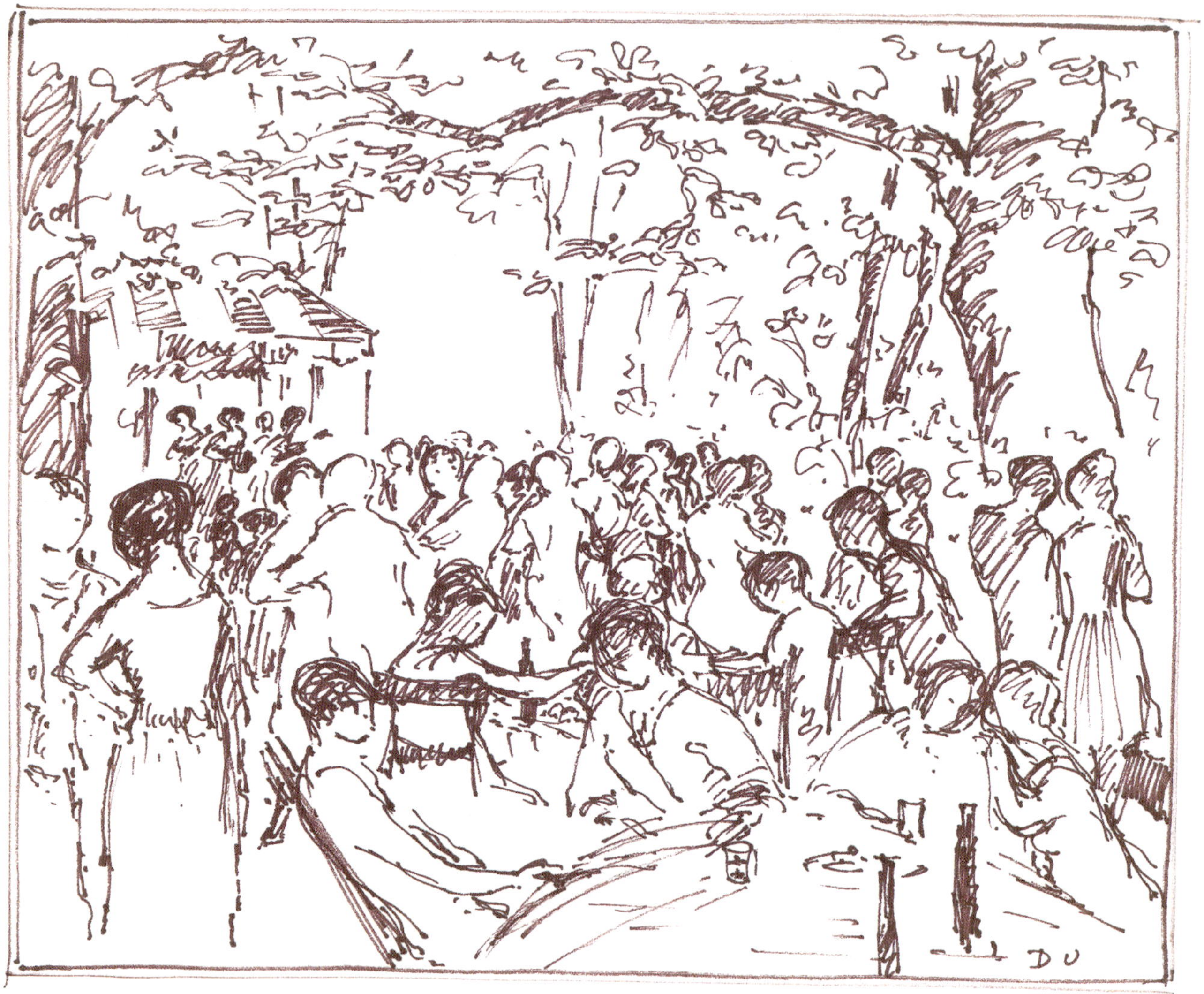

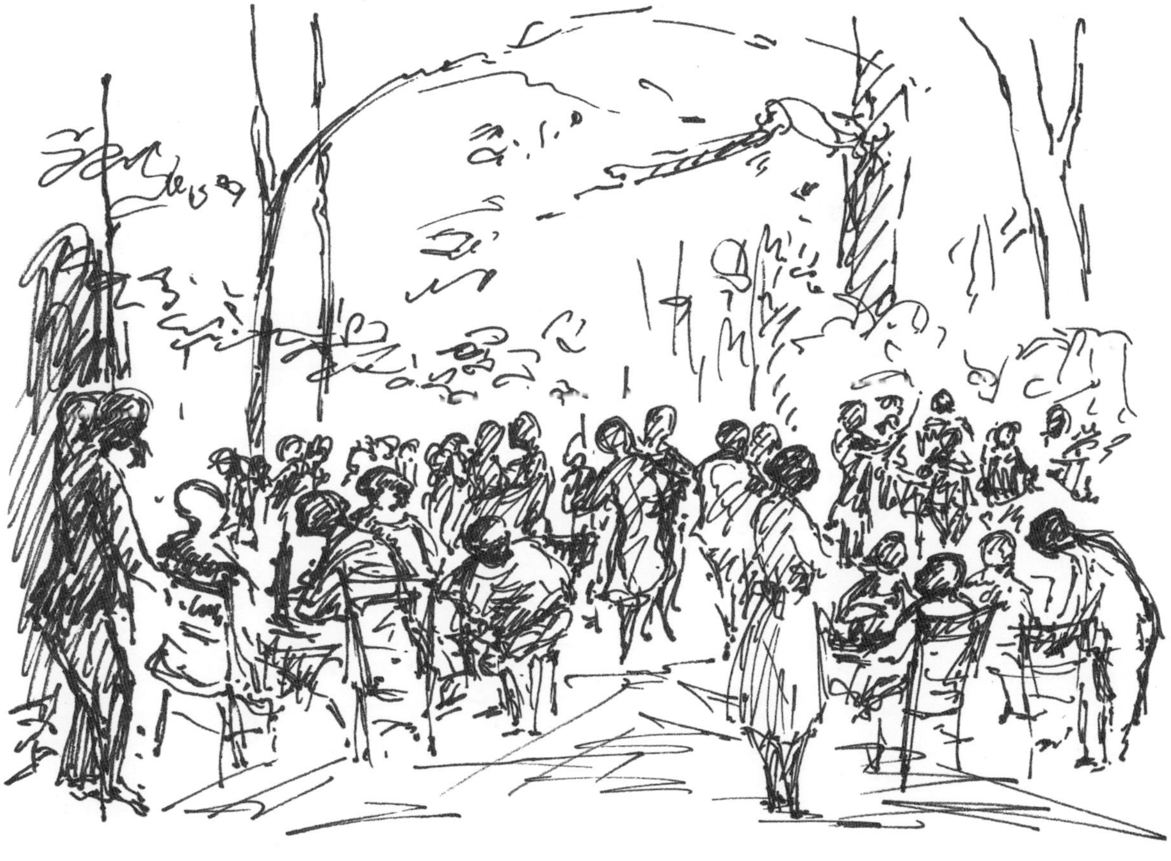

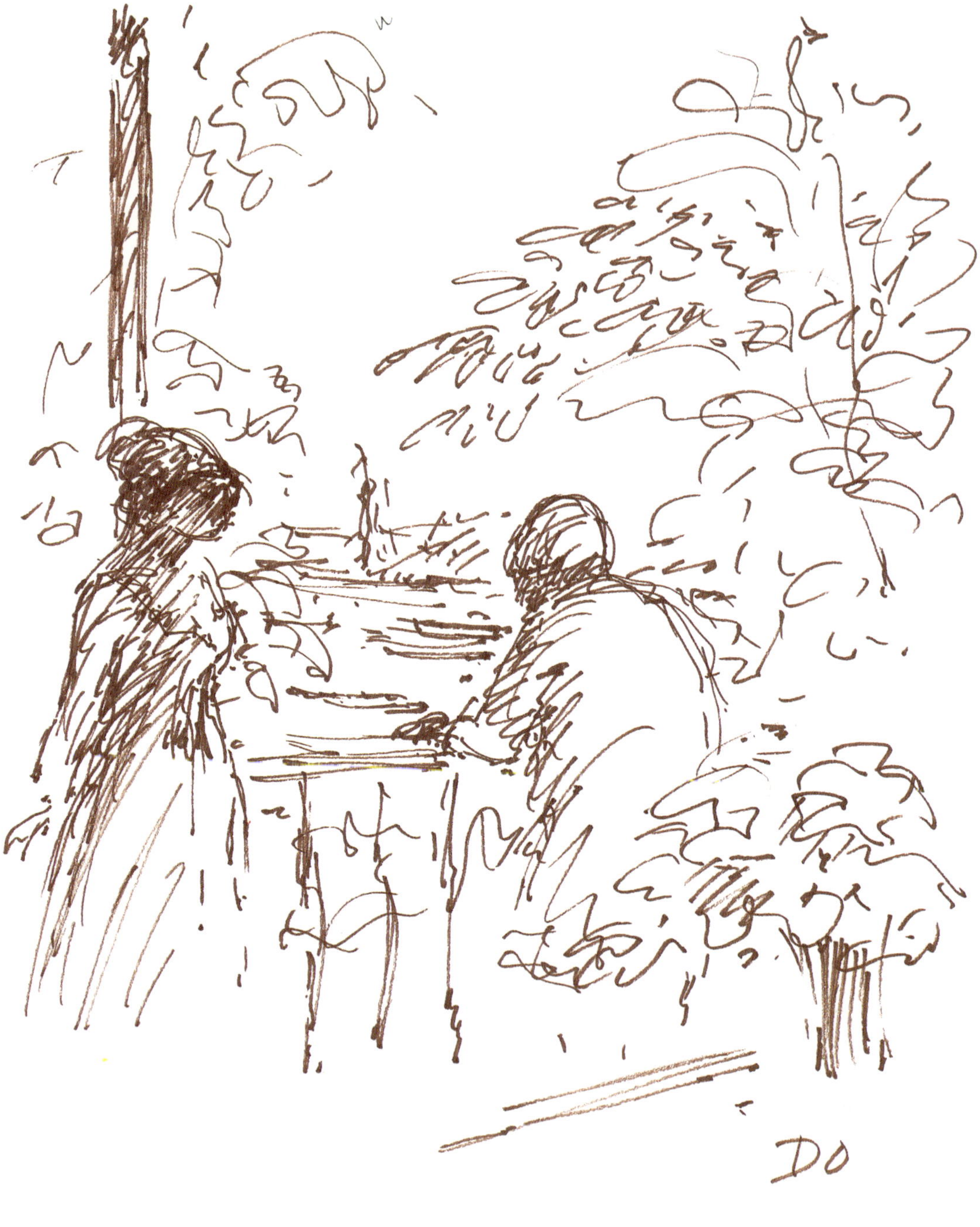
DO

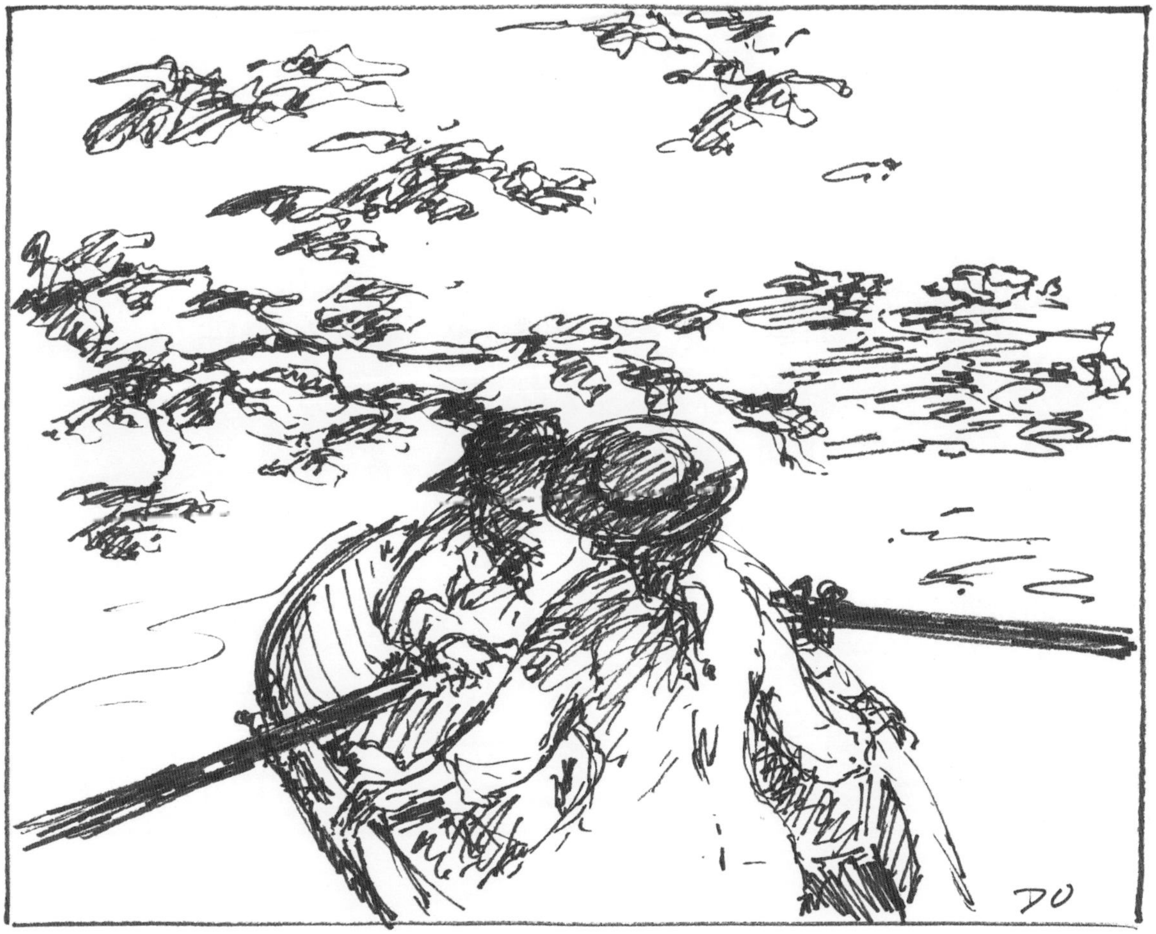
DO

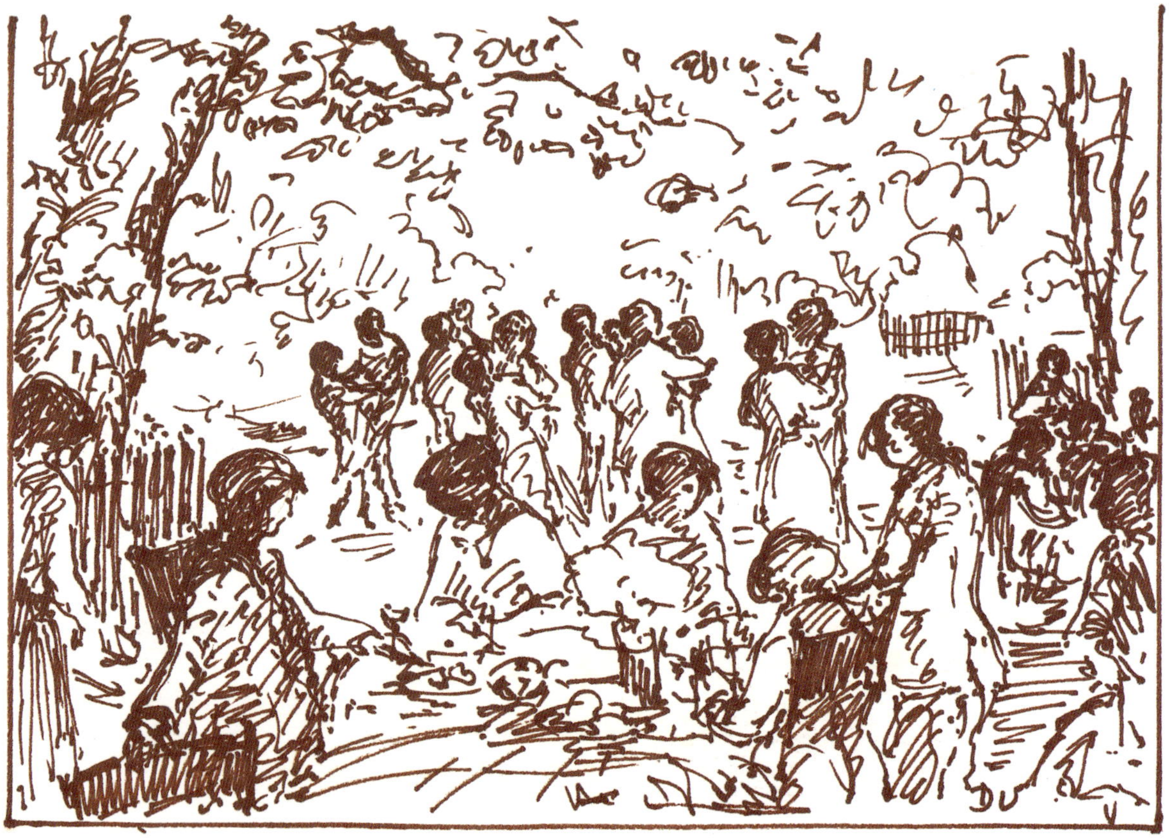

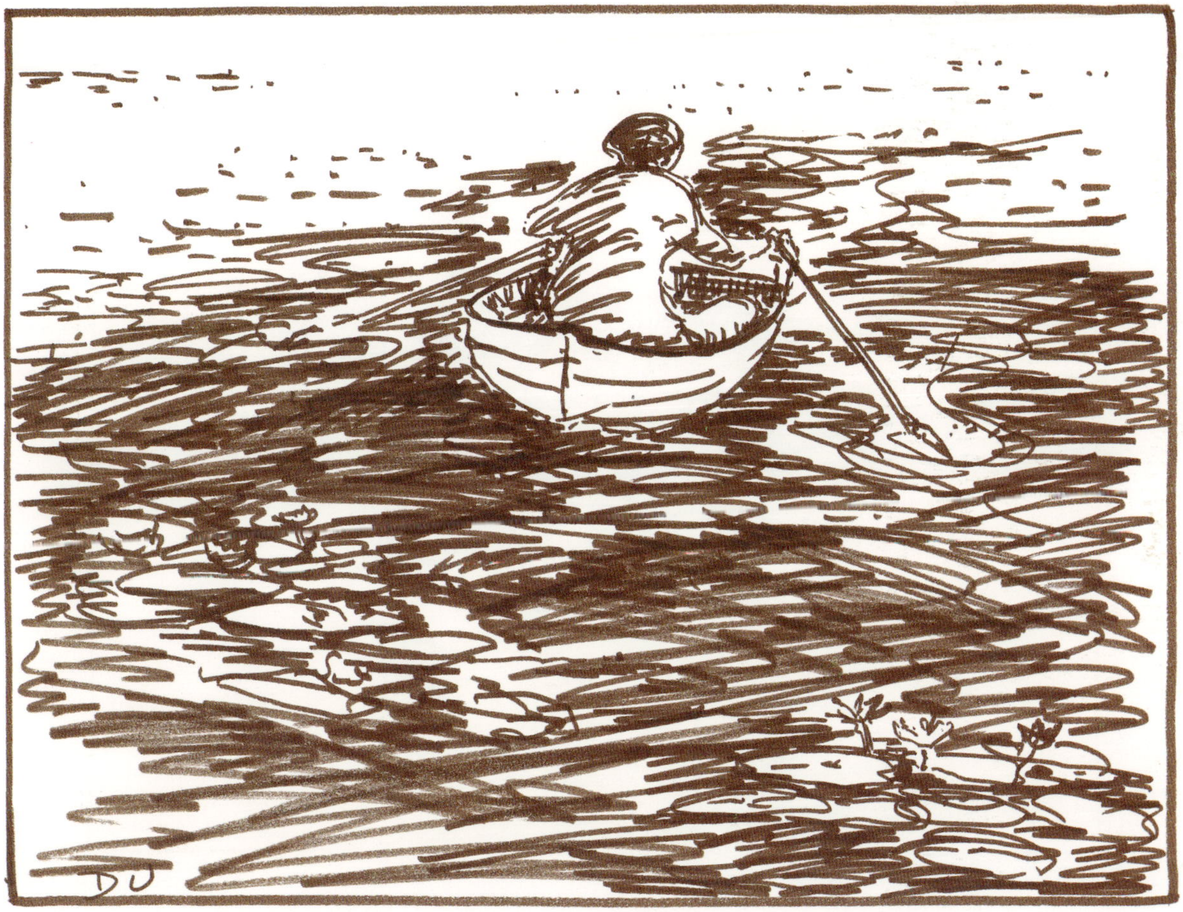
DU

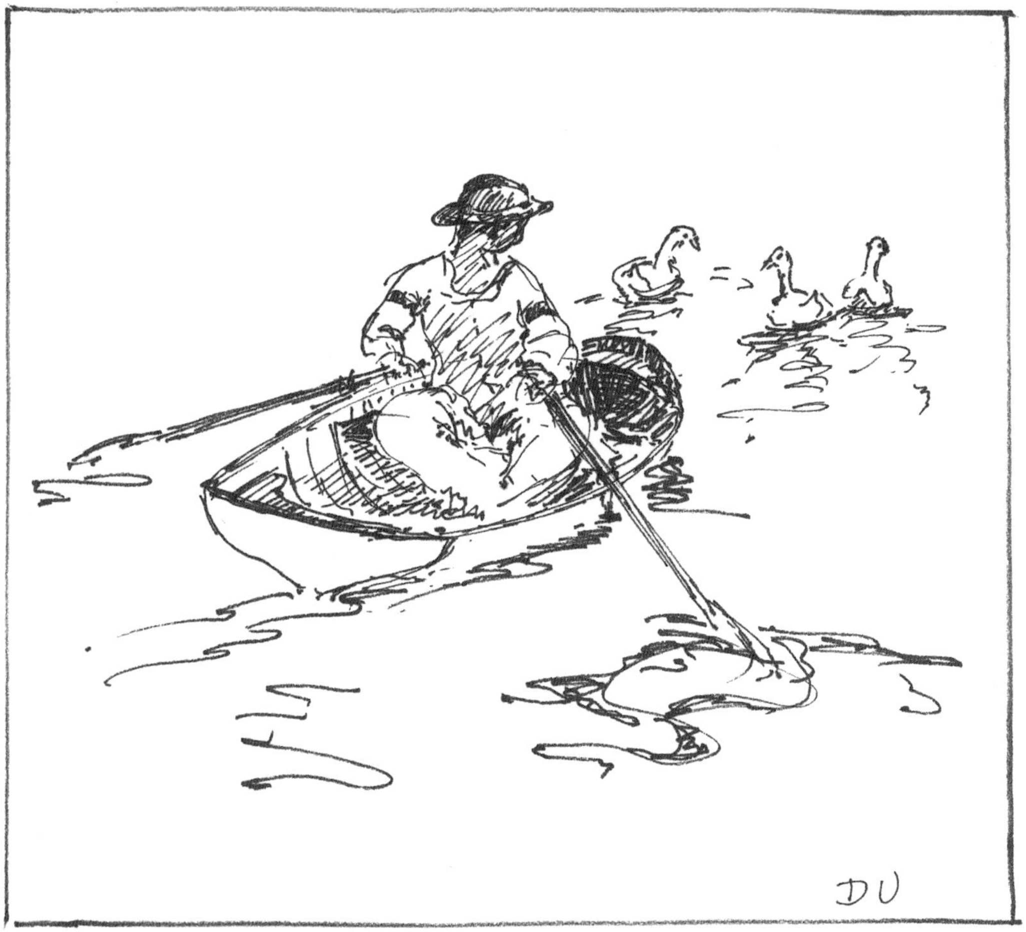

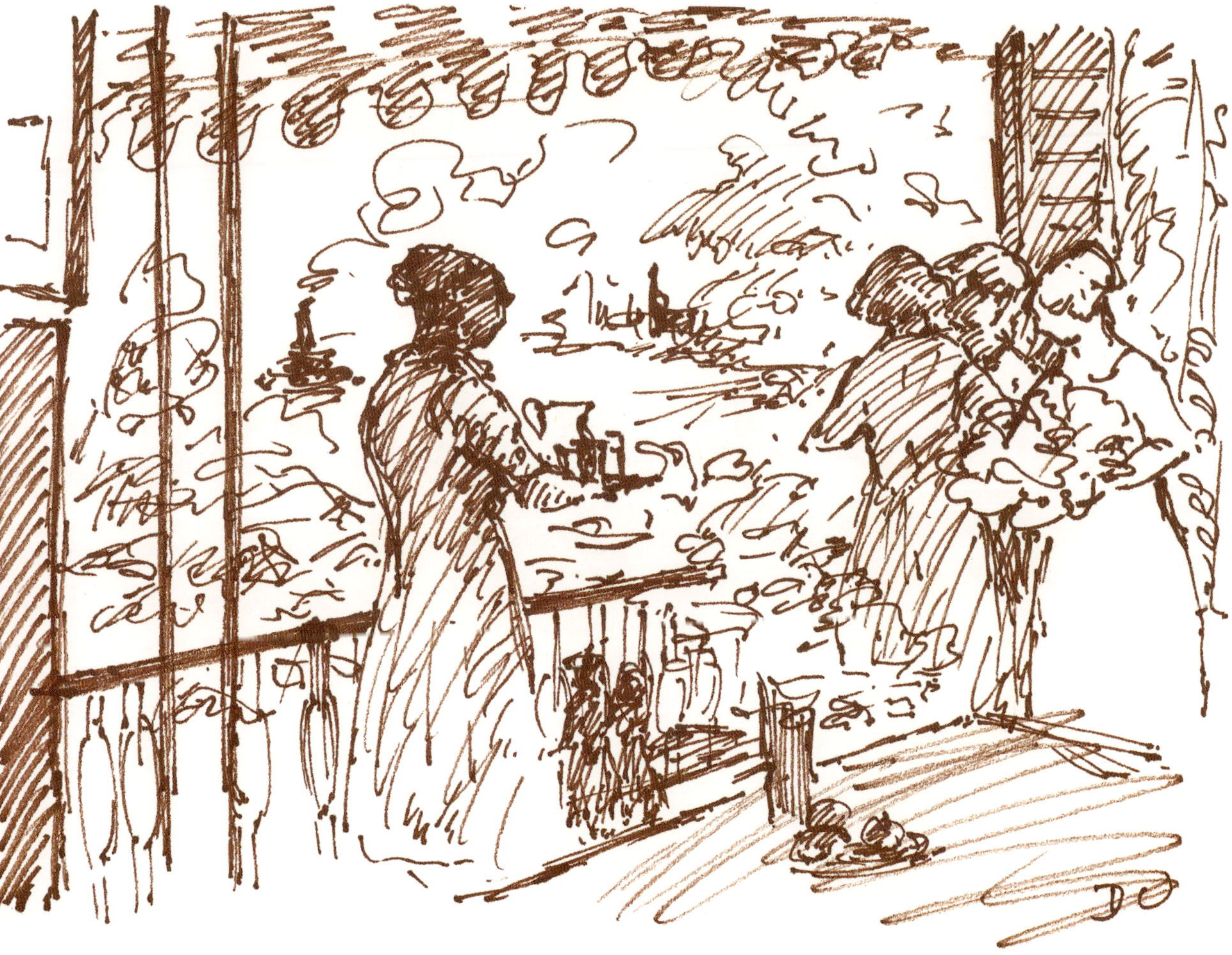

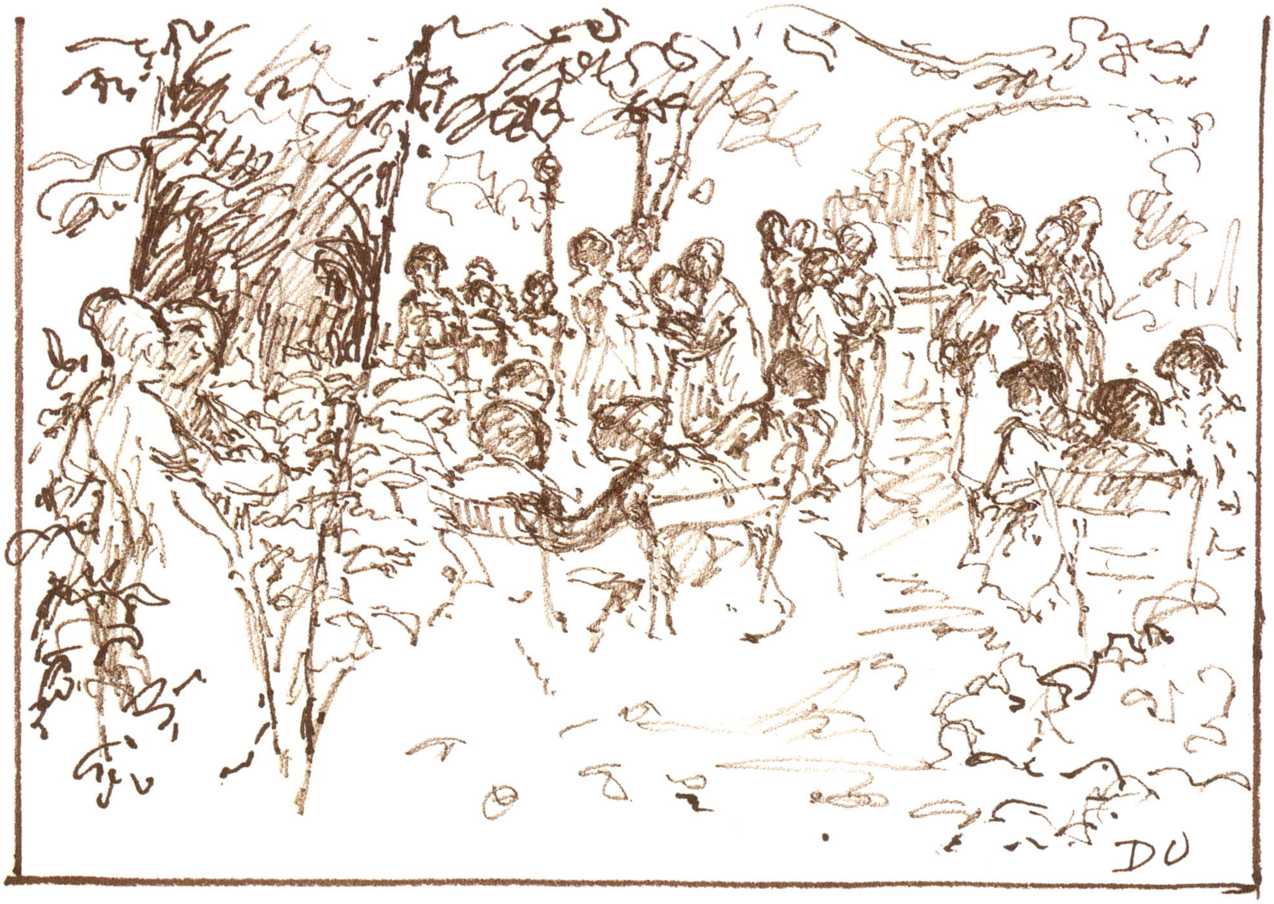
DU

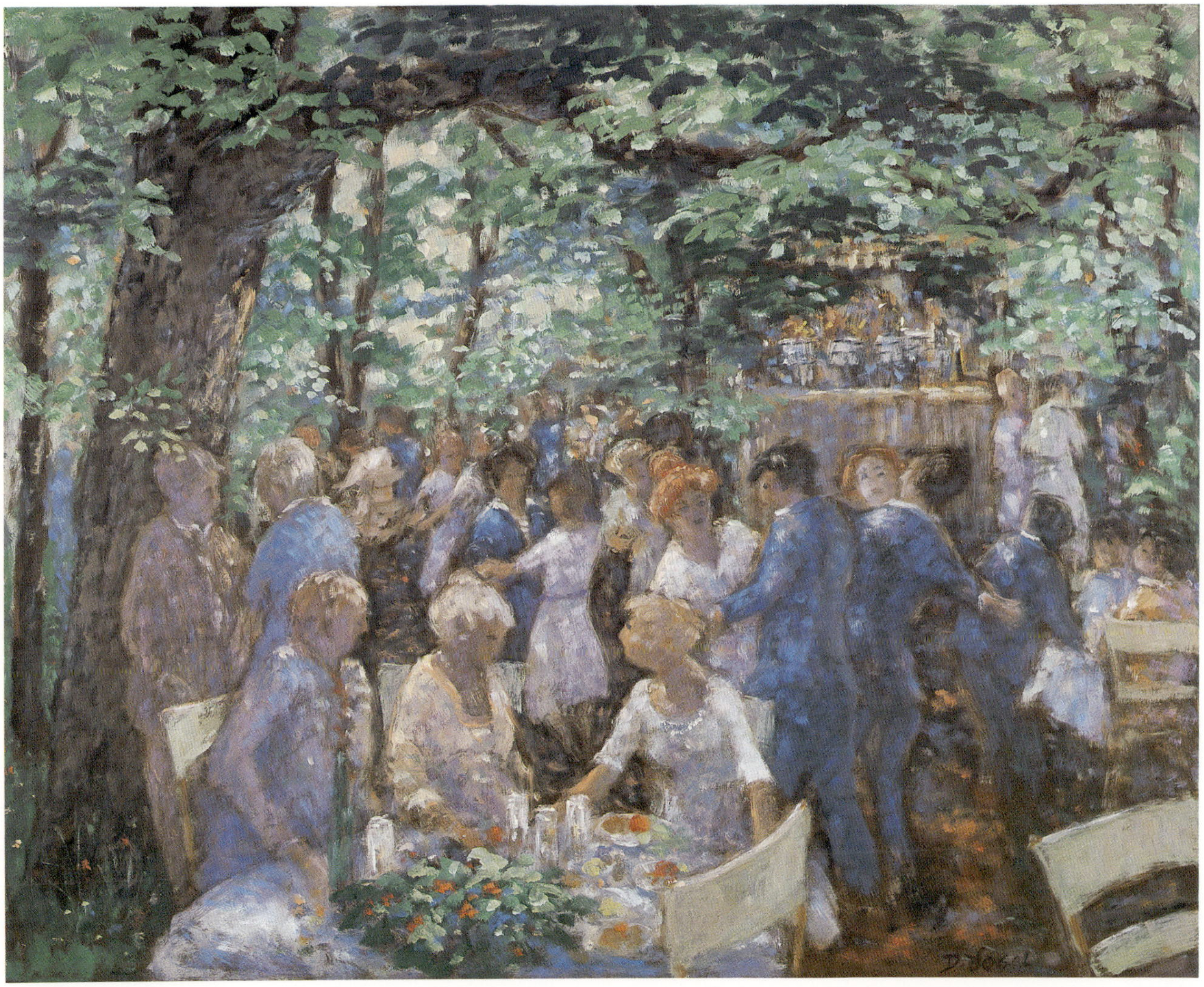

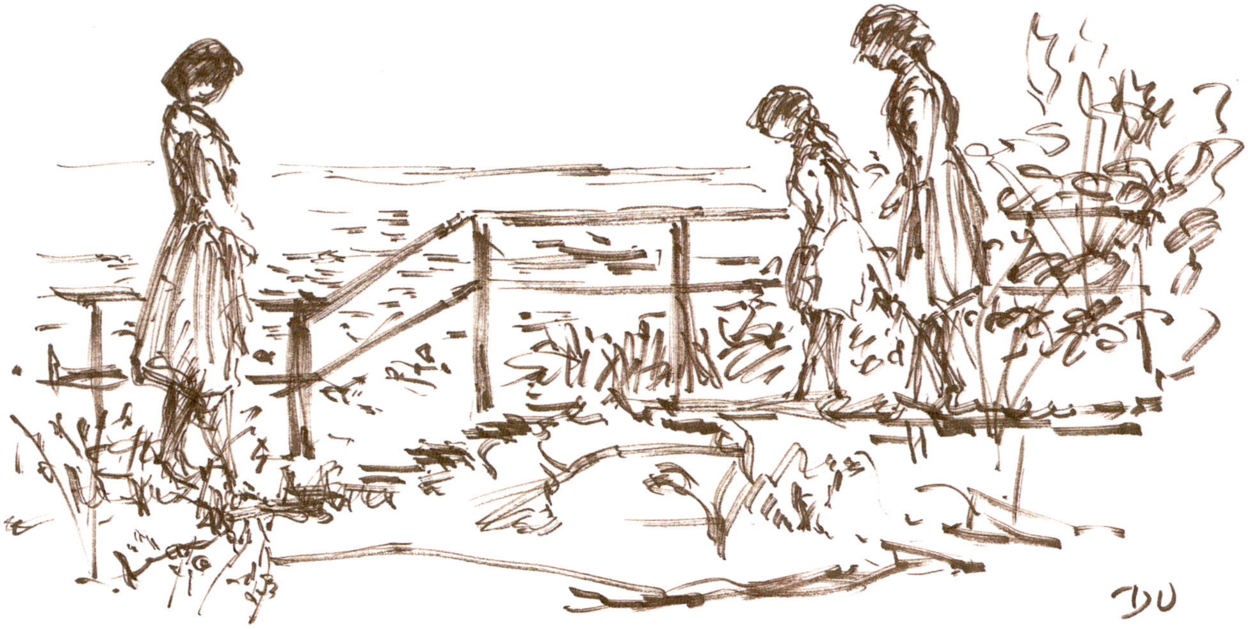

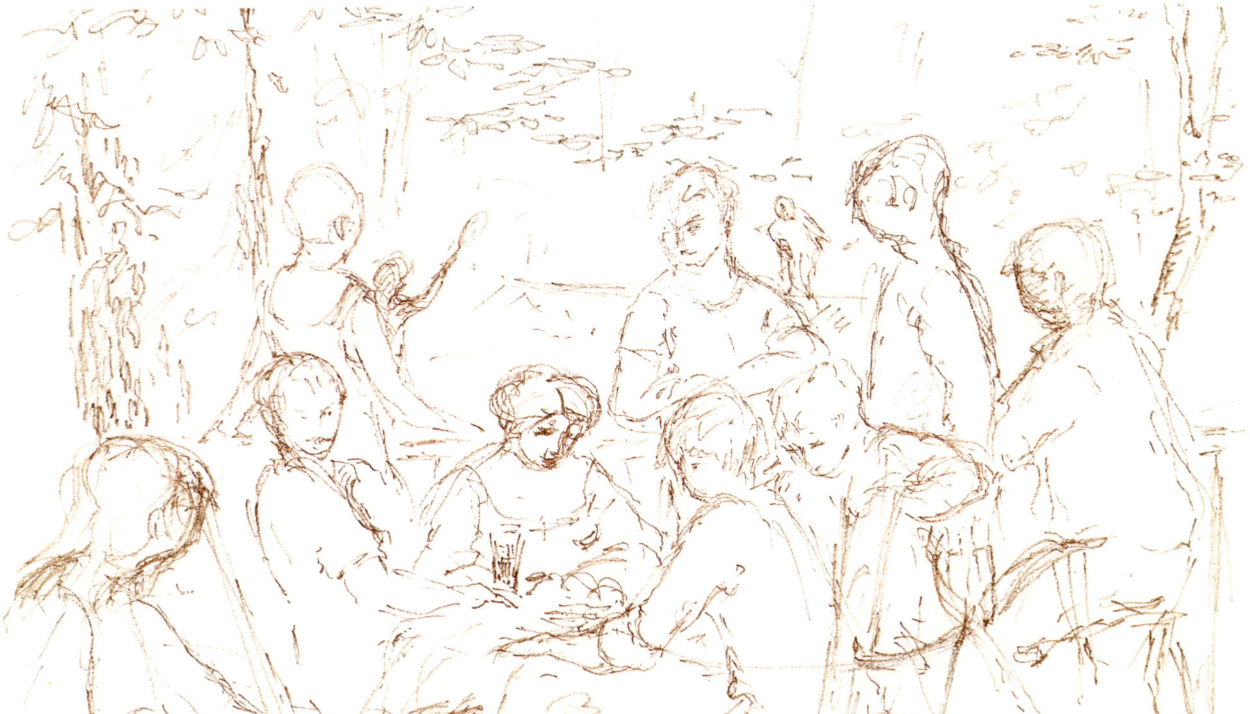

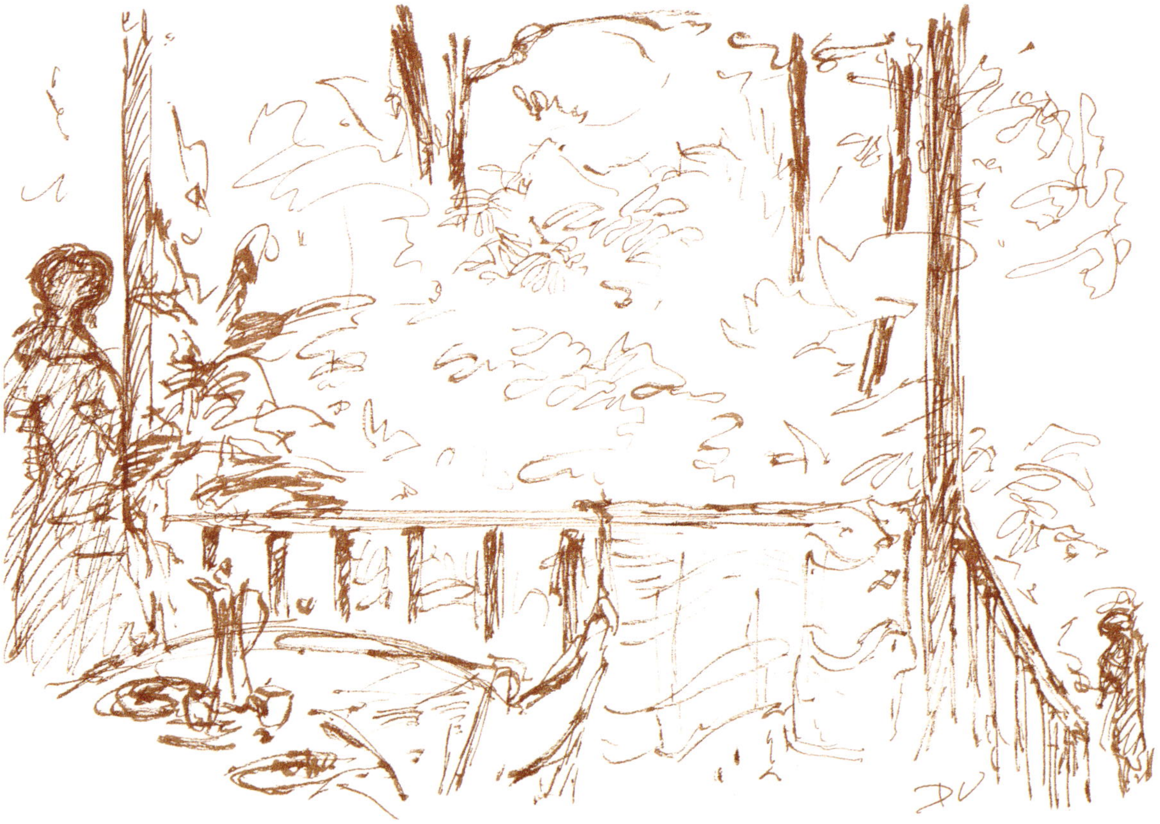

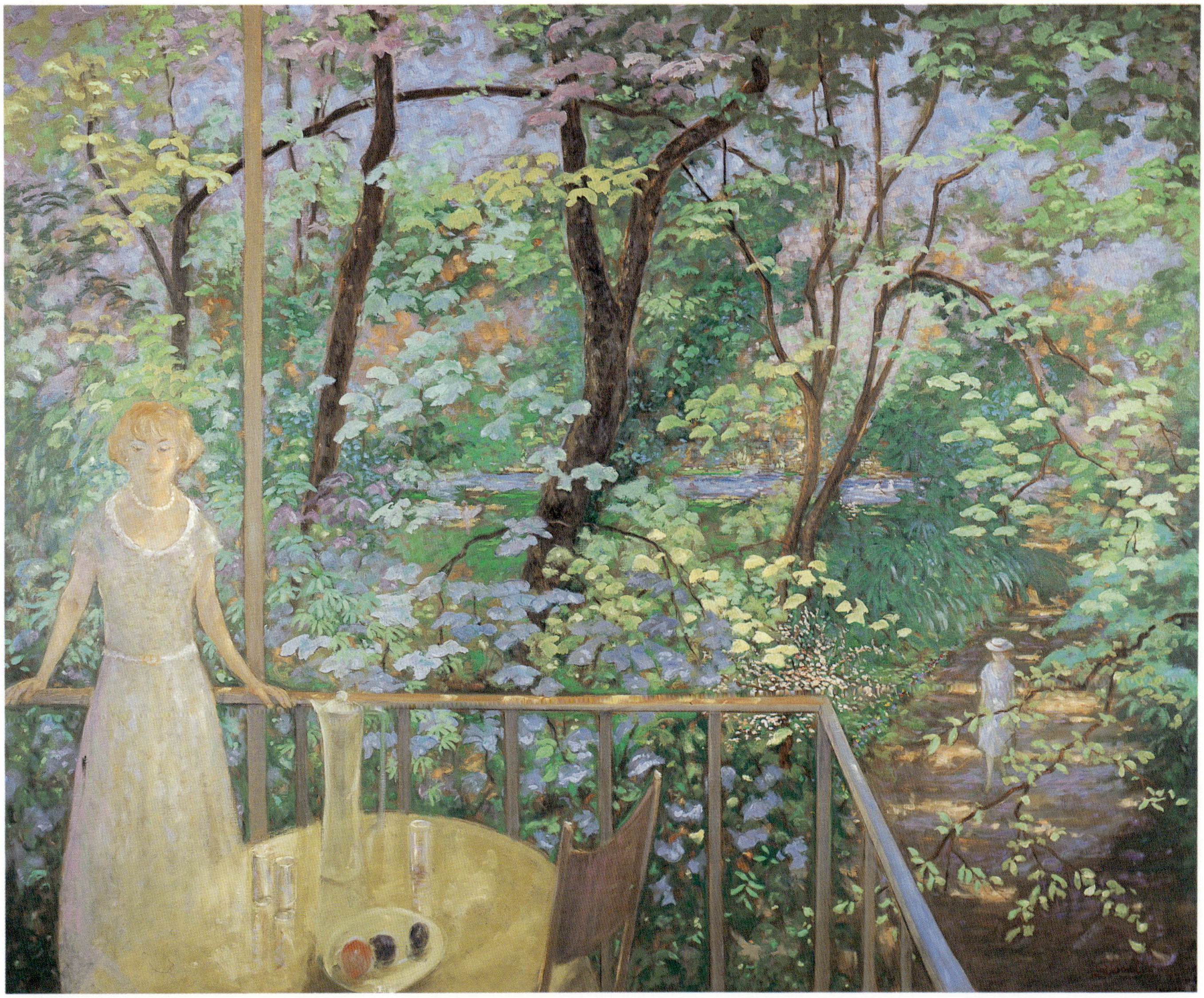

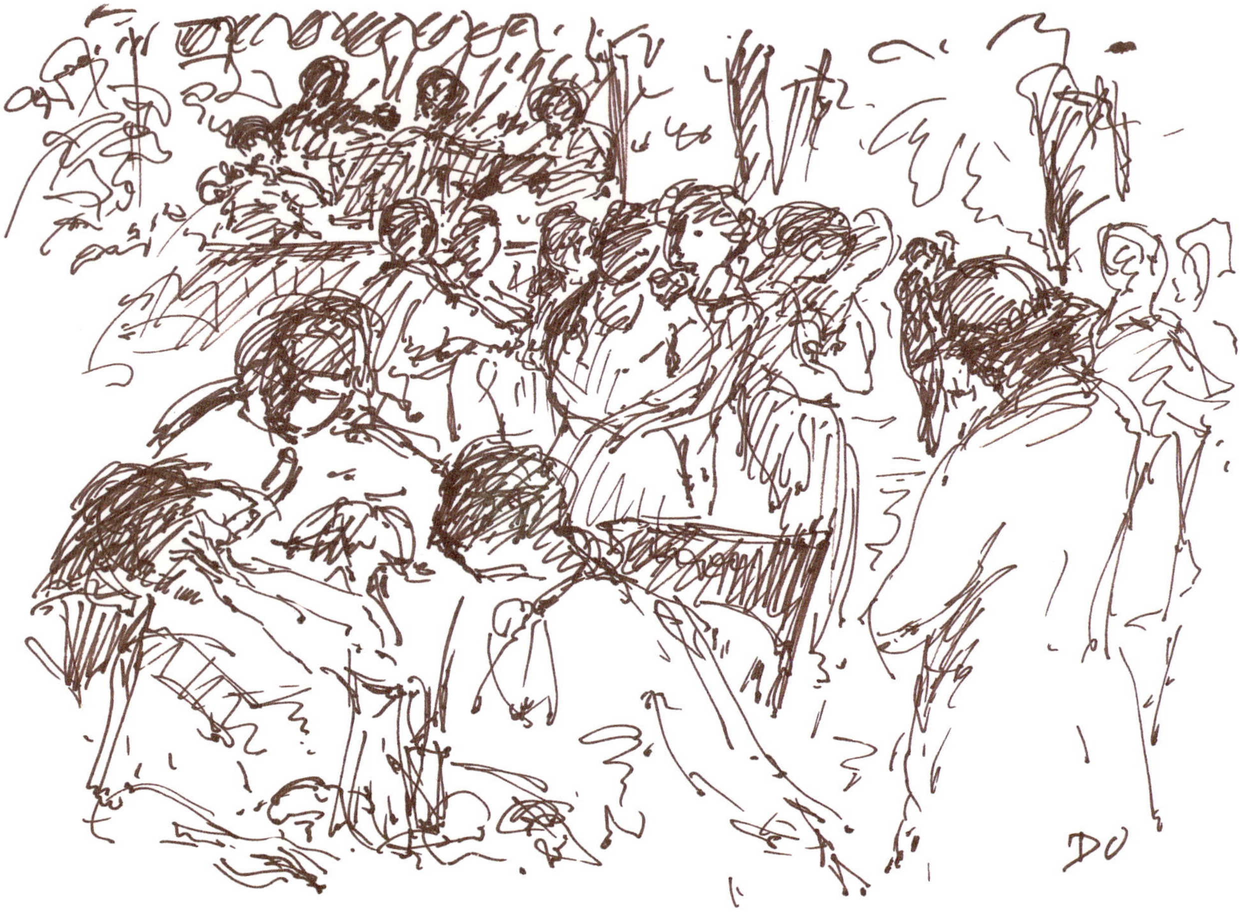

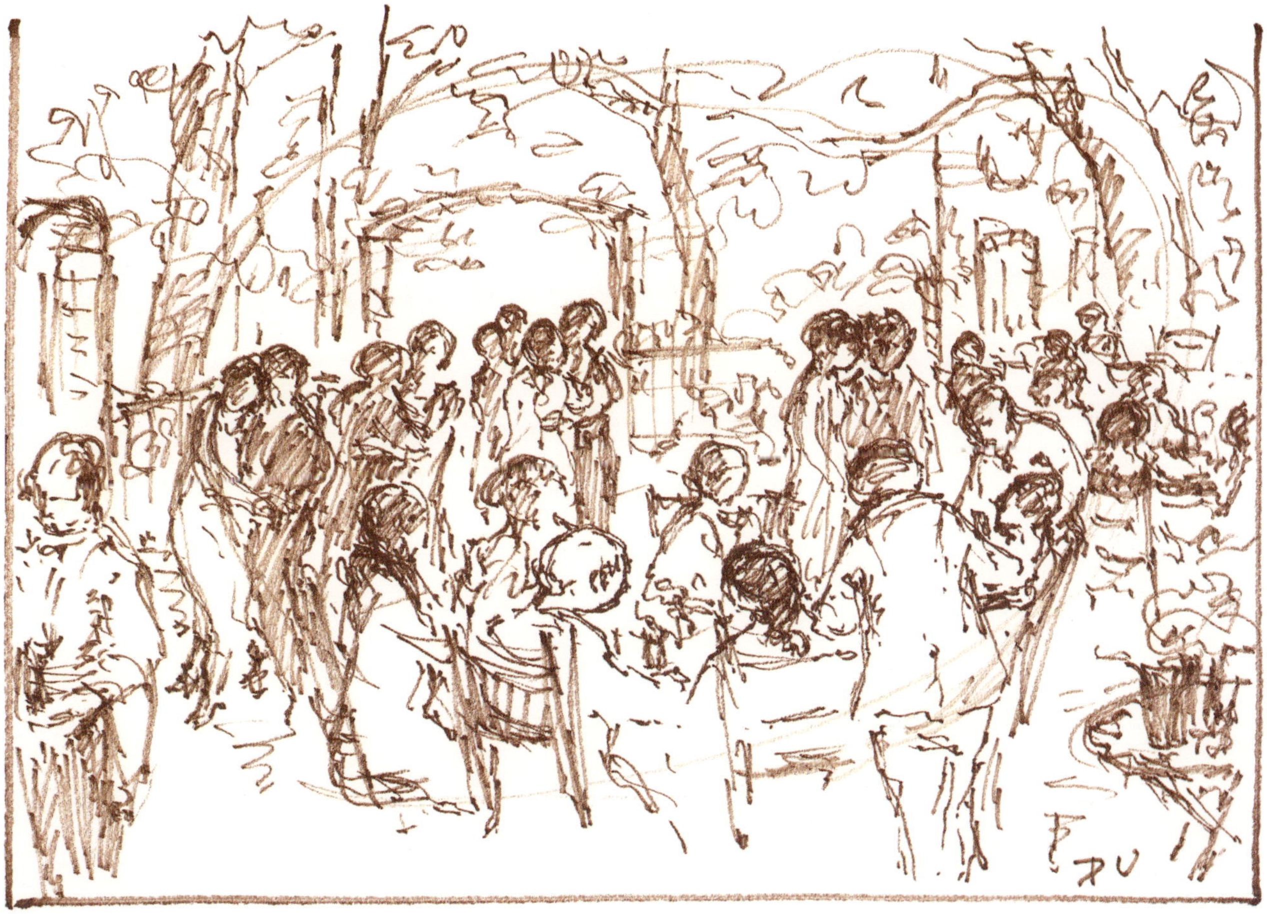

Part Three - Interiors, Exteriors

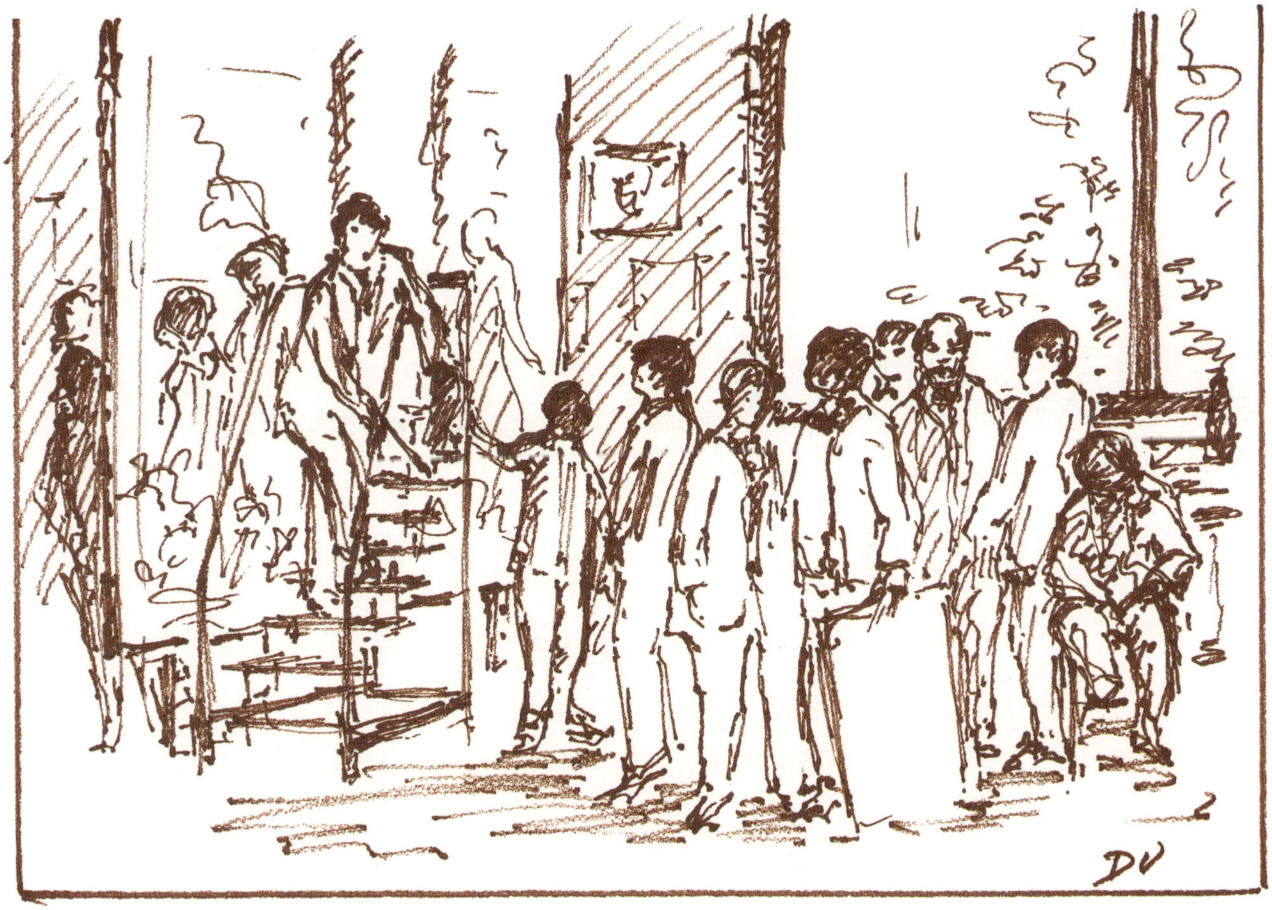

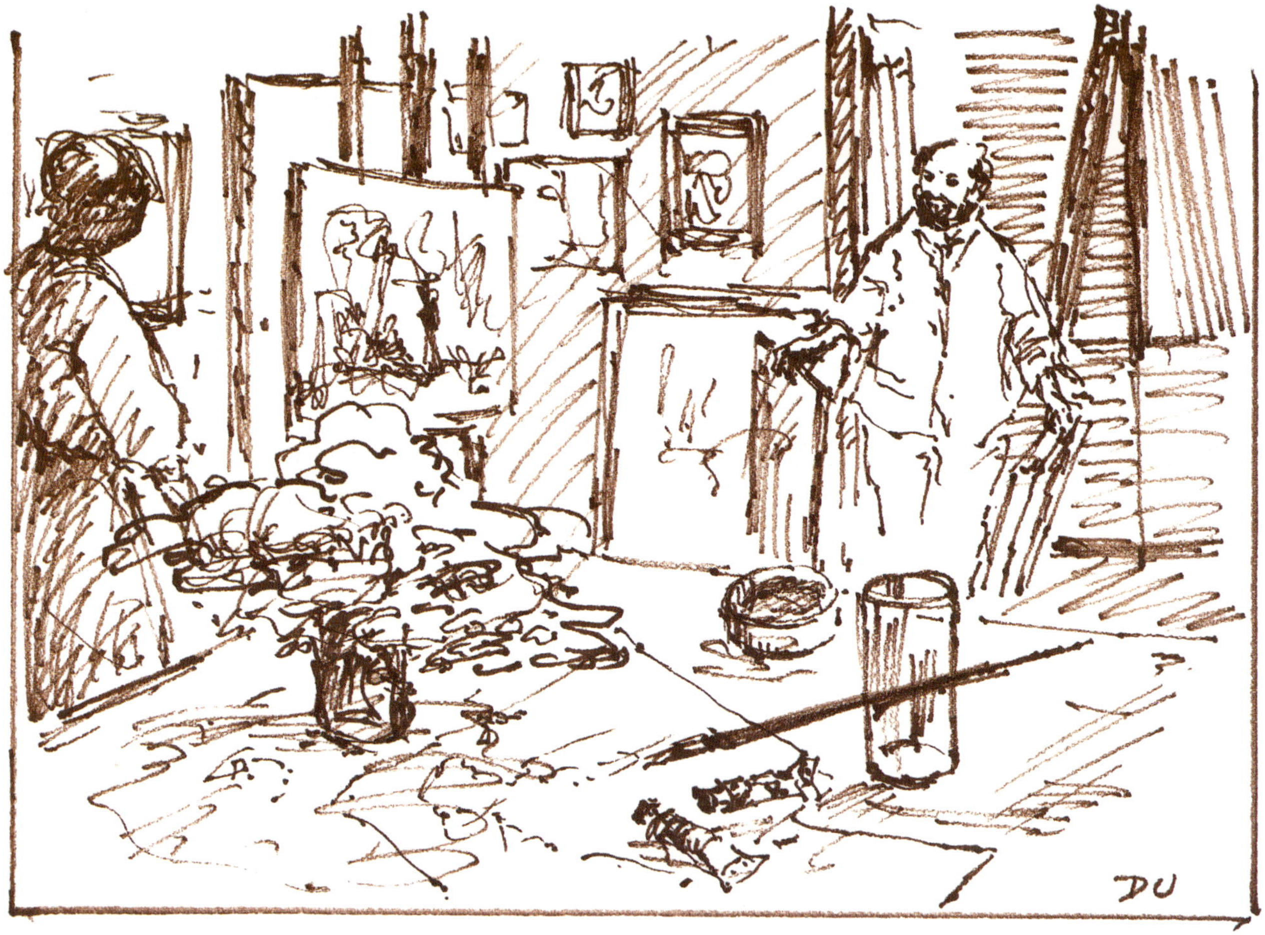
DU

The drawings reproduced here are mostly responses to the places in which I lived. They were many and varied. There were houses in various climates, apartments in great cities, a room in the rear of a theater, an abandoned kindergarten building, a room above a garage, one in a basement, and still another in an attic. None were as nice as my present home, its high ceilings and tall windows open on grounds shaded by tall trees that cast shadows in response to the morning and evening sun. Its off-white walls give nuances of changing intensity, ever-changing warm and cool tones. The bedroom and bath open onto a lush greenhouse that warms the spirit on even the coldest, bleakest day. Such an interior always suggests ideas for drawings.

It is far better to convey the expression revealing the personality than to duplicate the features.

Interiors offer the opportunity to employ still-life drawings, florals, and plants on tables with teapots, cups, and saucers of different textures and patterns. Such common objects can be joined with countless other items abounding in the house.

When a strong light invades the room, it fractures space, distorting objects in its path. It enchants the eye. It seems to ask the artist to freeze such moments and establish them forever on paper to share with others.

By drawing even the simplest, humblest objects around you, you can produce a unique work that possesses lasting value. Concern yourself always with the quality of the line as it moves. Each line has its own character and pace. Don't waste it. Make each line function to express your thought and response. You may not often succeed but when you do, you will know. That moment is your reward.

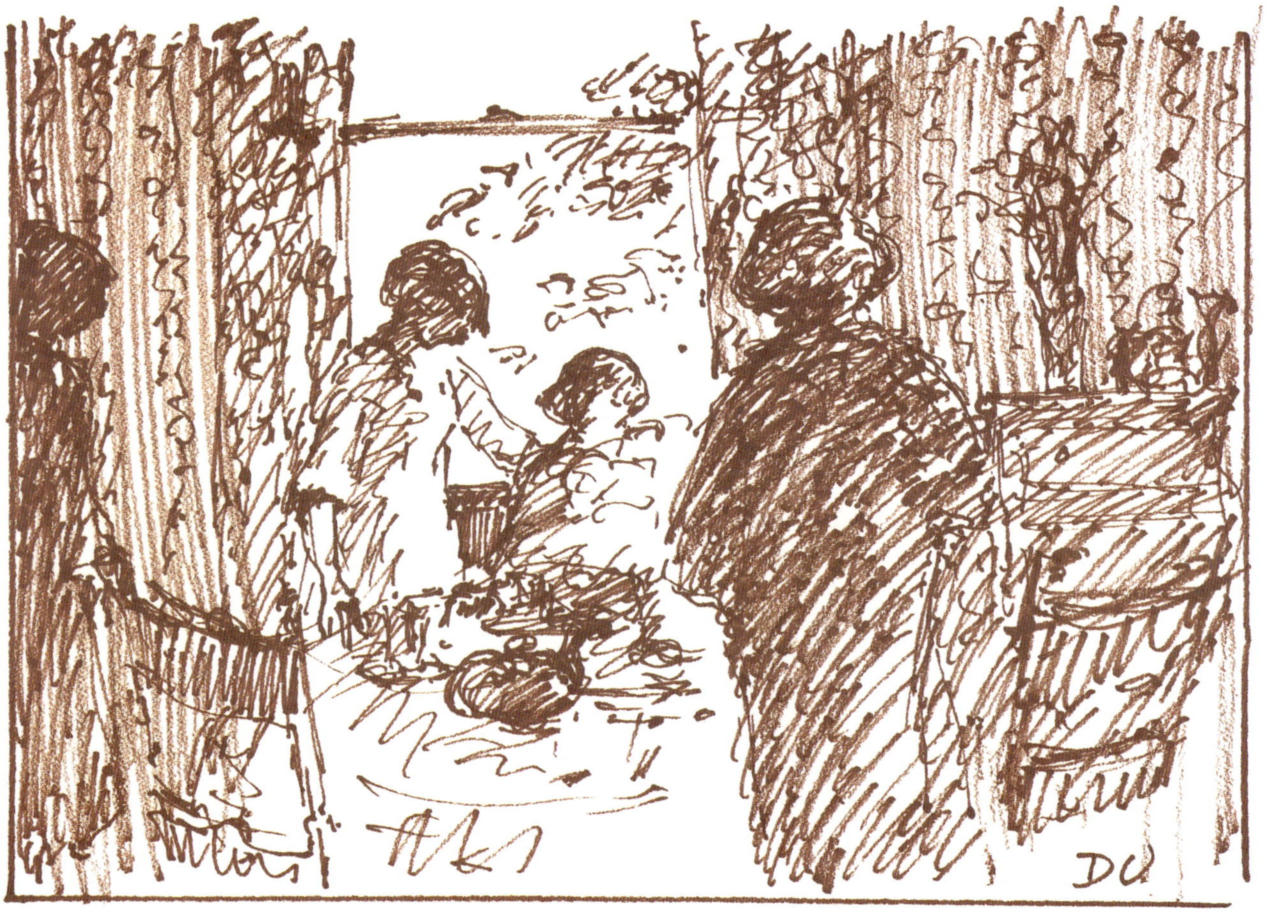

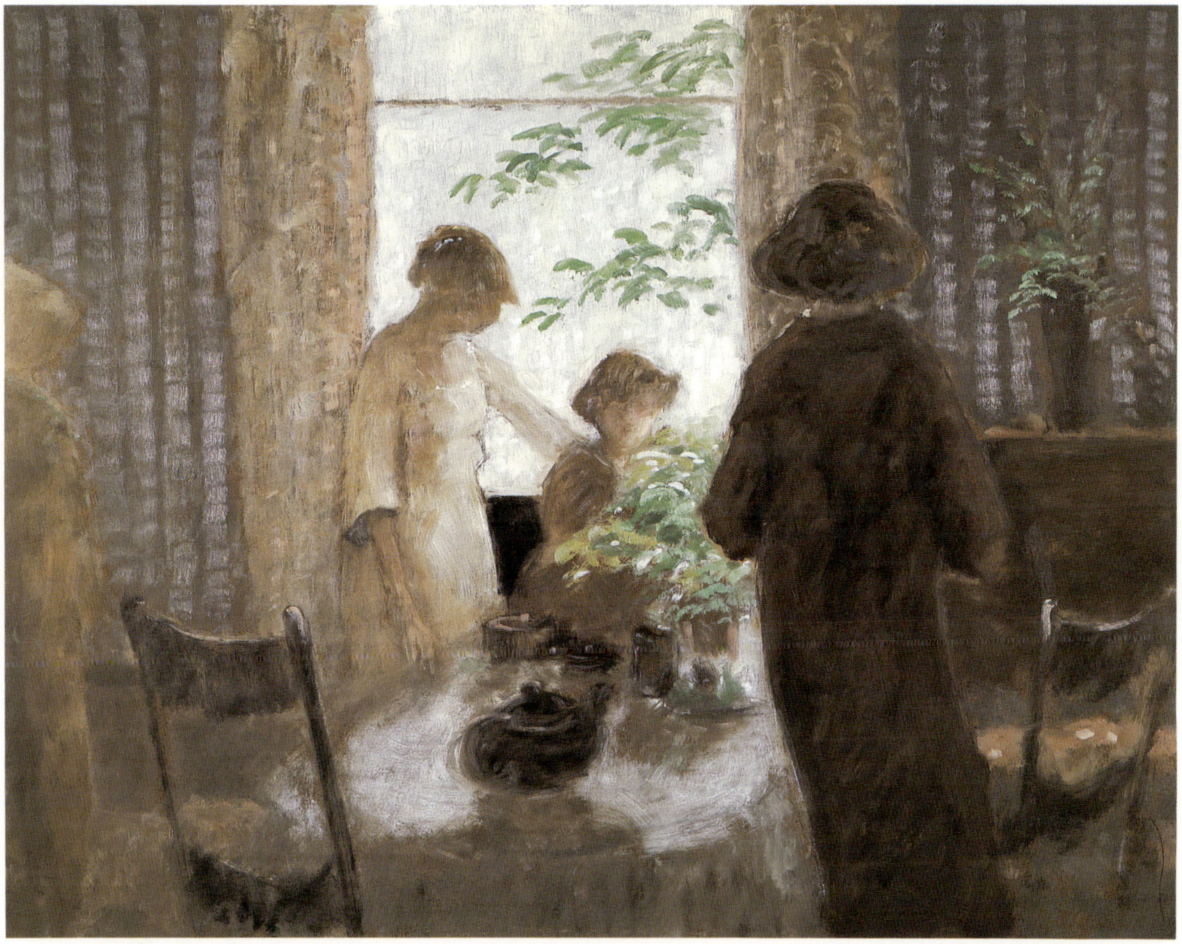

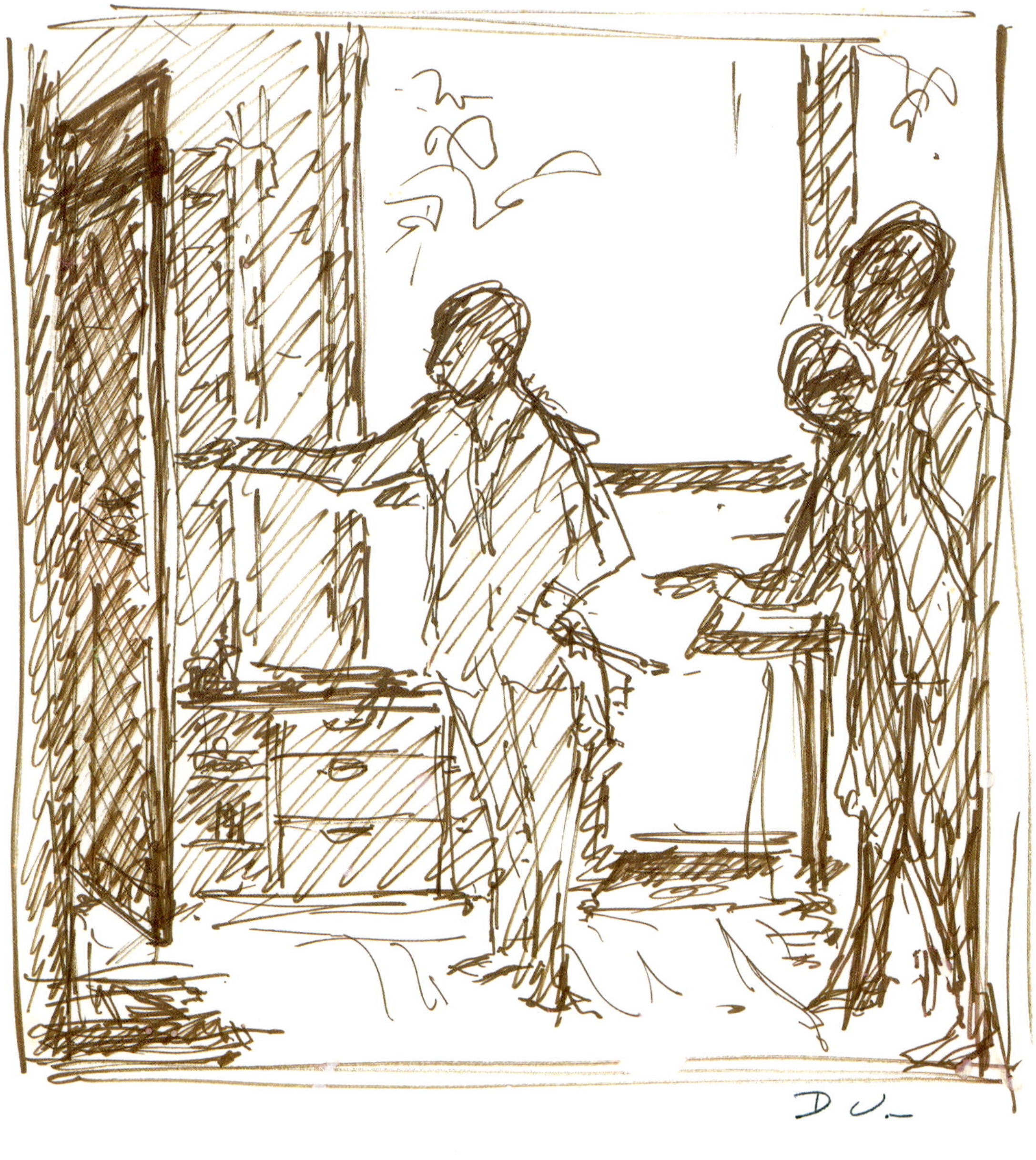

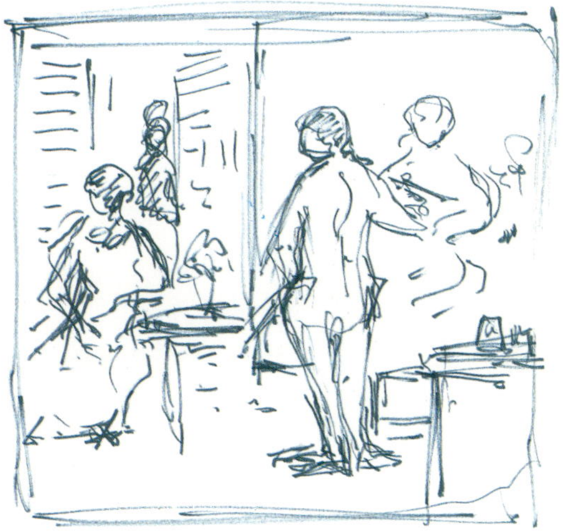

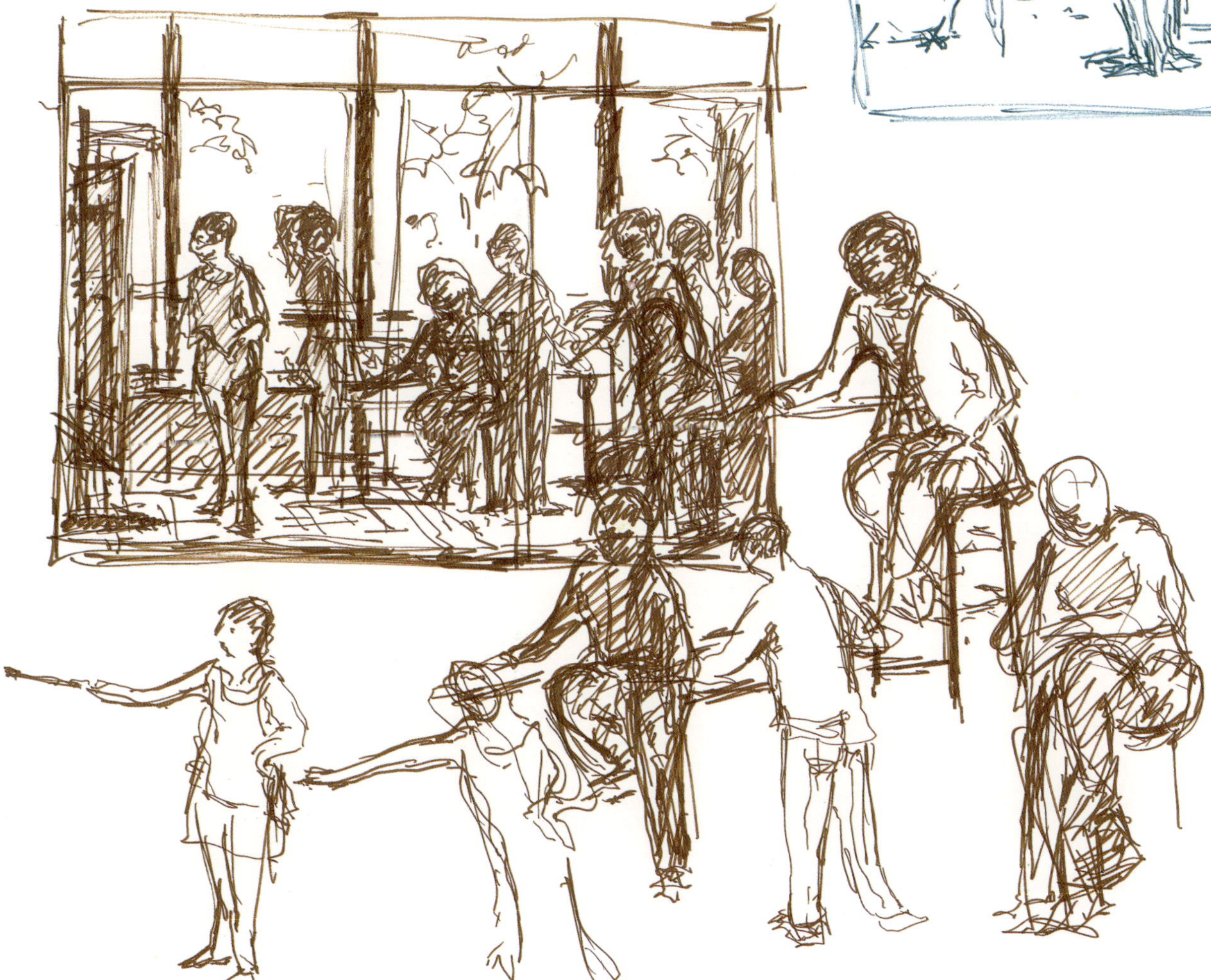

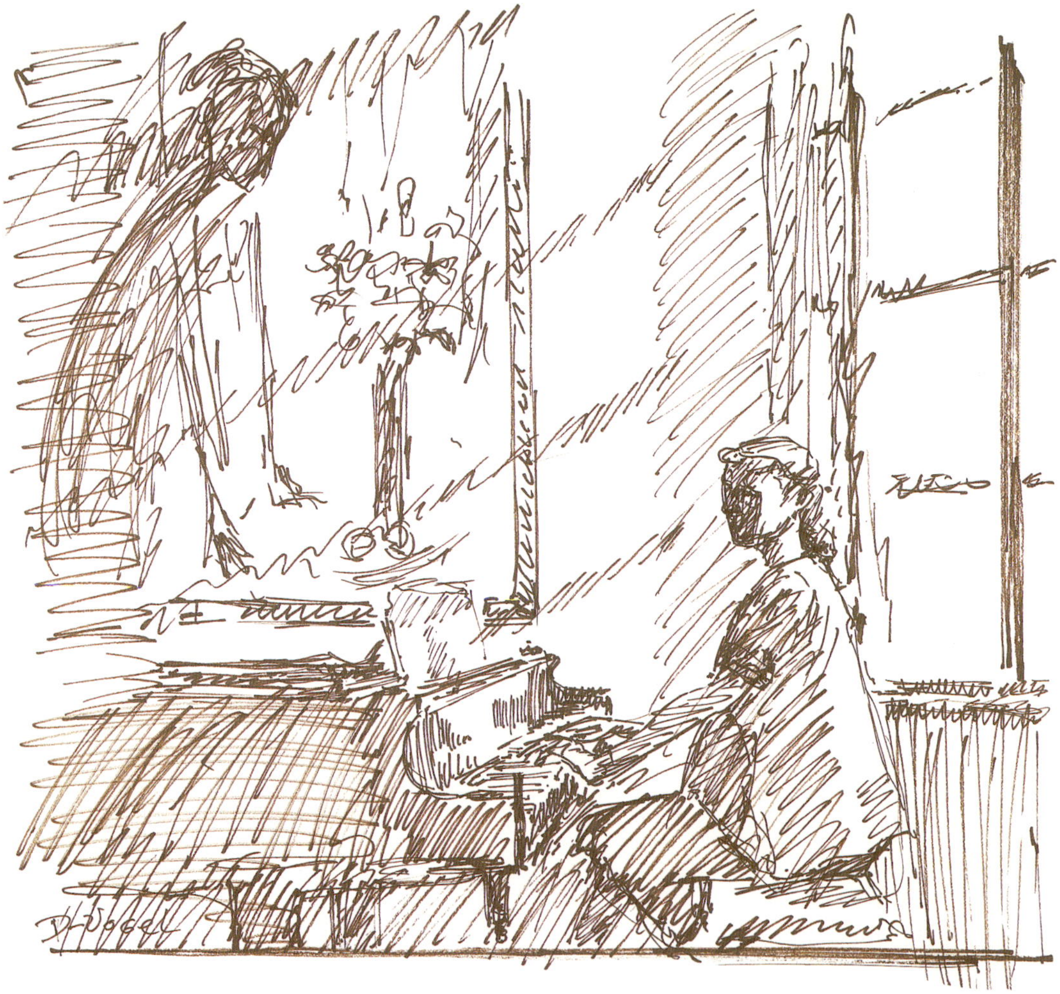

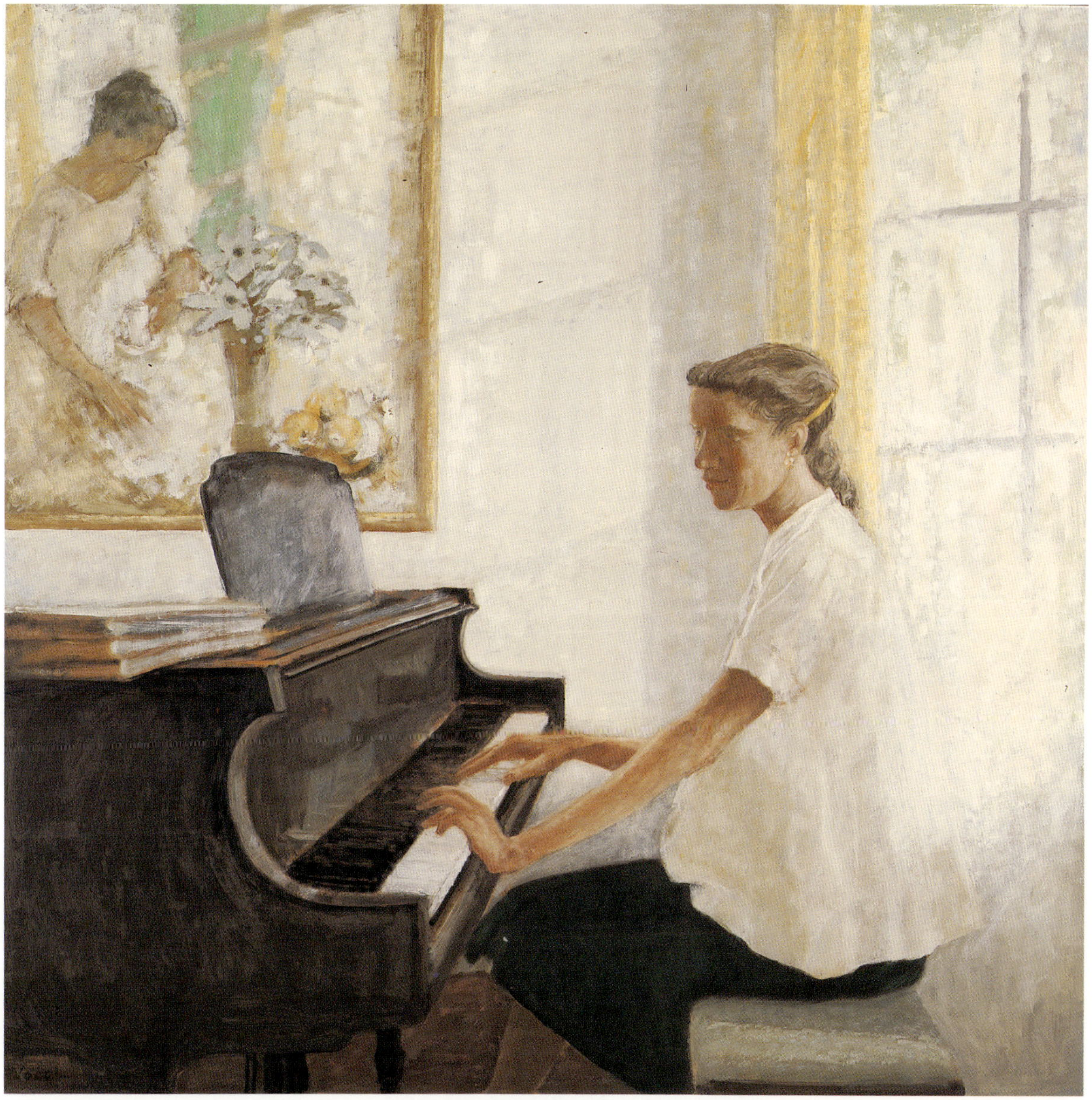

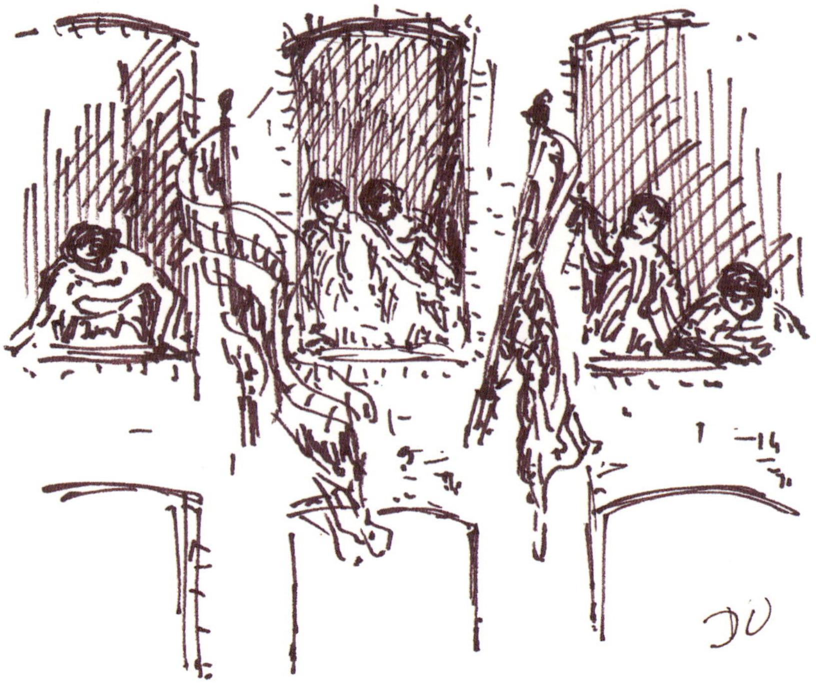
DU

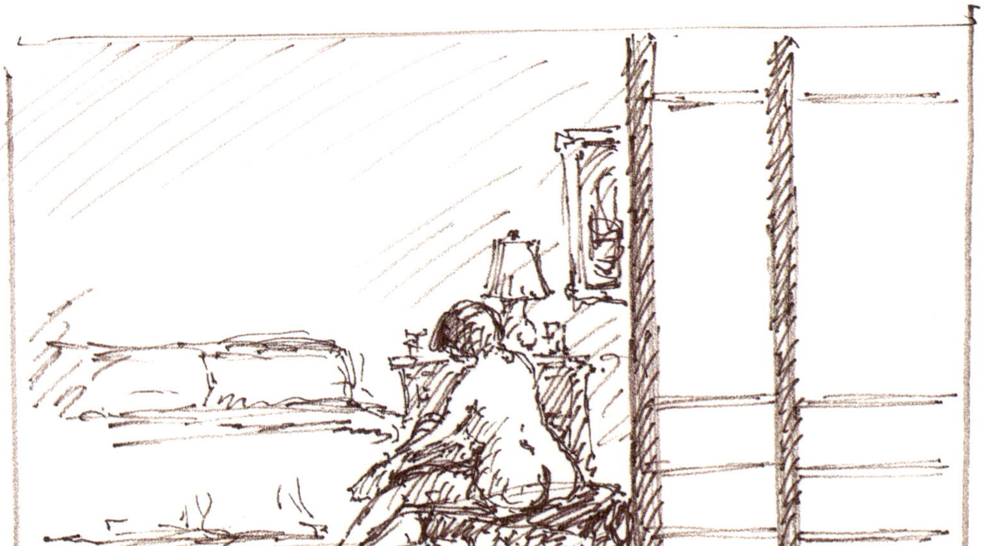
DU

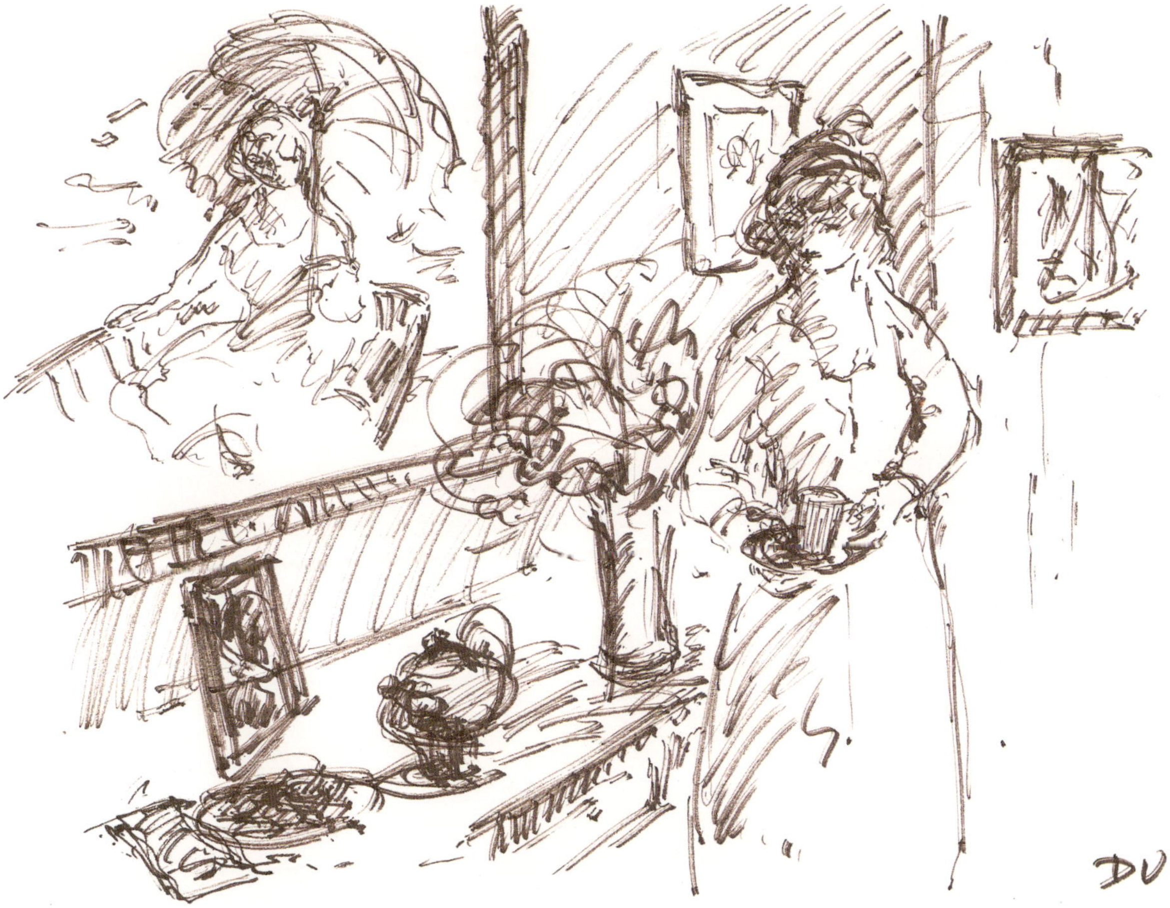
DV

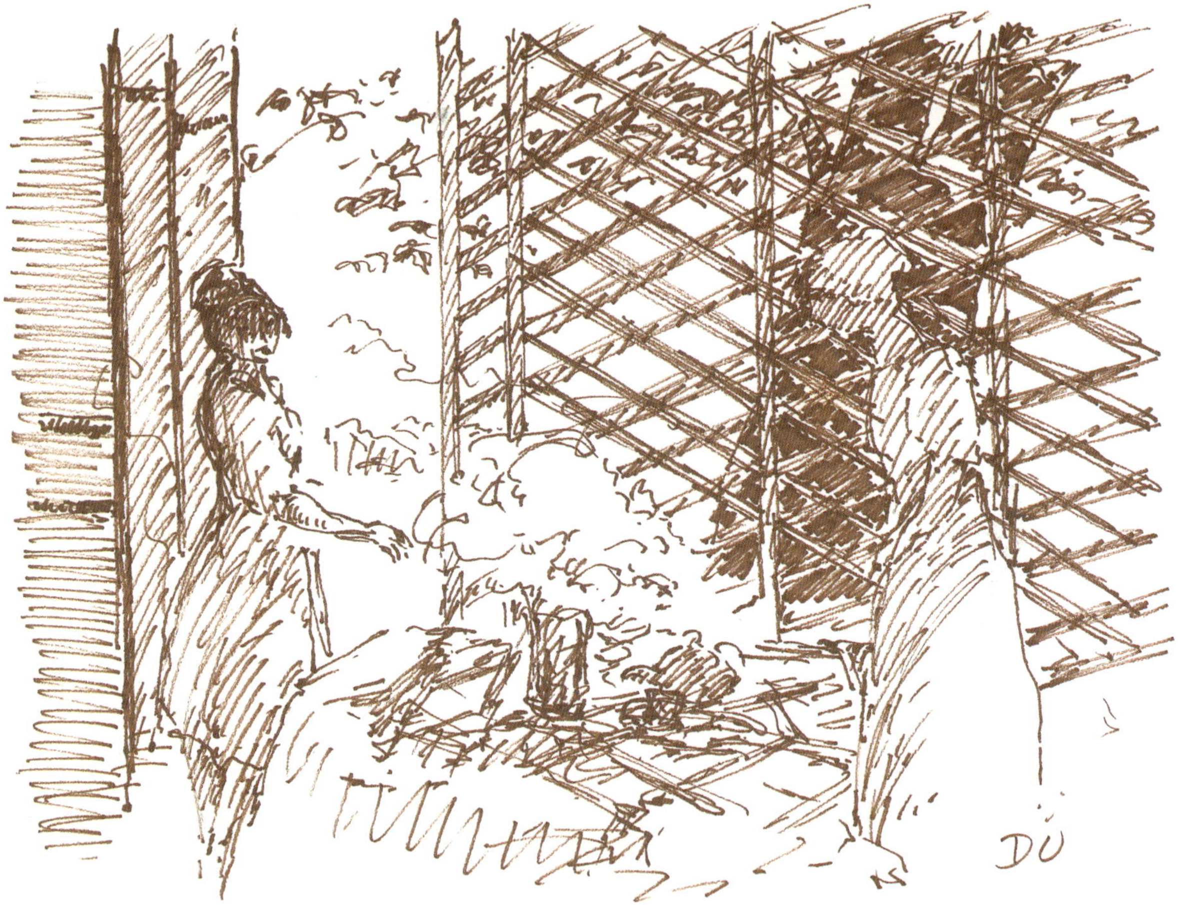

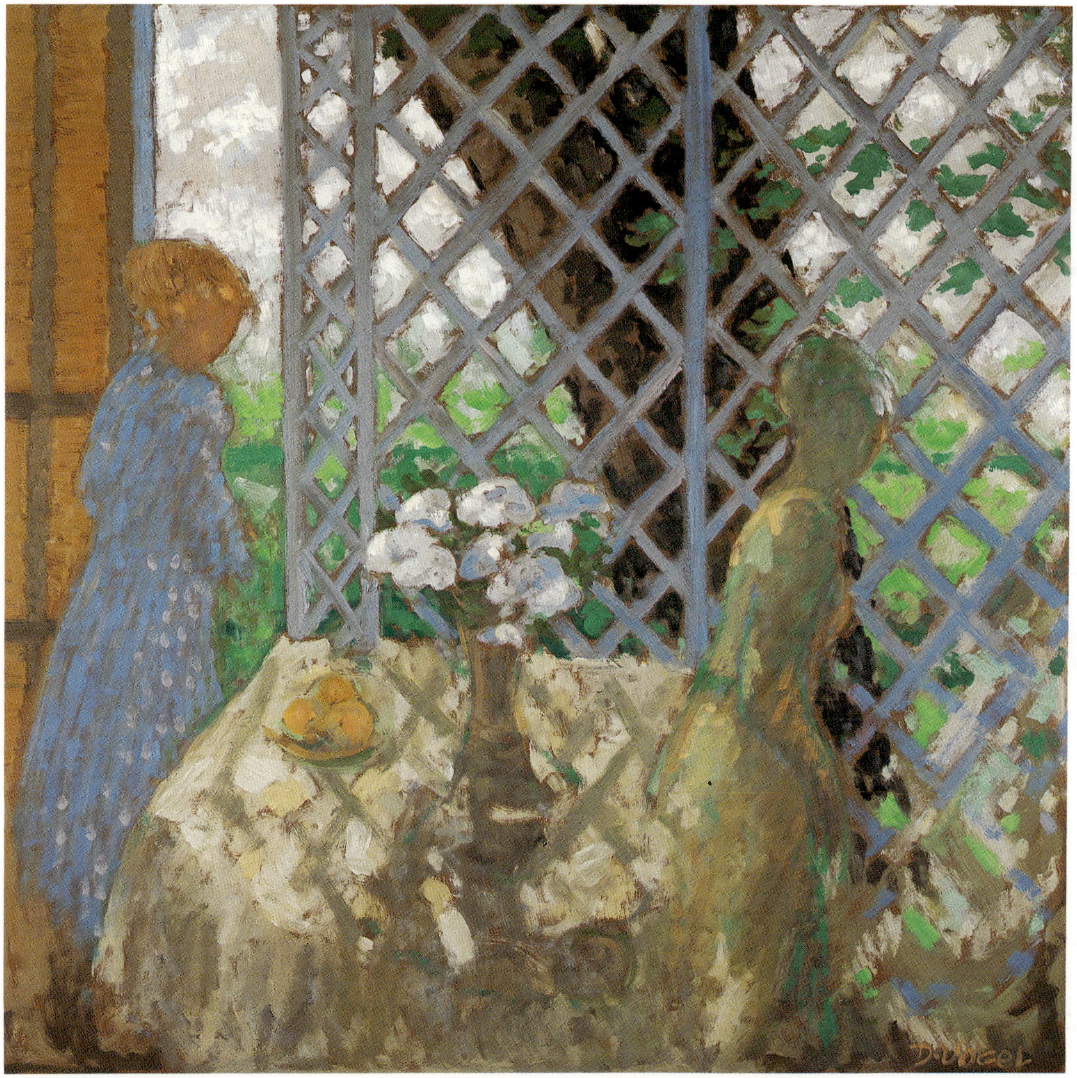

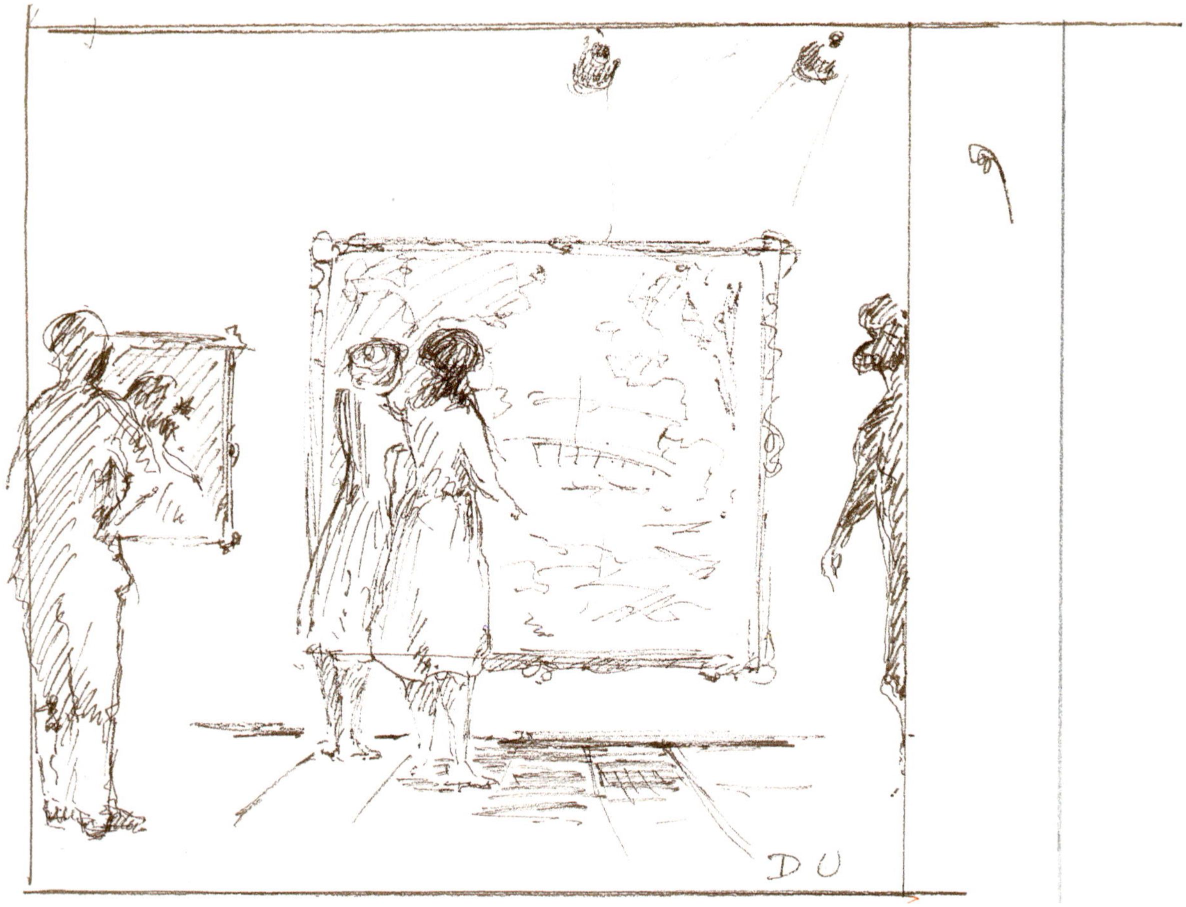
DU

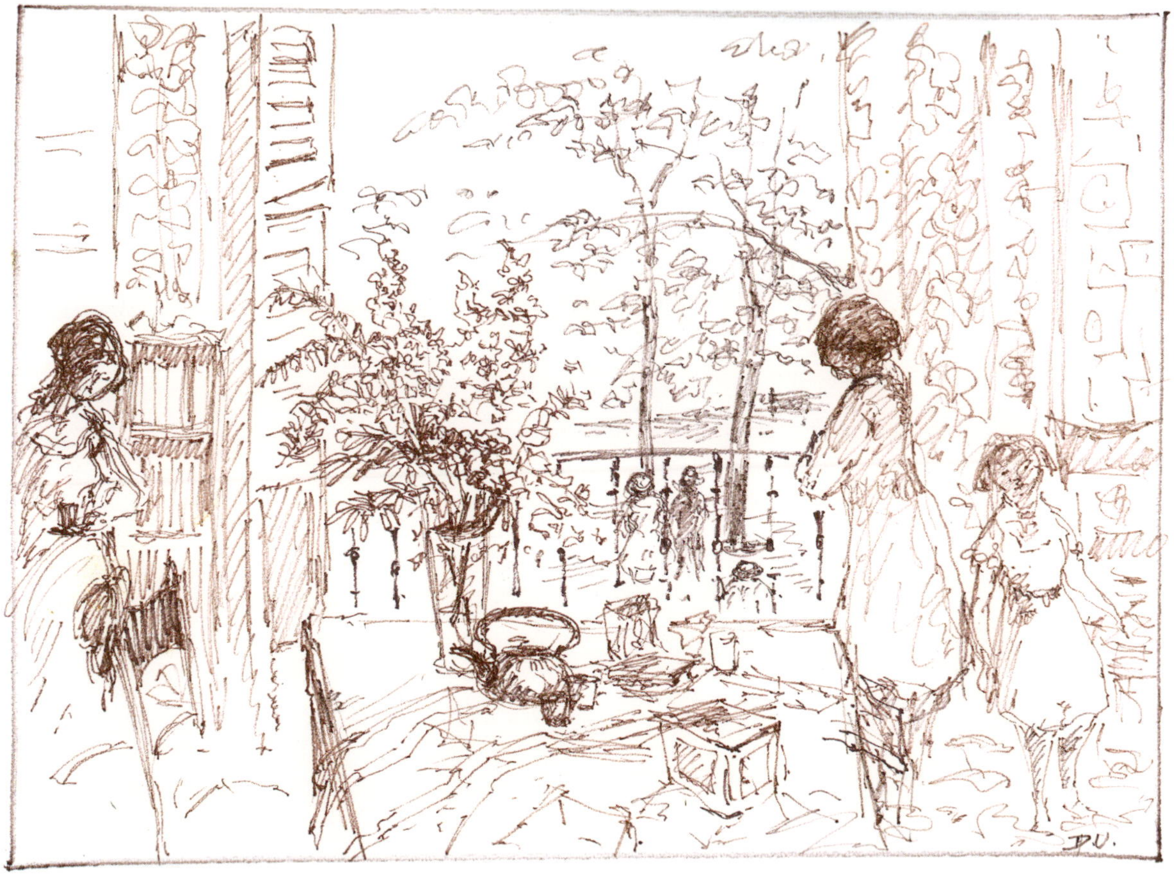

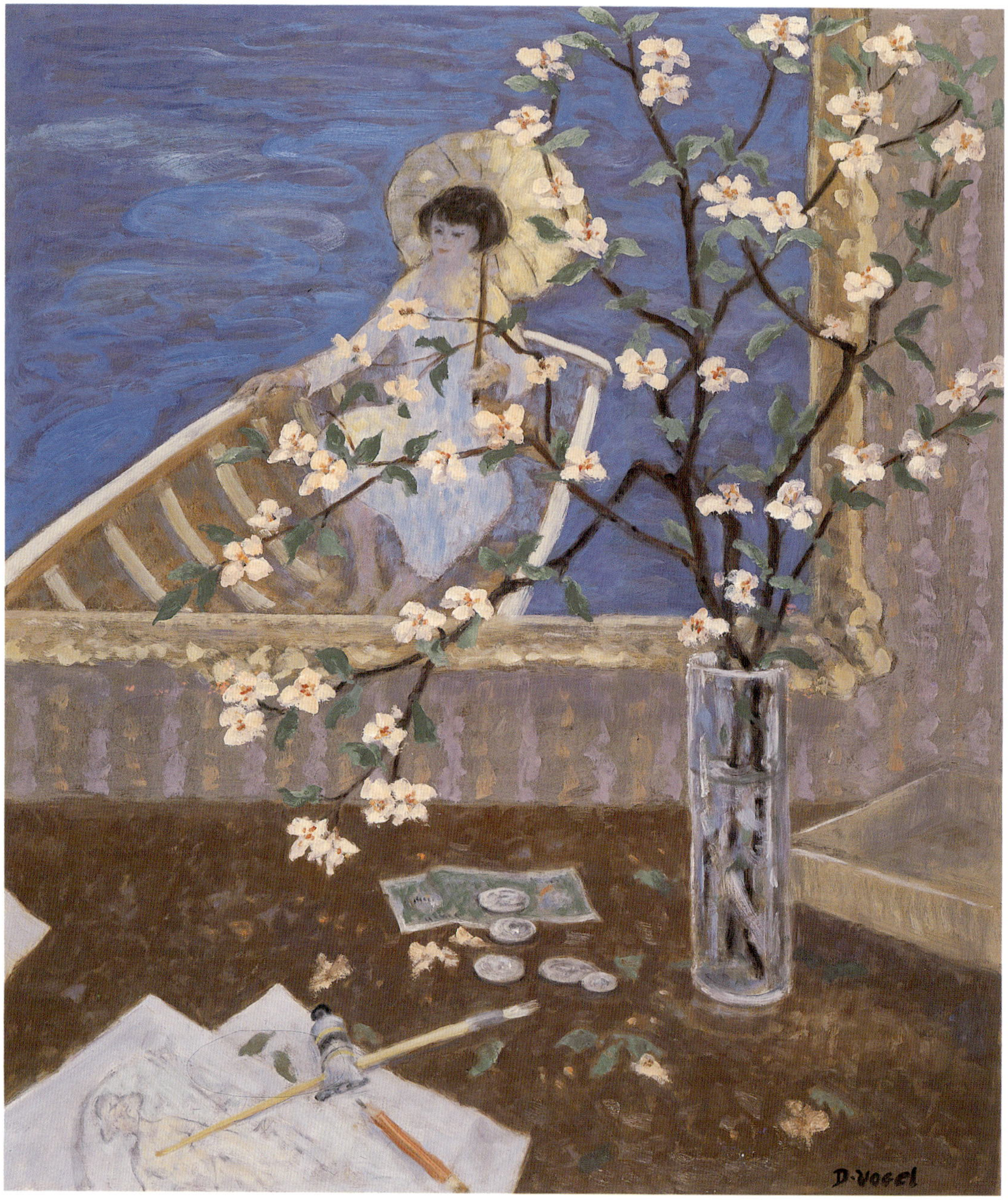
D.VOGEL

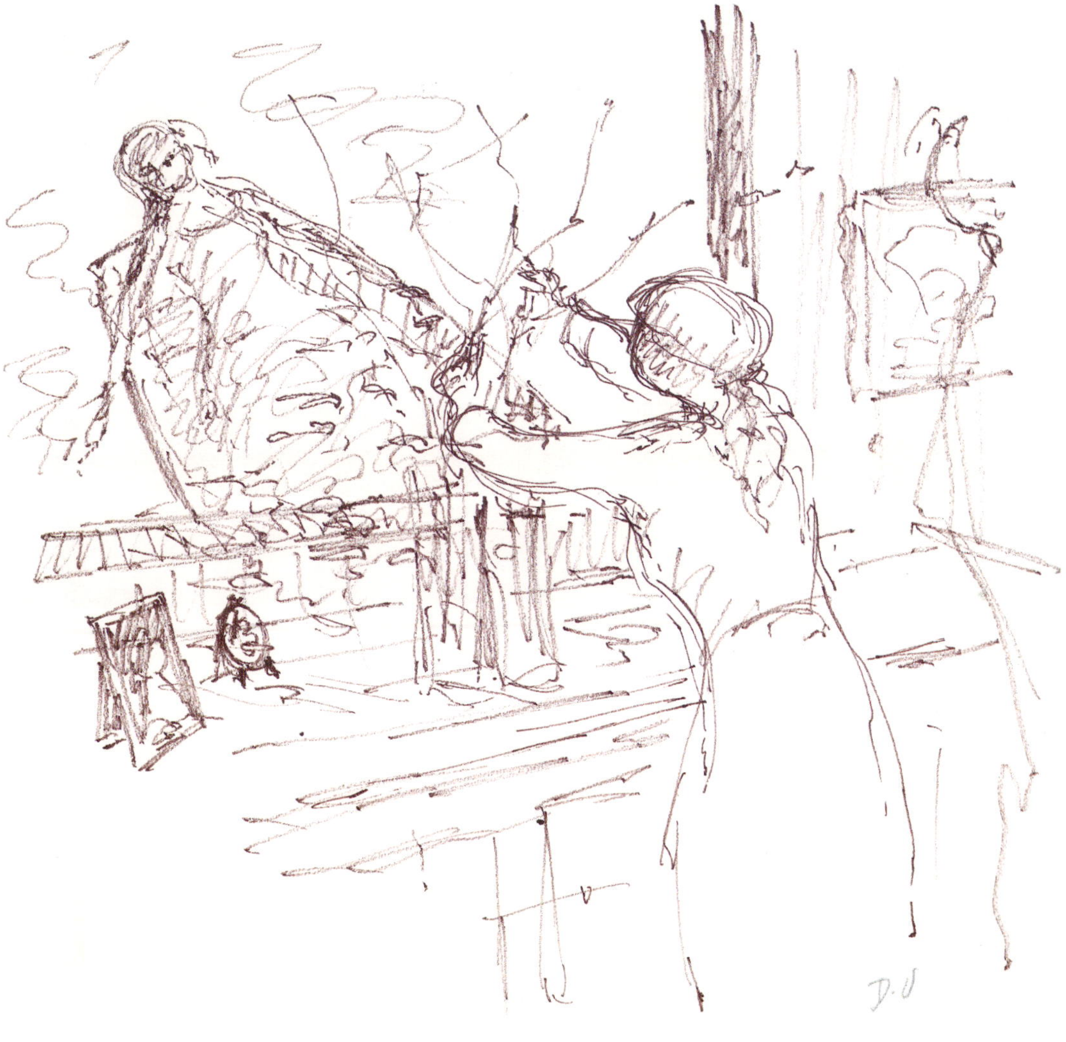

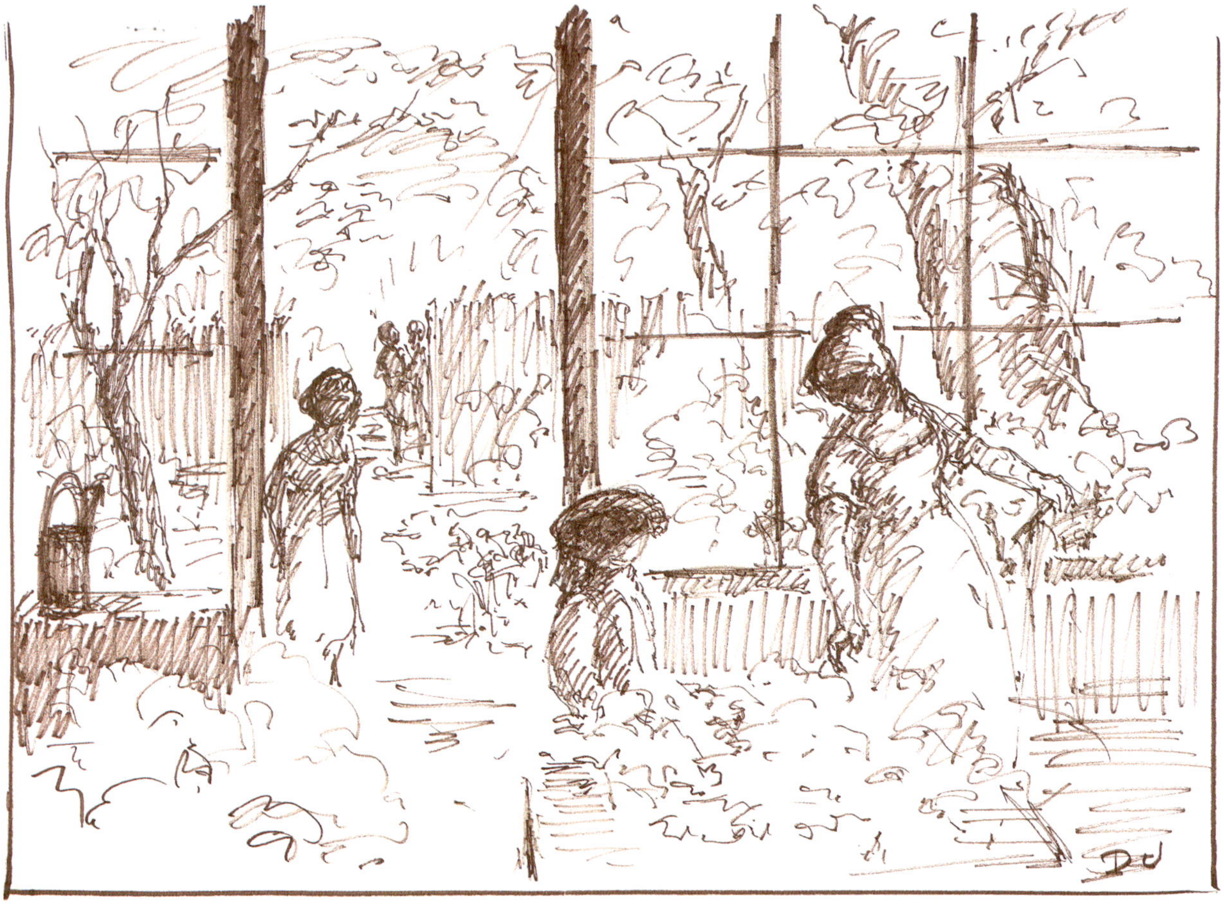

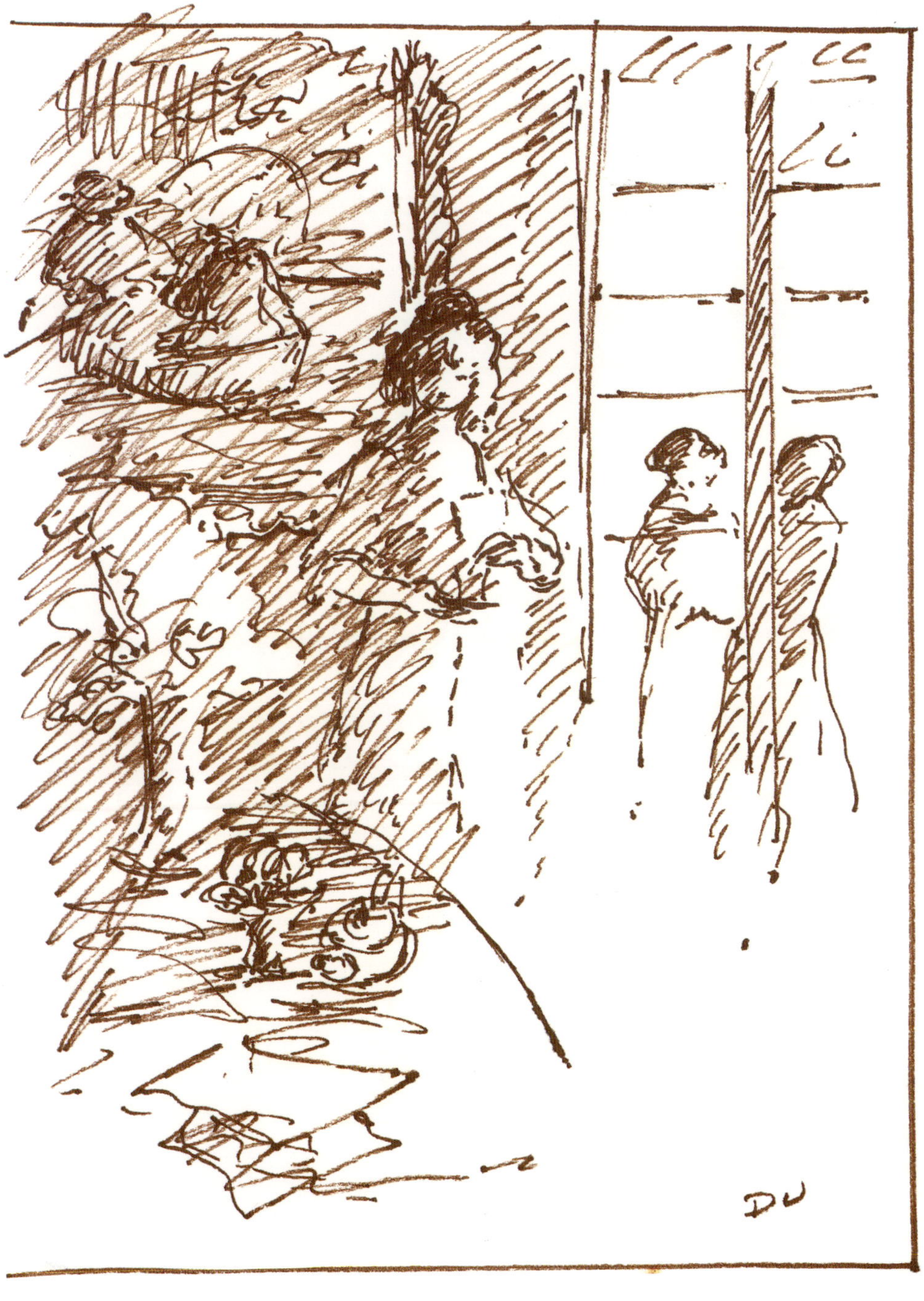
DW

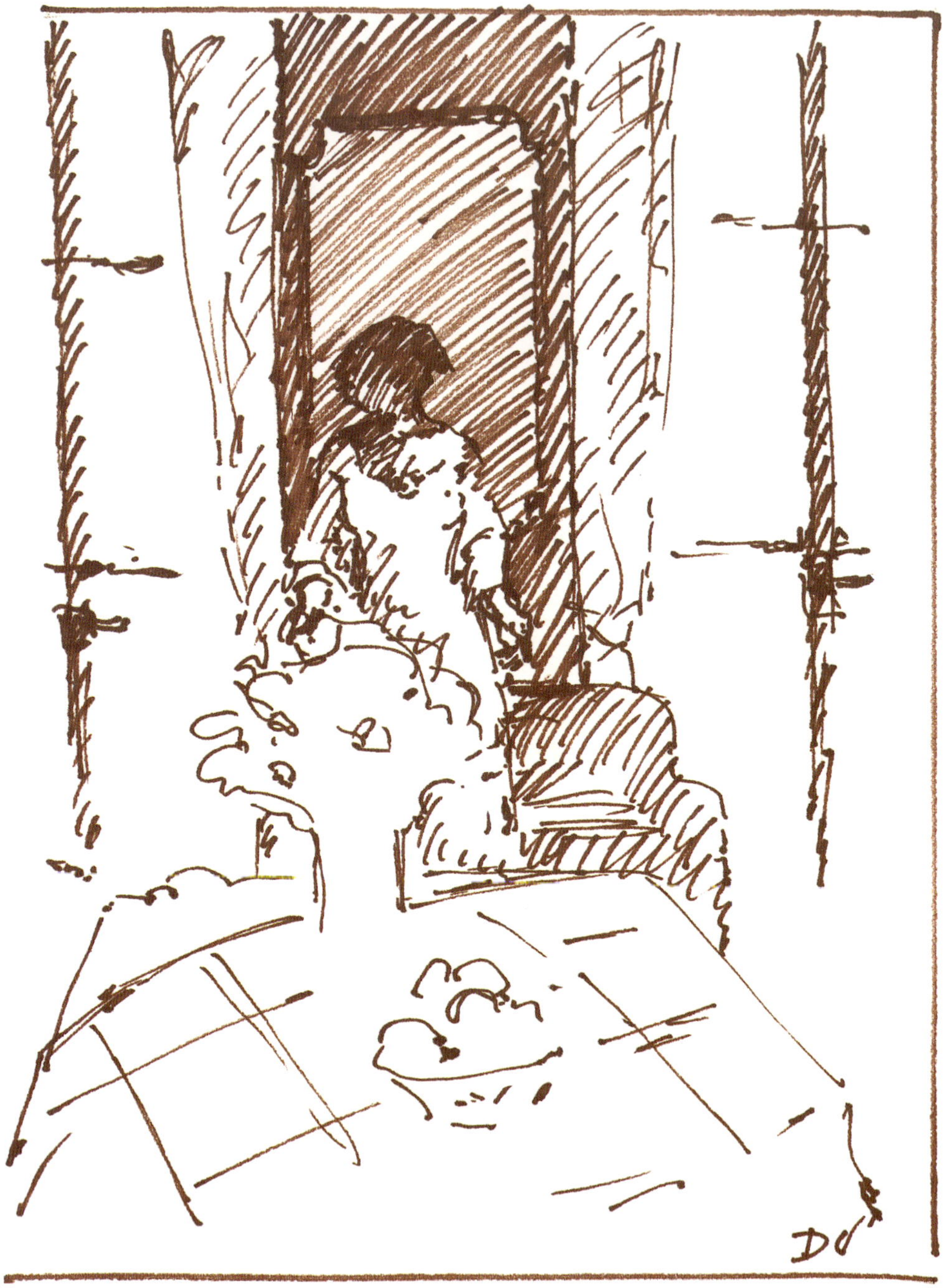

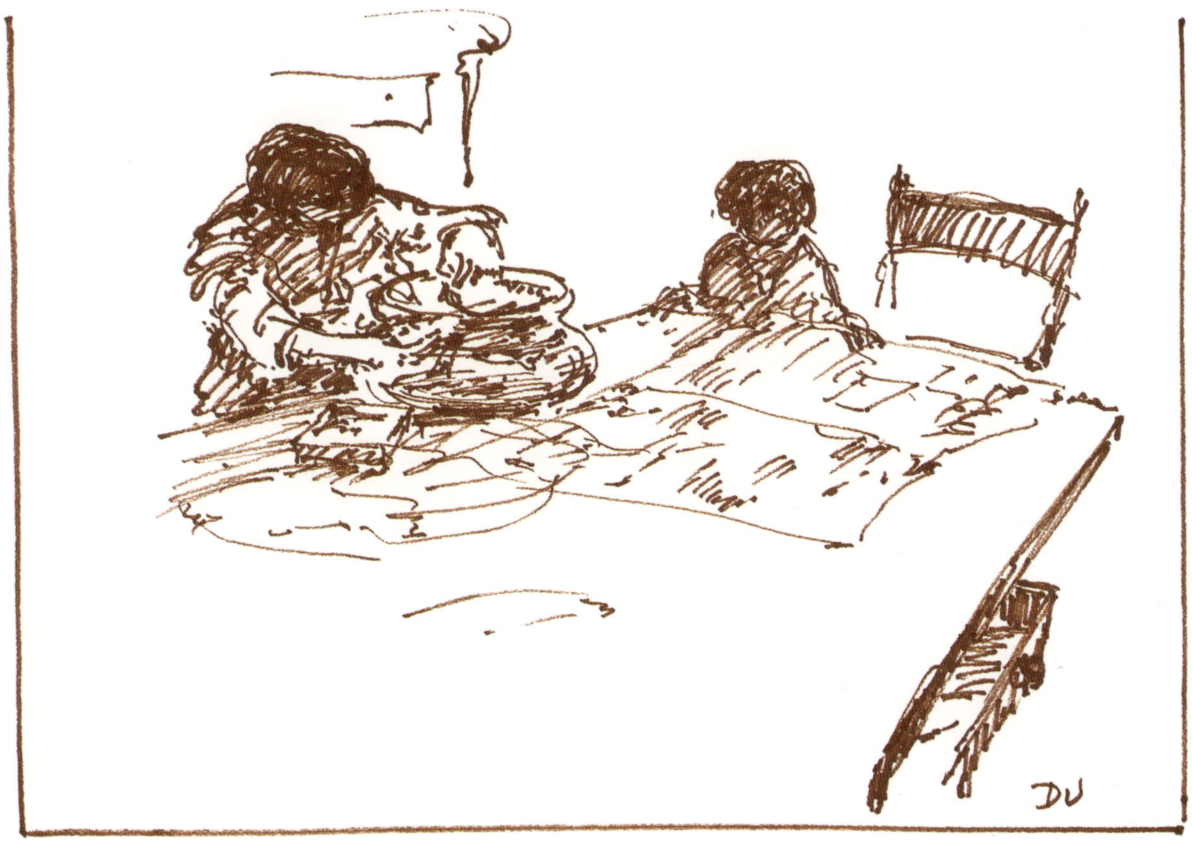
DU

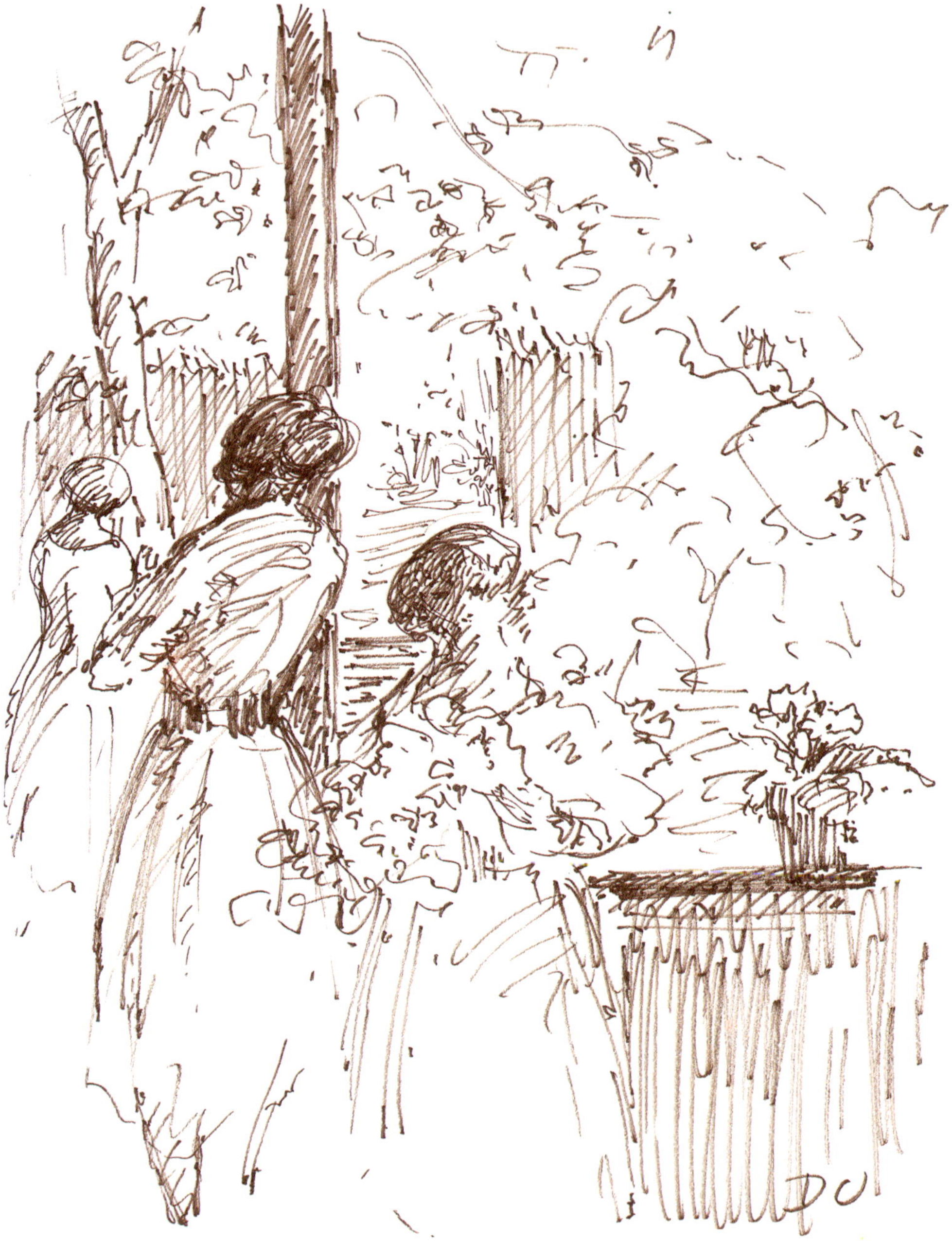

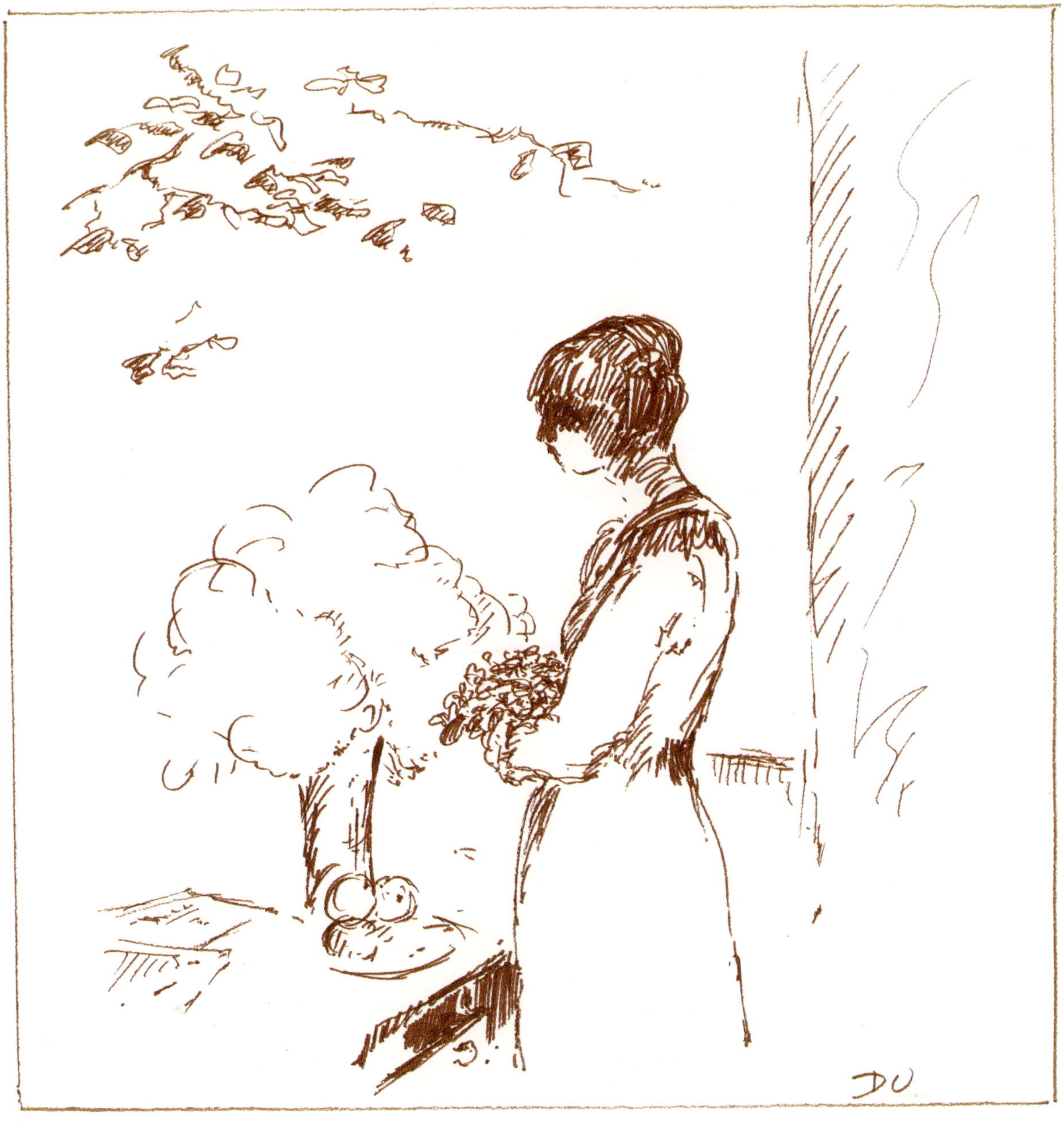
DU

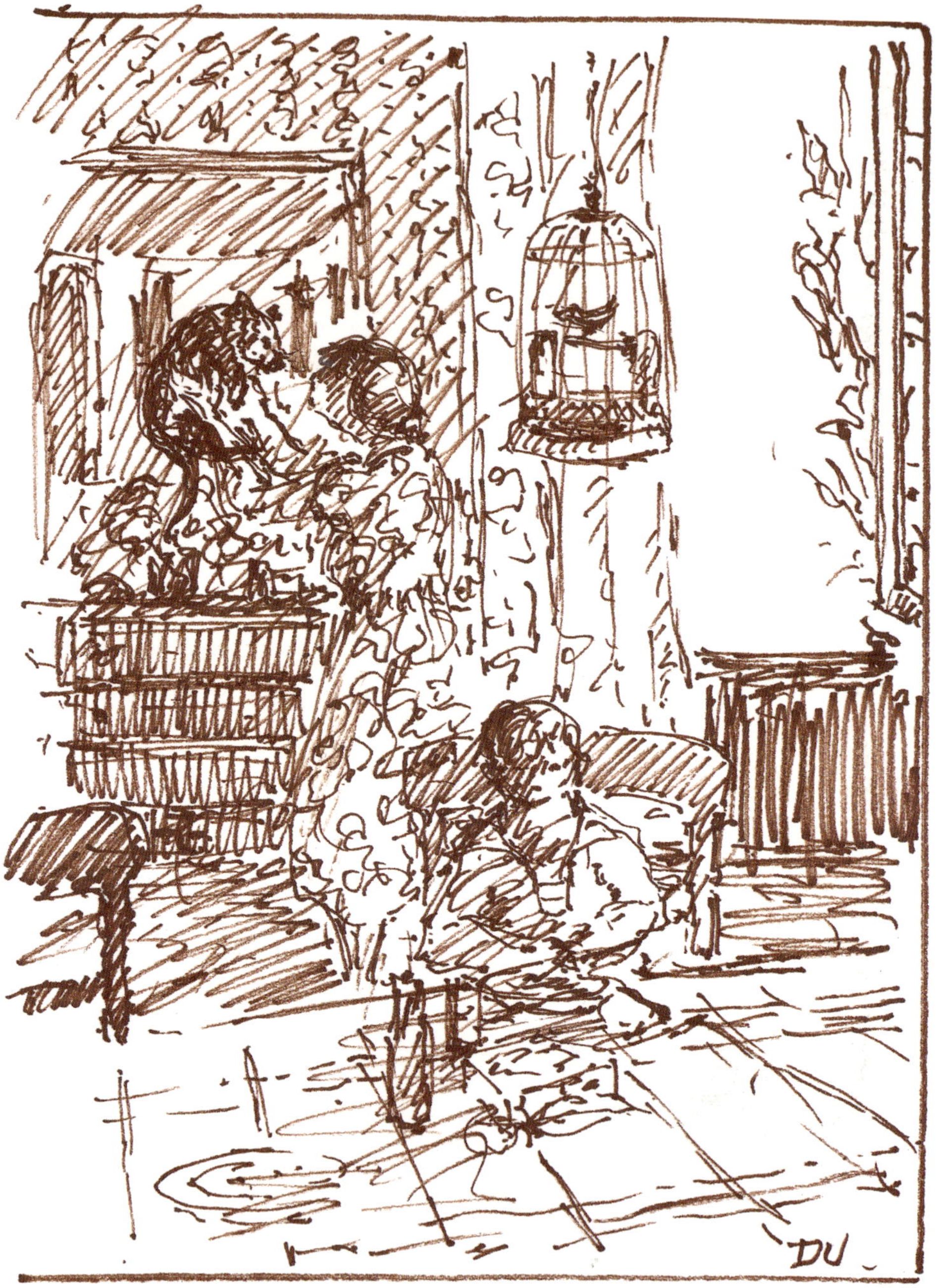
DU

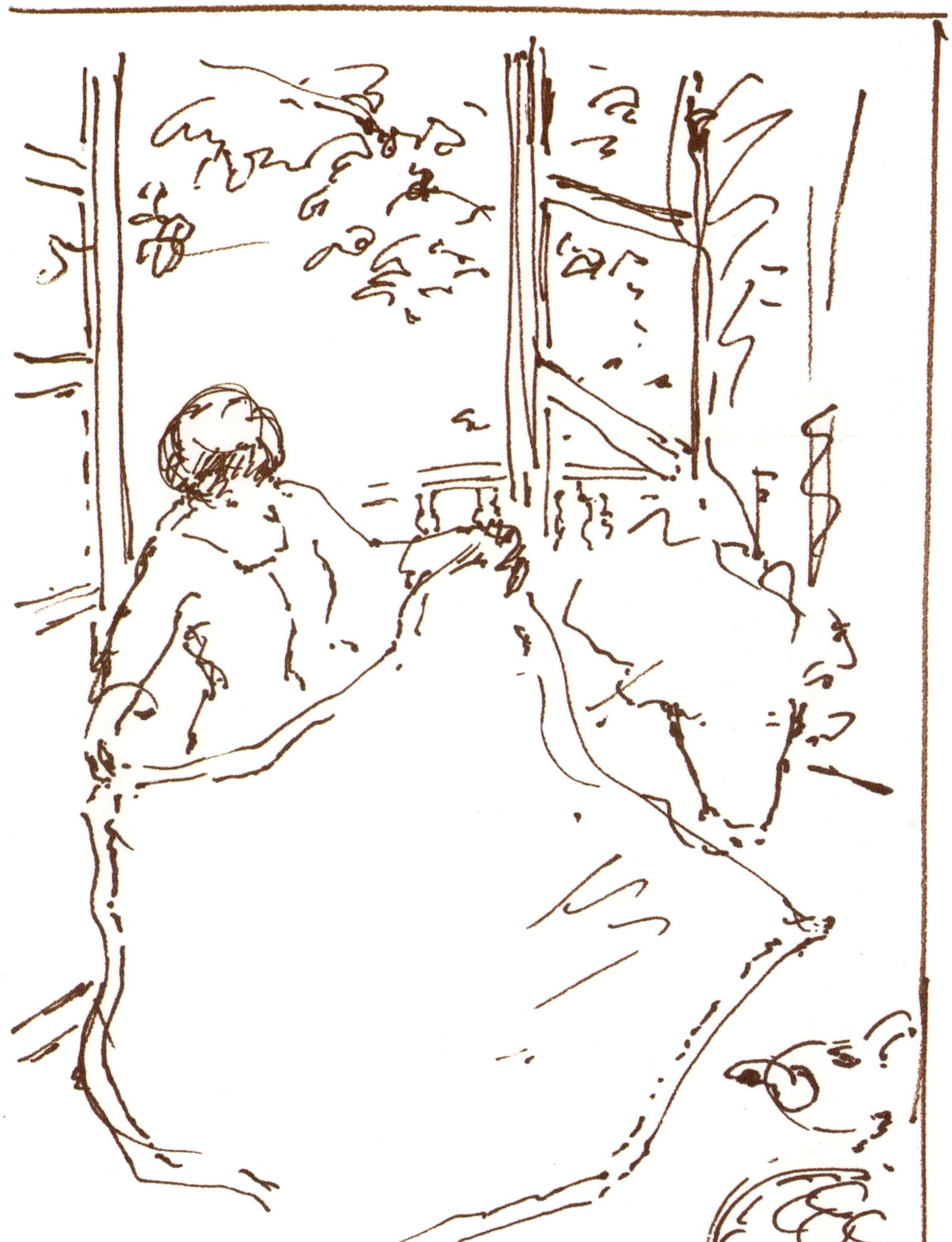

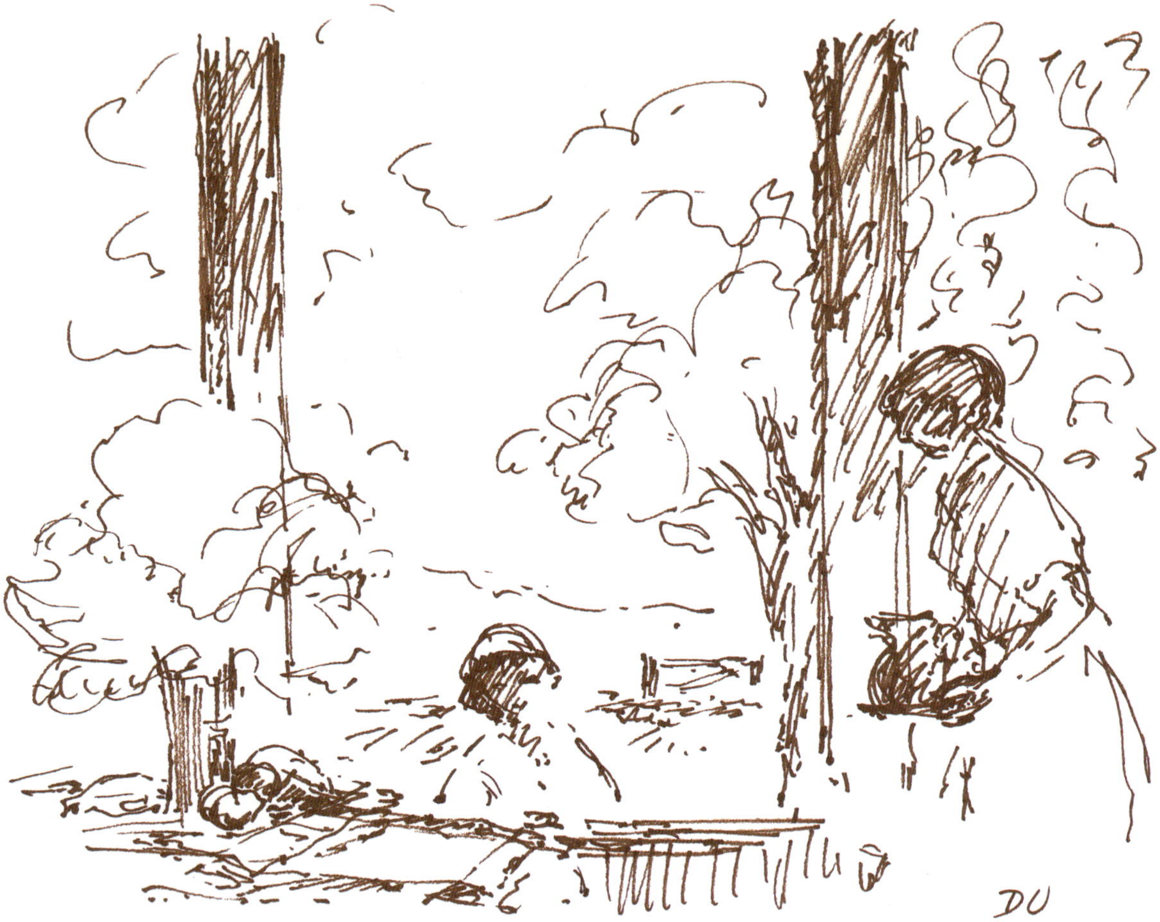
DU

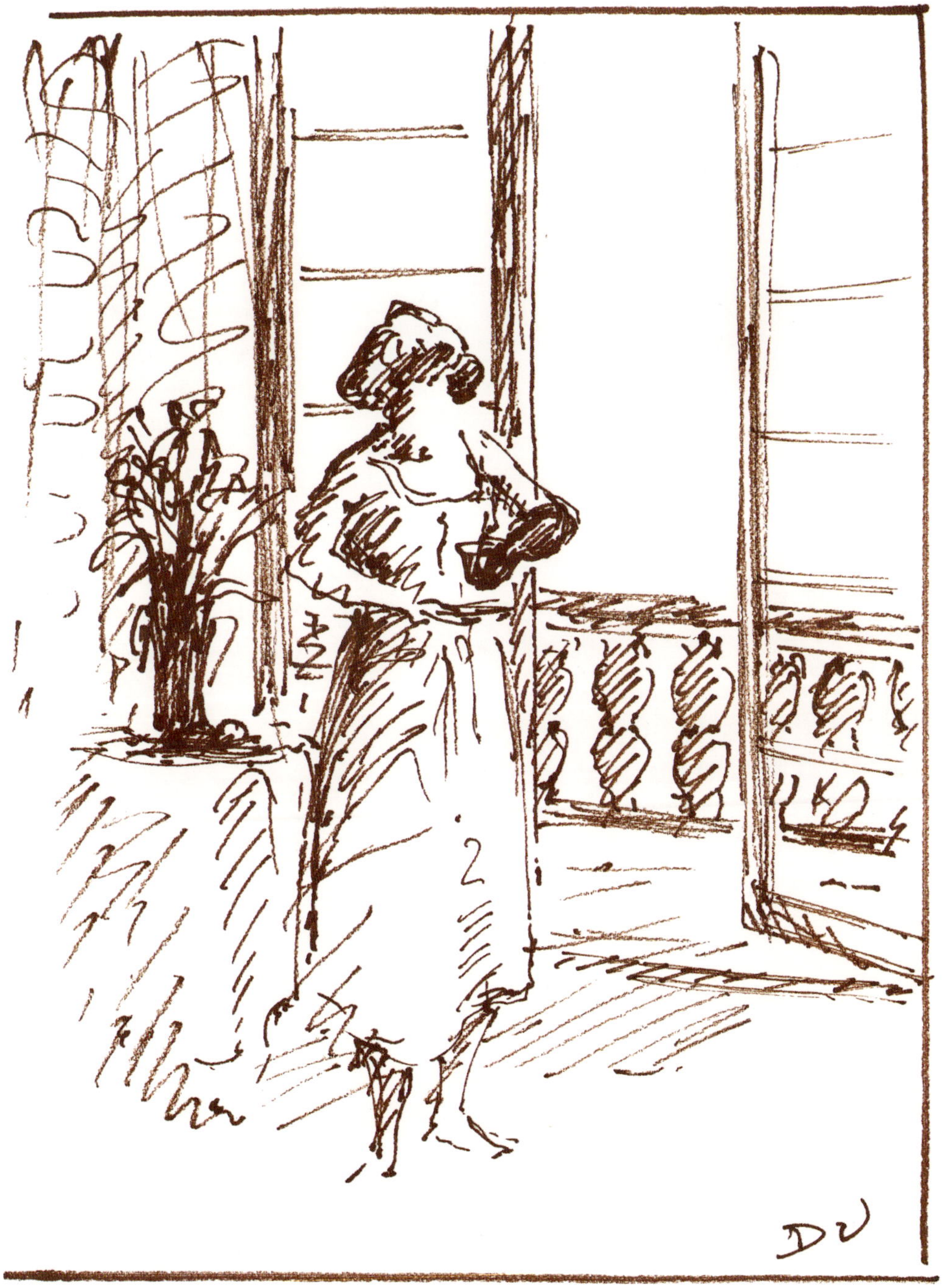
DV

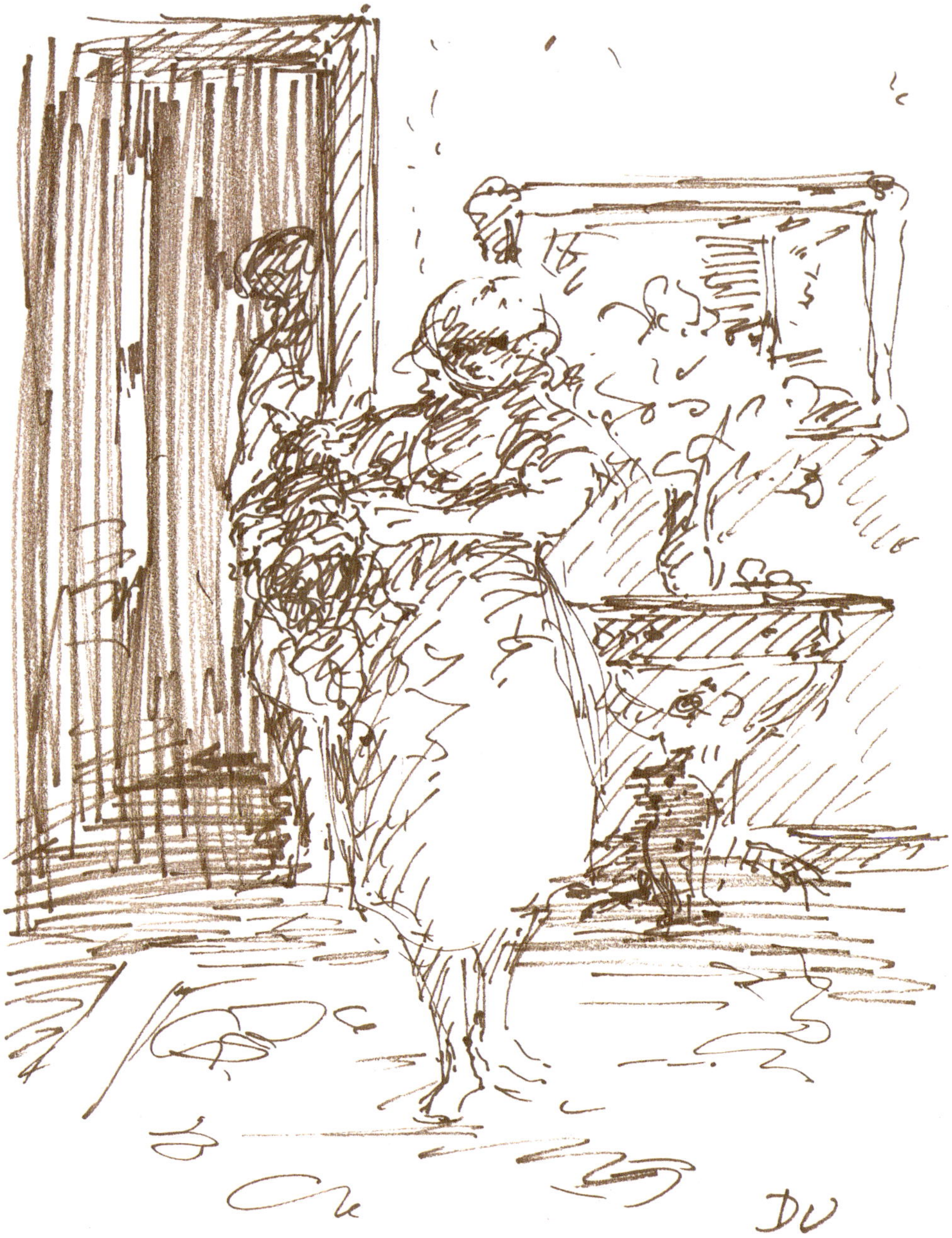

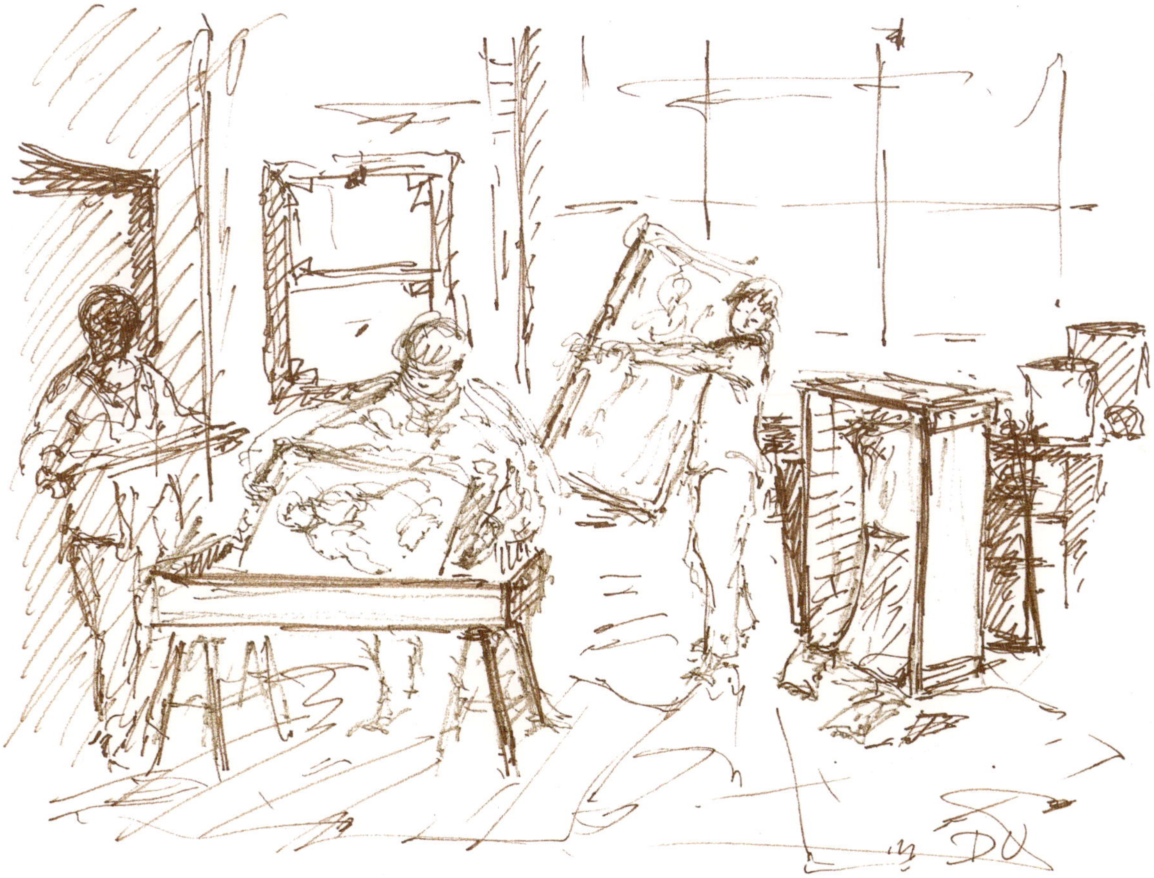

Part Four - Music

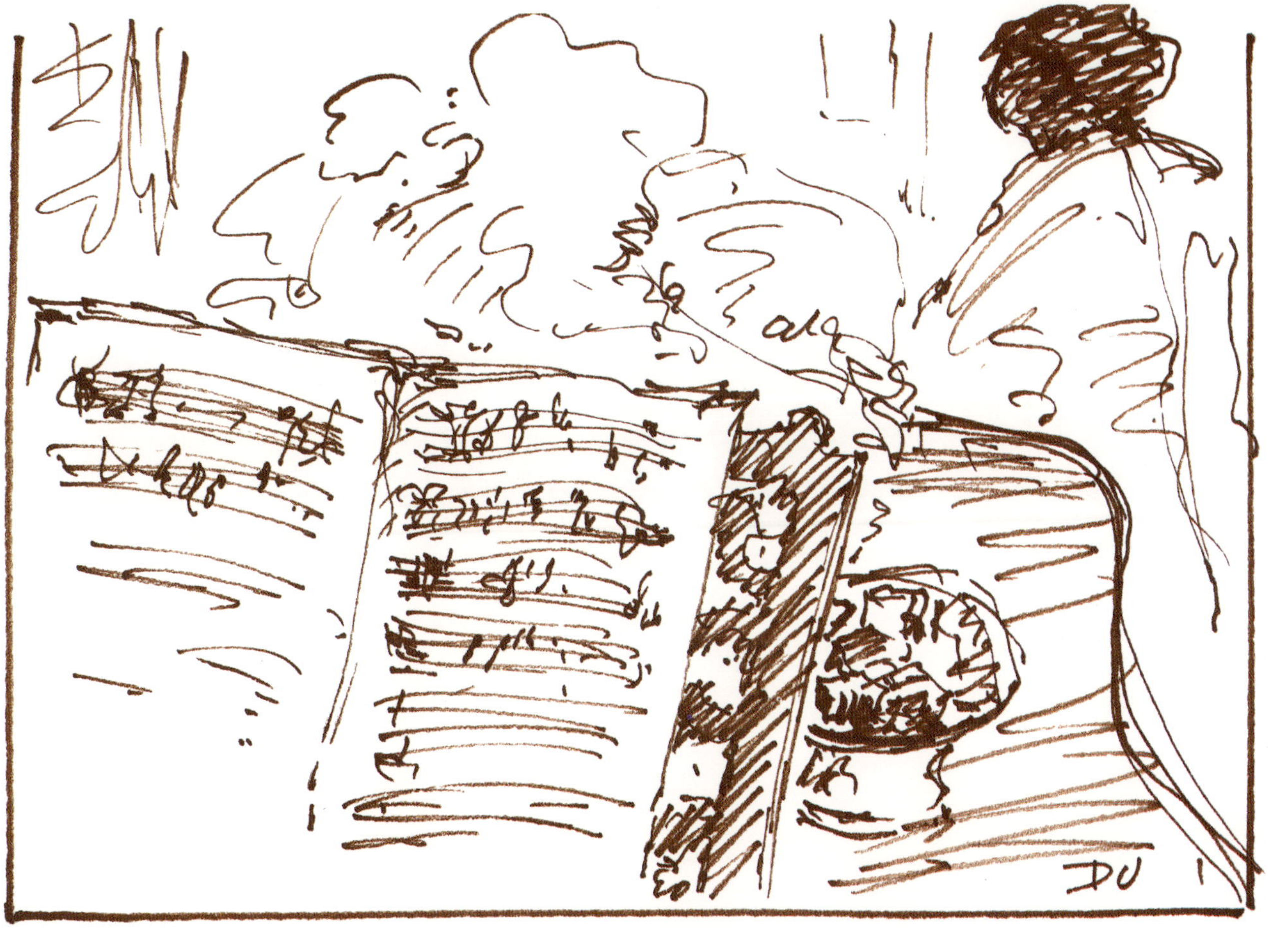

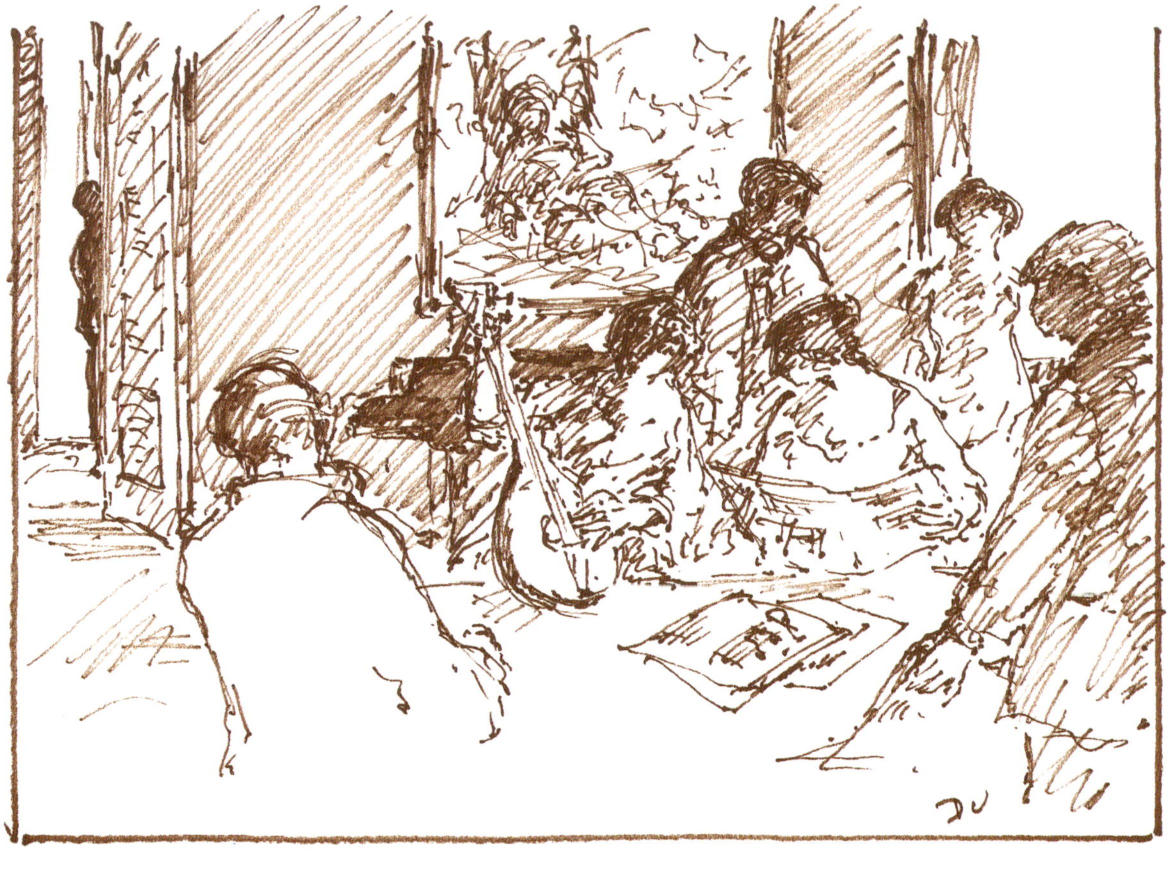

We have been blessed with the gift of five senses, each developed to varying degrees according to personal capabilities and interest. Perhaps the oldest pleasure man has responded to is sound. It may have been the rhythmic striking of bleached bones against a rock that started it all. No matter; the sounds we enjoy today fill an important part of each day of our lives.

The pleasure of both making and listening to music is a theme I have often used in my drawings. The fascinating shapes of instruments seem to invite the pen to render them. But for me, the gathering of figures to perform together has a special meaning. These drawings are wholly invented. They are not intended to be accurate in any way other than in expressing the spirit of the event. To capture the sound is the challenge. It is expressed in these drawings by the attitude of the performers and the tonal value of the setting, as well as by the instruments used.

Music is a very important part of my life, and I am most grateful for the opportunity and luxury of having as company while I work, a hundred piece orchestra, accompanied by beautiful voices, performing an opus composed by a great master. Humbled, I offer my simple drawing and painting with grateful thanks.

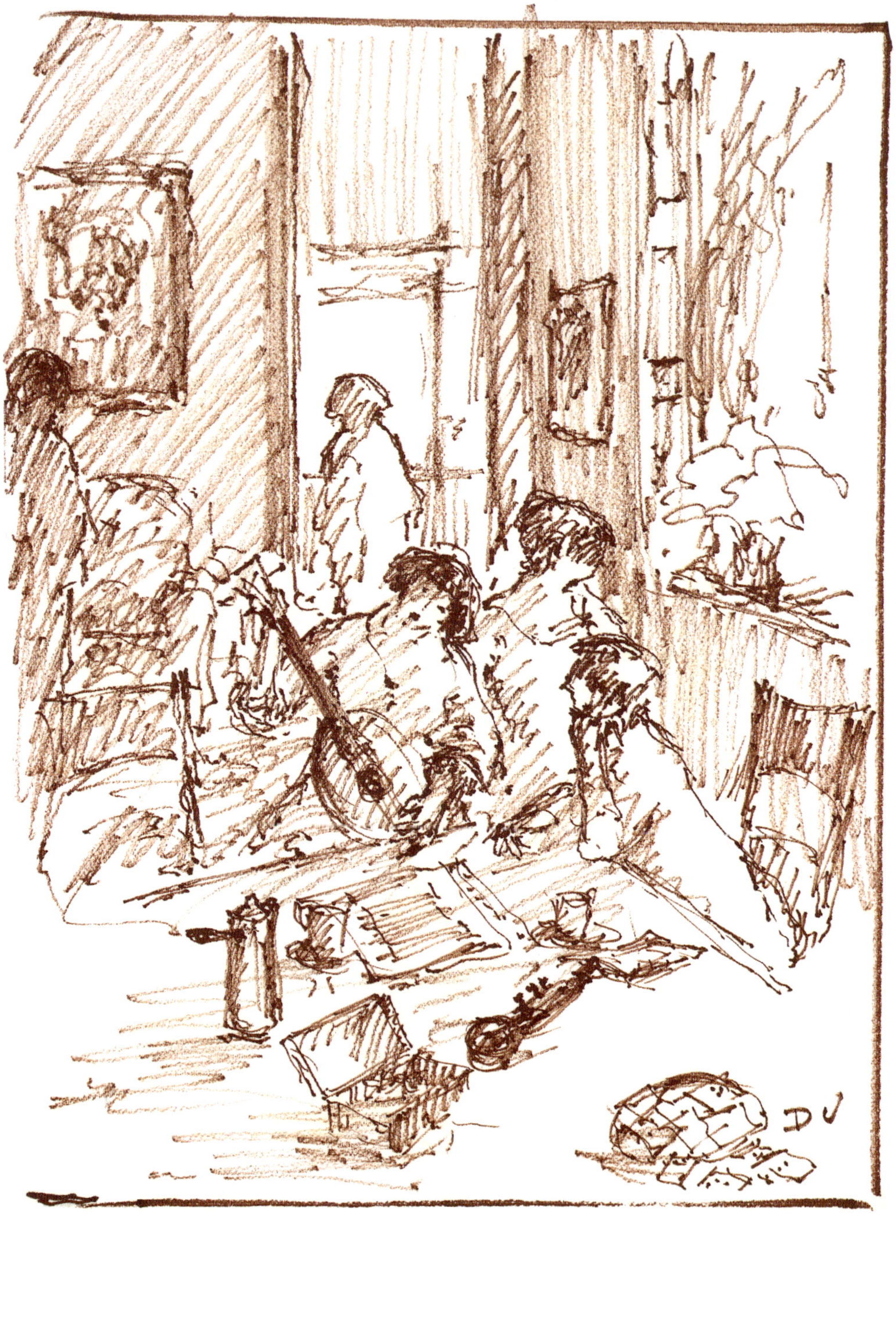

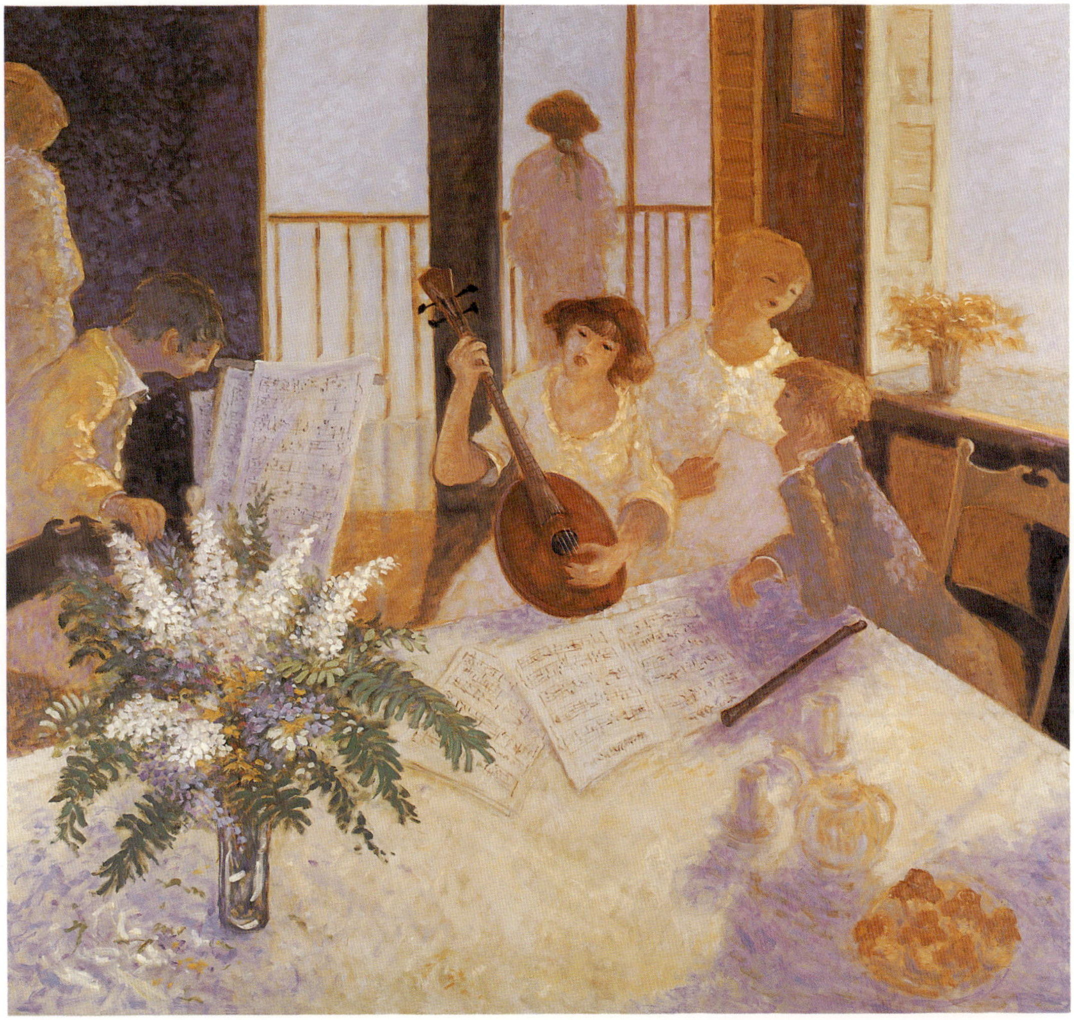

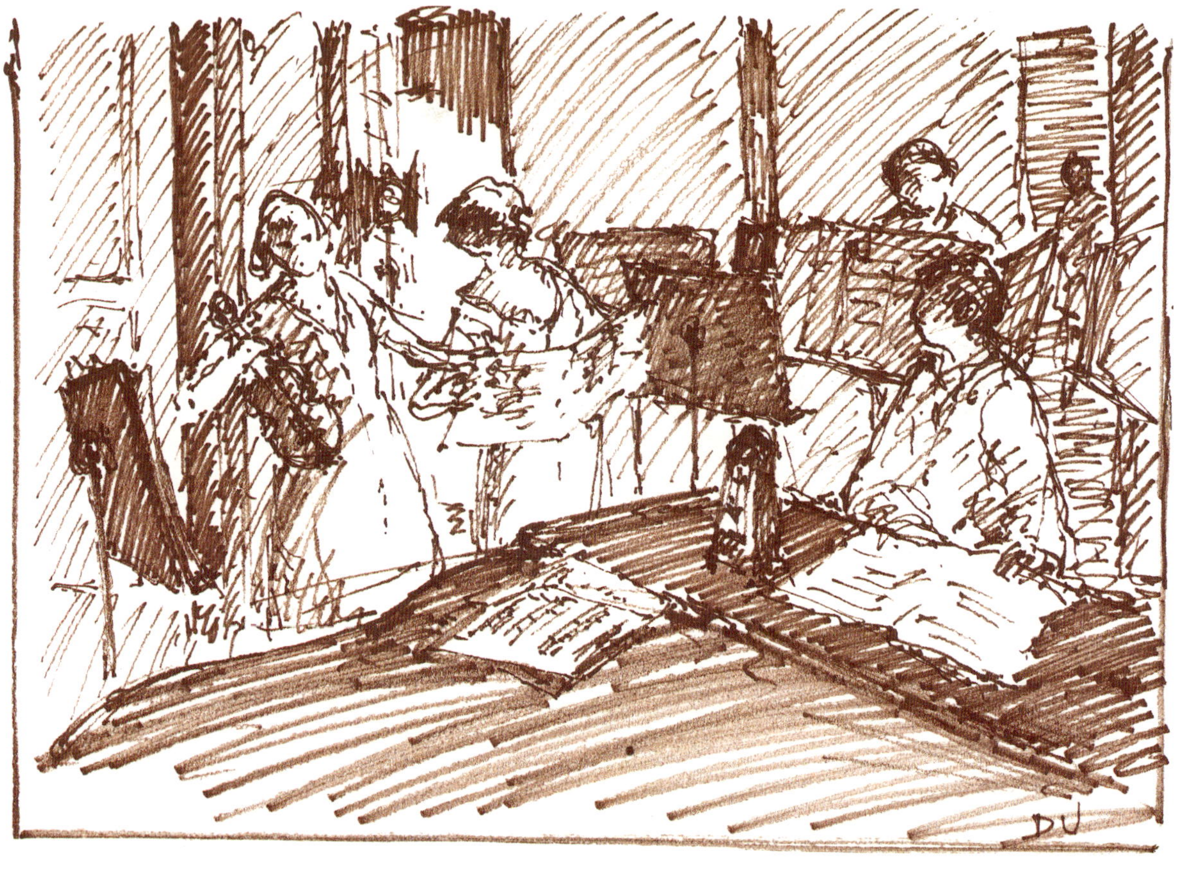

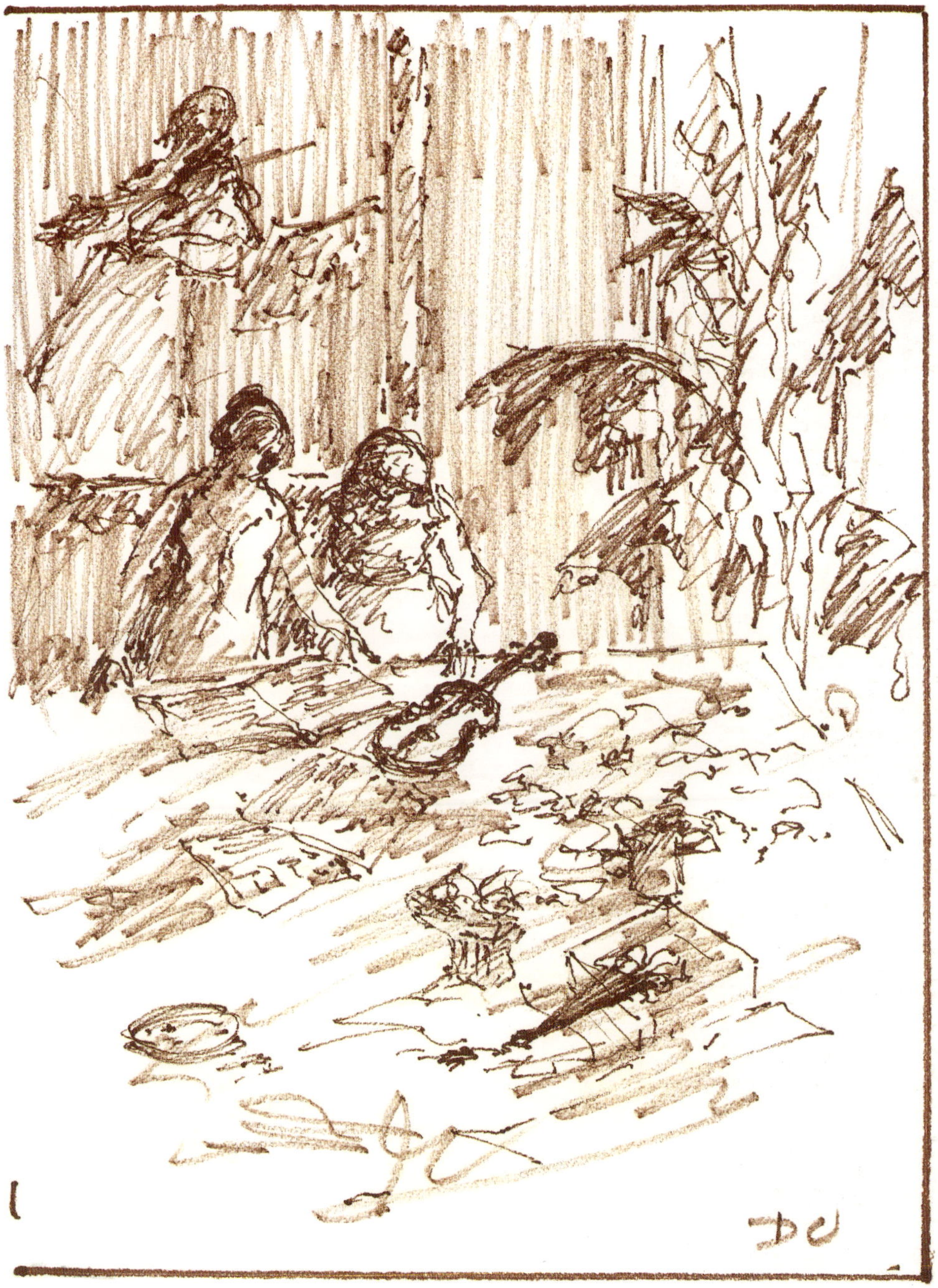

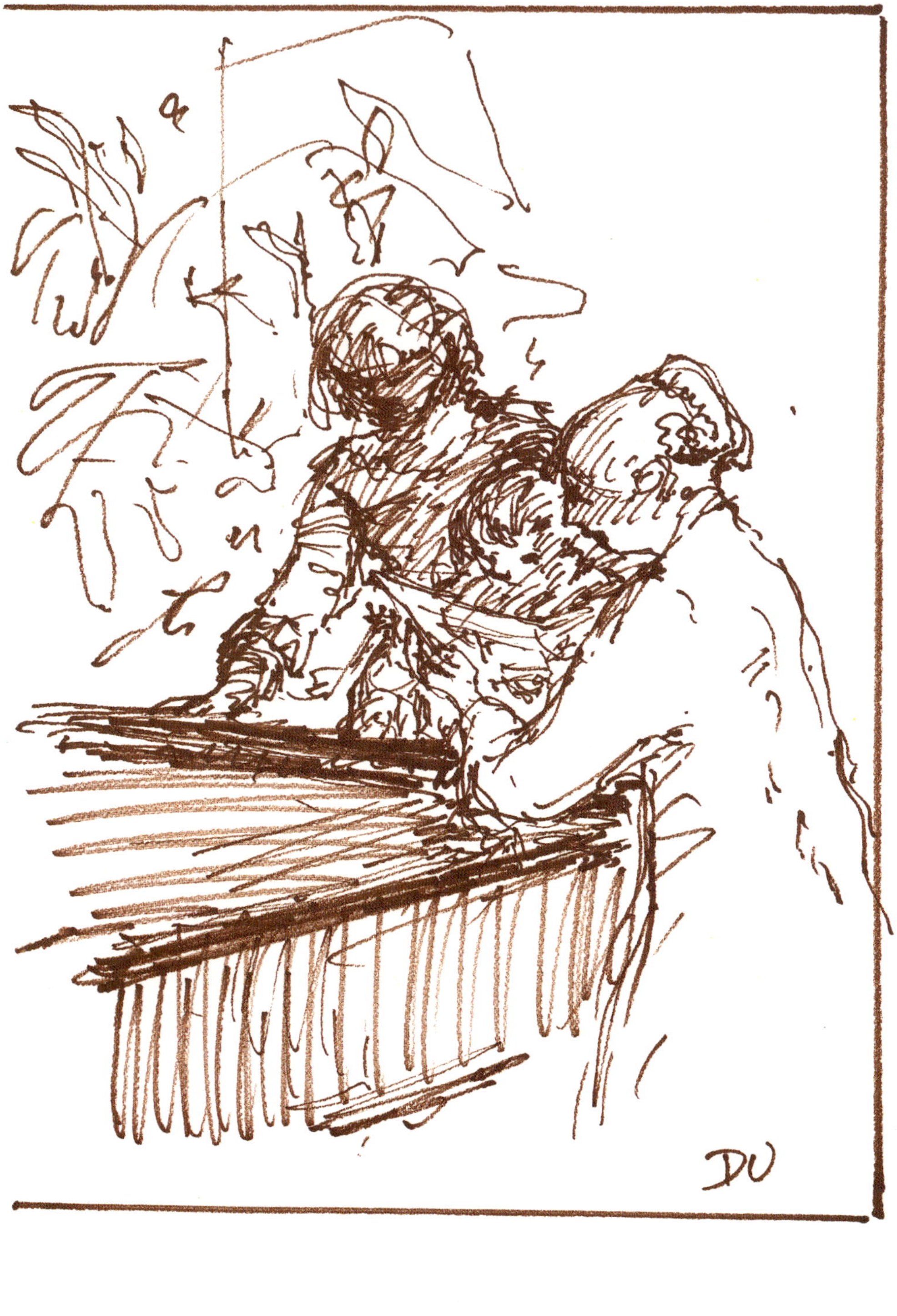
DV

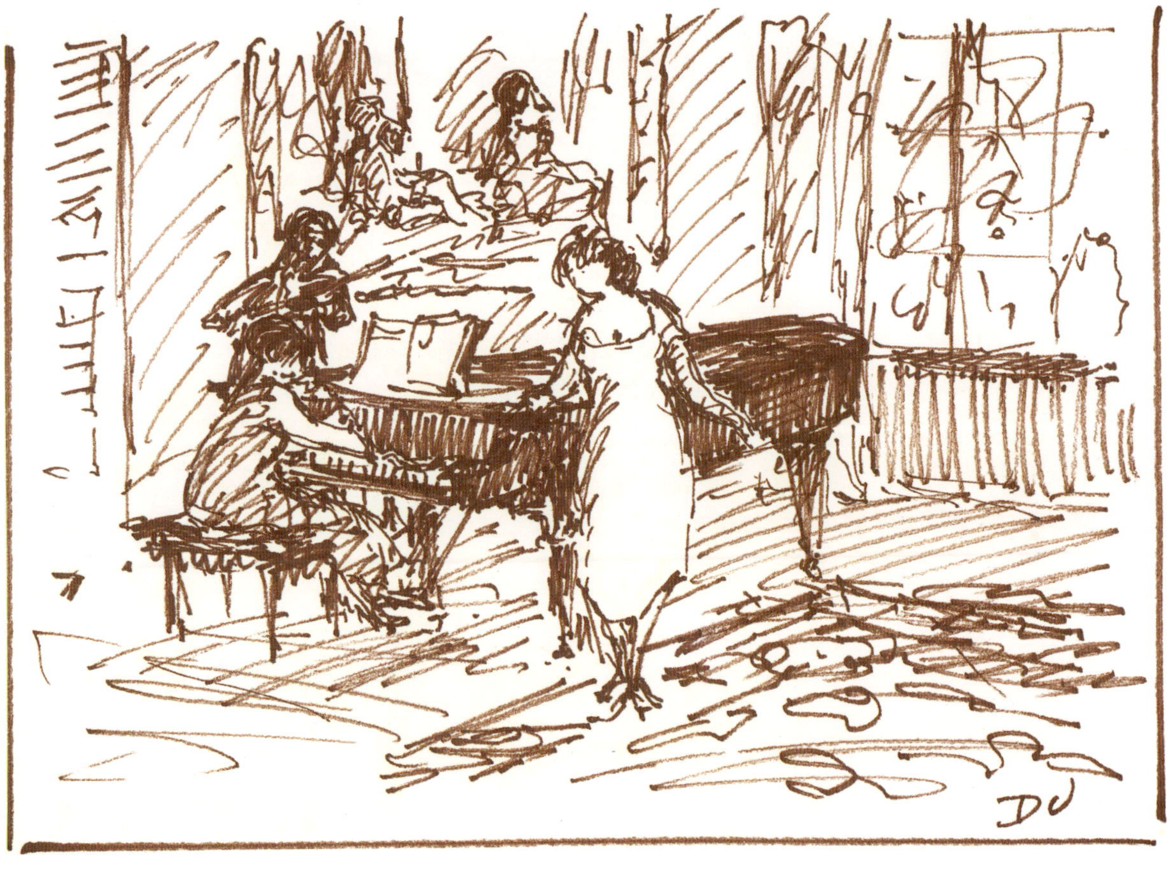

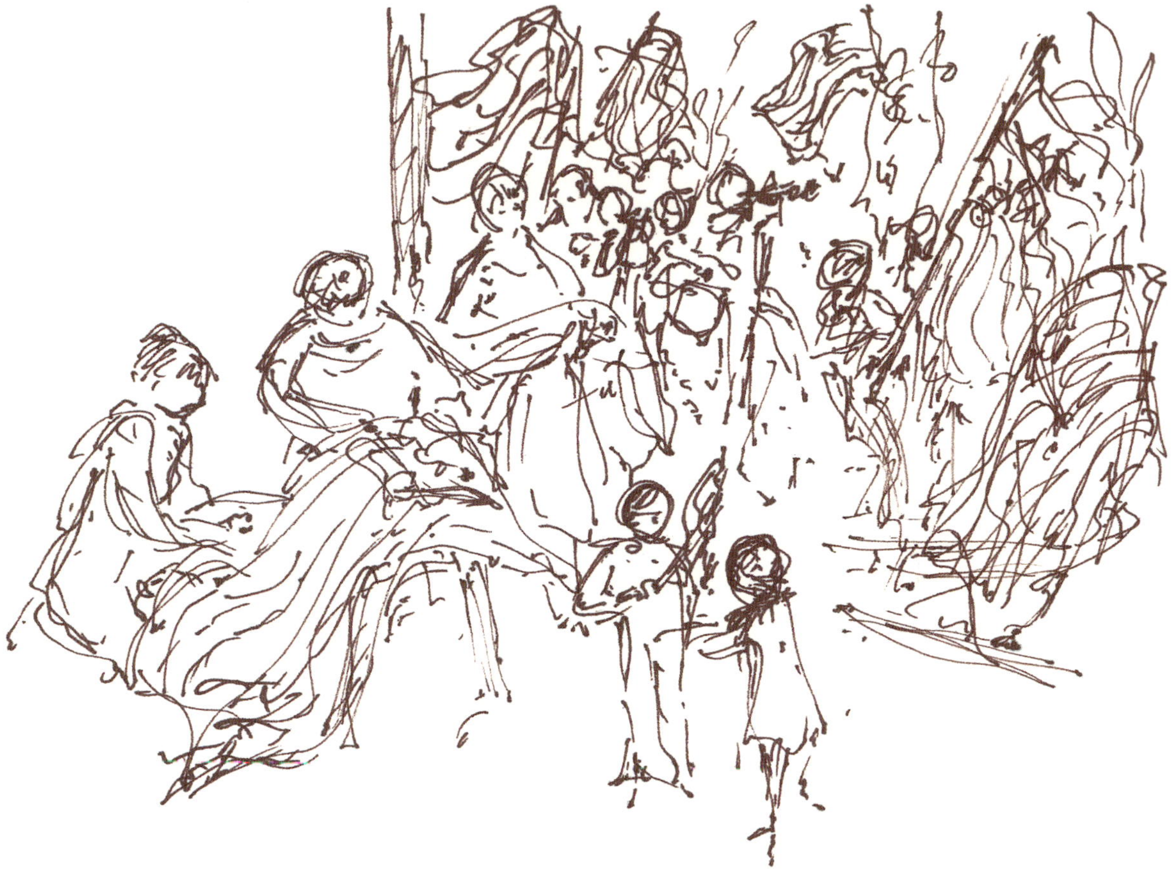

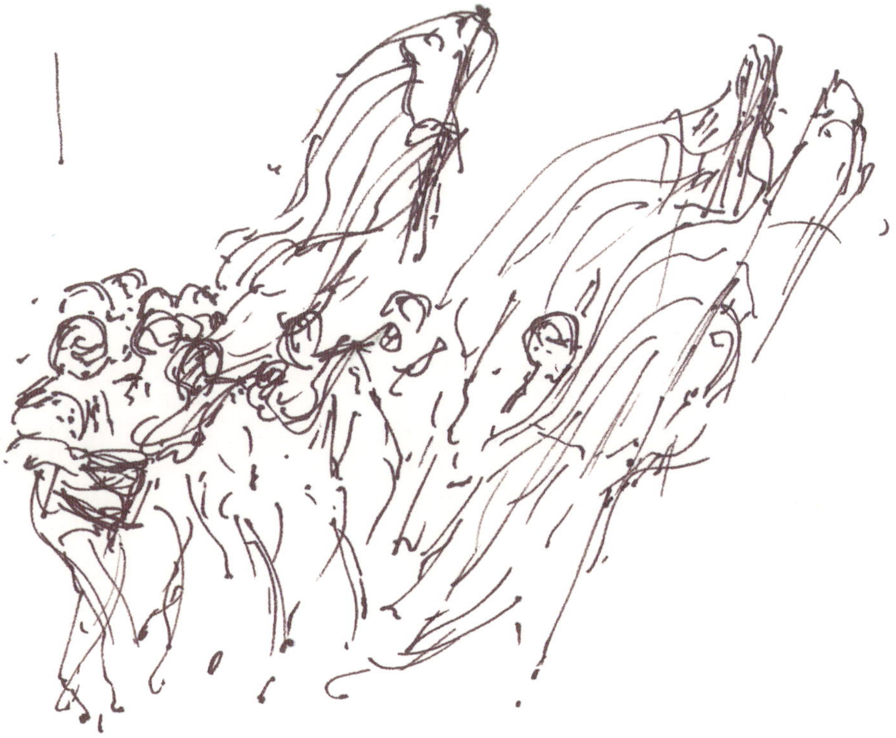

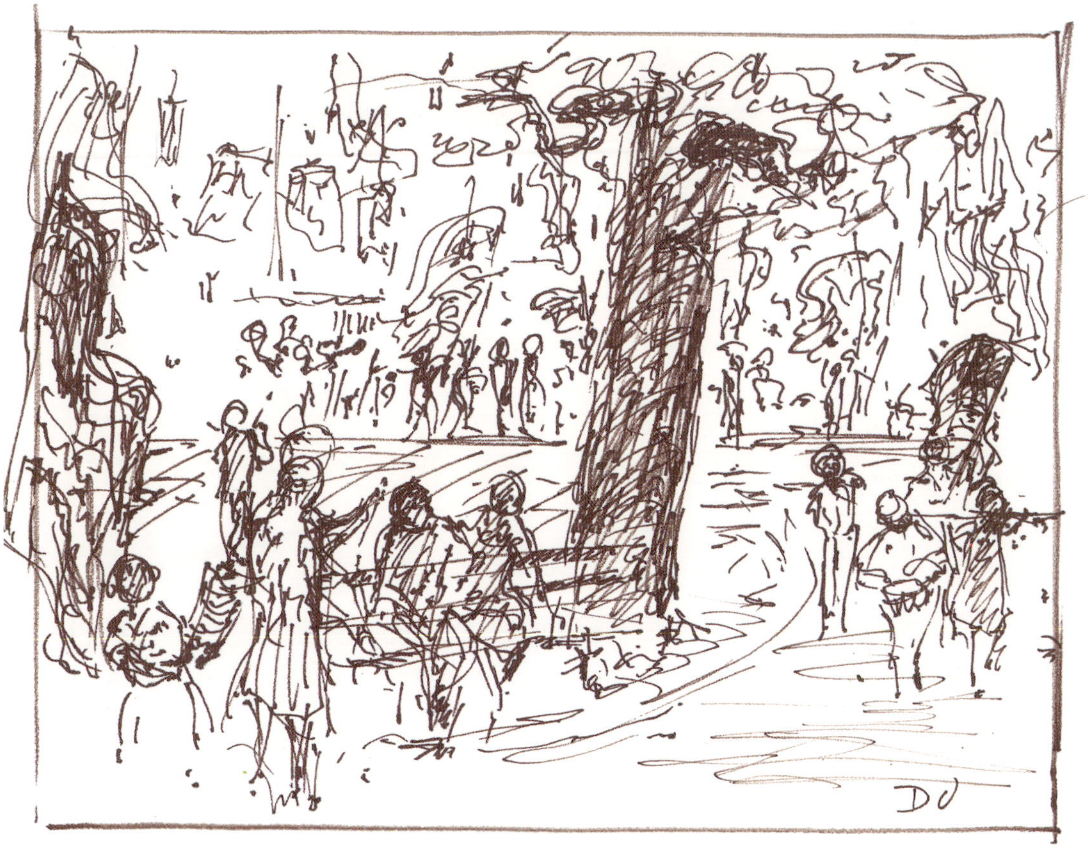

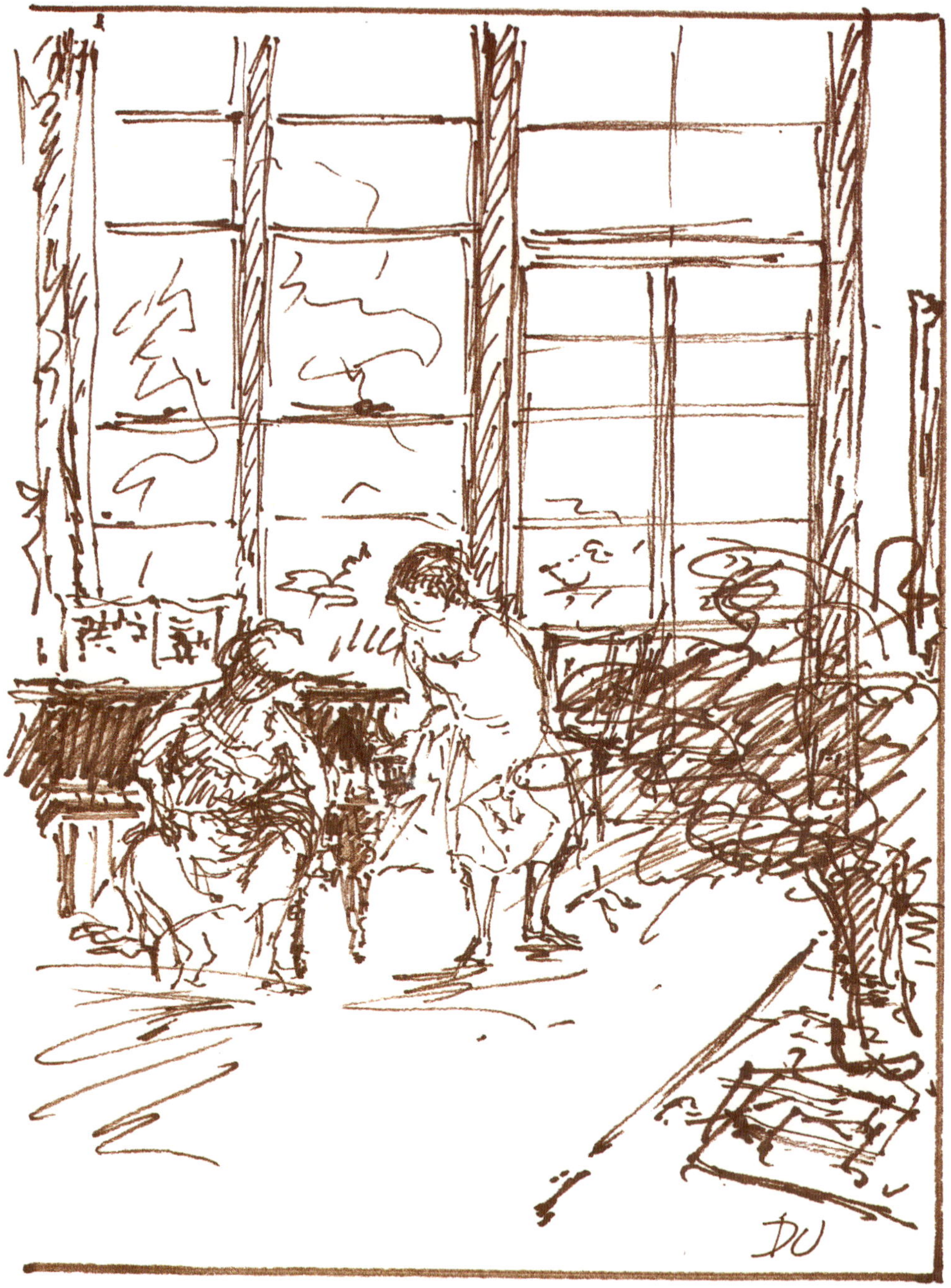

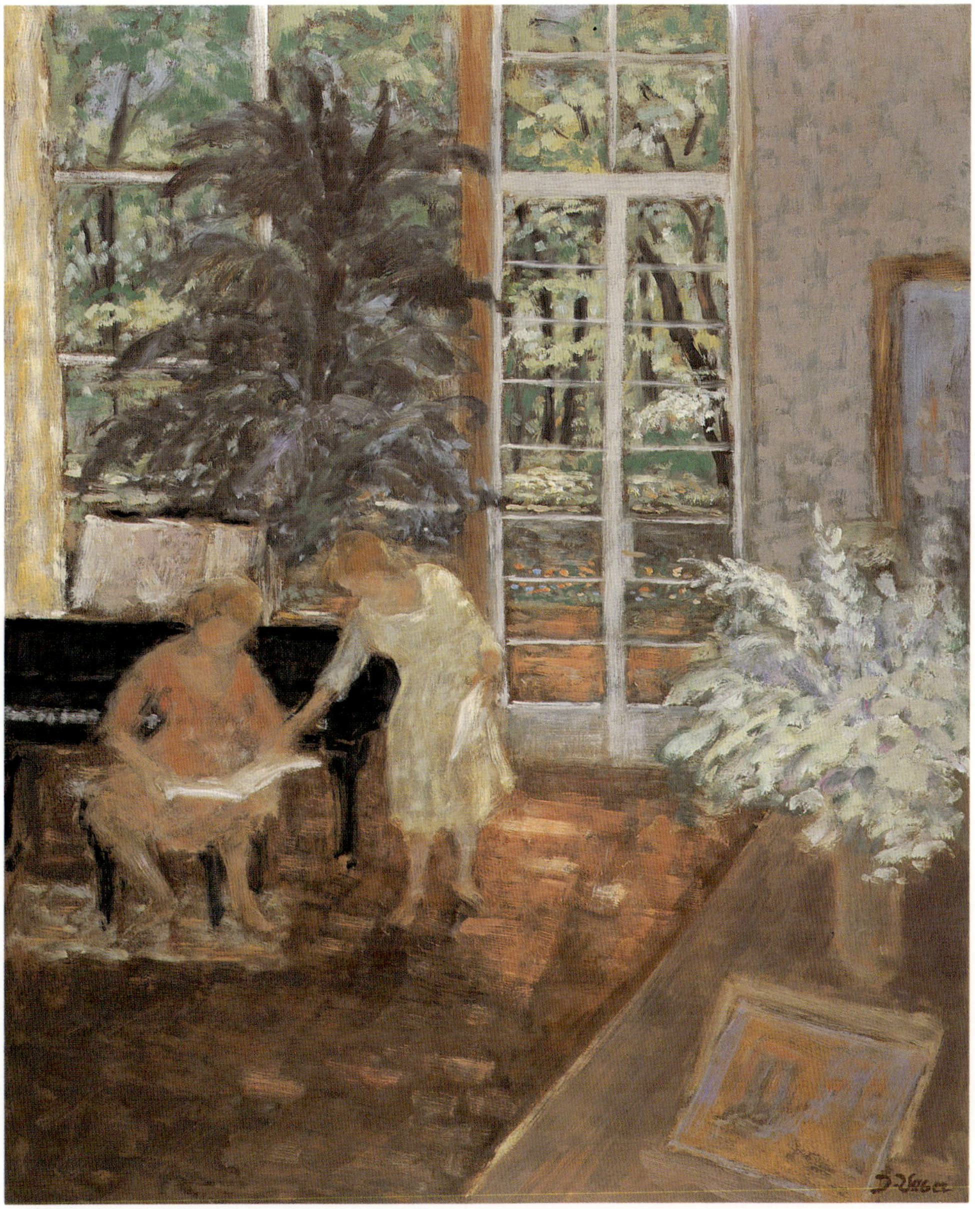

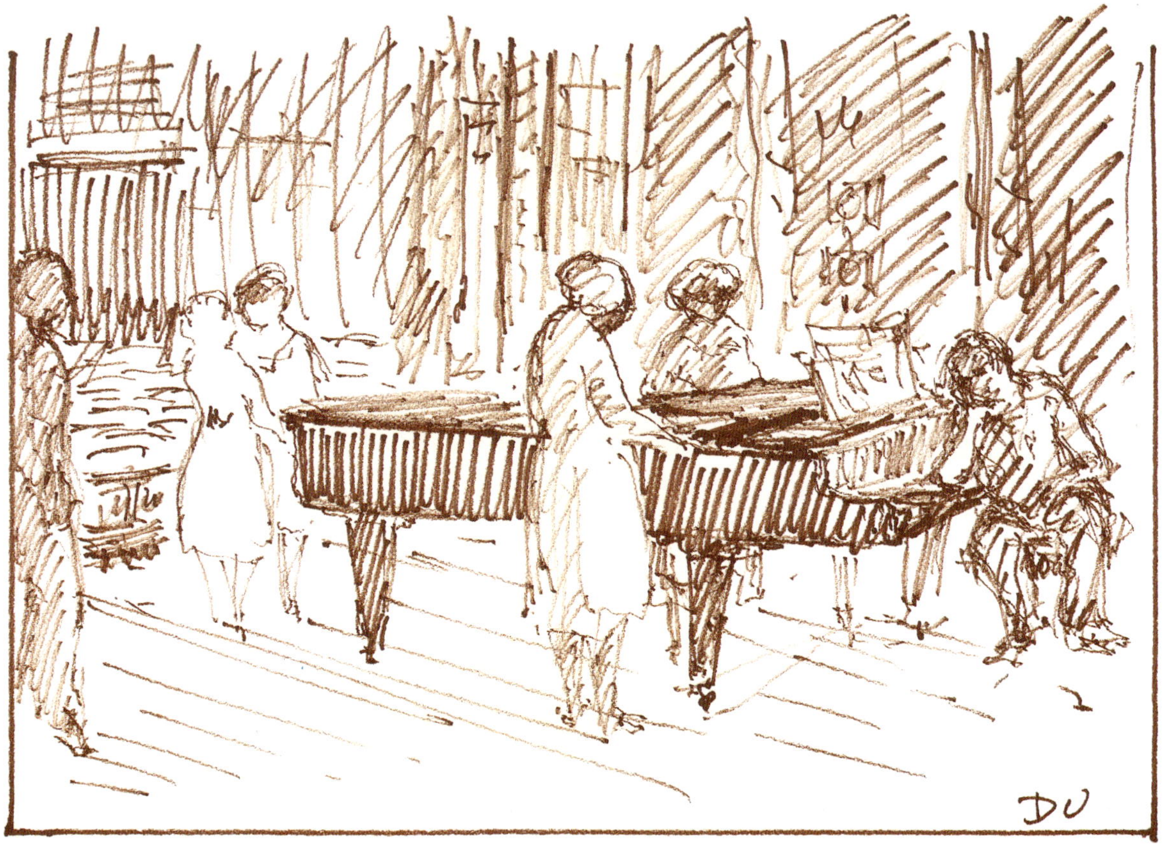
DU

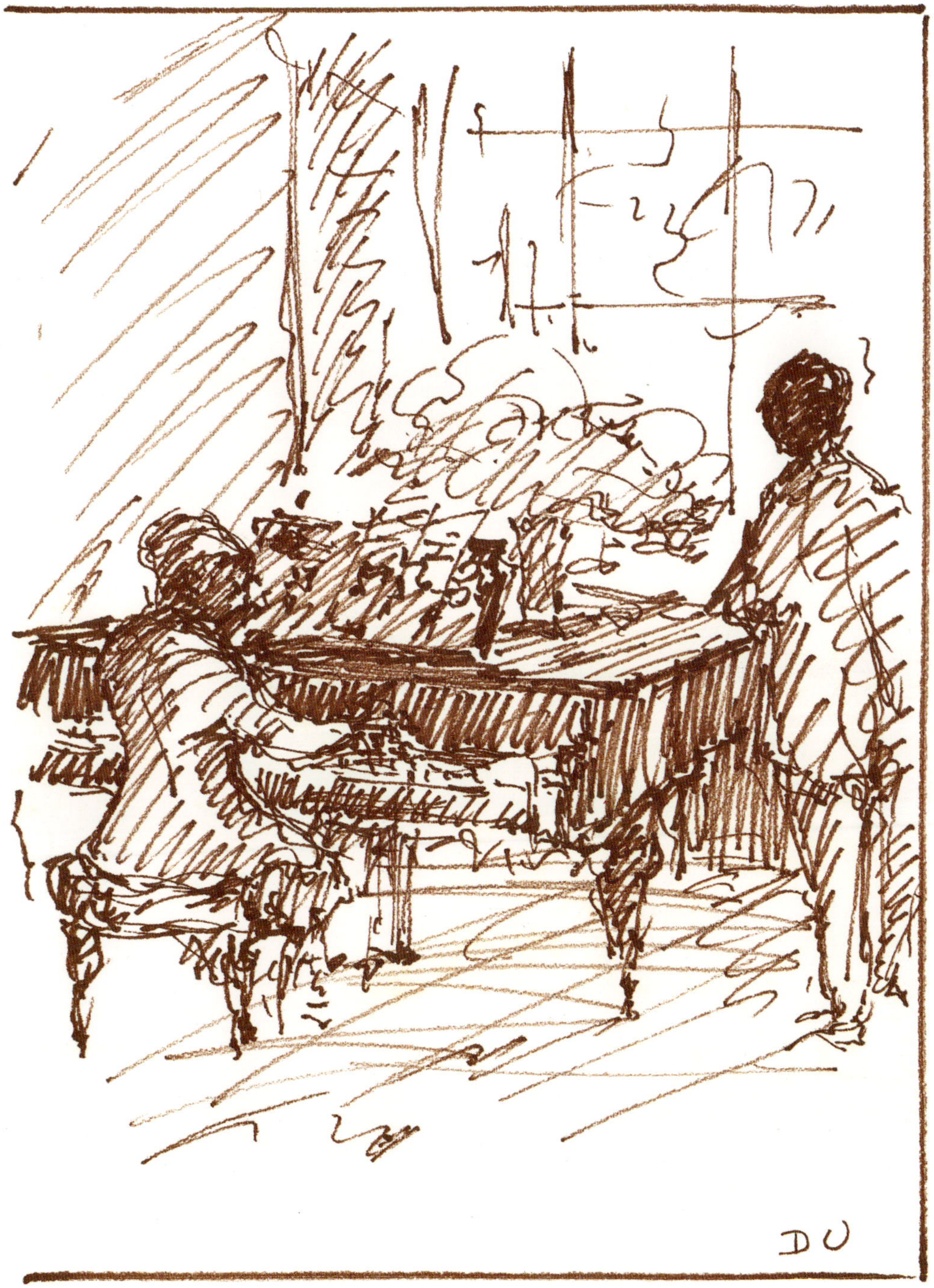
DU

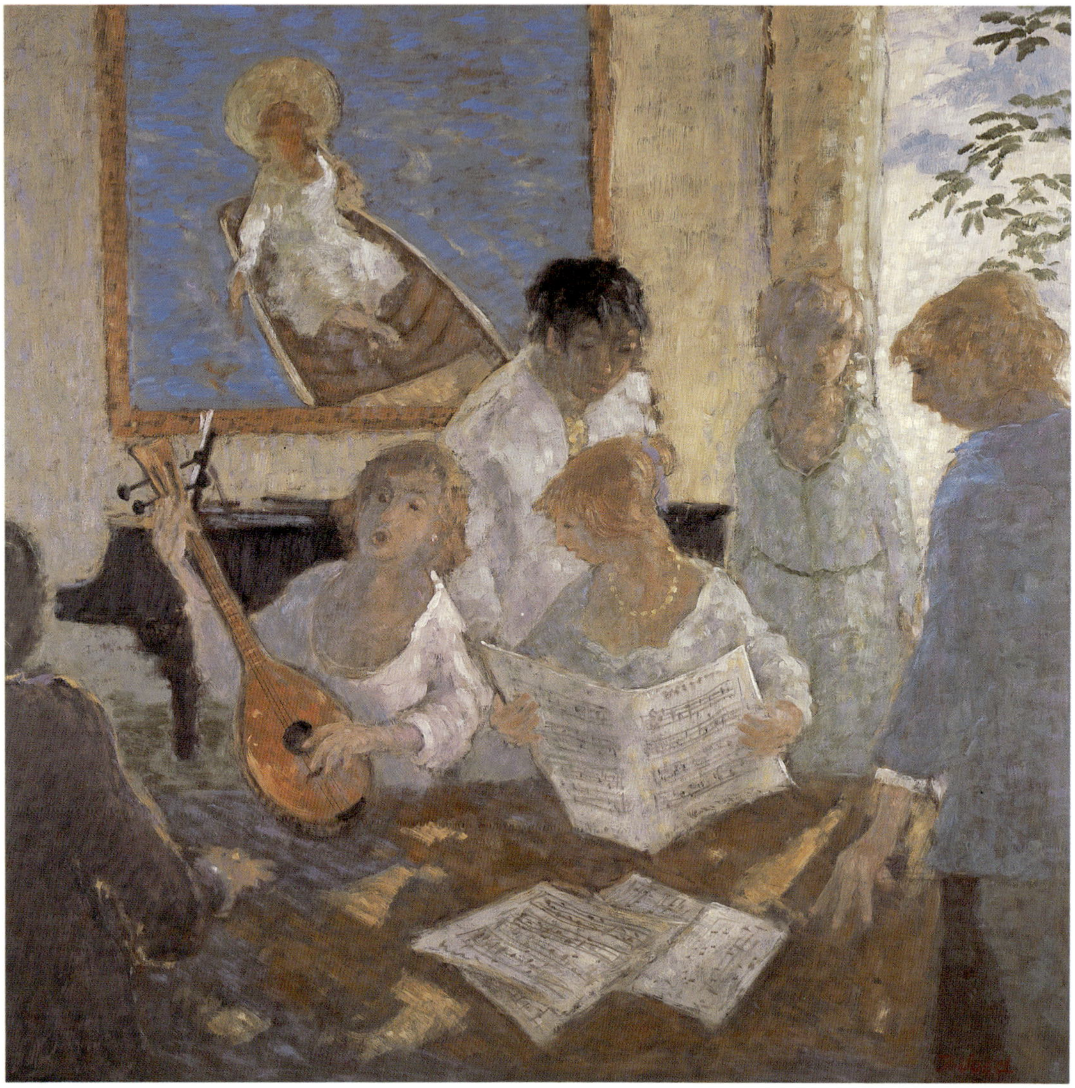

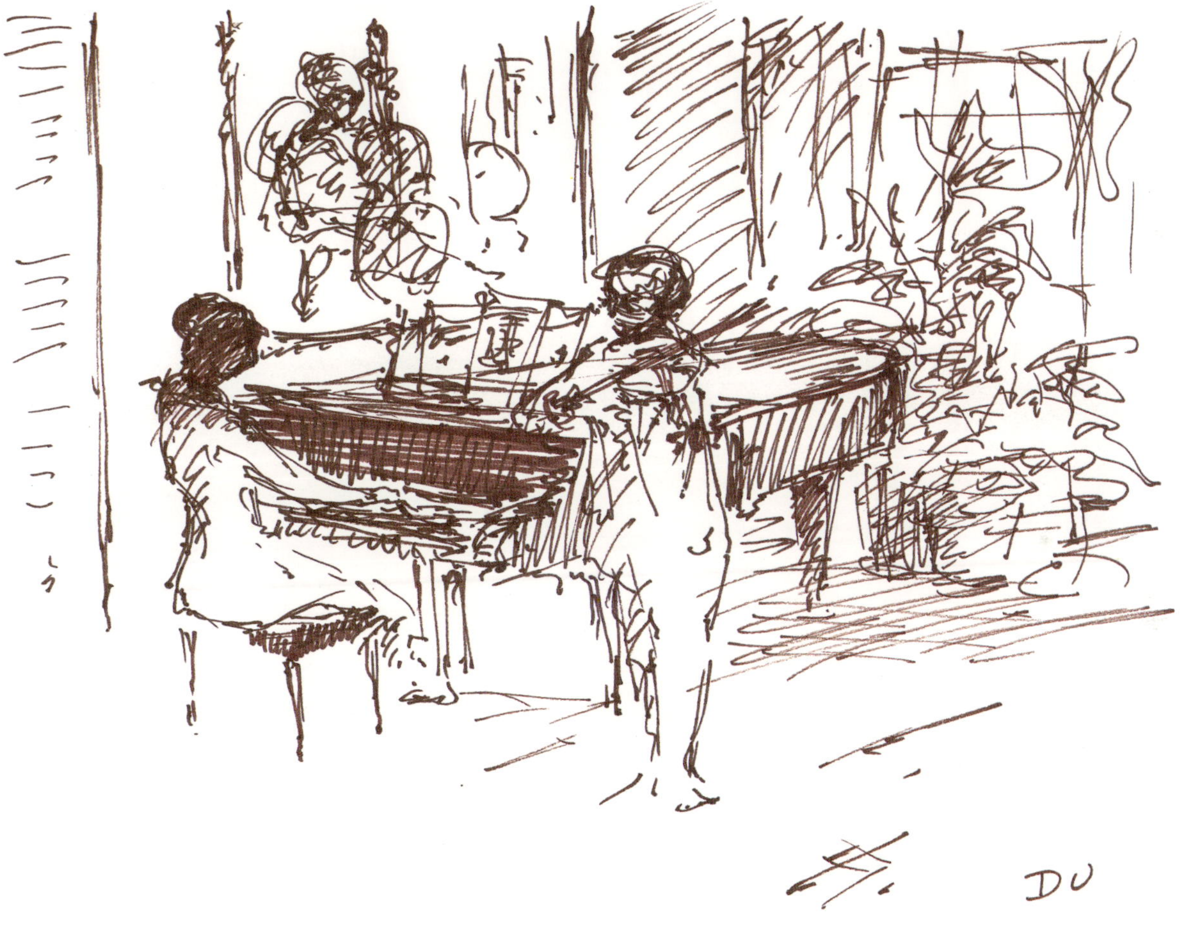
DU

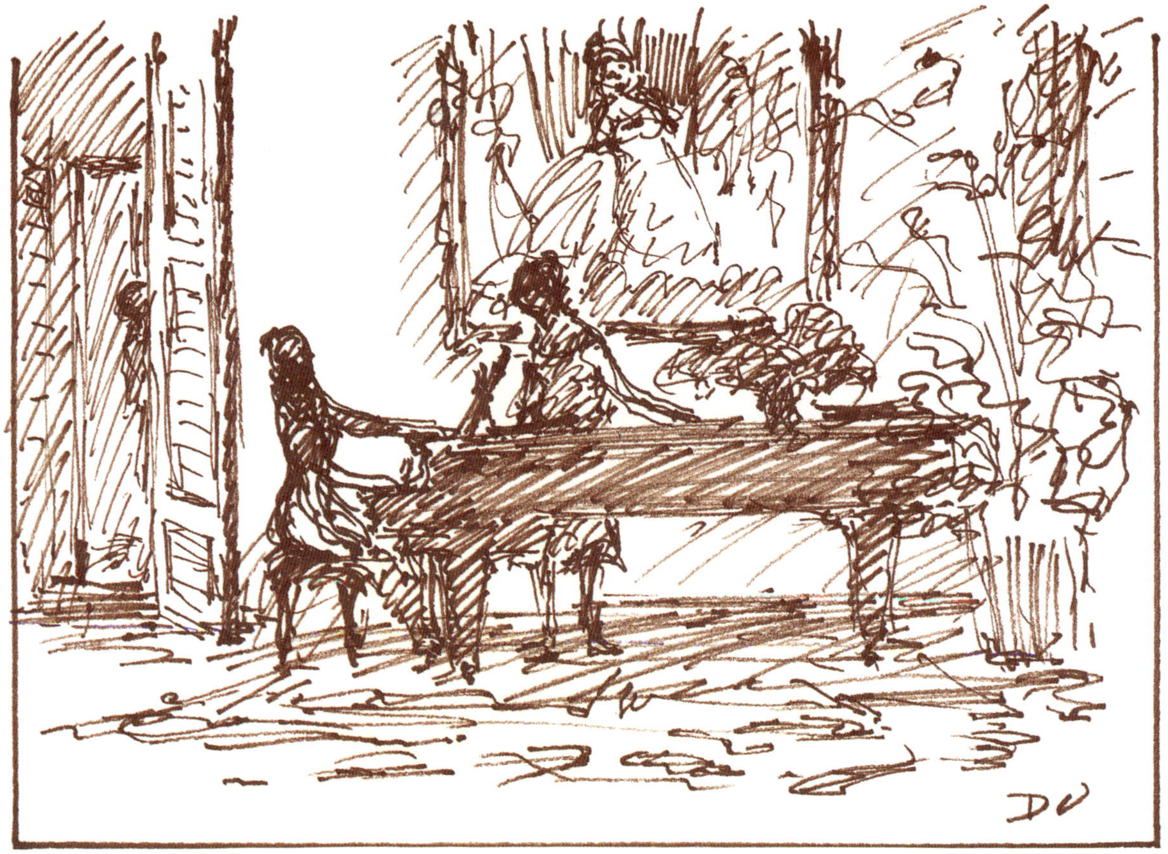

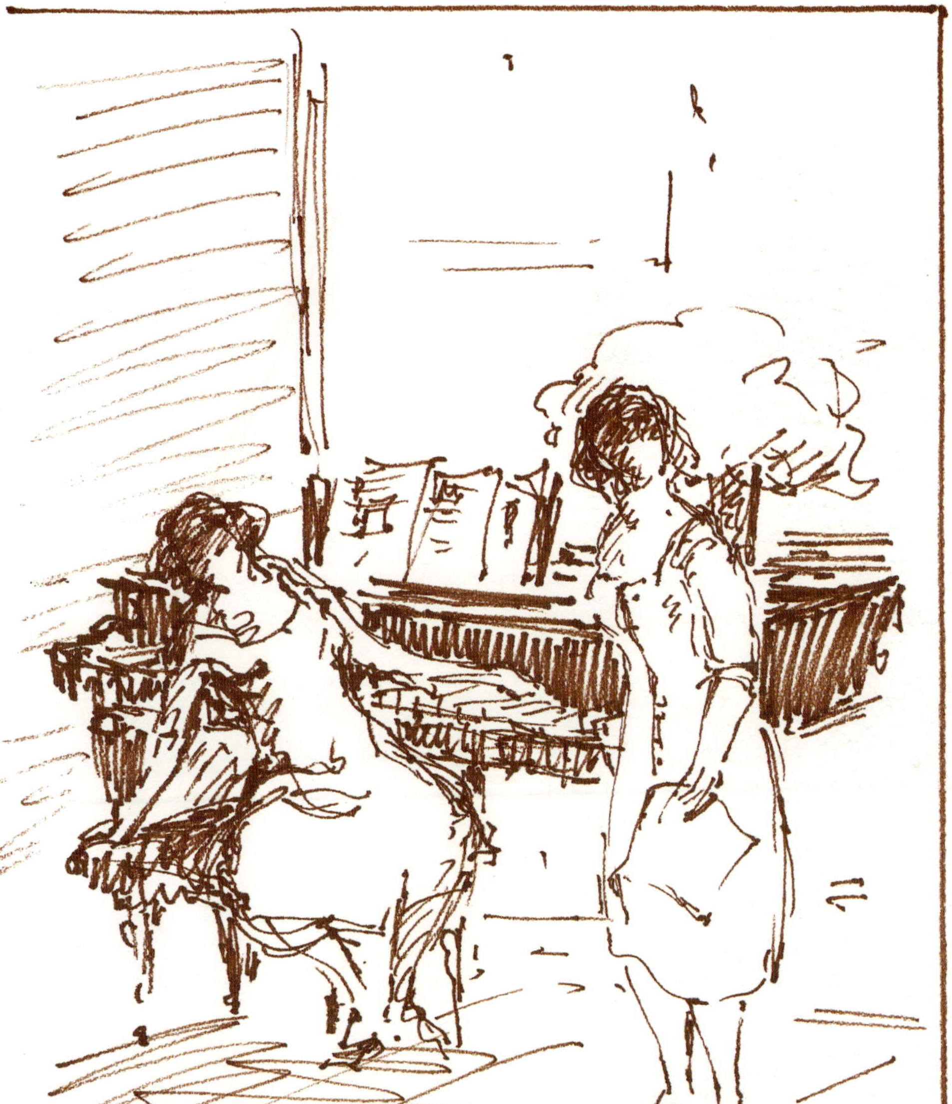

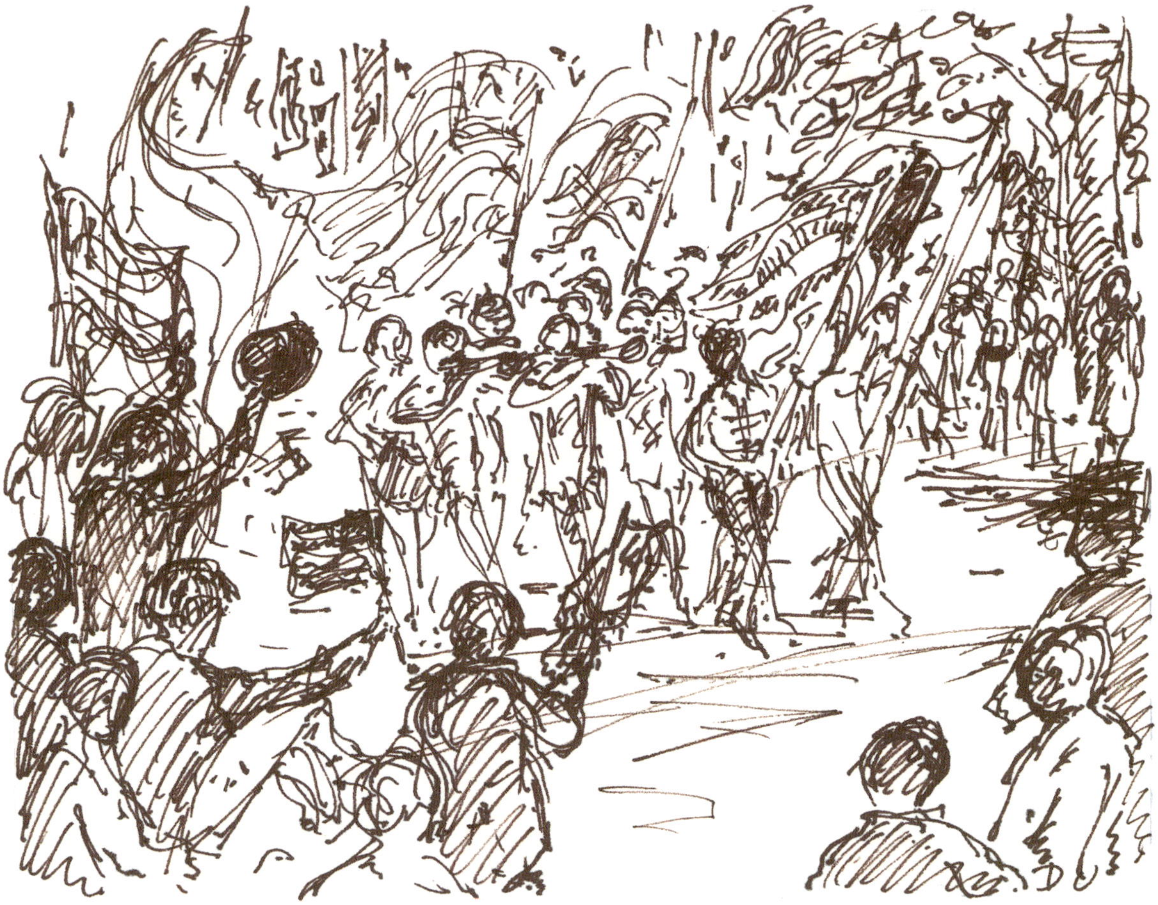

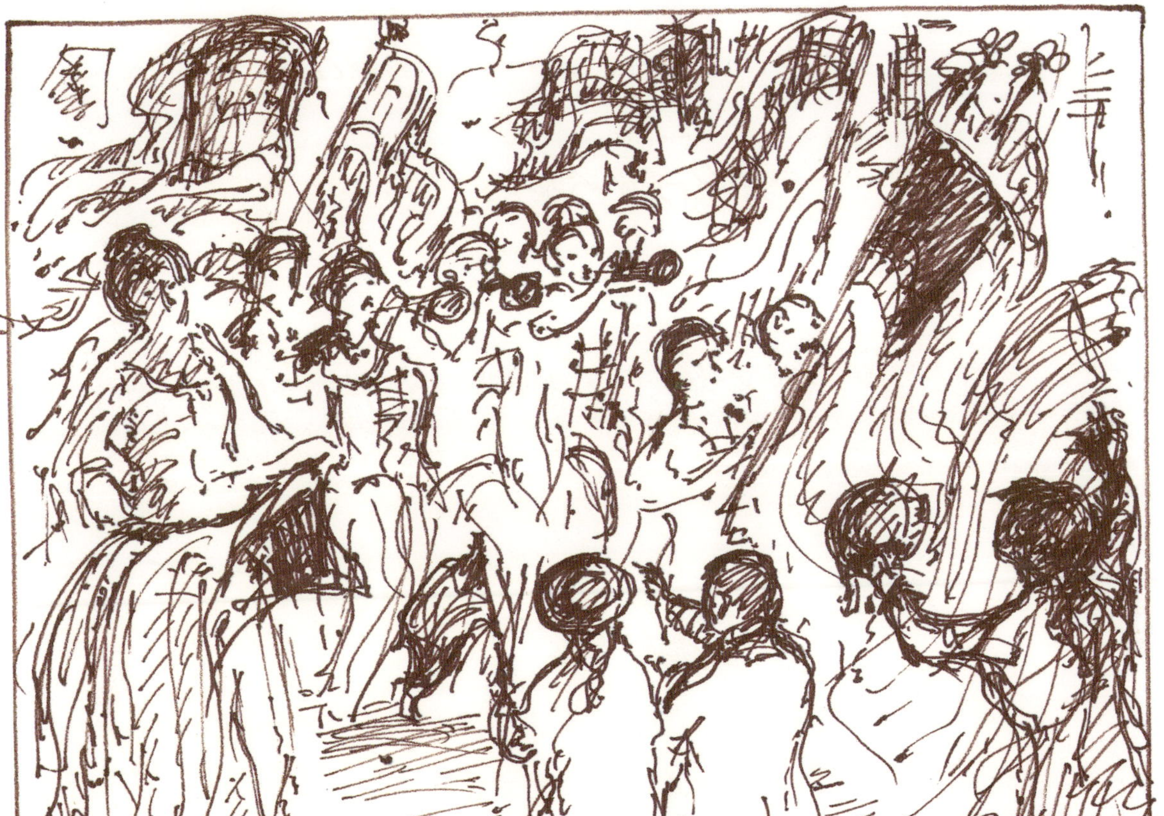

Part Five - The Greenhouse

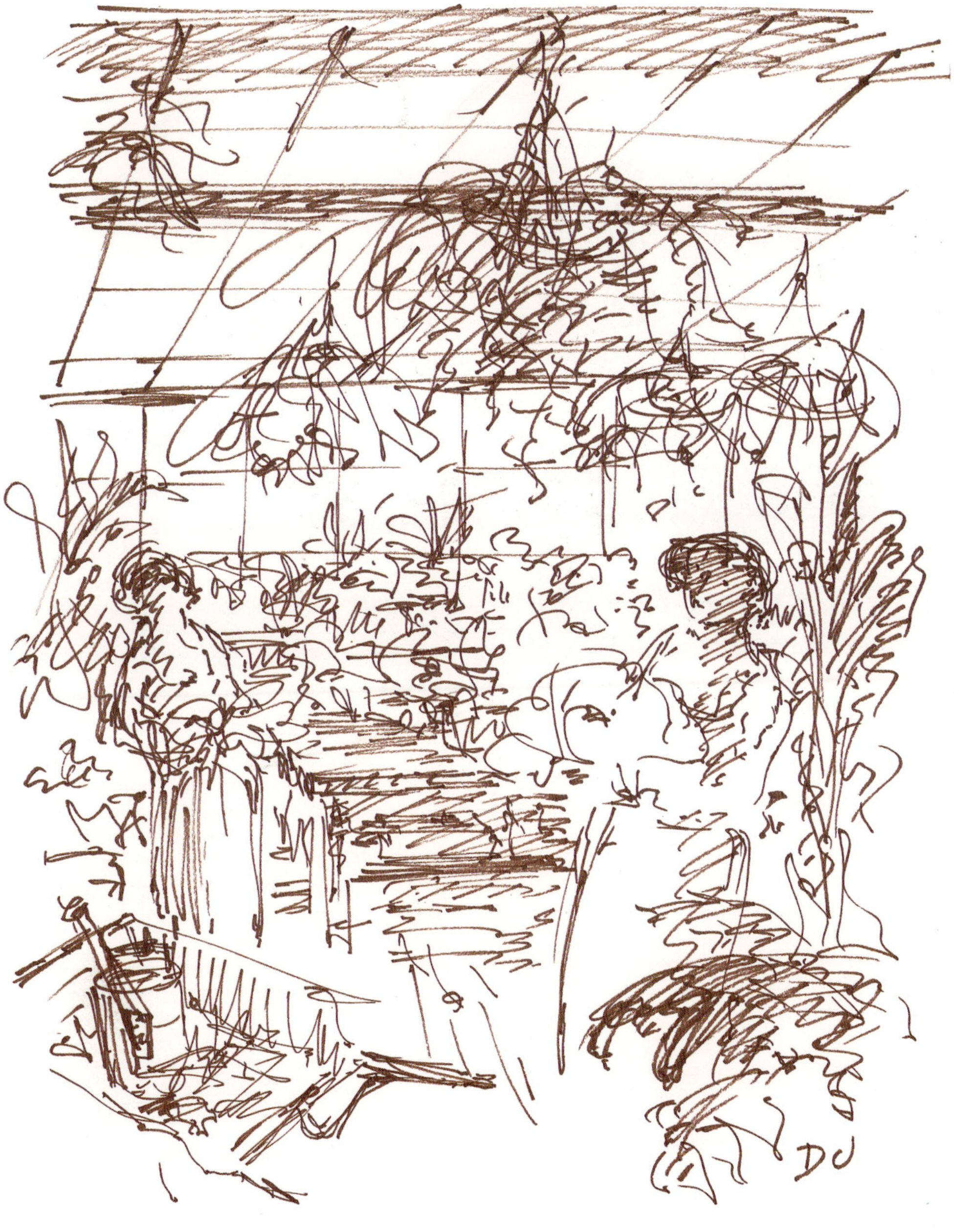

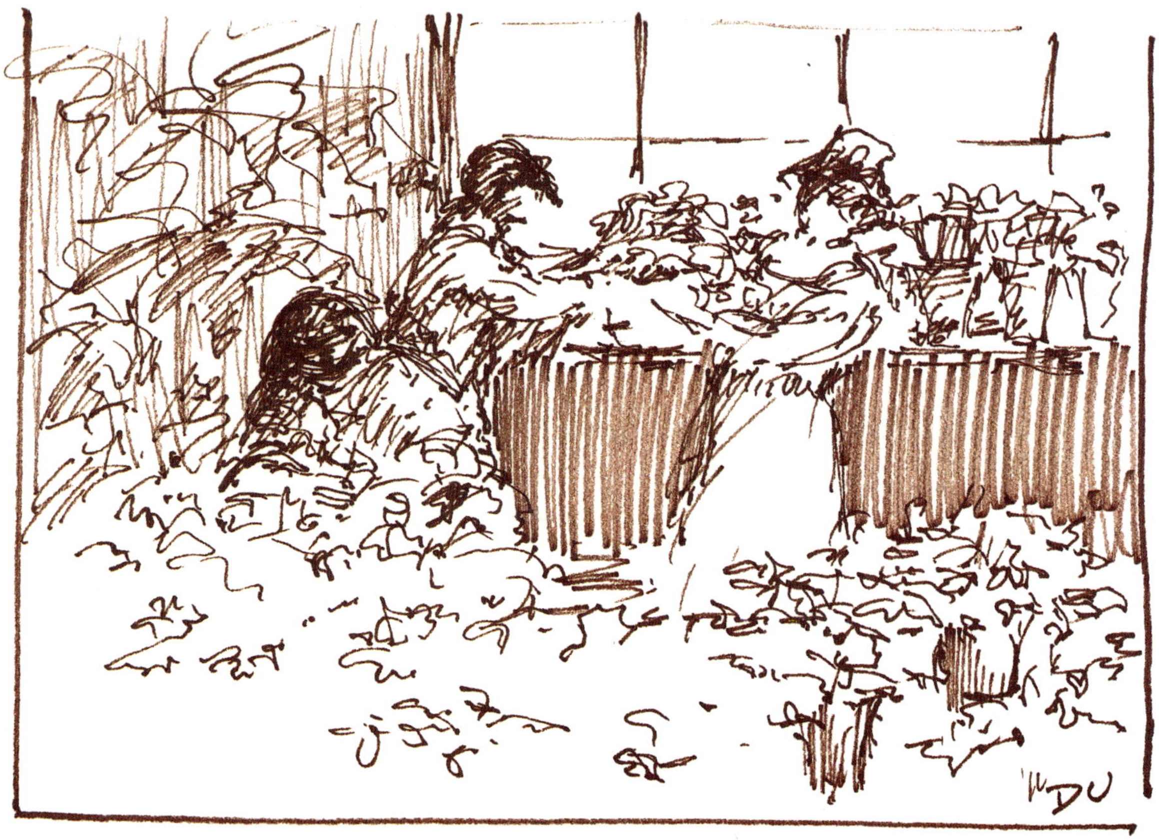

Painters often work in themes. In time, critics and historians refer to an artist's body of work as his such-and-such period. For example, Picasso's work is divided into periods classified as the blue, classical, negro, cubist, etc. Other artist's works may be designated by location or subject matter.

An artist might become intrigued with a drawing just done or one revisited that had been put aside years before. It was by chance that the greenhouse theme began to appear ever more often in my work. It was a natural subject to pursue, for having visited numerous such structures throughout the years, I was well acquainted with their variations. There were the simple, private greenhouses such as one that joins my bedroom, those of commercial growers of flowers and plants, and the grand structures of glass and steel that are interior gardens.

It is not a fragment that interests me but the essence of the whole.

For me, subject matter was never a great problem in itself. As one who is concerned about nature and the human response to it, I find that the greenhouse has fulfilled my needs for years now and no doubt will continue to do so in the future. Surprisingly enough, it was not the plants, or flowers, or the figures as much as it was the qualities of light flooding through the multi-paned glass panels that captured my attention.

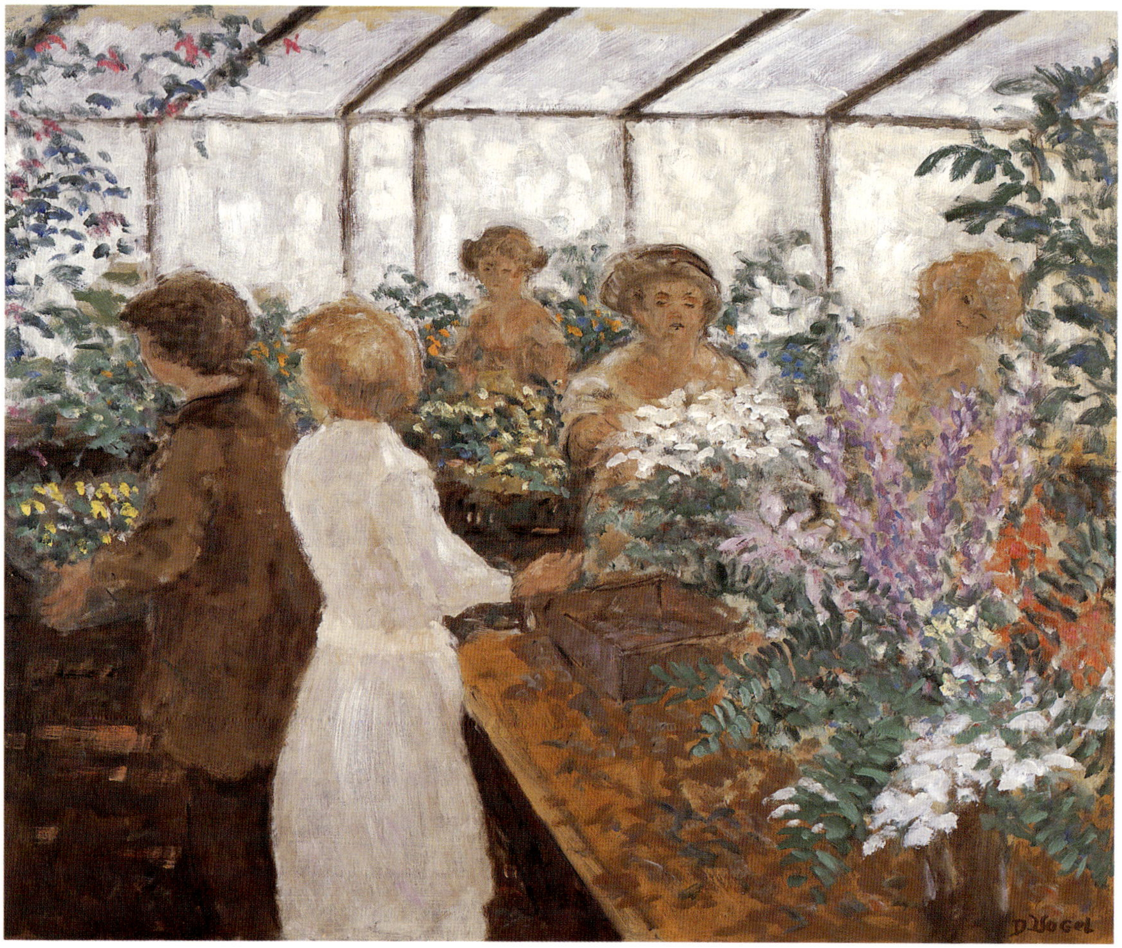
D Vogel

The greenhouse opened a wealth of ideas that have served well. What Monet reaped from his lily pond, the glass houses have offered me. Still it is the drawing and the resulting painting that matter, not the subject. I use this theme to capture the essence of place, with emphasis on the lovely, mysterious light that invades it. The greenhouses encase the working figures in attitudes of movement, and the forms add to the tensions, contributing interest to the composition.

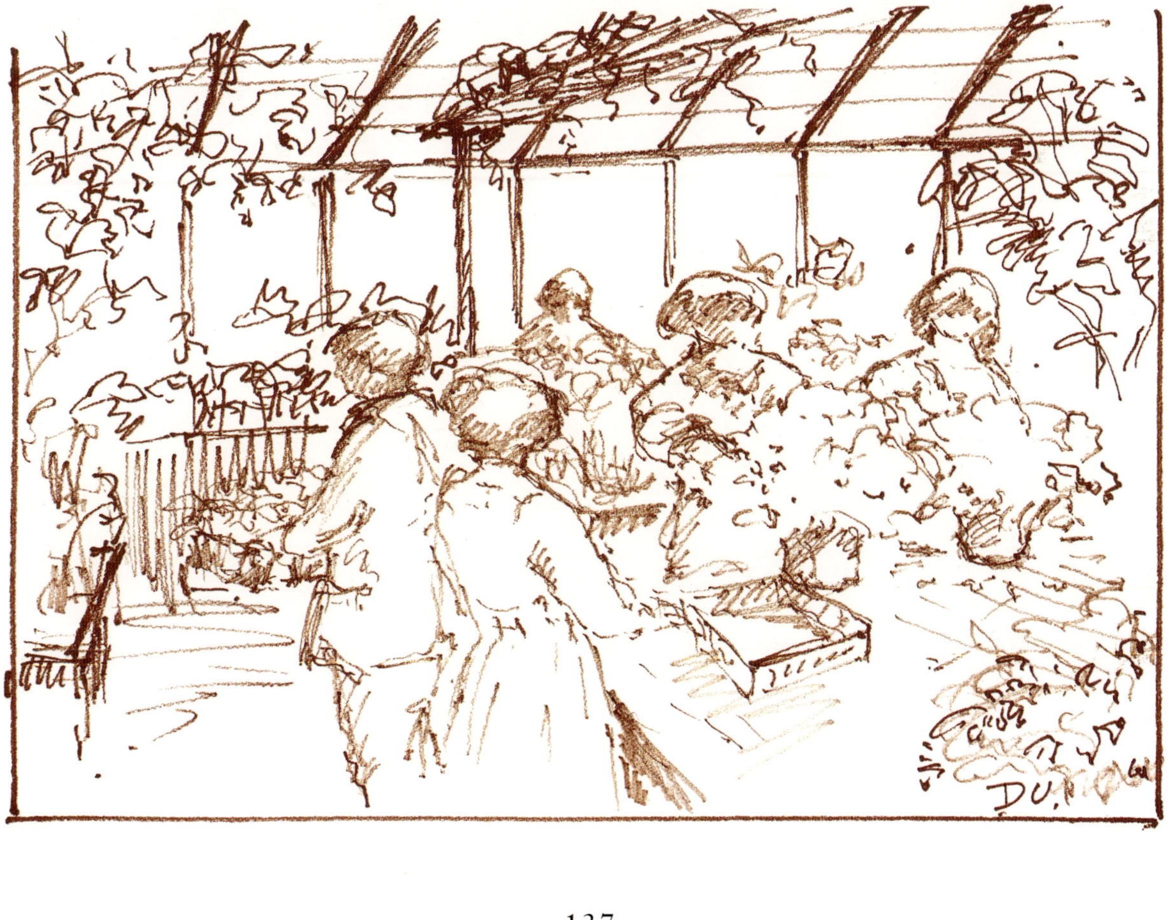

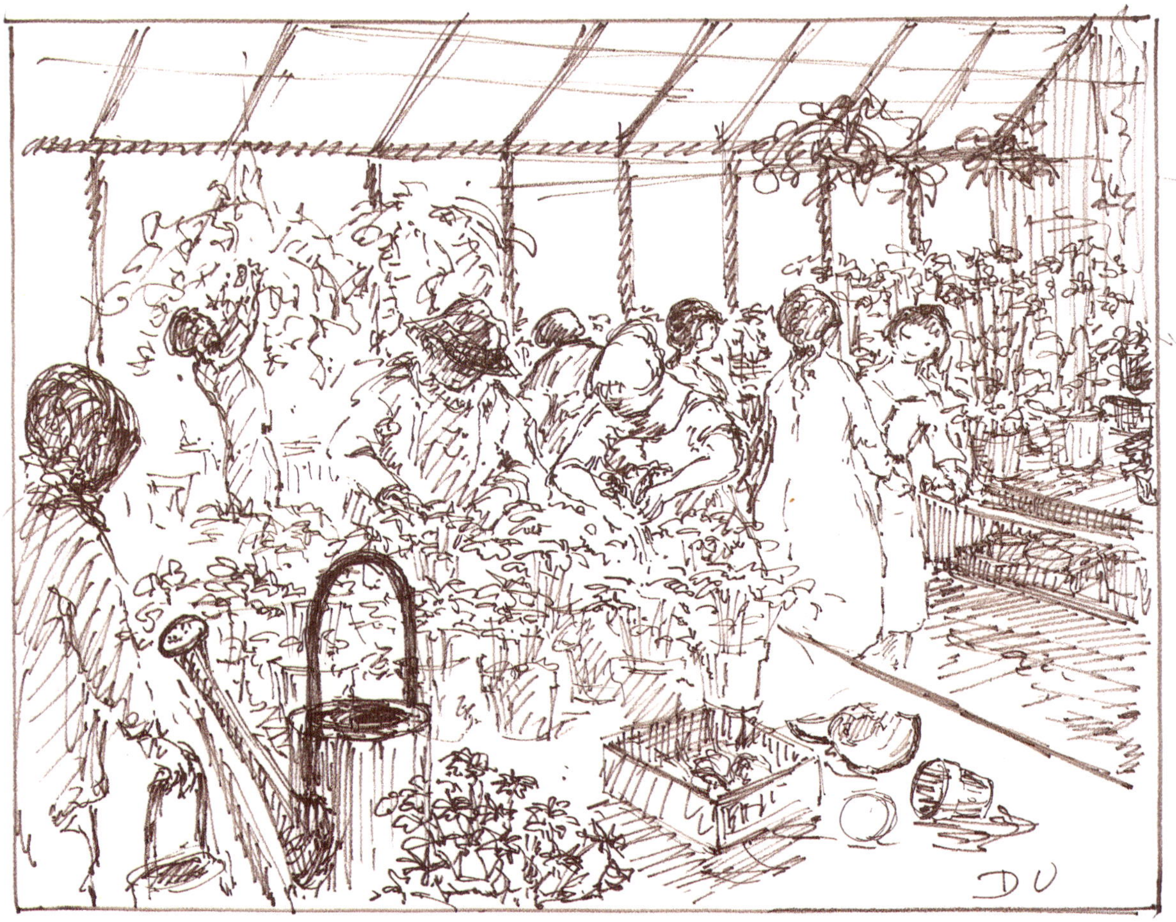
DU

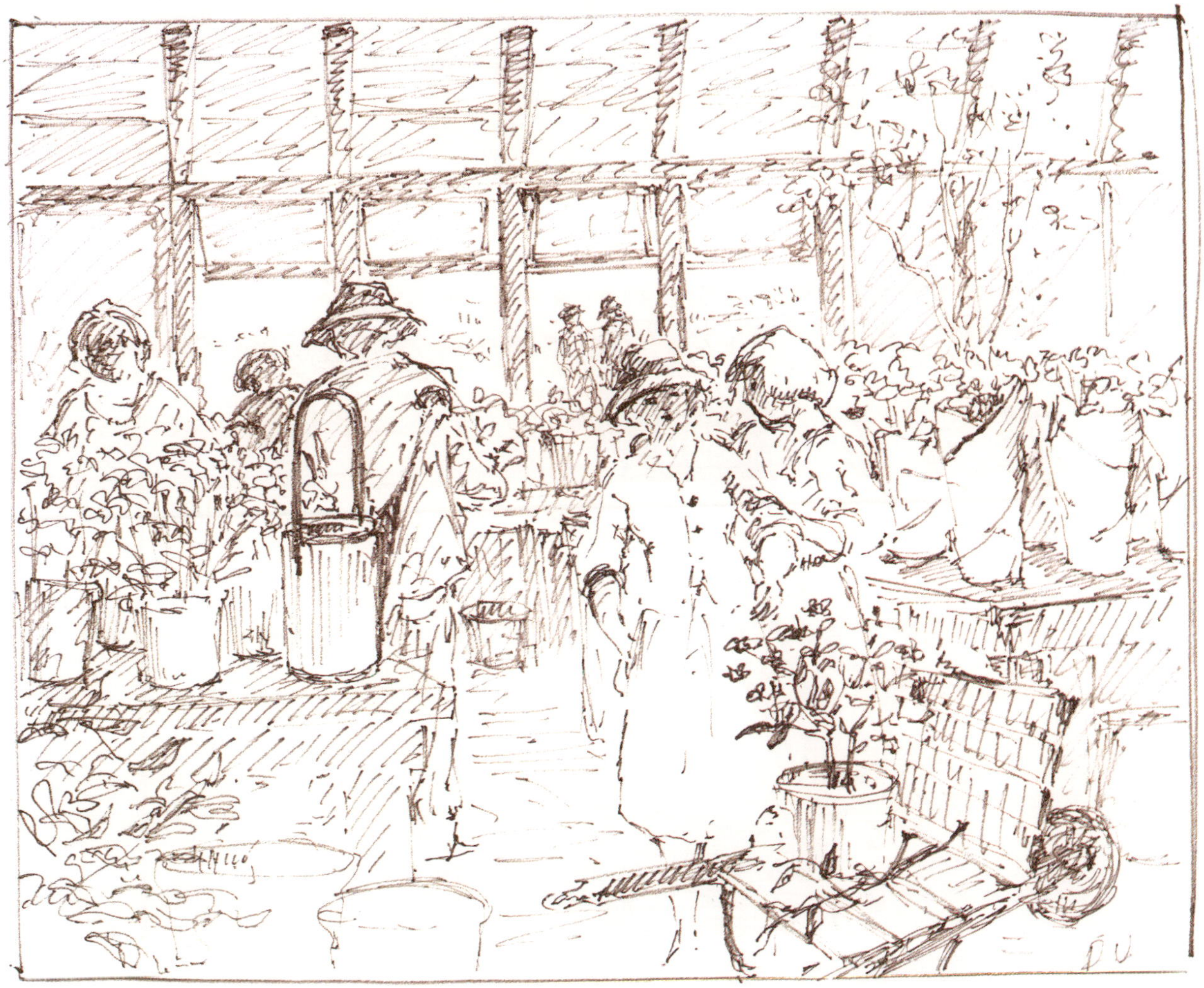

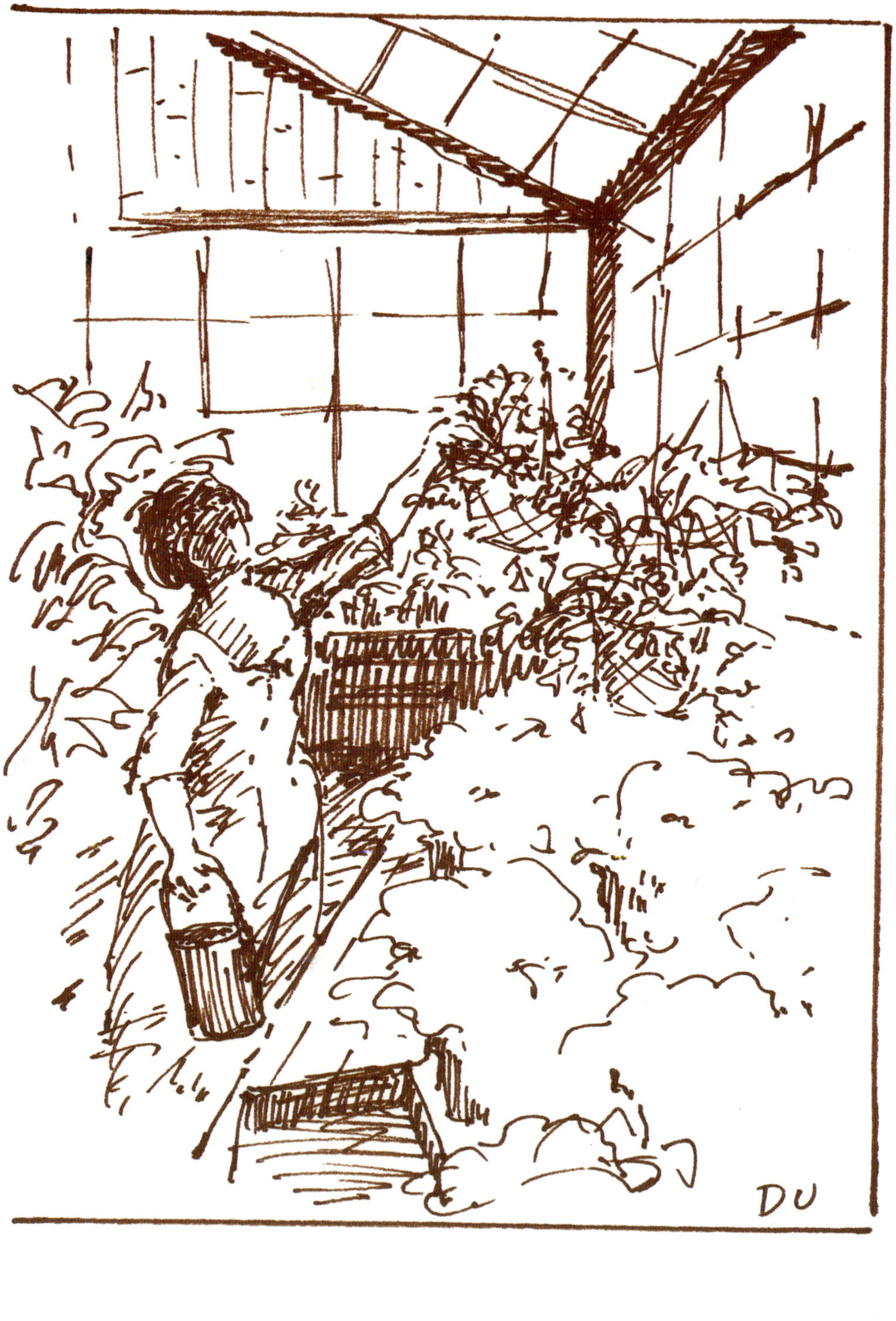
DU

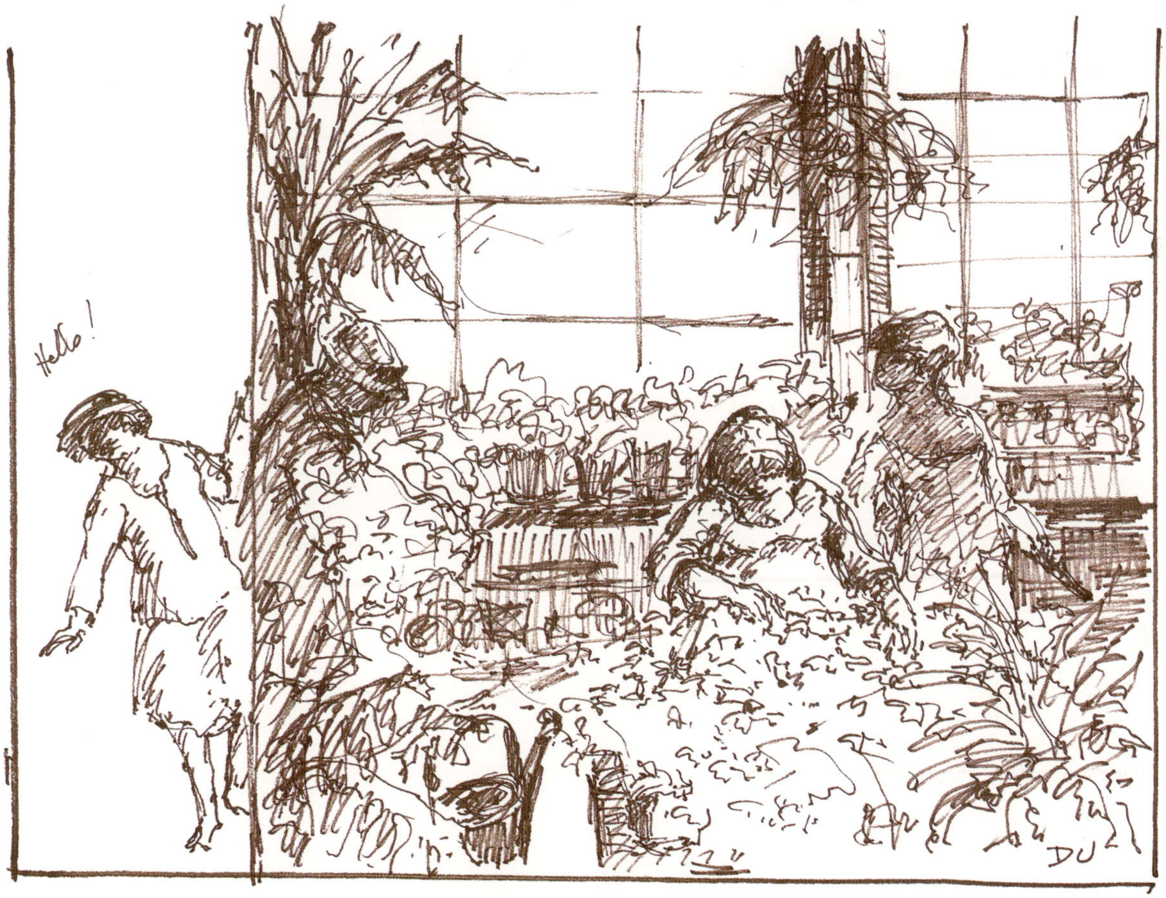
Hello!
DU

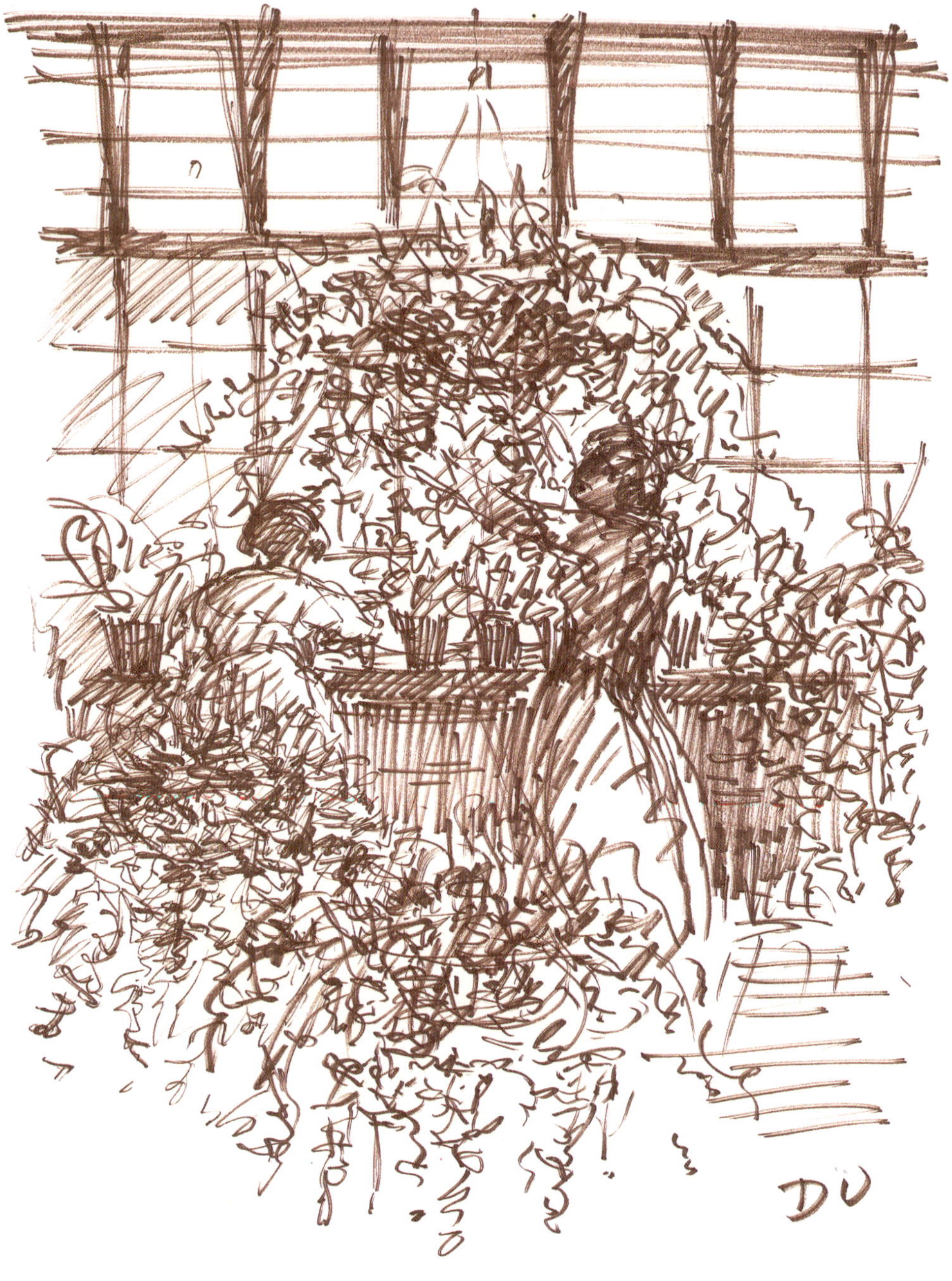
DU

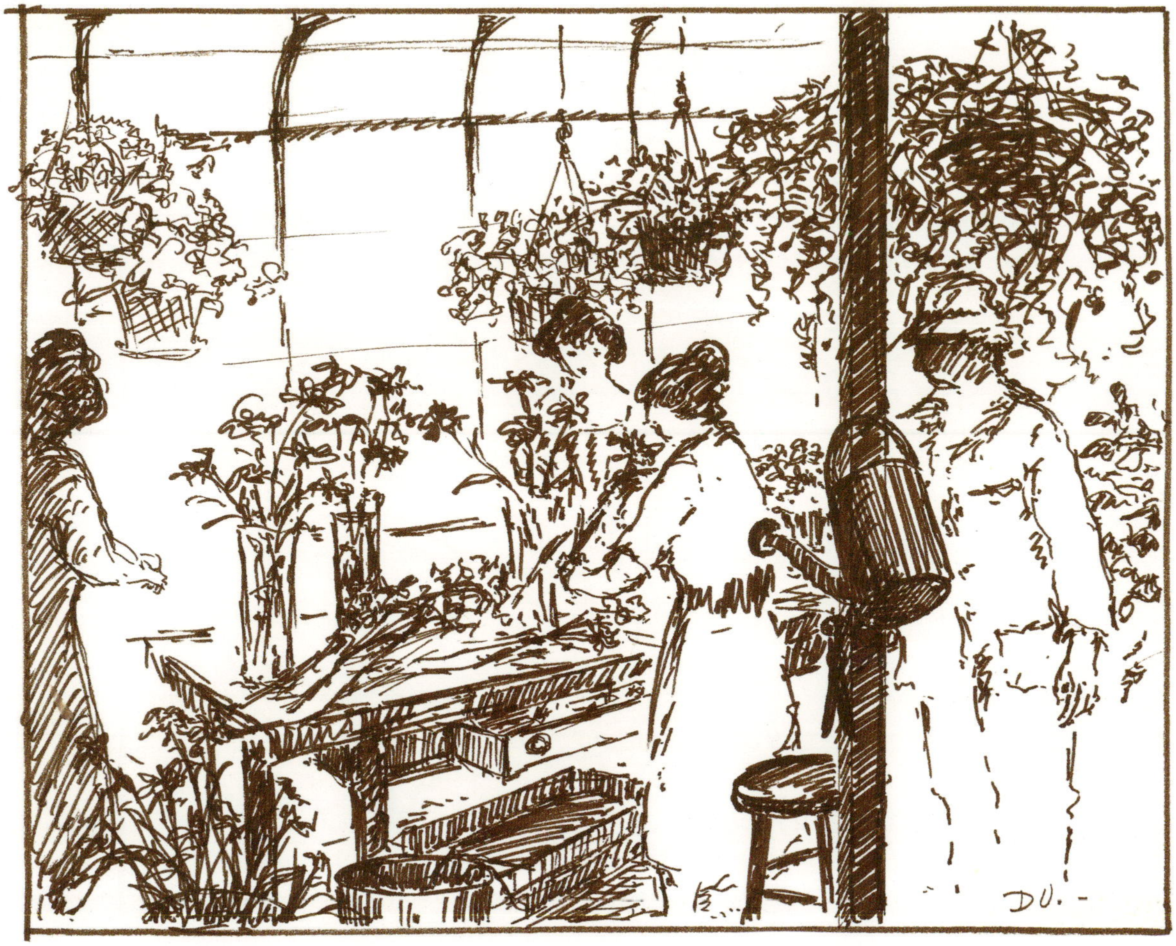
DU.

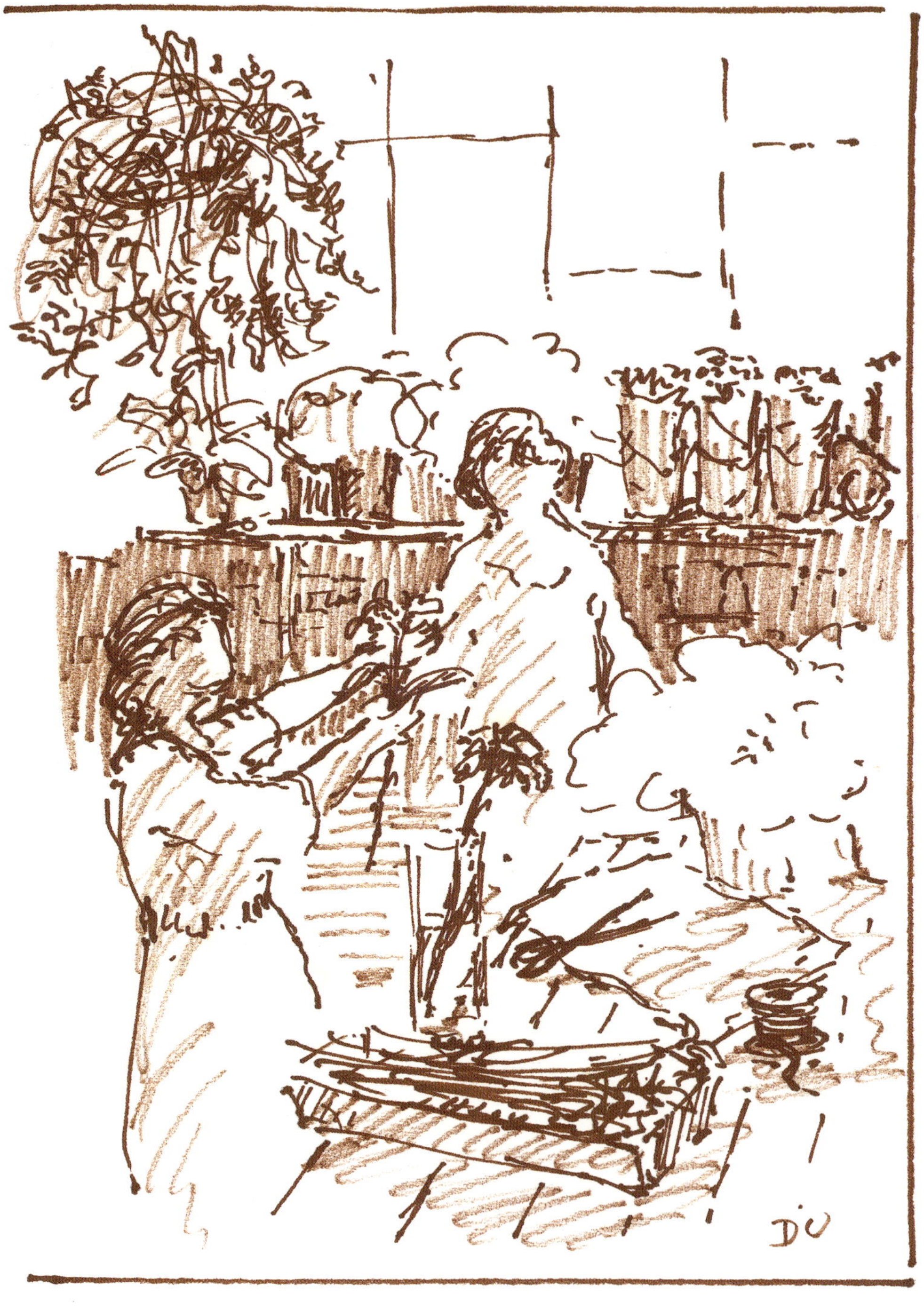

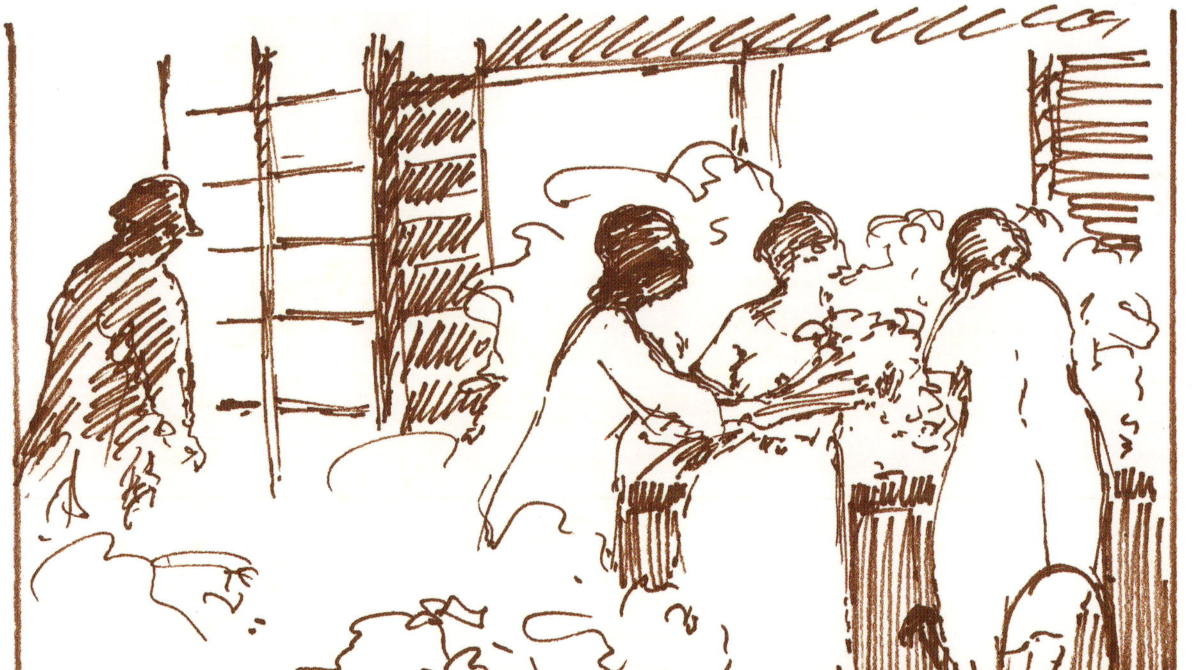

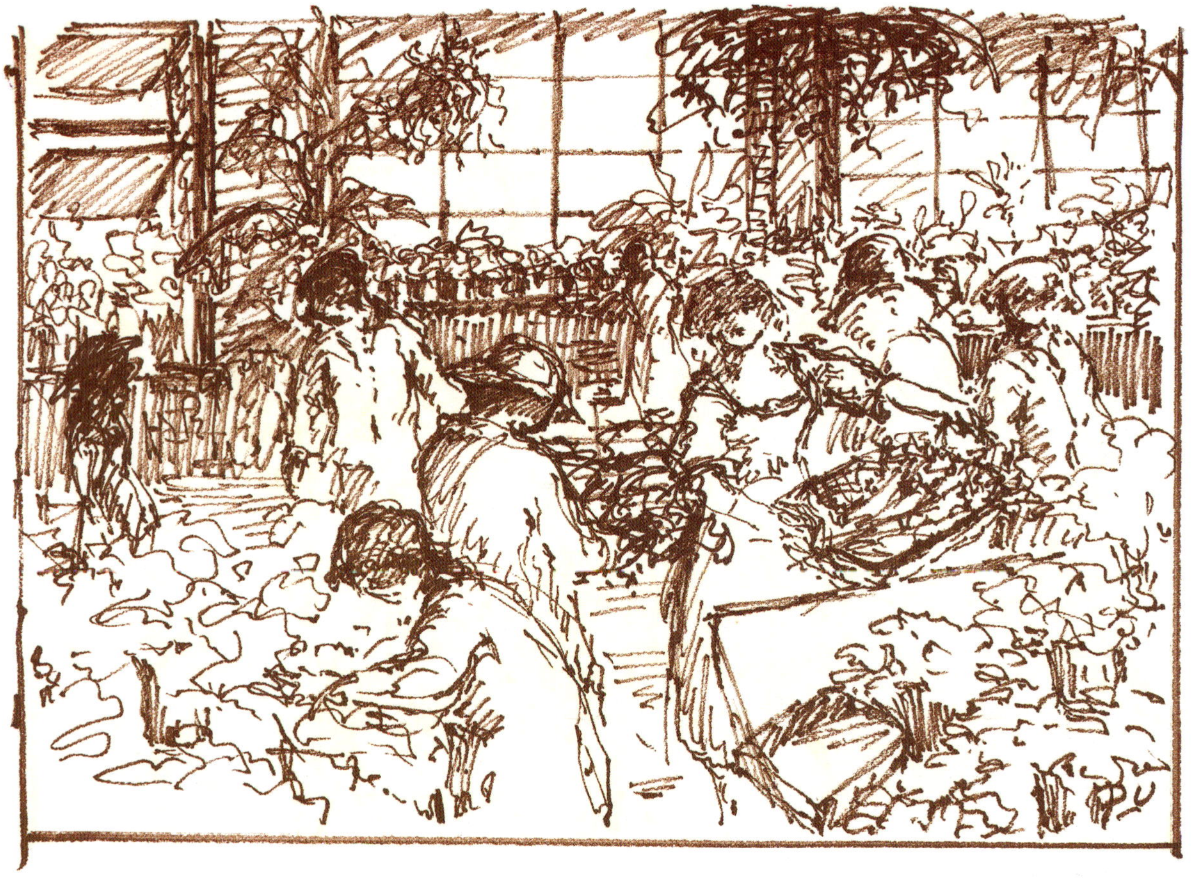

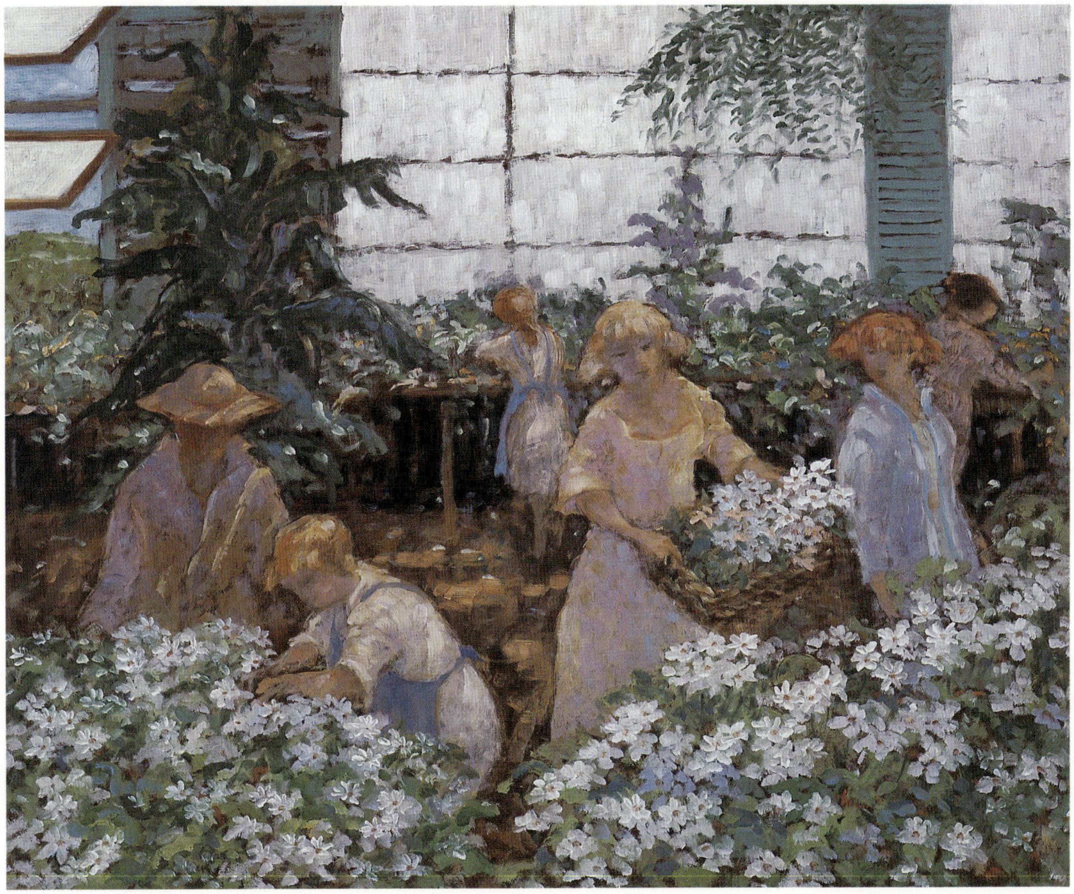

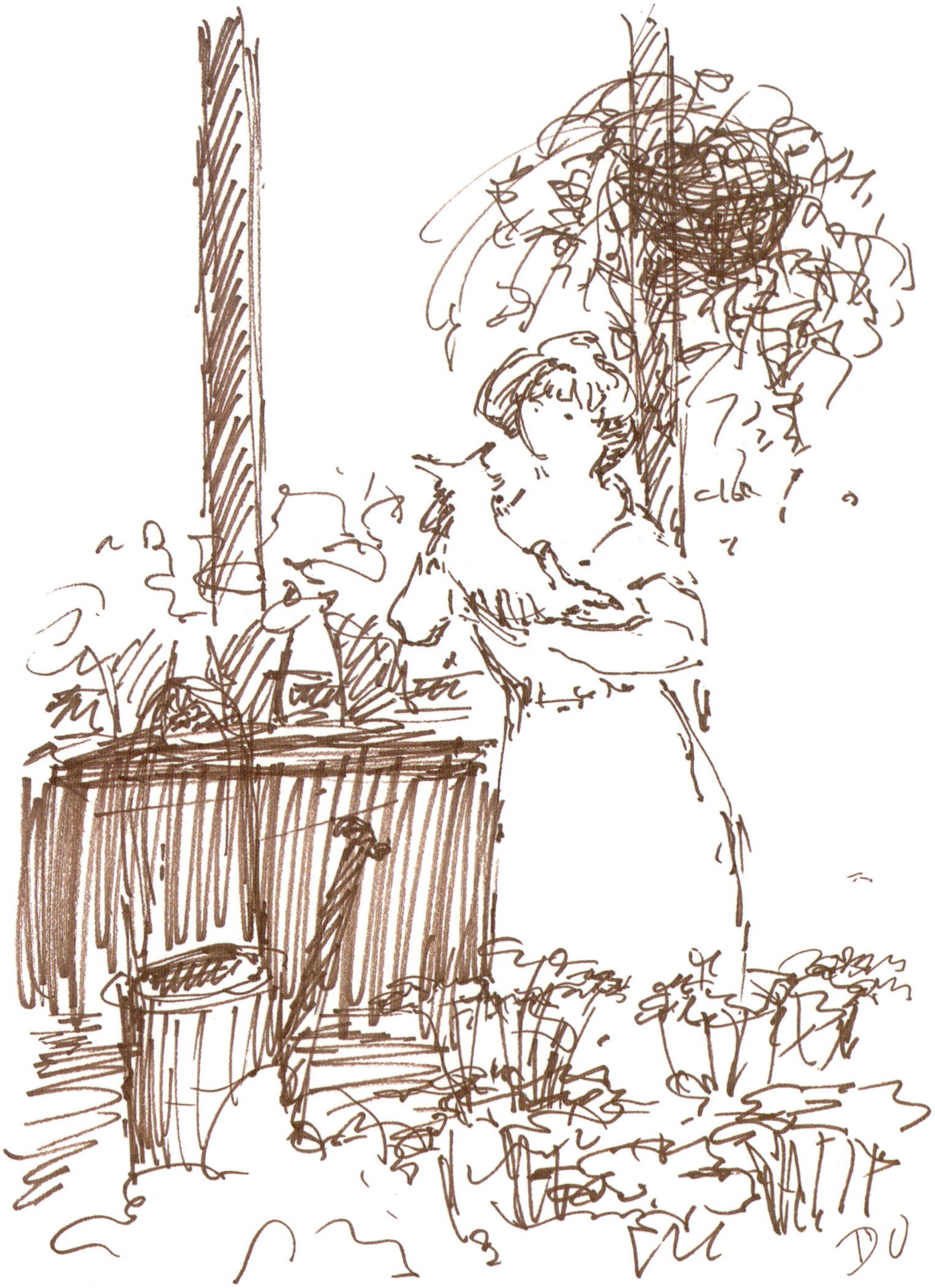
DU

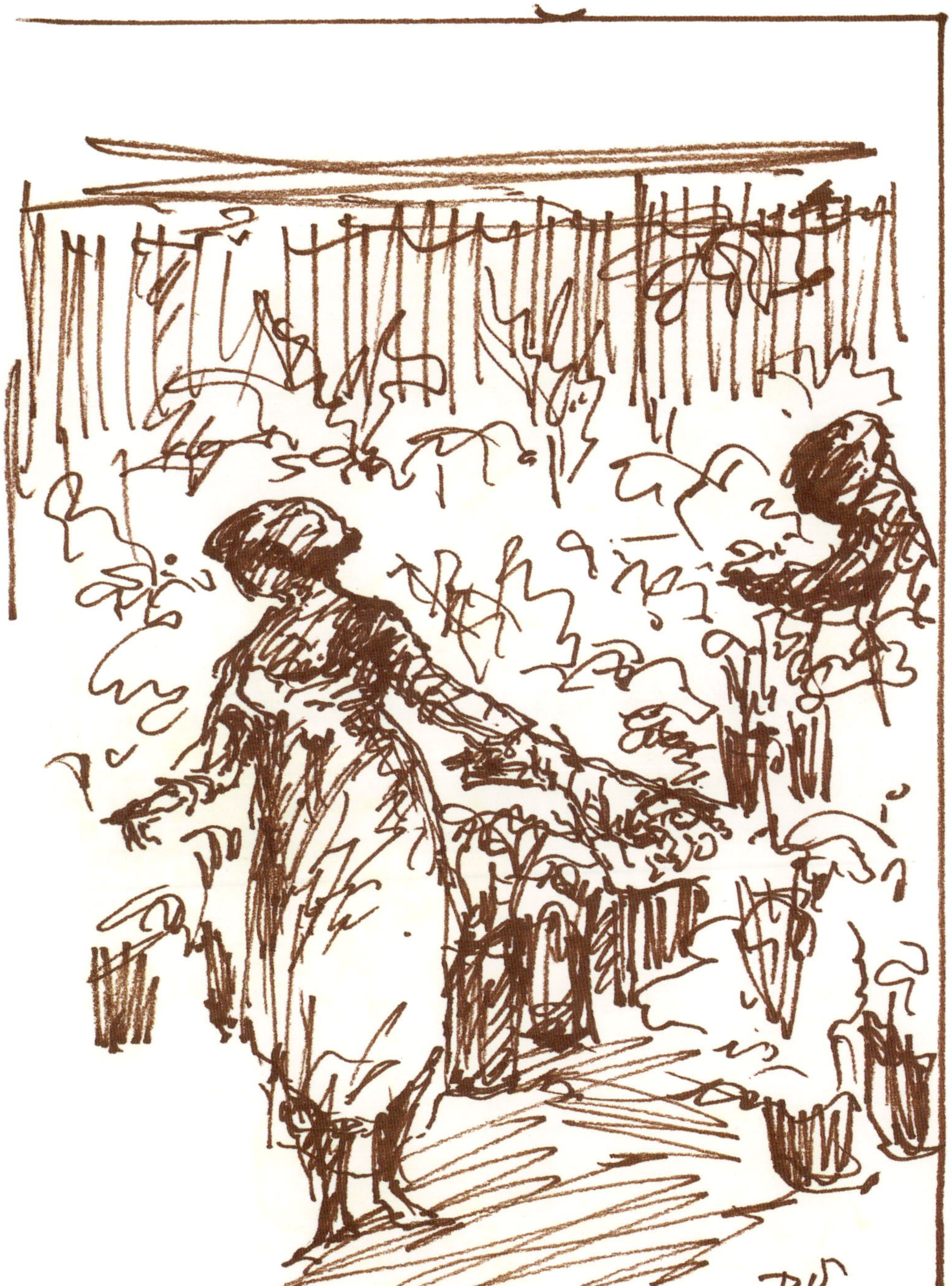

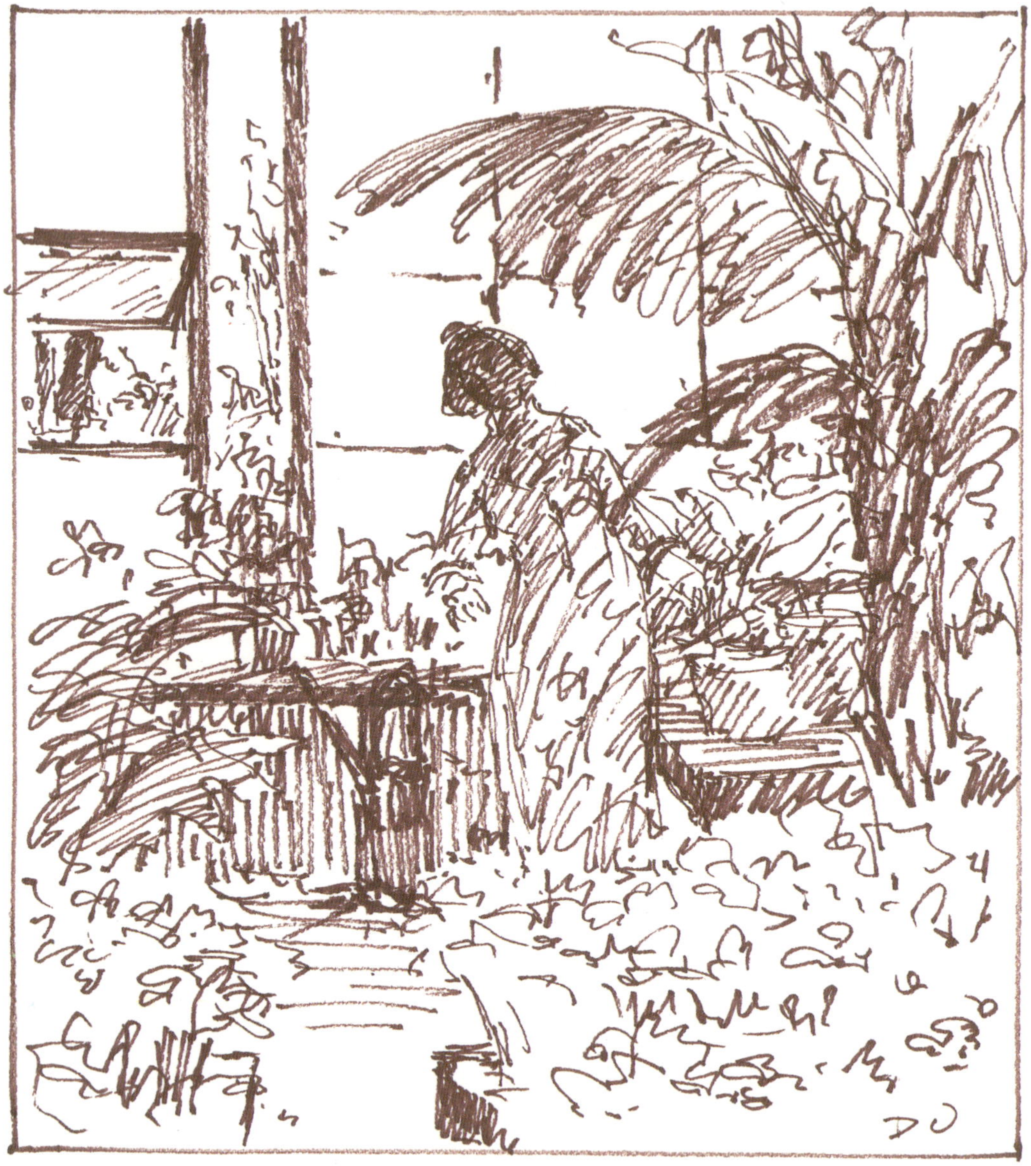

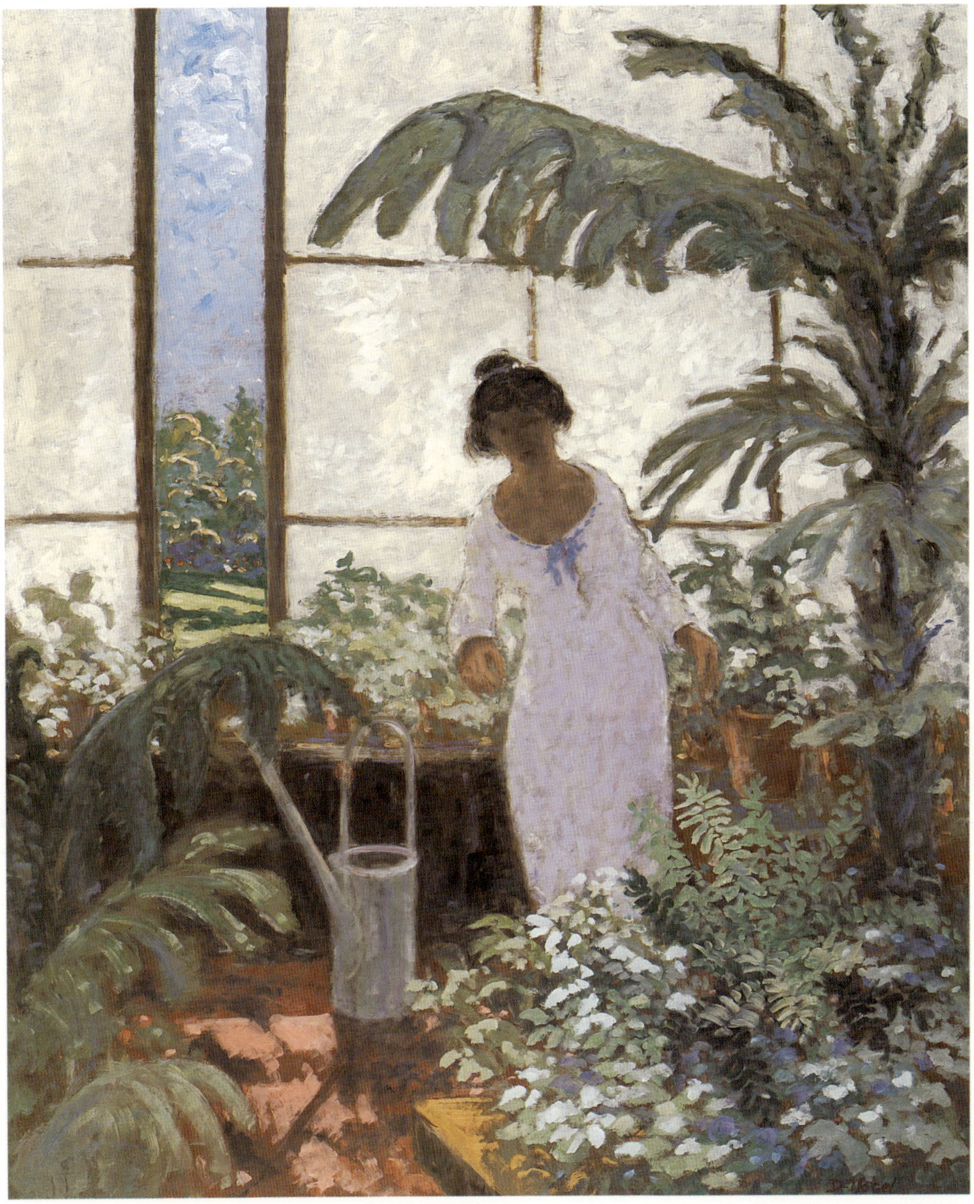

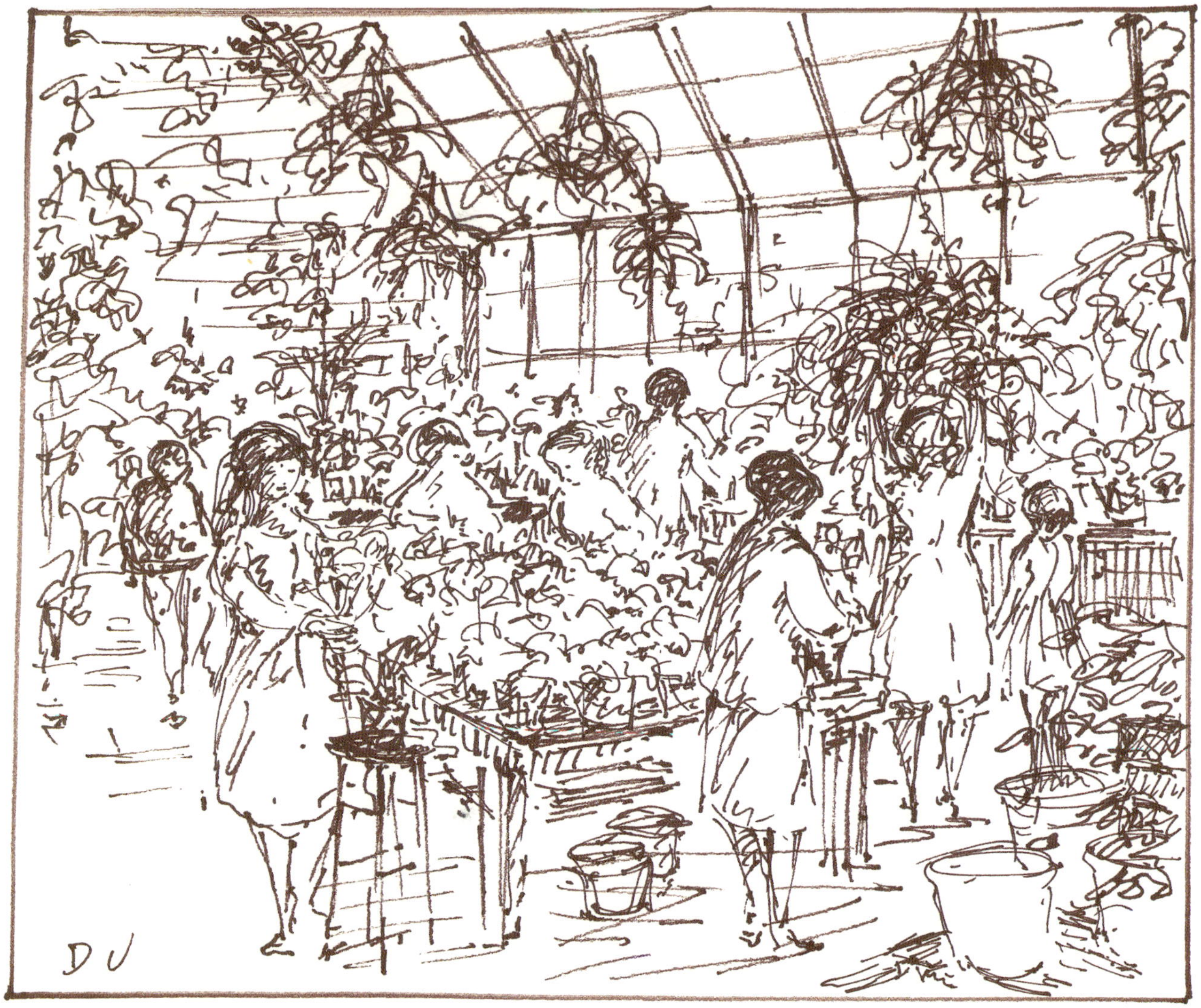
D U

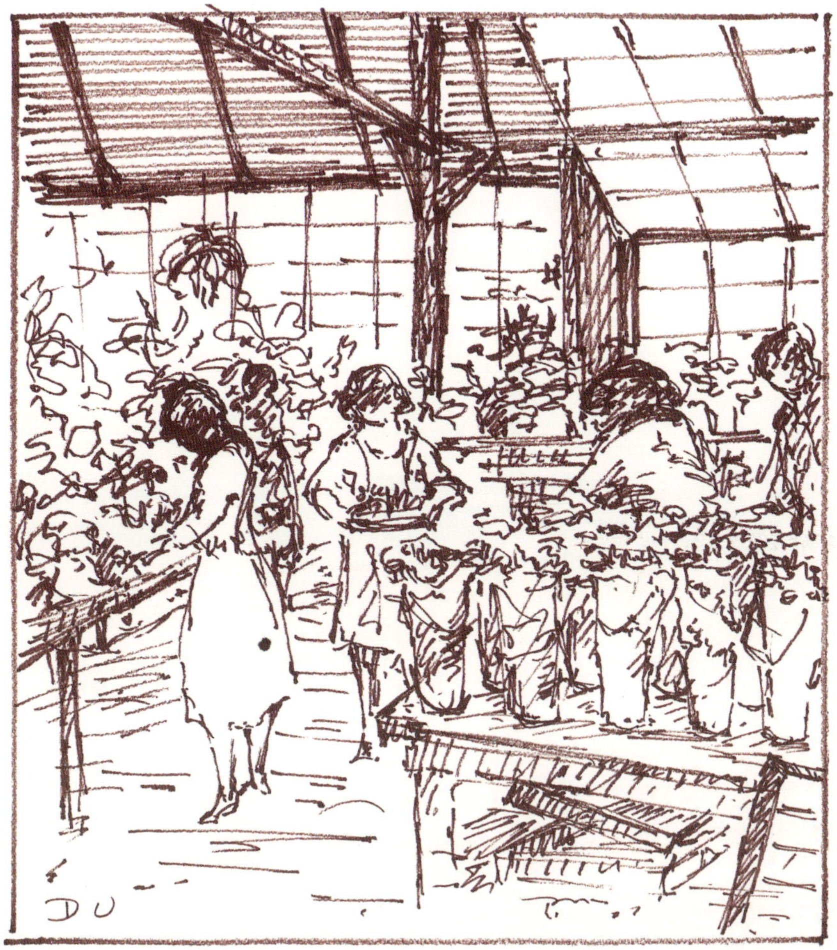
DU

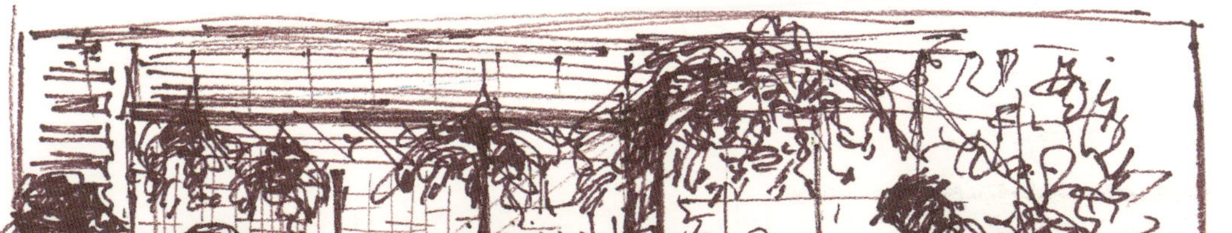

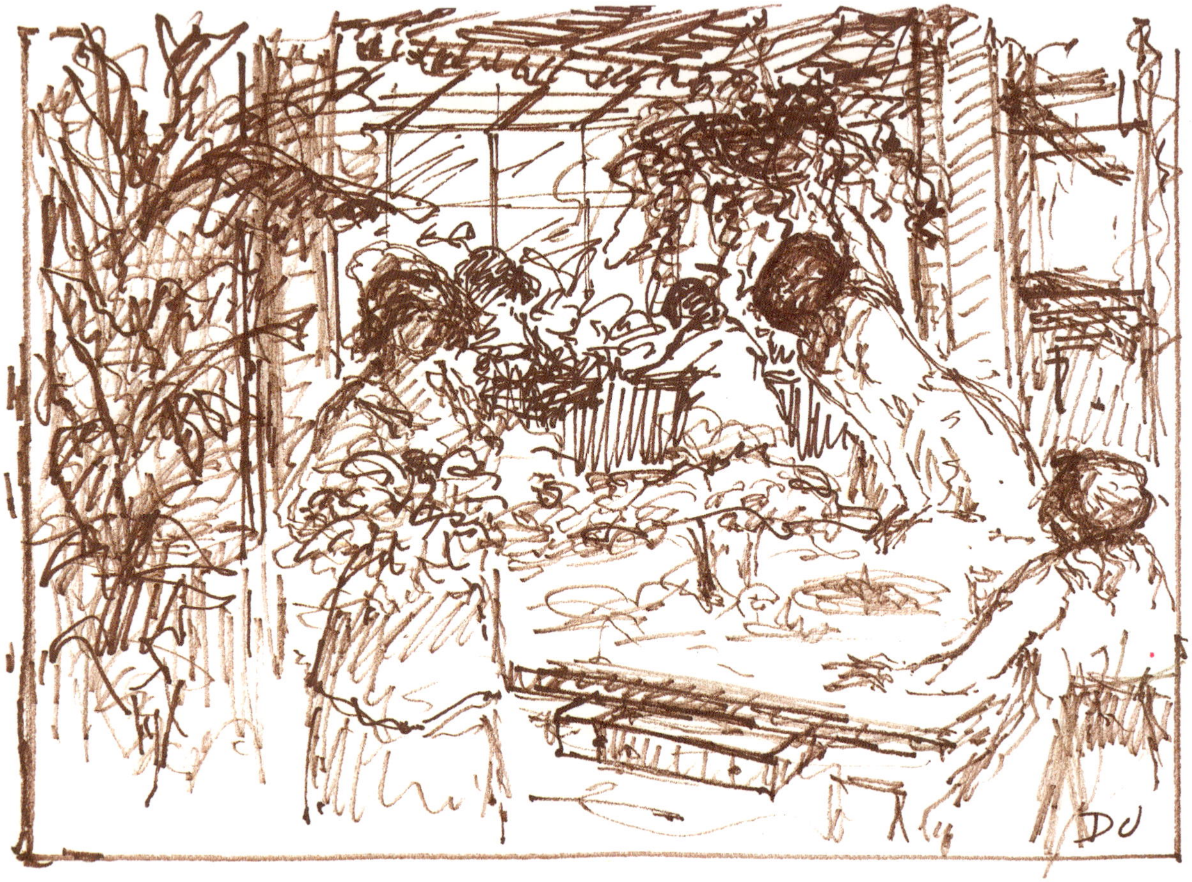

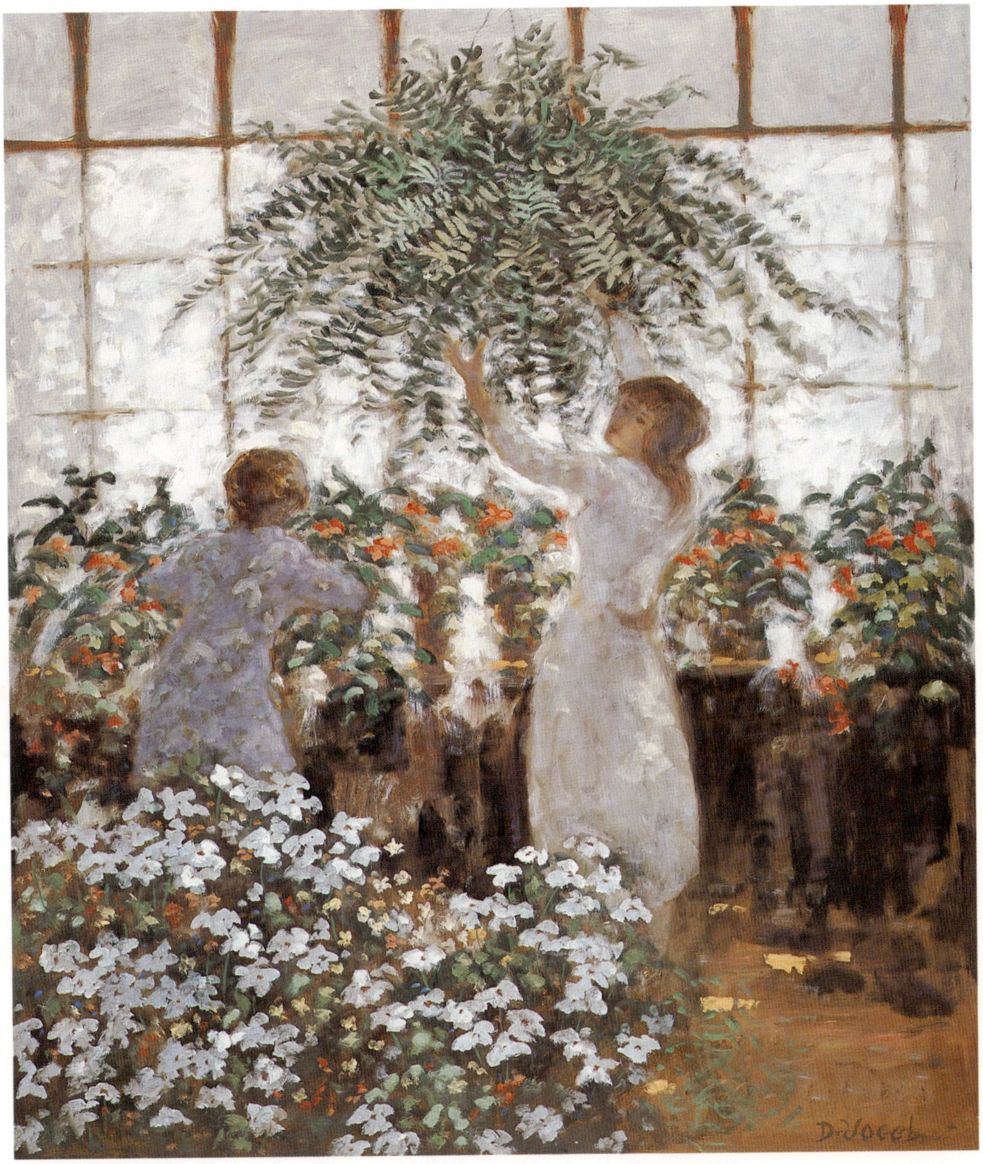
D.Vogel

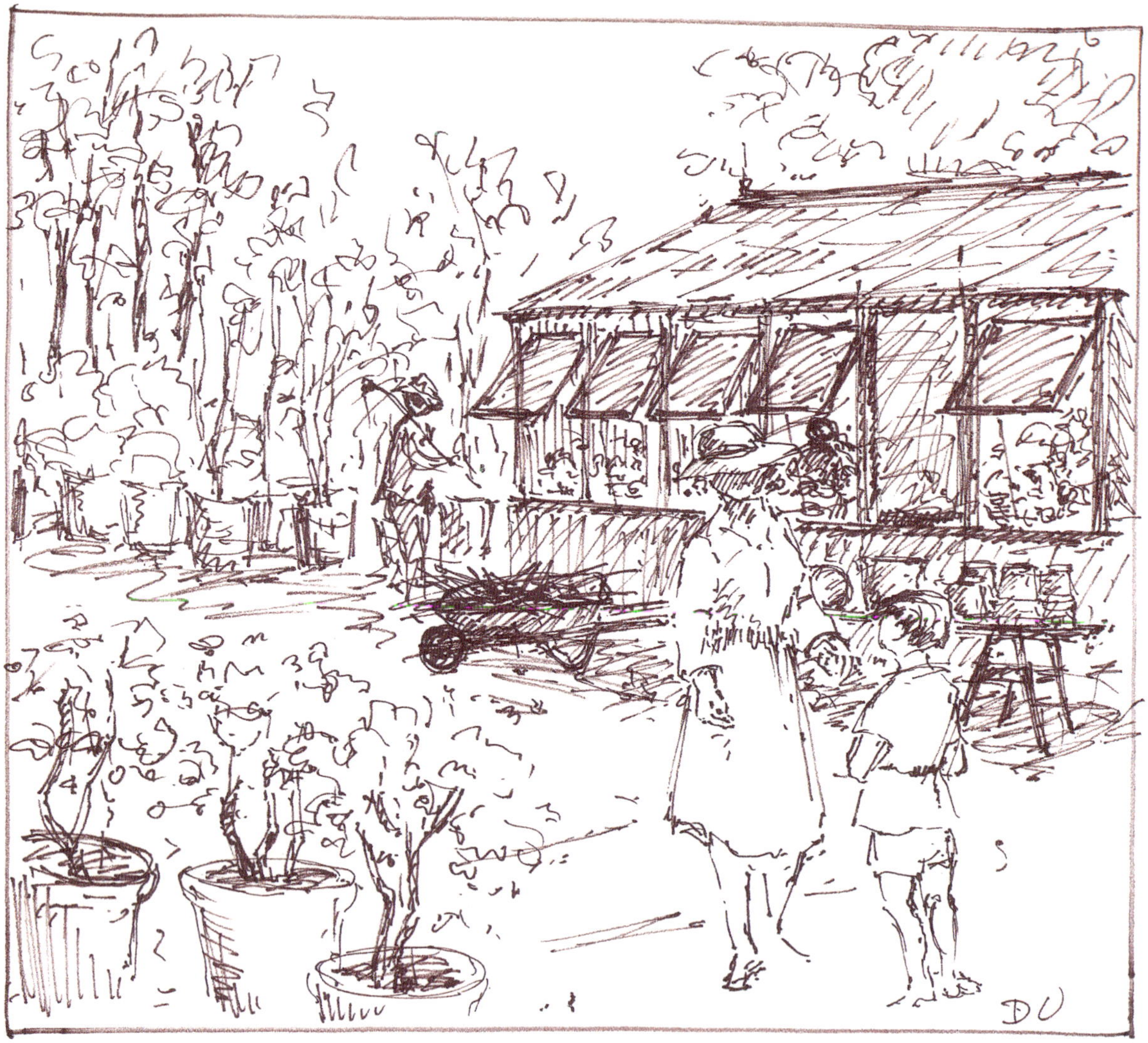
DU

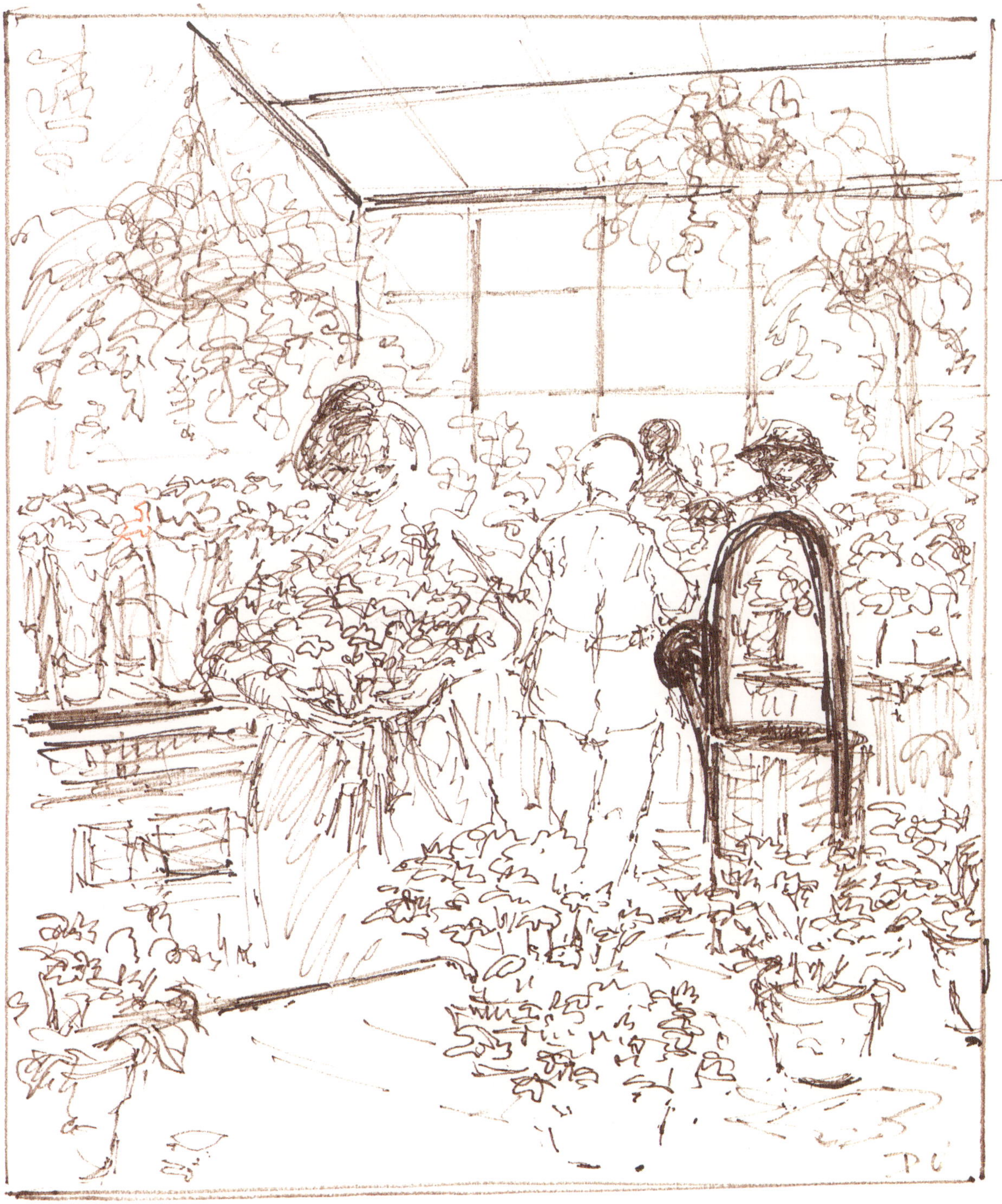

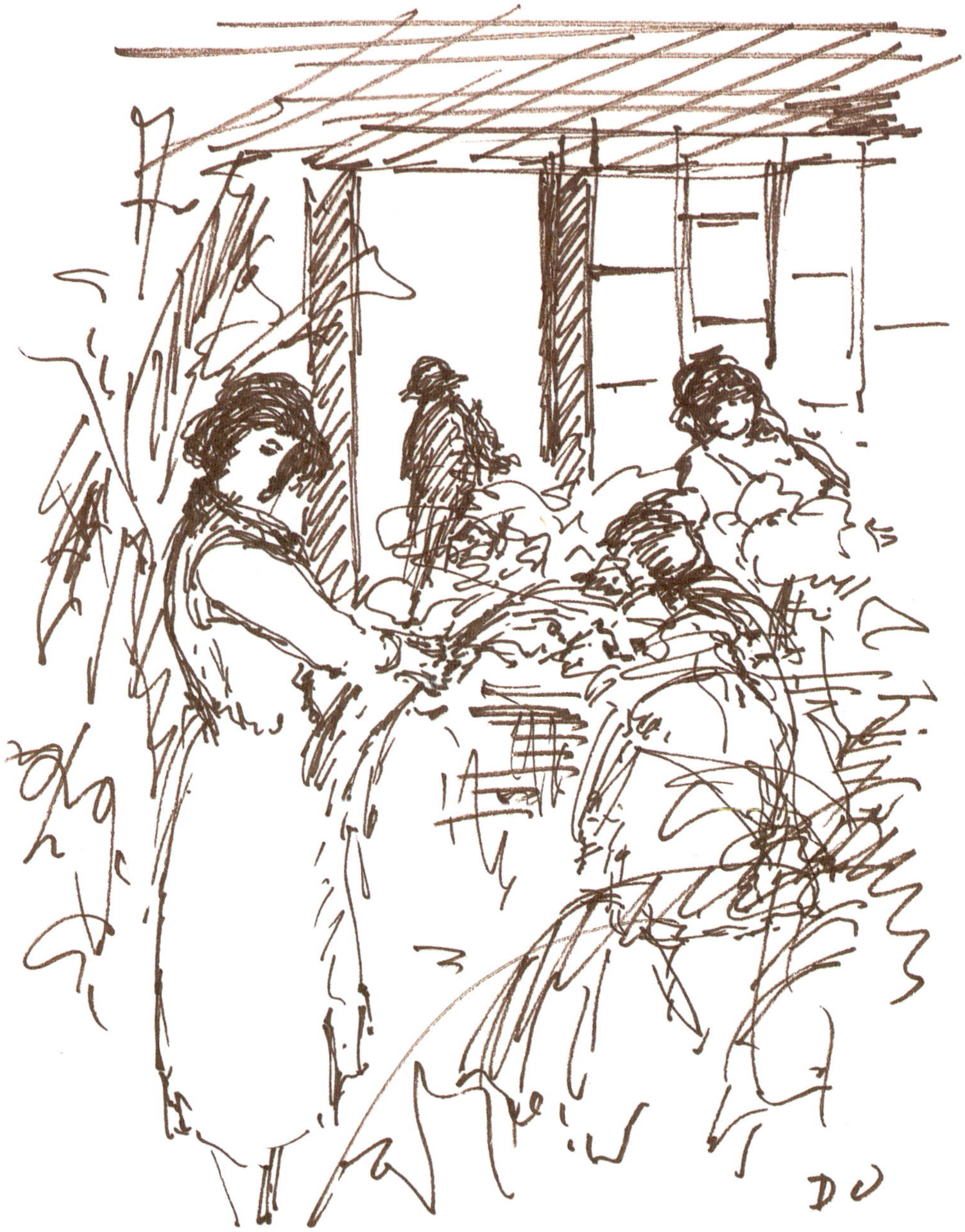

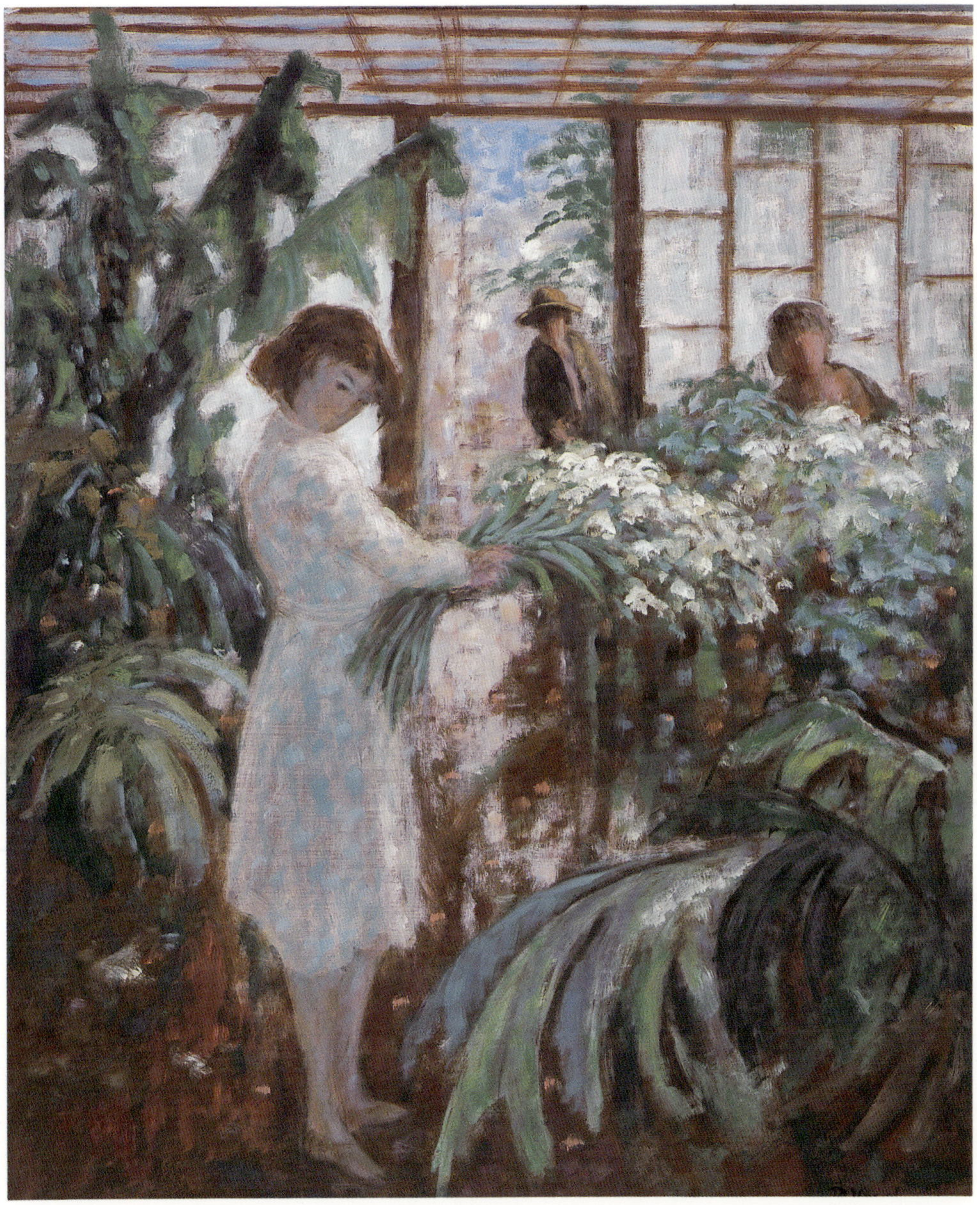

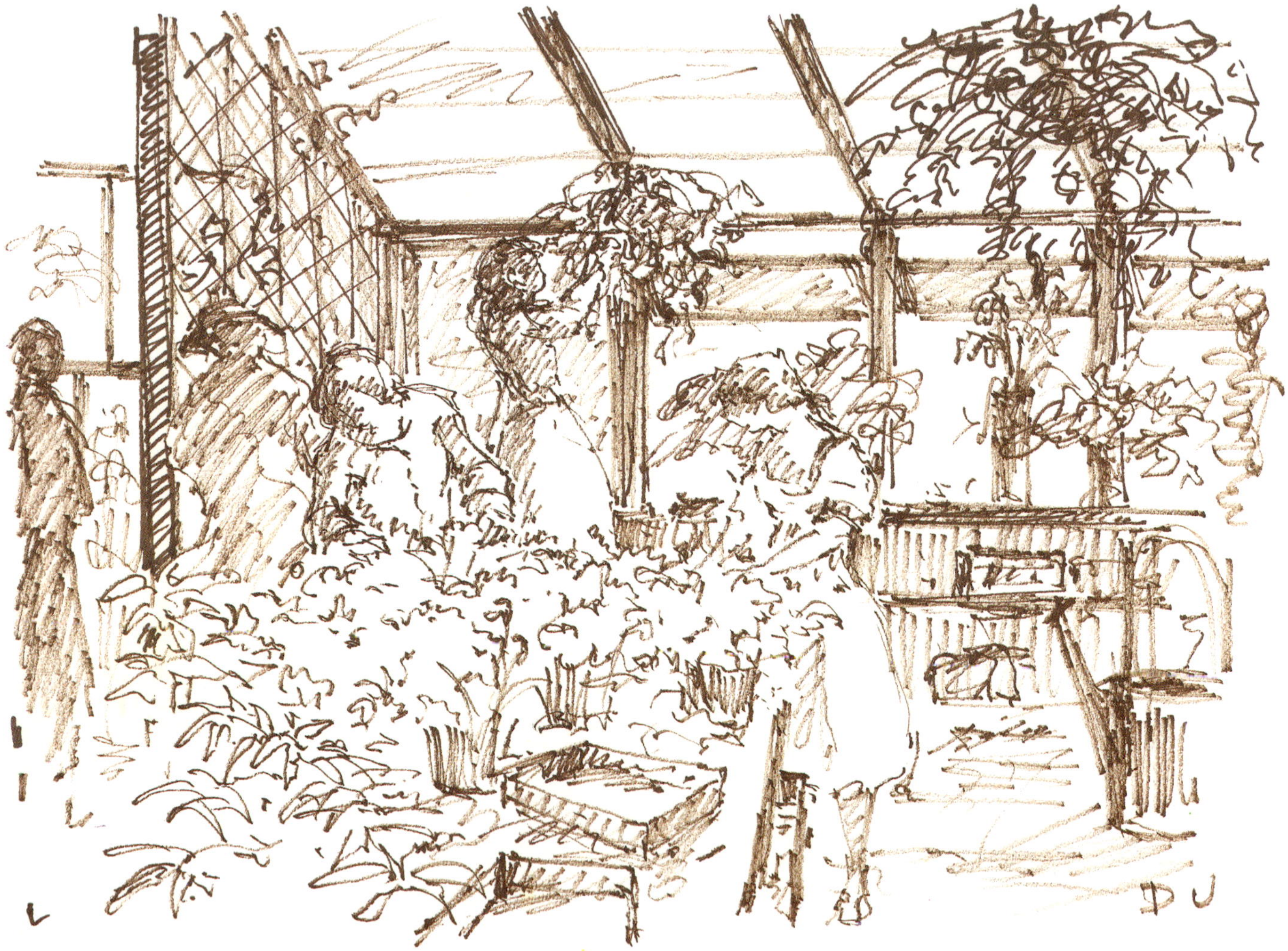
DJ

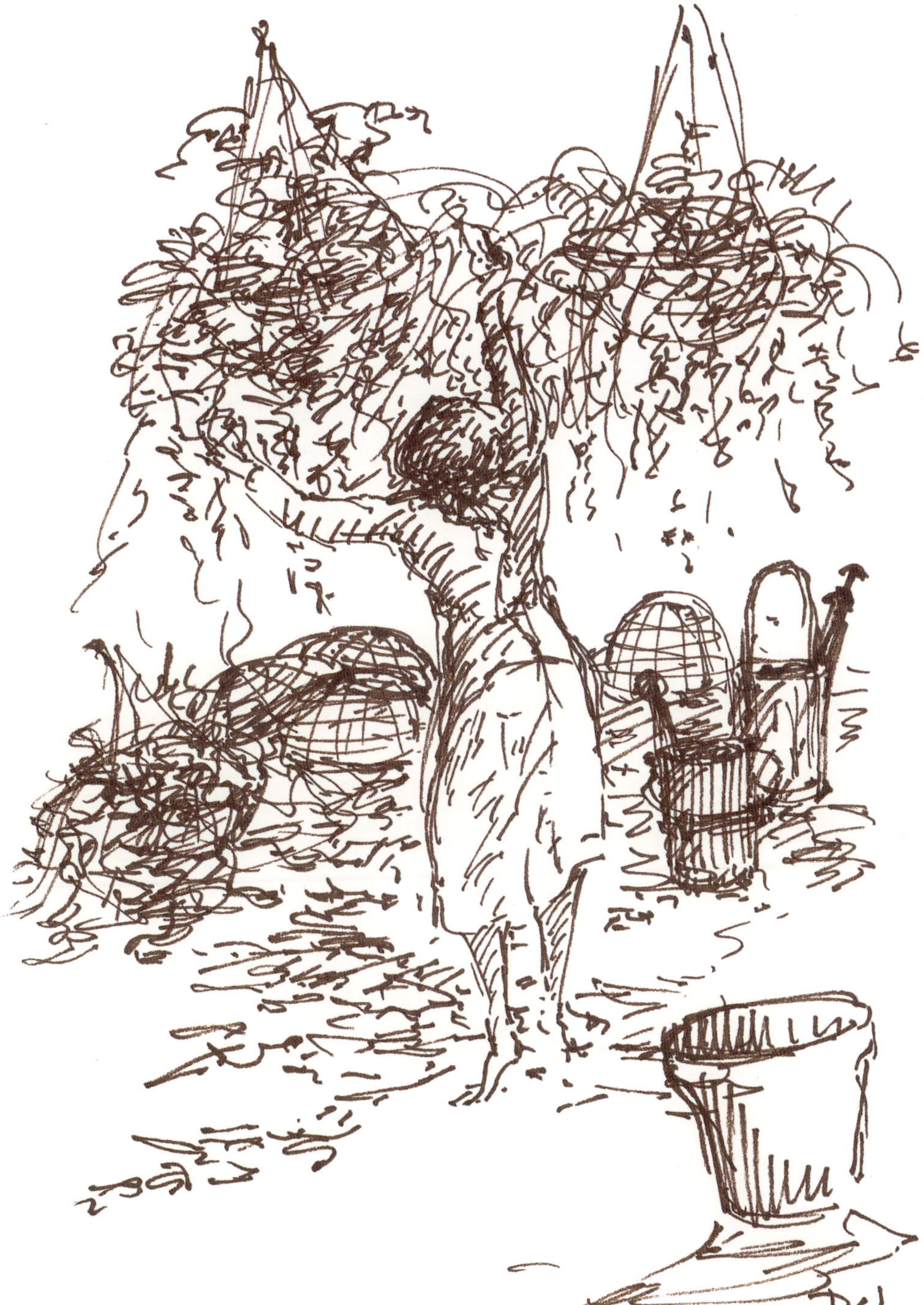
DU

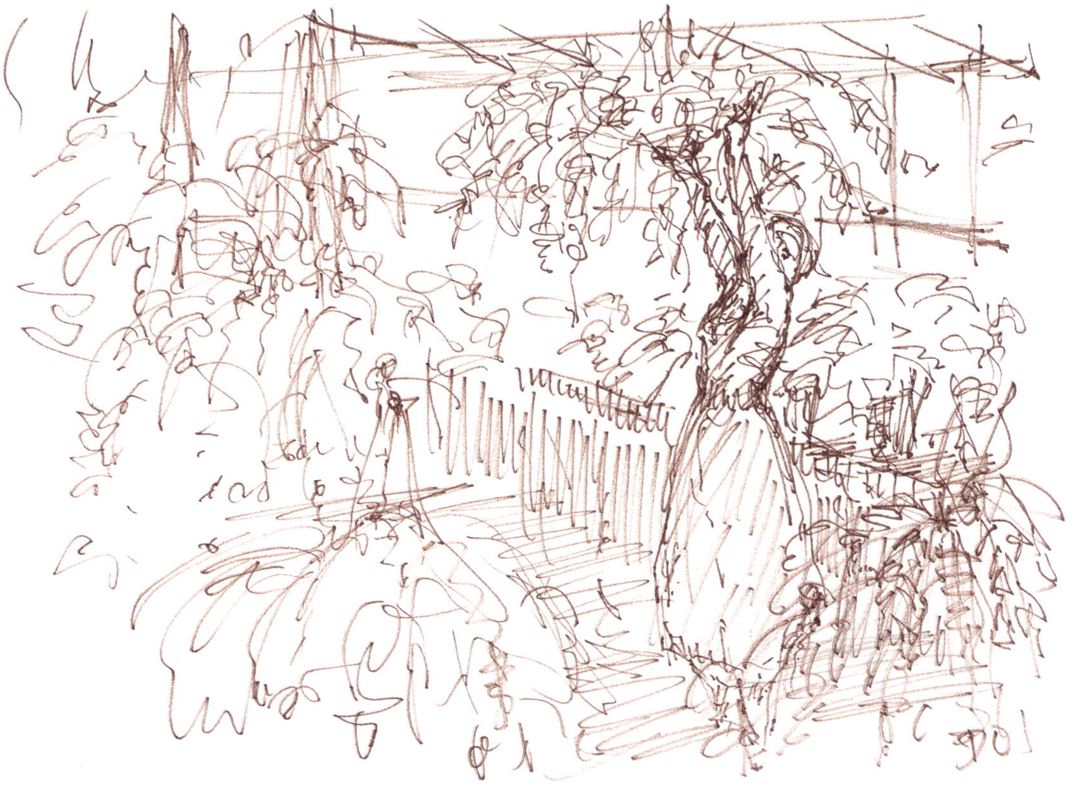

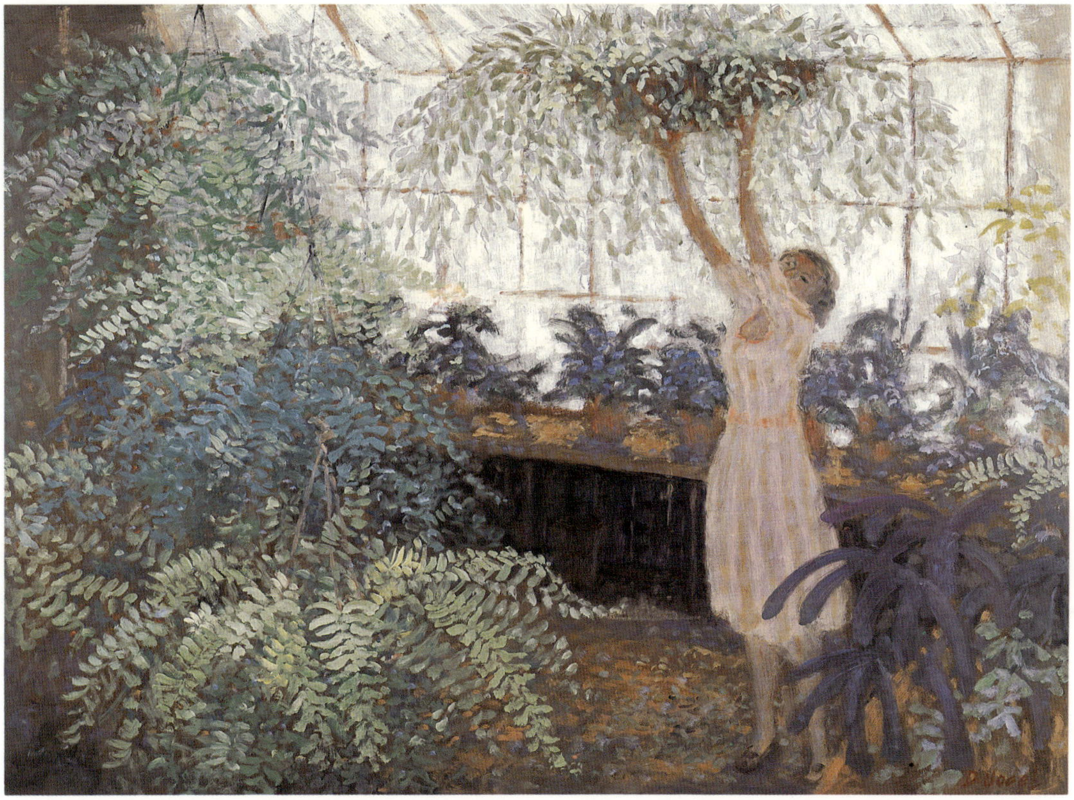

Part Six - The Figure

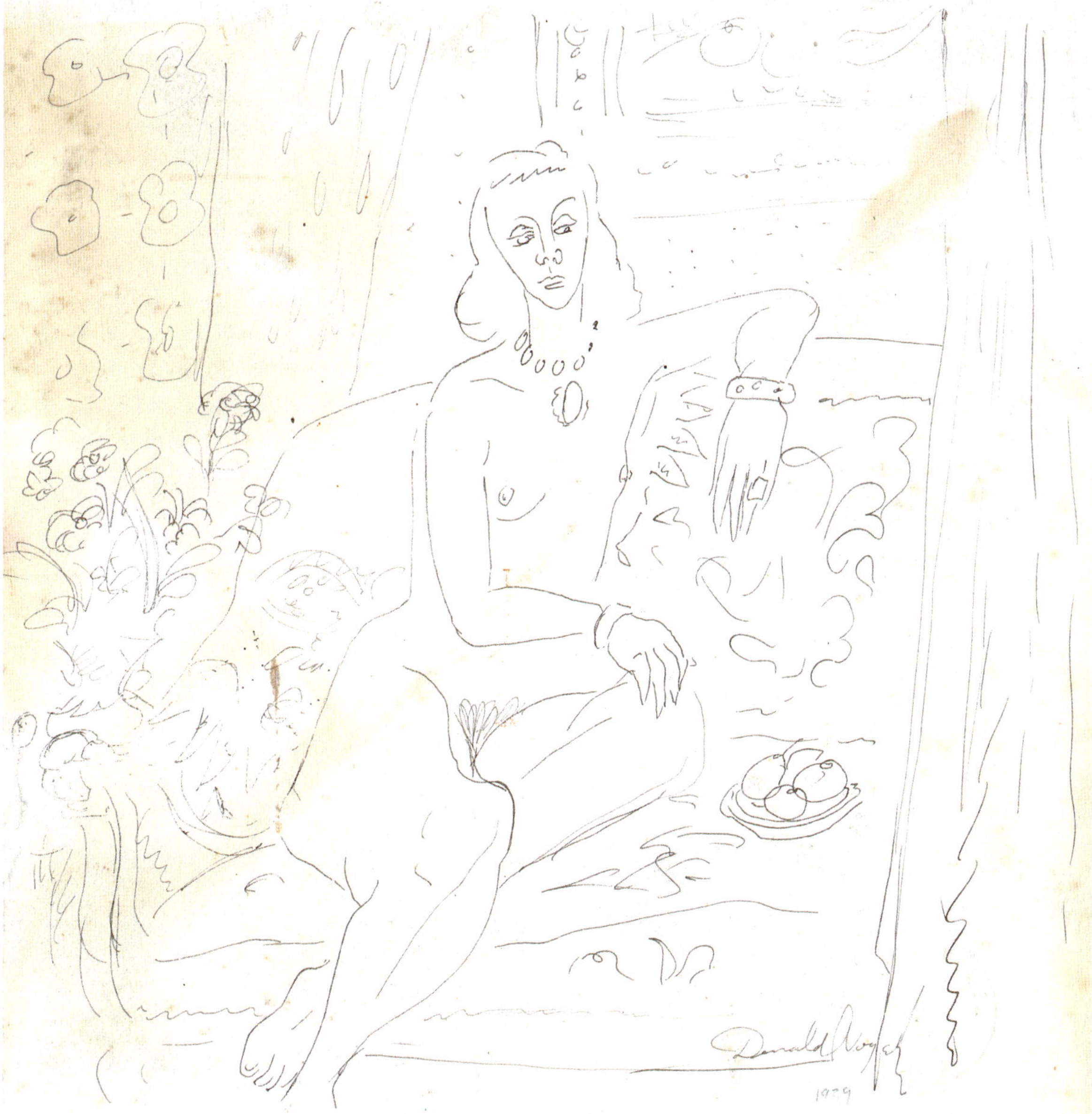

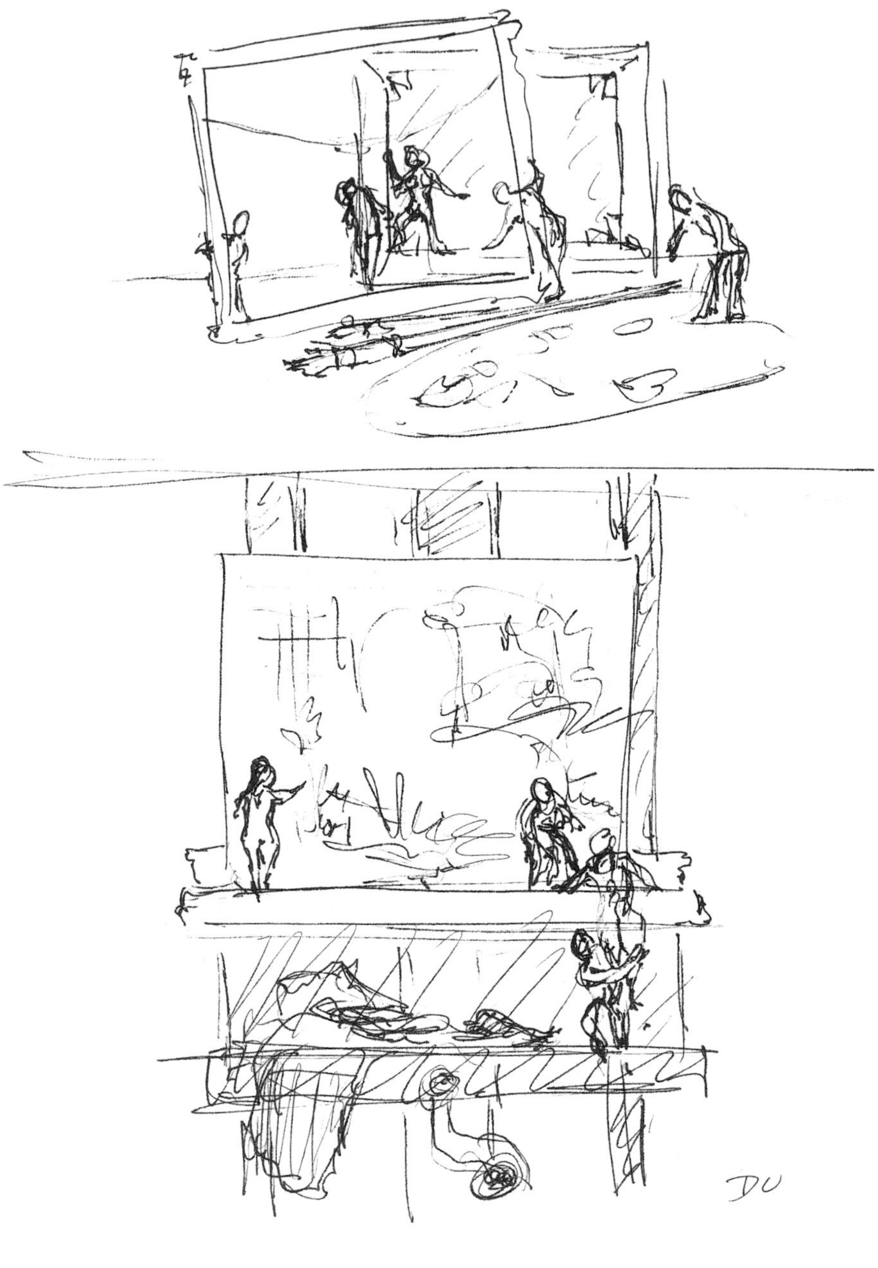
DU

The highest order of pleasure is beauty. The greatest reward of intellect is beauty.

In school, most young would-be artists spend a good part of their student days drawing from live models. Working countless hours, they consume pads of newsprint and reams of charcoal paper to create images of nude figures in every imaginable position. After hundreds of quick sketches, or slow and long ones, drawing the figure still holds a fascination.

When I started, tradition demanded that a student first spend a year drawing from the cast before working from the model. So three nights each week, after traveling by trolley and bus, this fourteen year-old spent three hours drawing plaster heroes. Those dead, white, unyielding sculptures gave me little inspiration. What I learned, however, was a discipline I appreciated only years later. Much was required before the charcoal could respond to the exciting, living, moving, responsive figure.

Then the time comes when you try to forget the discipline of rendering and begin to express what you feel. This is when the drawing becomes personal. It gains an identity that is yours and no one else's. When this happens, the model gets in the way. Turn your back on it and make the figure a form that functions as part of the composition, but still retains its identity.

A figure drawn with a very few lines often suggests an attitude far better than a figure fully rendered. By suggesting, you invite the viewers to participate in the drawing, allowing their imaginations to complete it. Thus, they become part of it. What you suggest is their invention, and your suggestion is recognition of their sensitivity to respond.

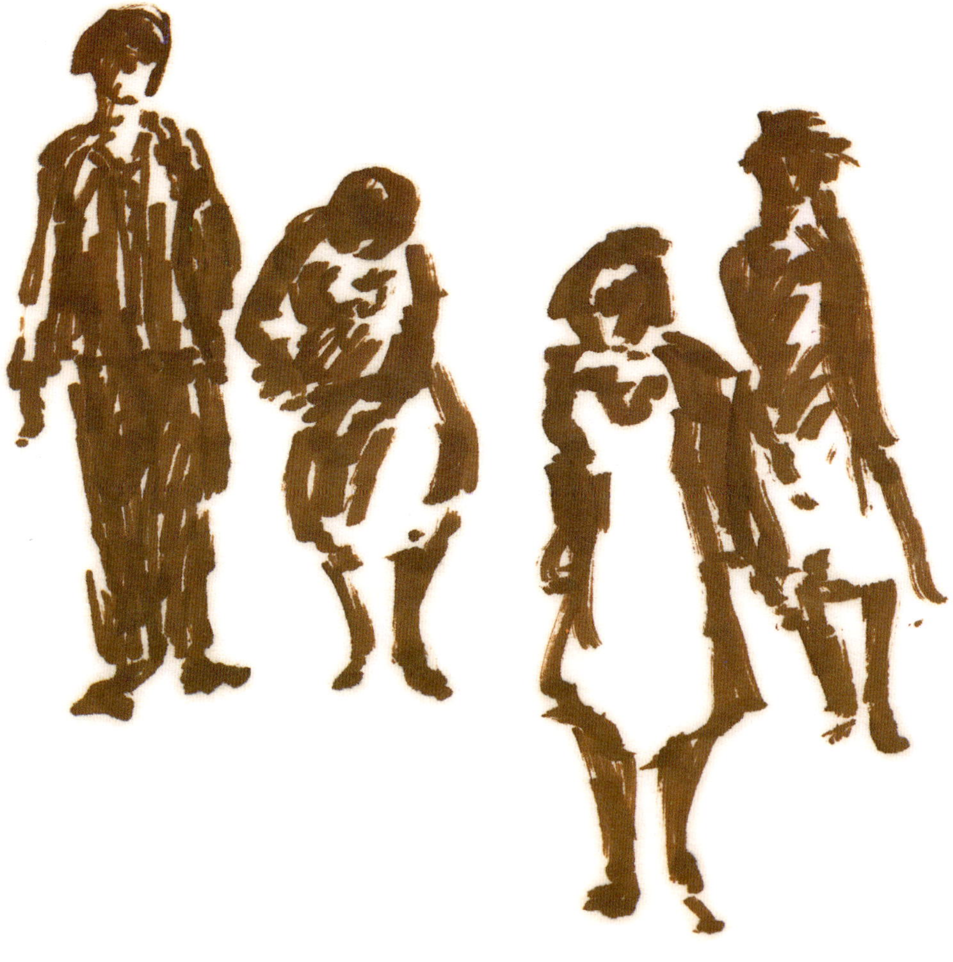

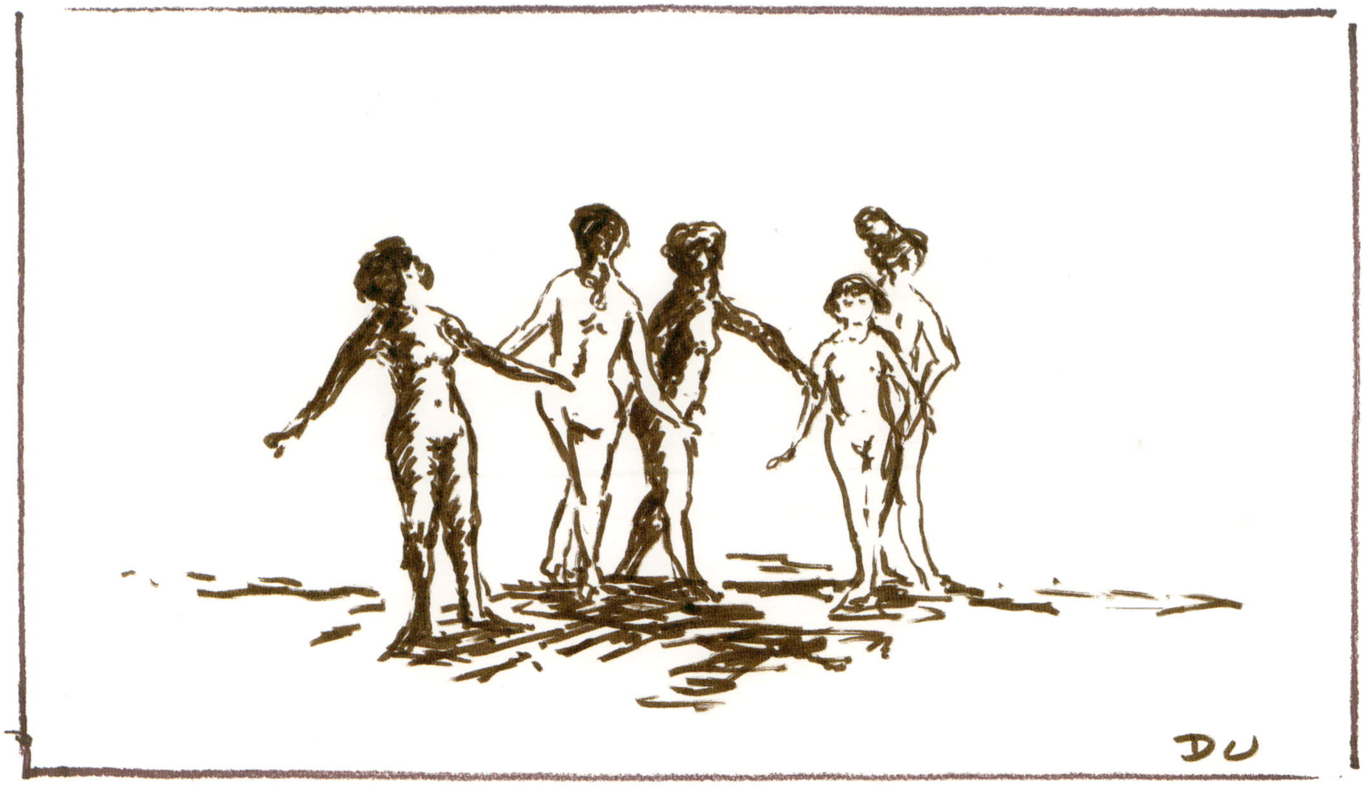
DU

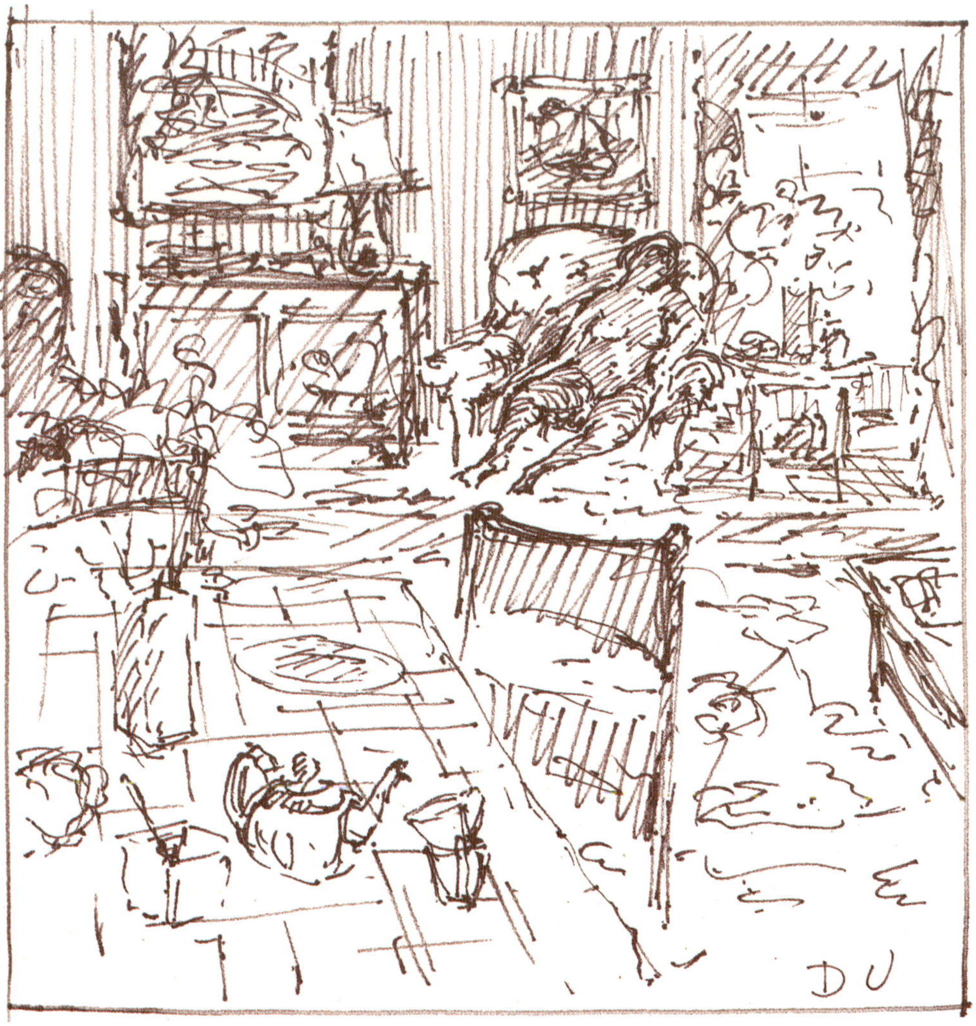
D U

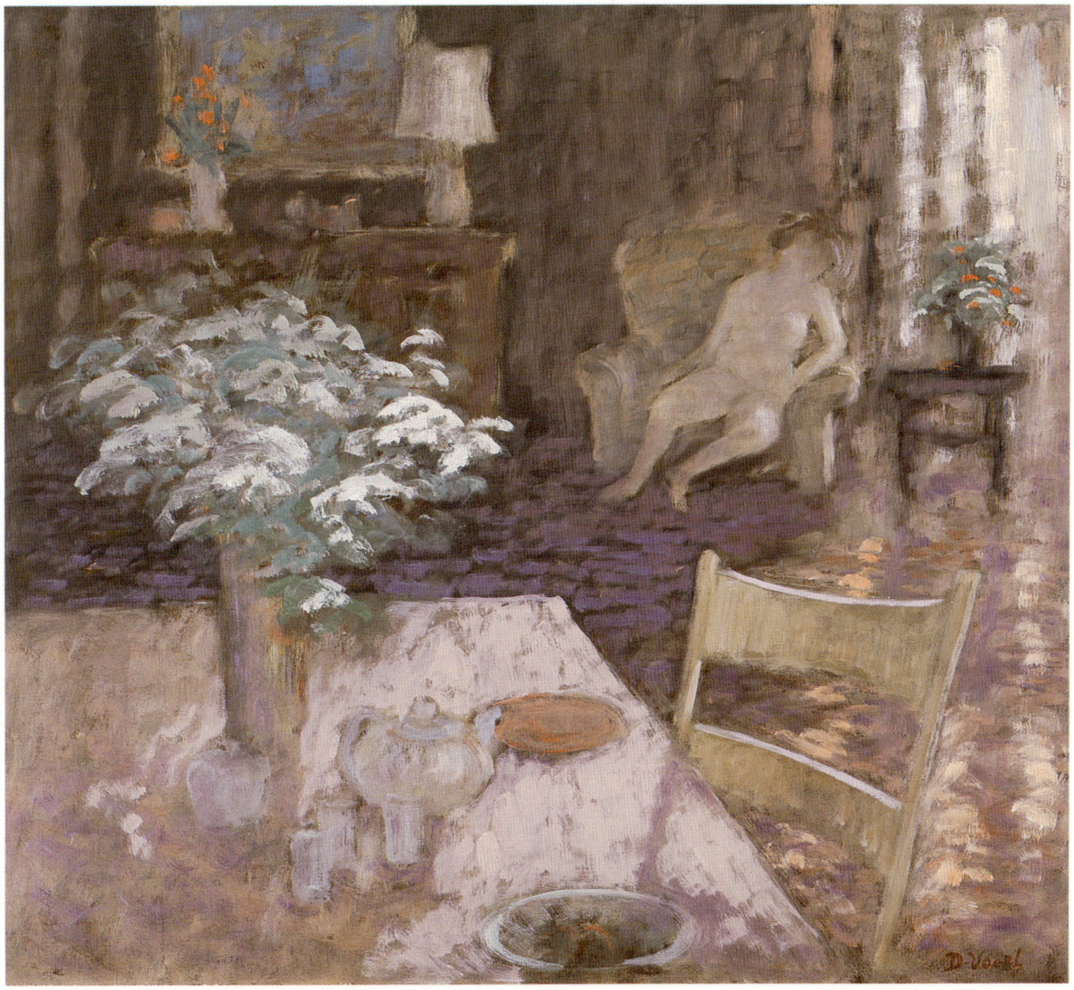

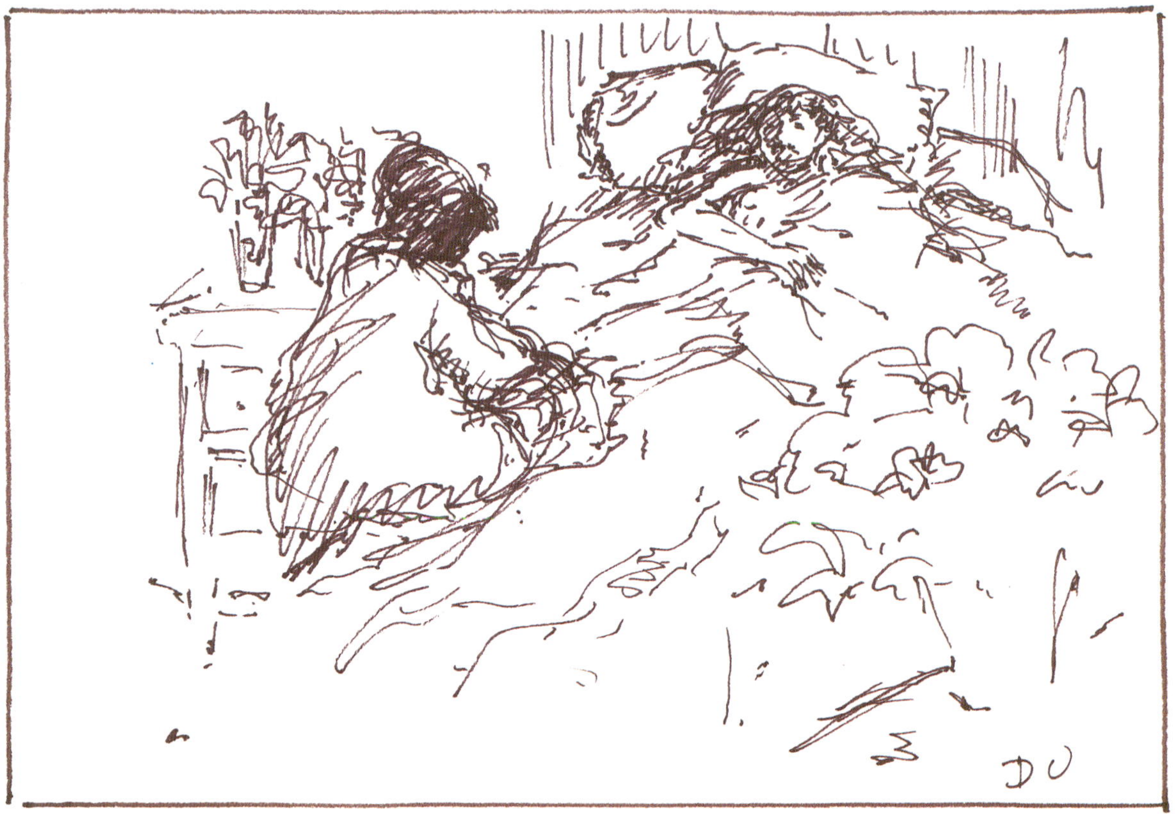

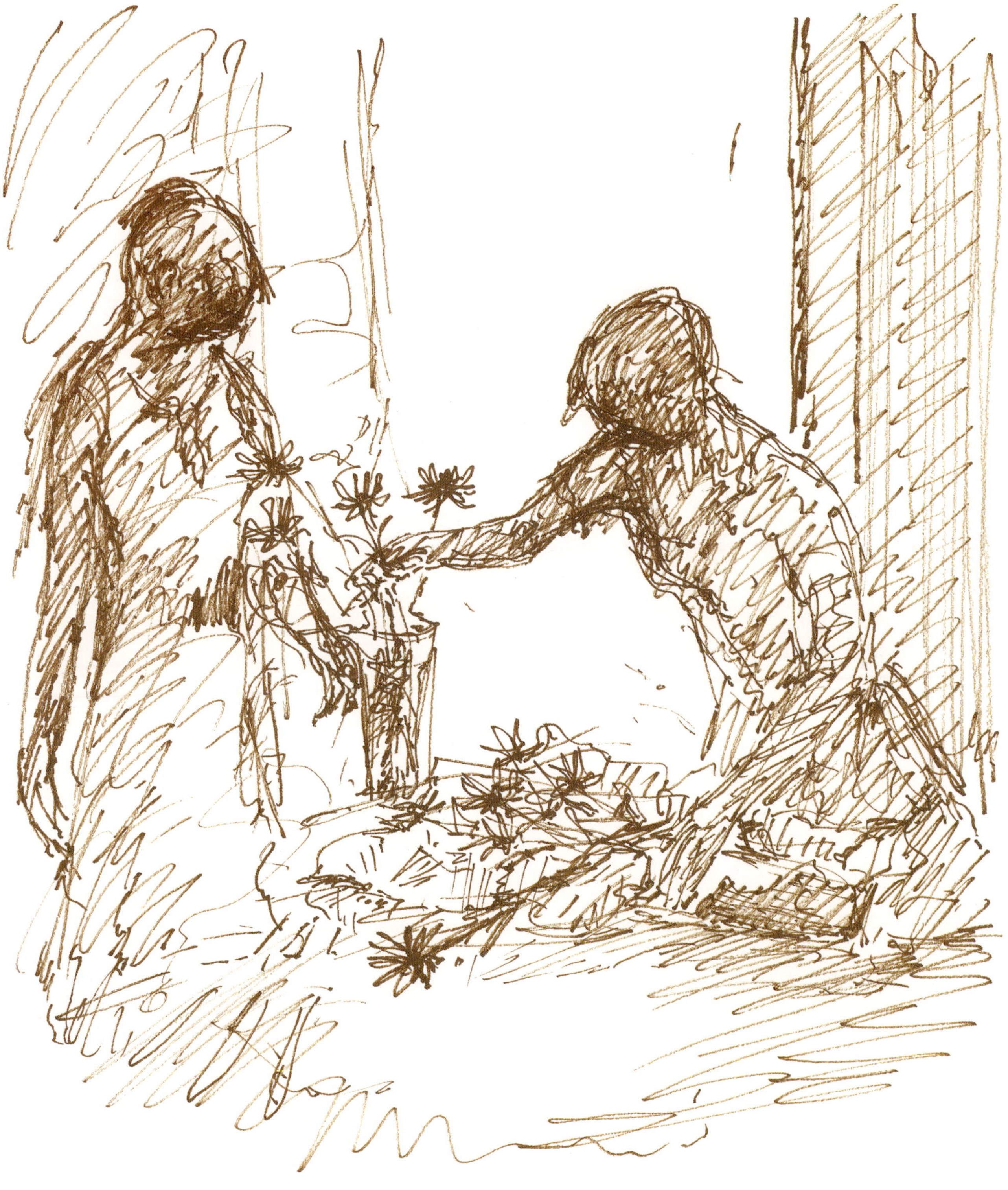

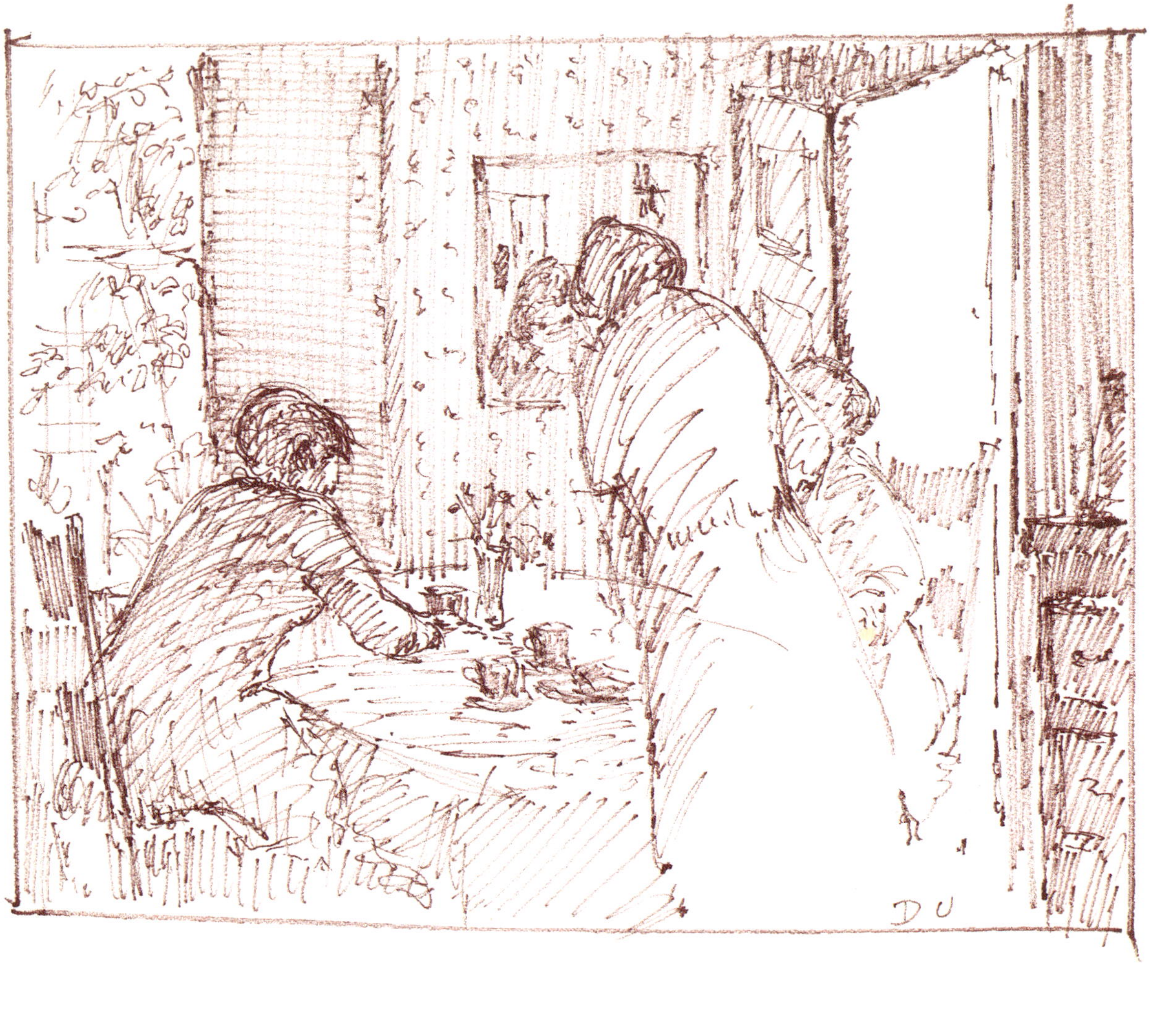
DU

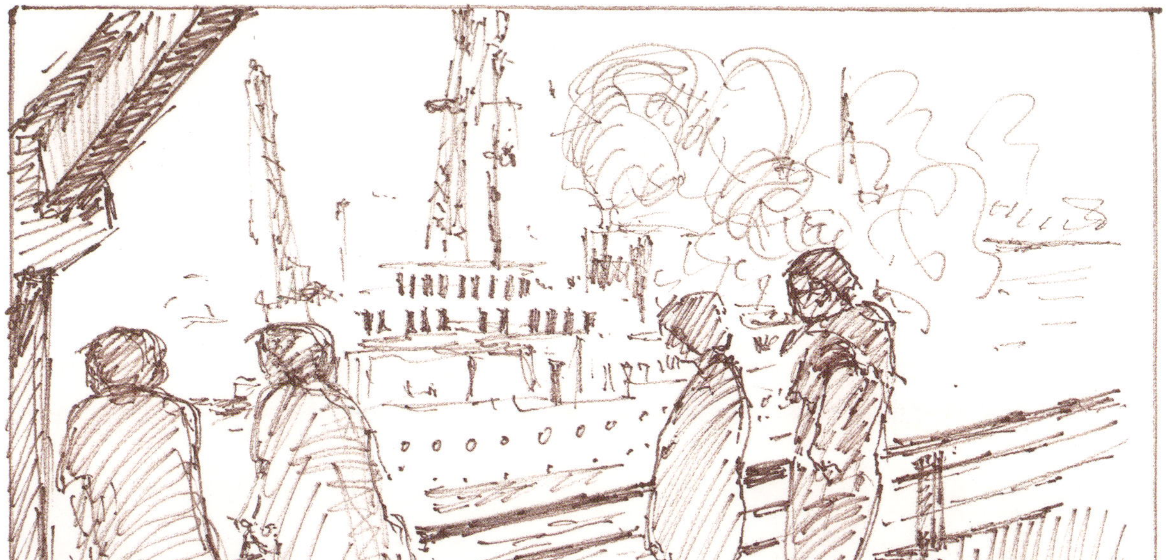

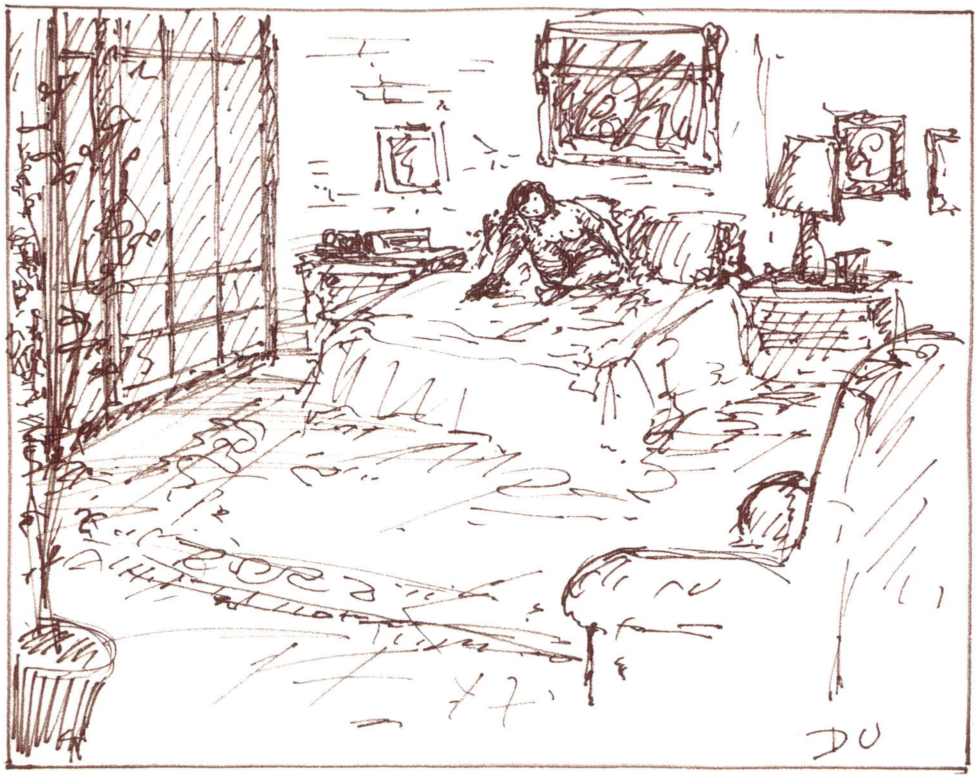

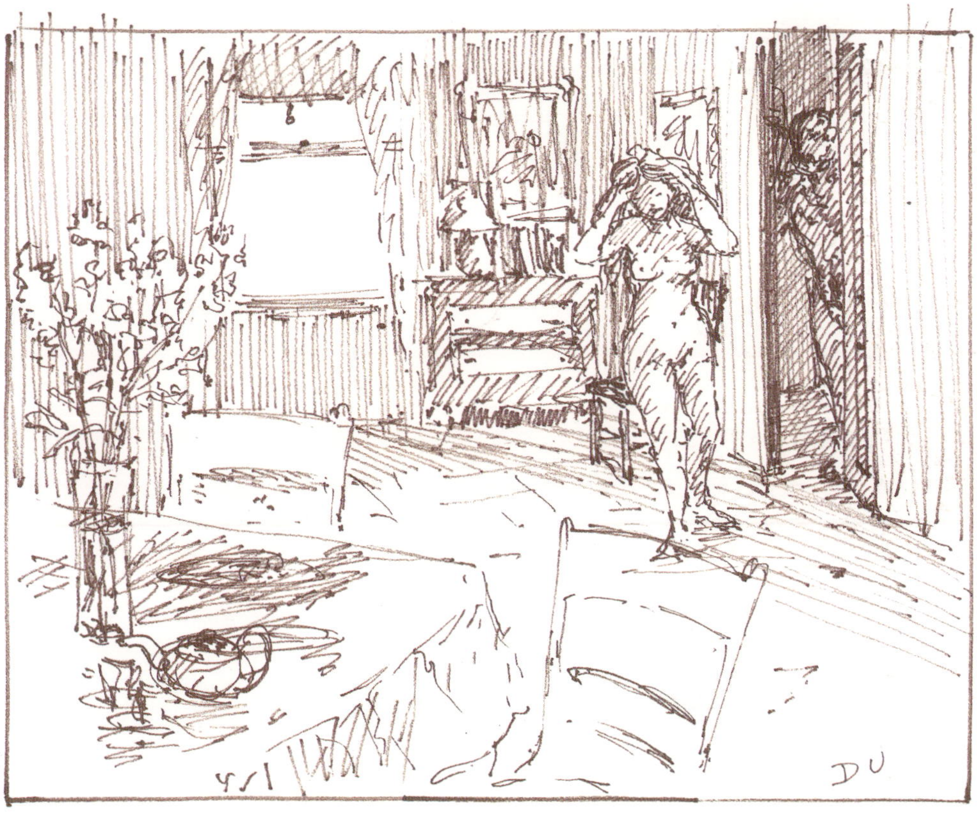

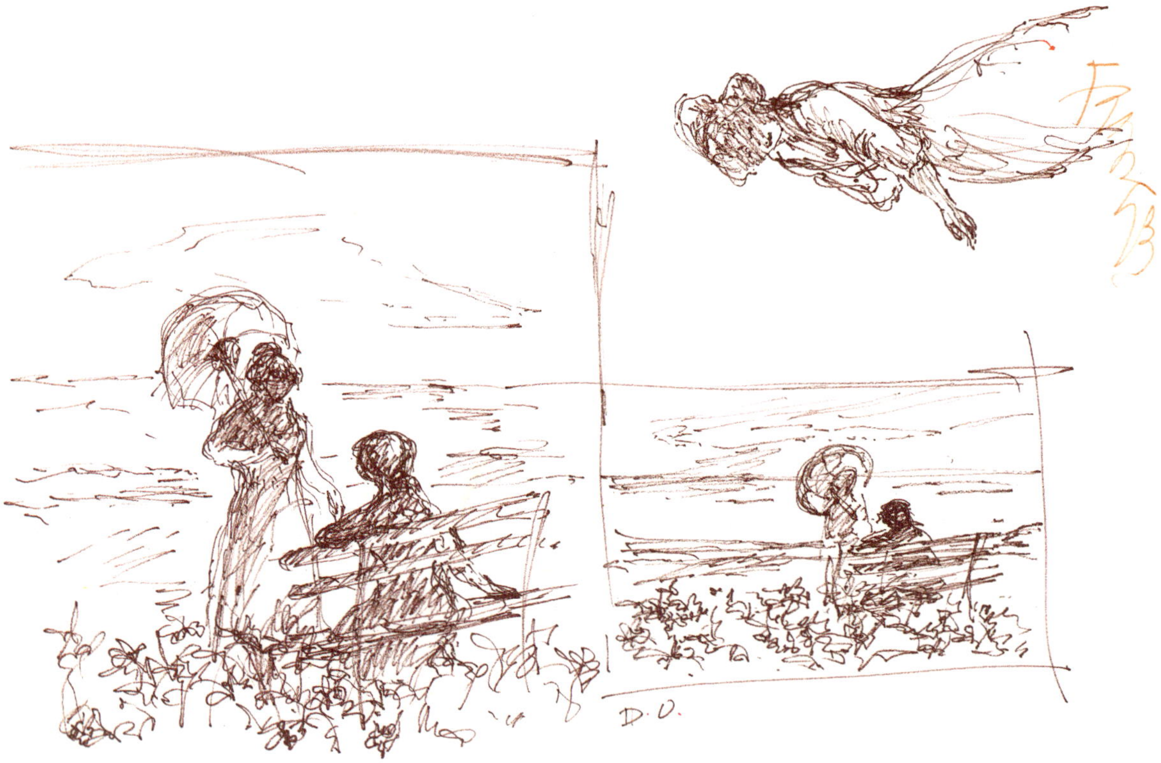
D.O.

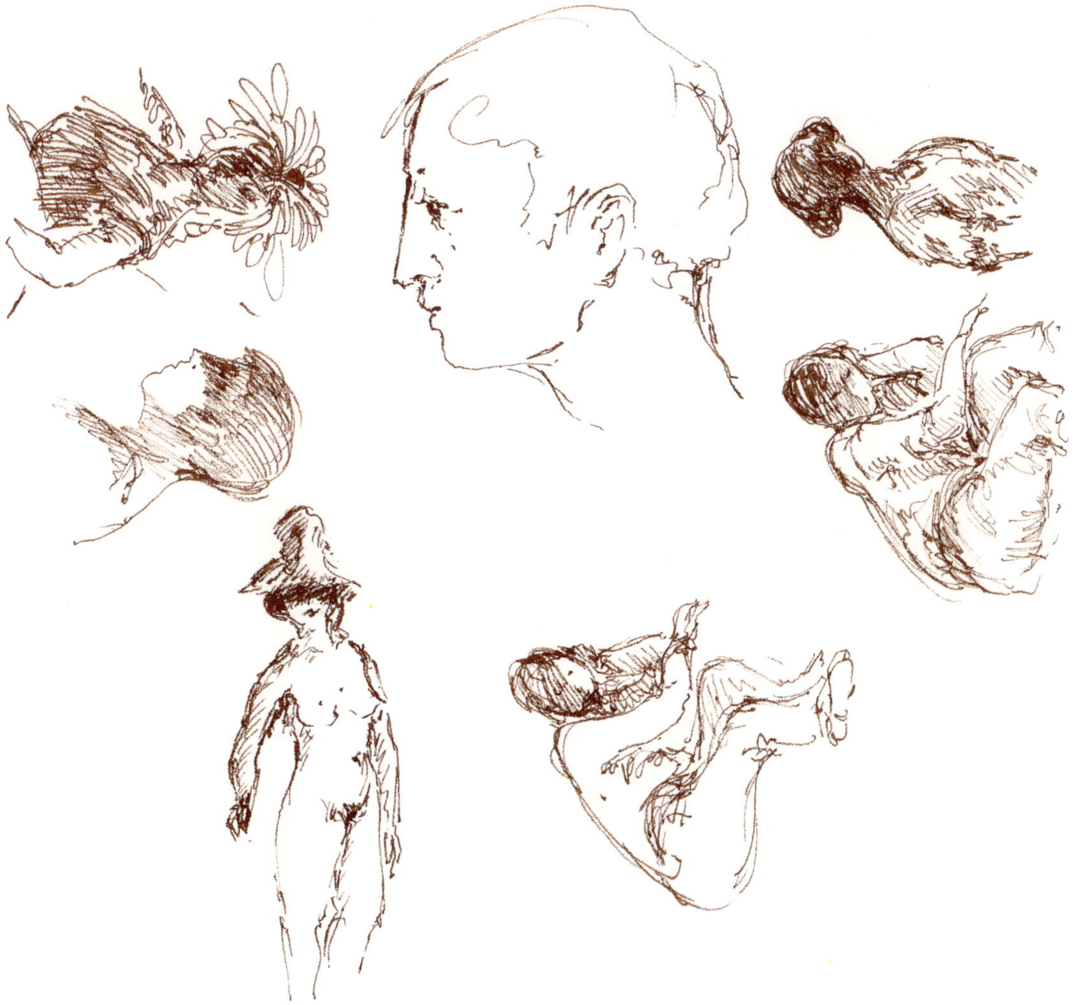

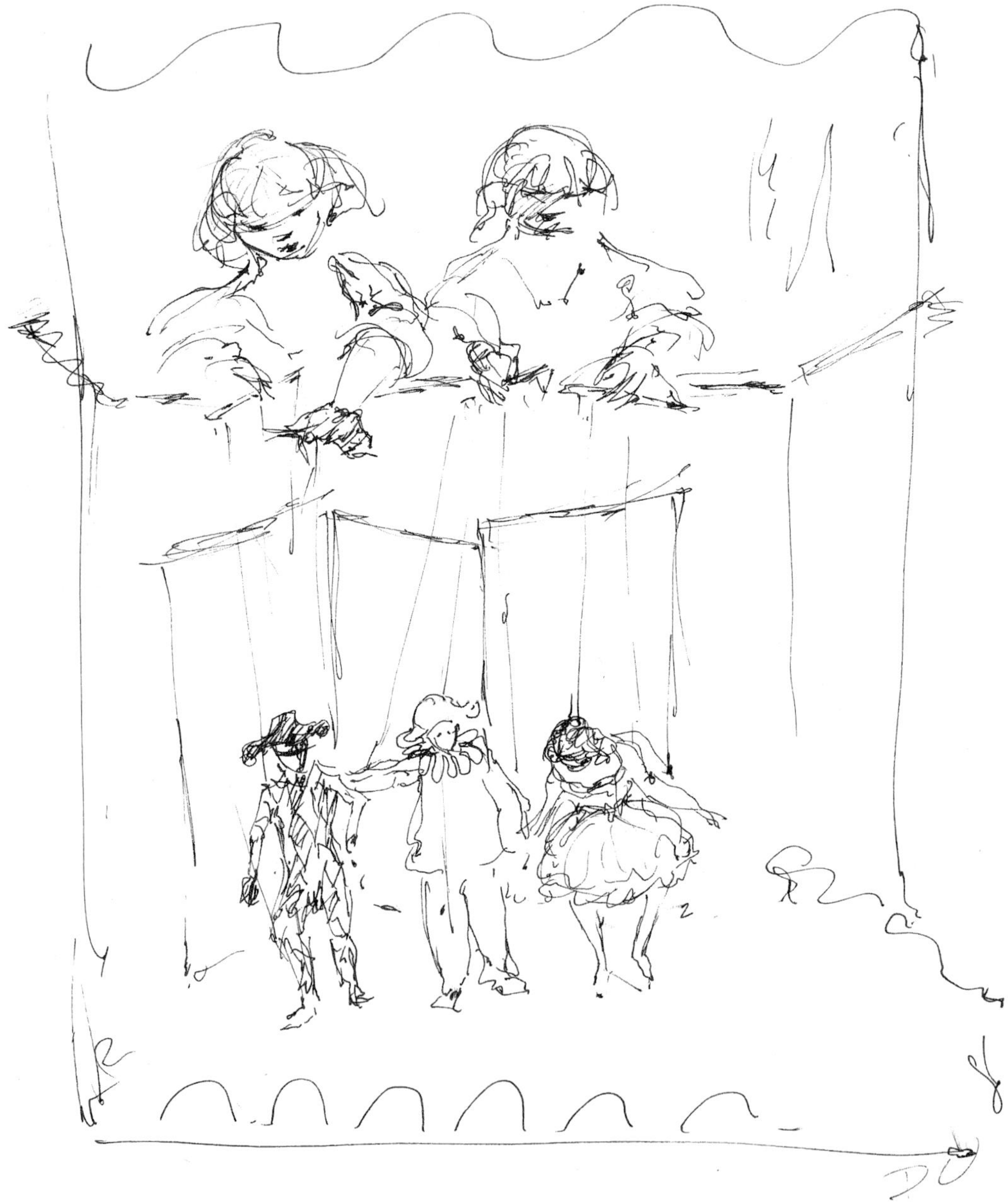

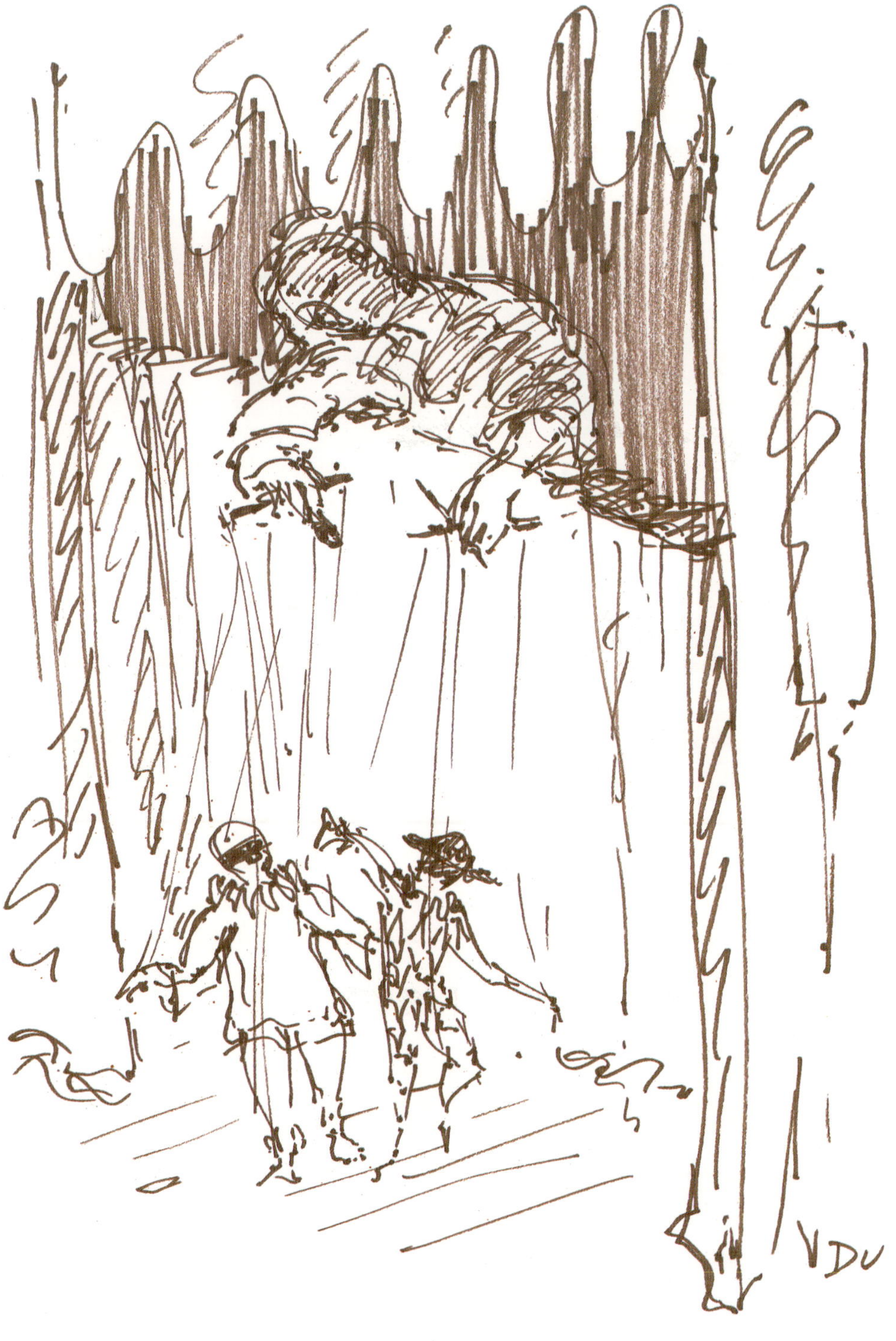
VDU

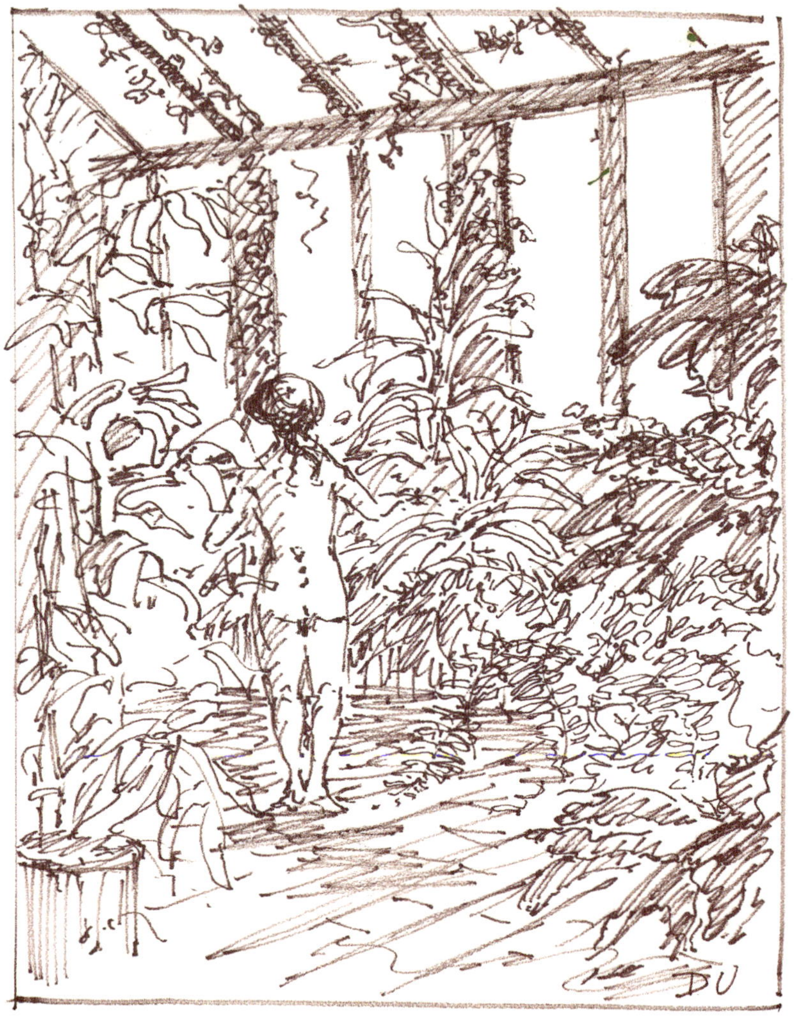
DU

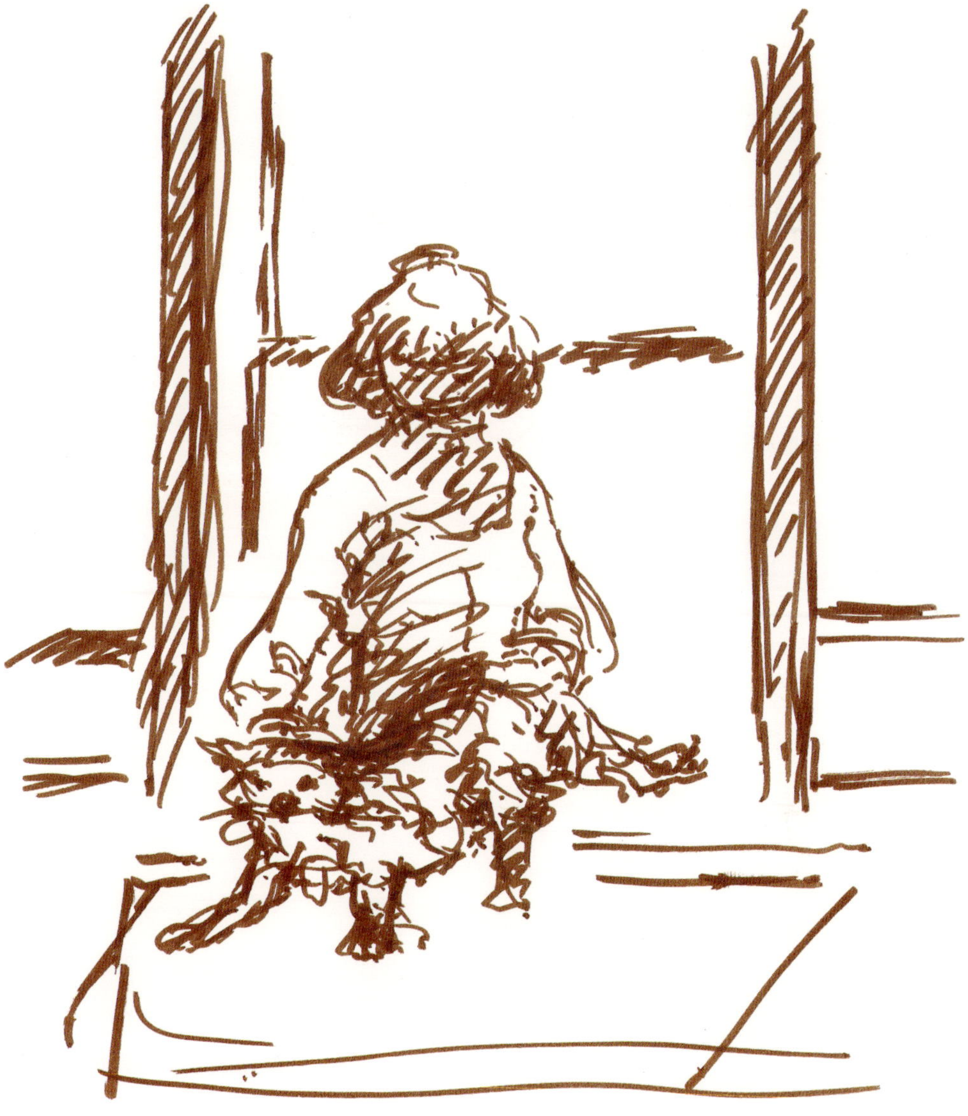

Part Seven - Still Life

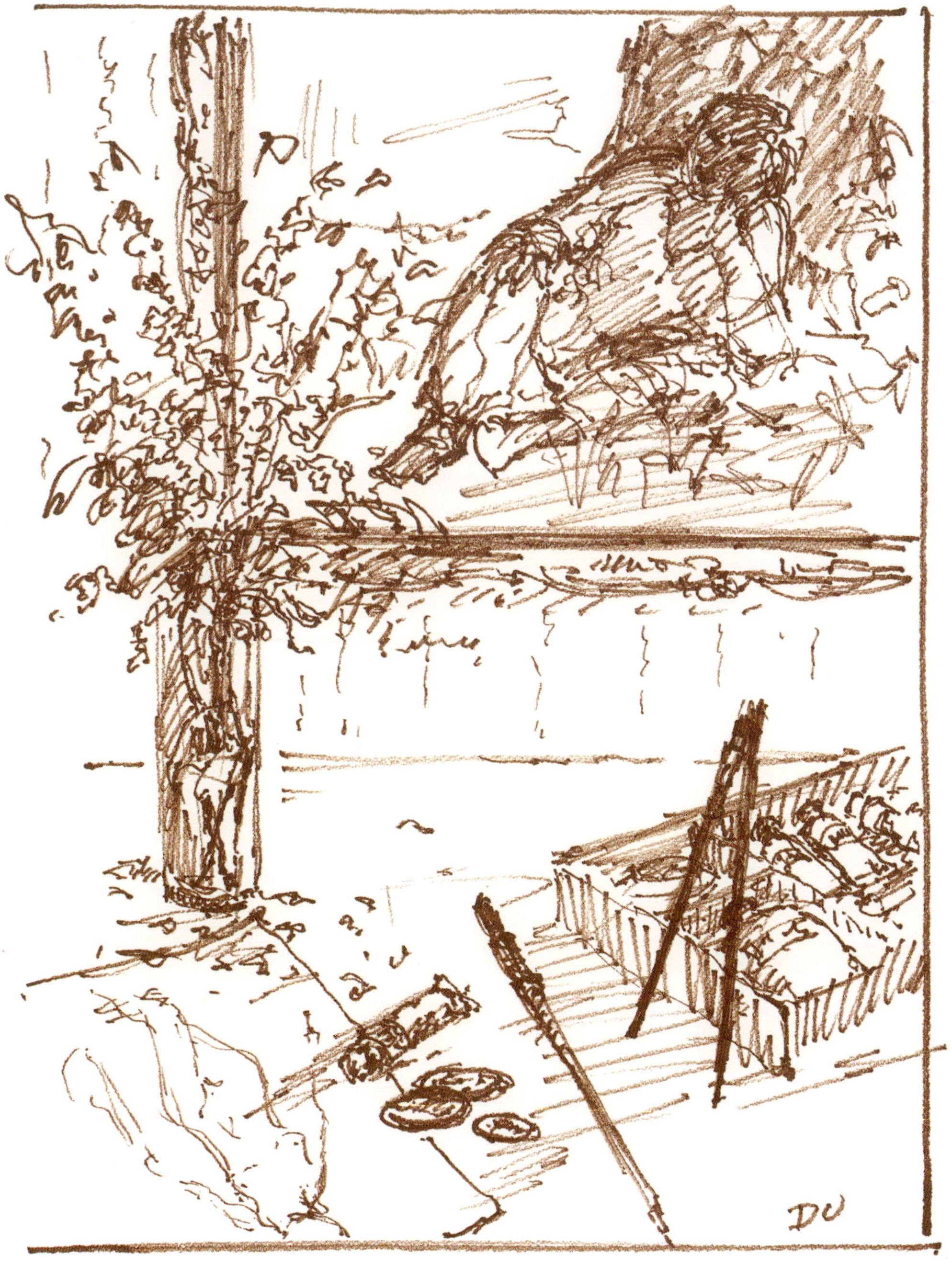

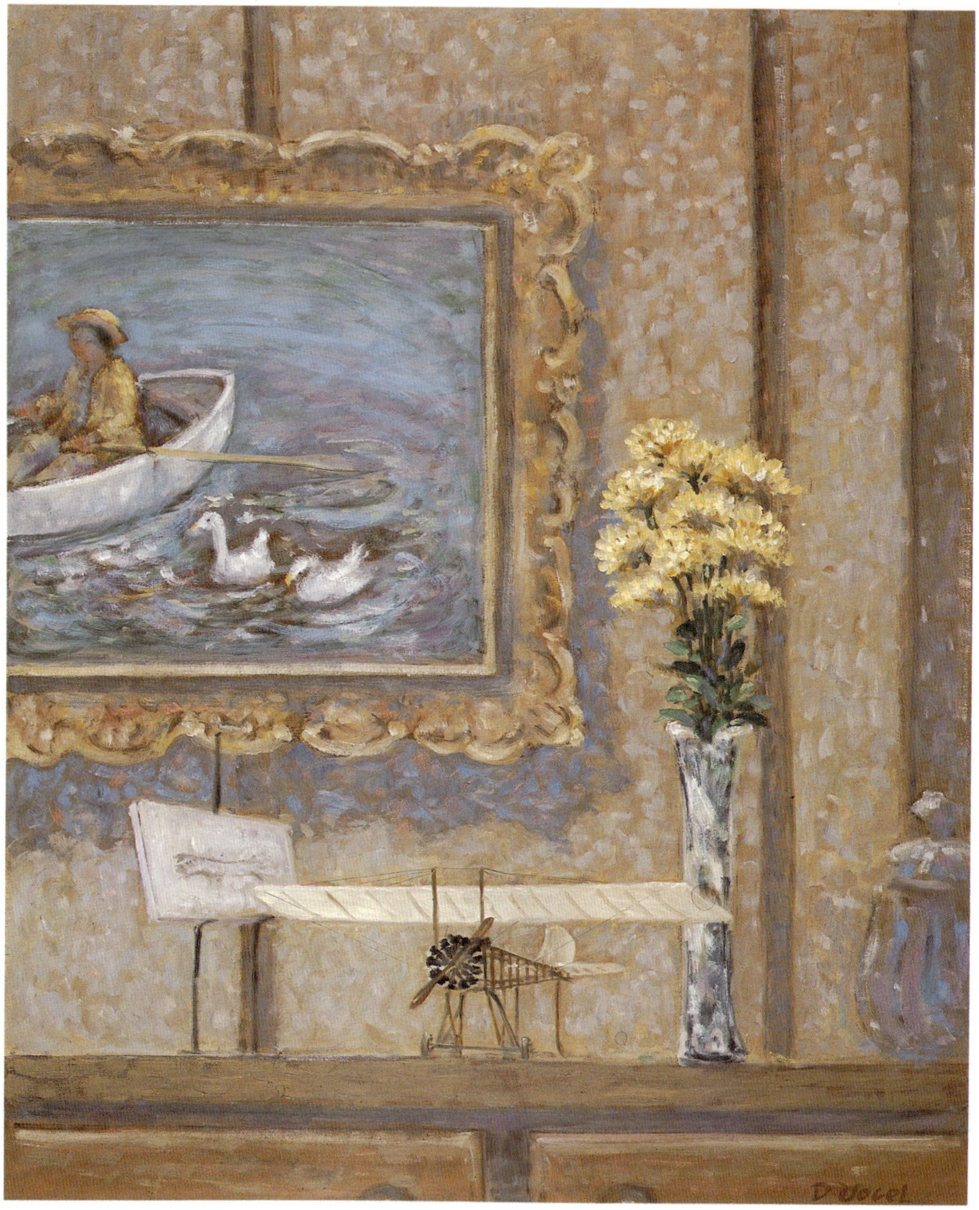

Now and then a change of pace is rewarding. In drawing the still life one usually sets a group of objects on a table, hangs or drapes a piece of fabric, and perhaps adds a flower or two in a vase. Then the task is to translate the arrangement into another dimension, creating tensions from existing forms and using the negative space. To understand the possibilities of producing a good still life, I suggest you look at works by Cezanne and Morandi. They should both inspire and humble you. Note at first glance the total simplicity of their work, but don't be fooled, for in time you will marvel that such control is possible.

Here, I share a different approach to the subject content, such as drawing in the painting and painting in the drawing. Usually, the objects in these works are invented; those that exist are not arranged, but are employed when the need for their shapes is felt. As in other paintings and drawings, the subject content is secondary to what is done with it. It is possible to draw a still object and make it lock into another object or space. If you understand it here, revisit the other works and see when, where, and how such happens.

For myself, innovation and style take care of themselves. When one is honest to his muse, creativity prevails--but only then?

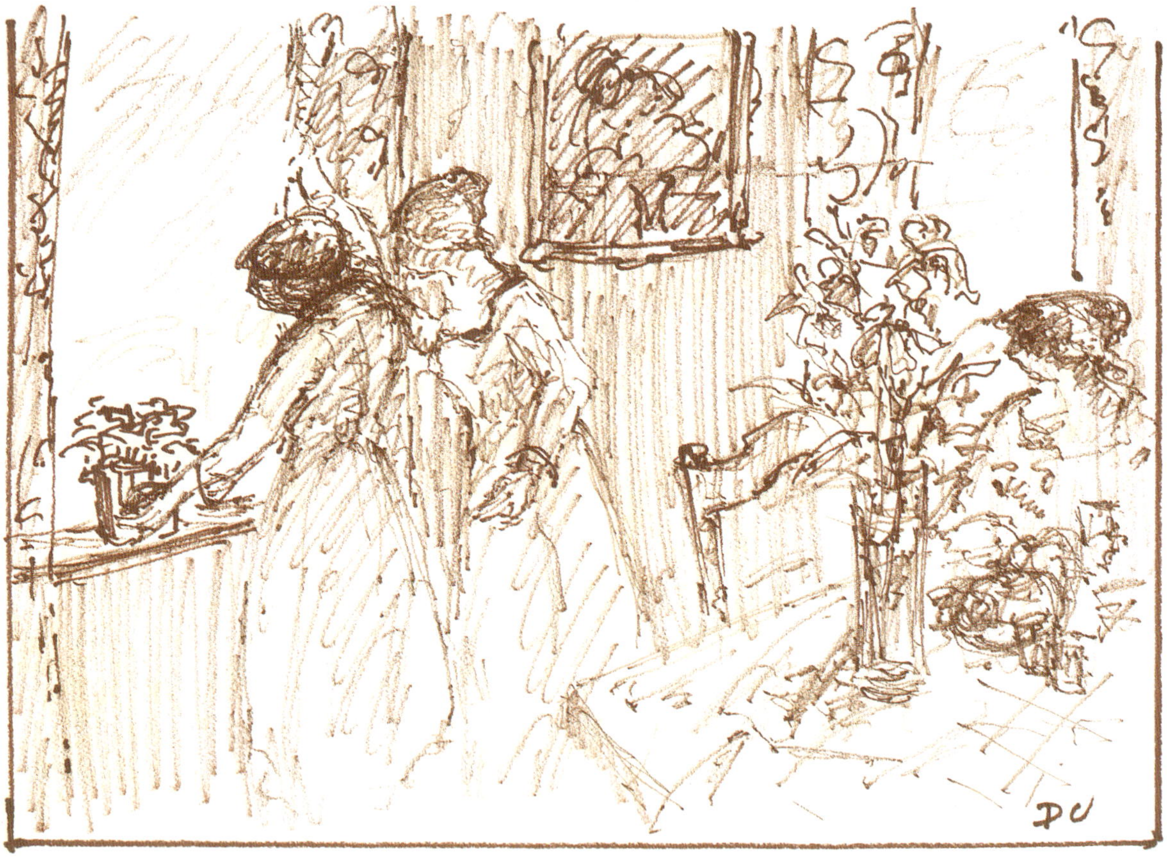
DC

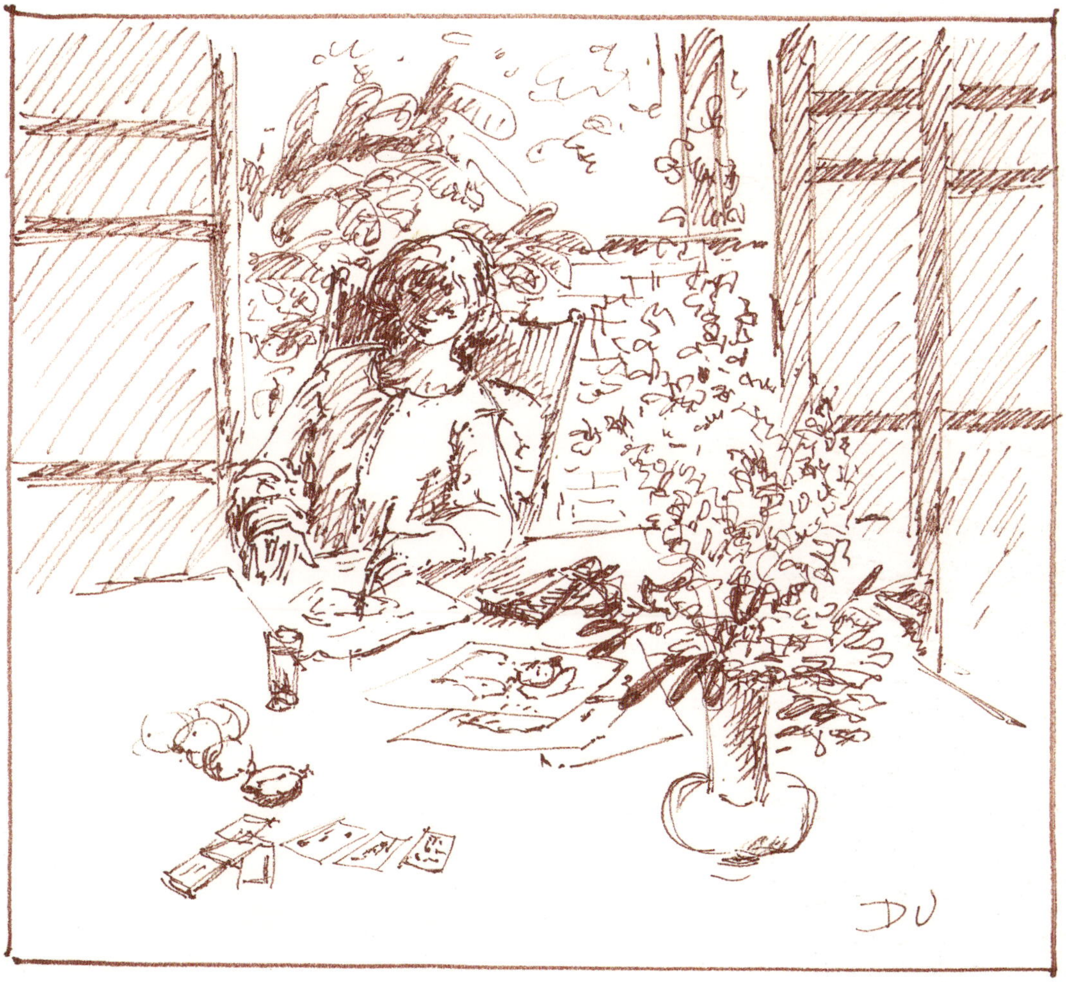
DV

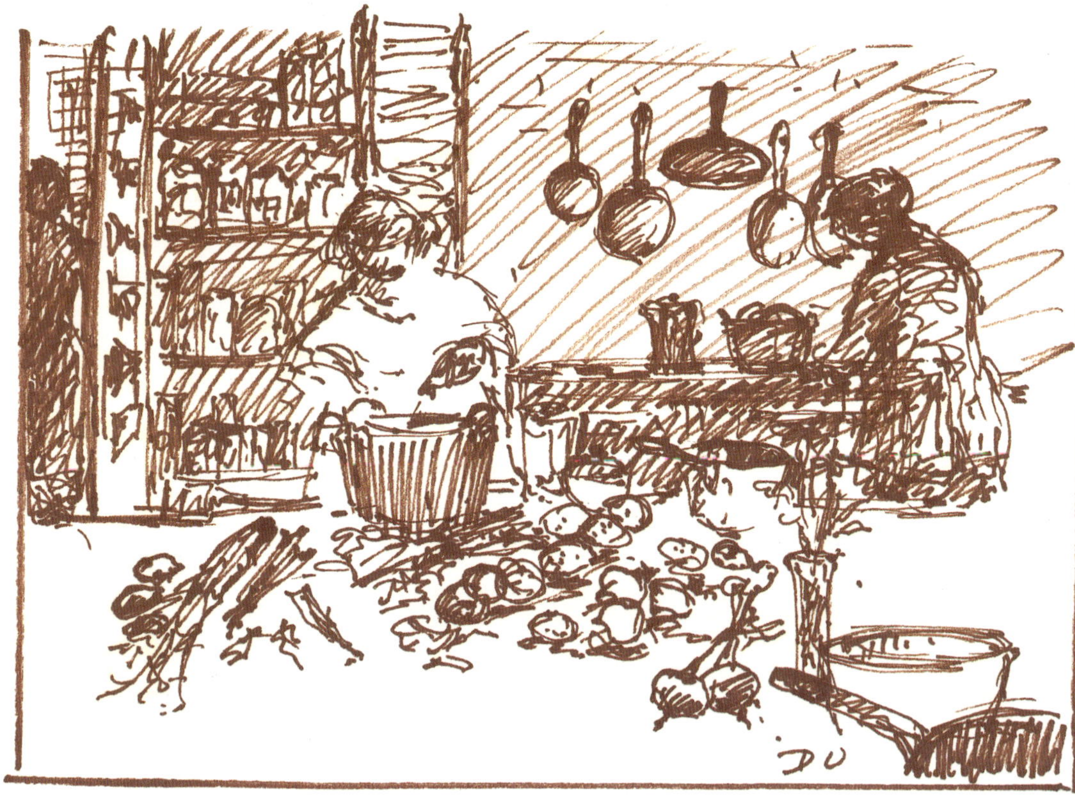

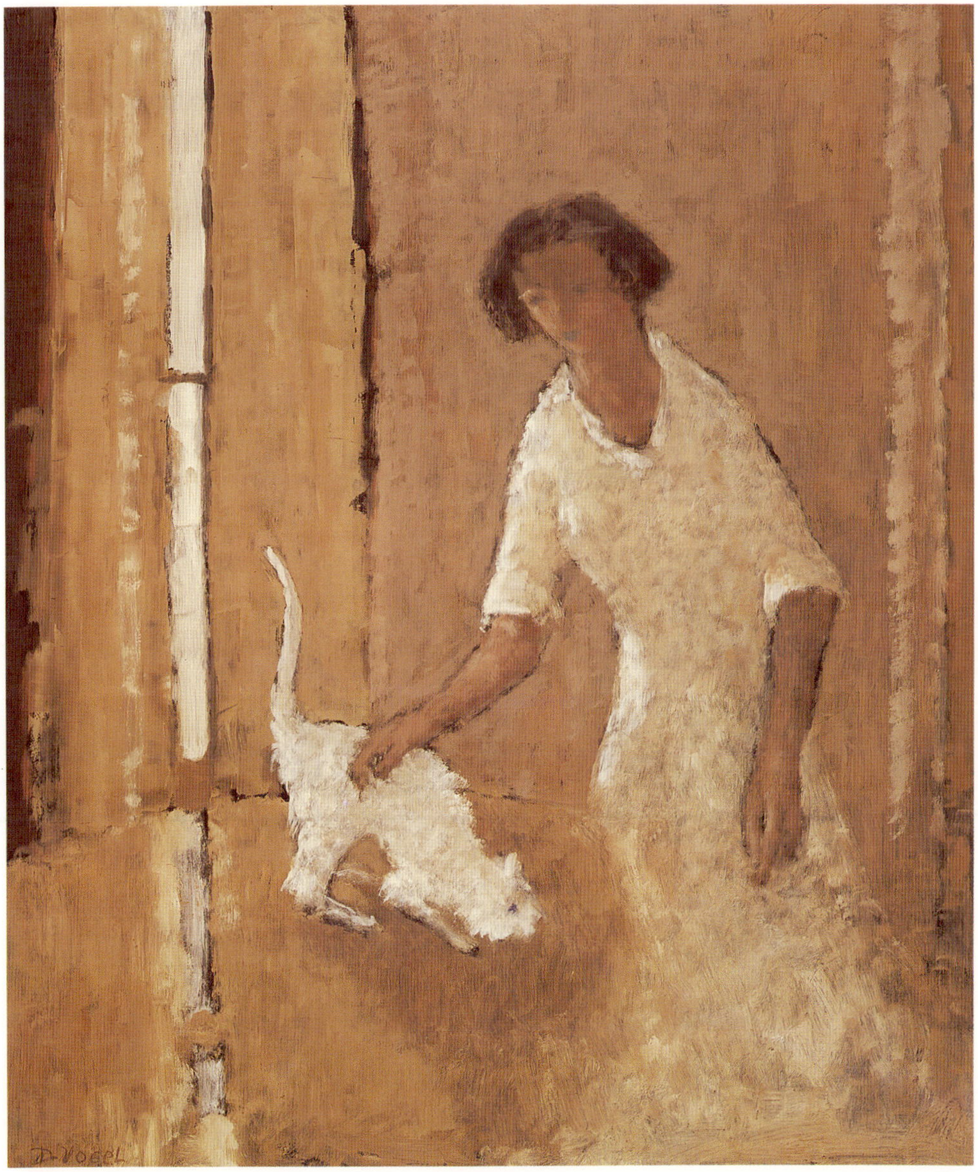

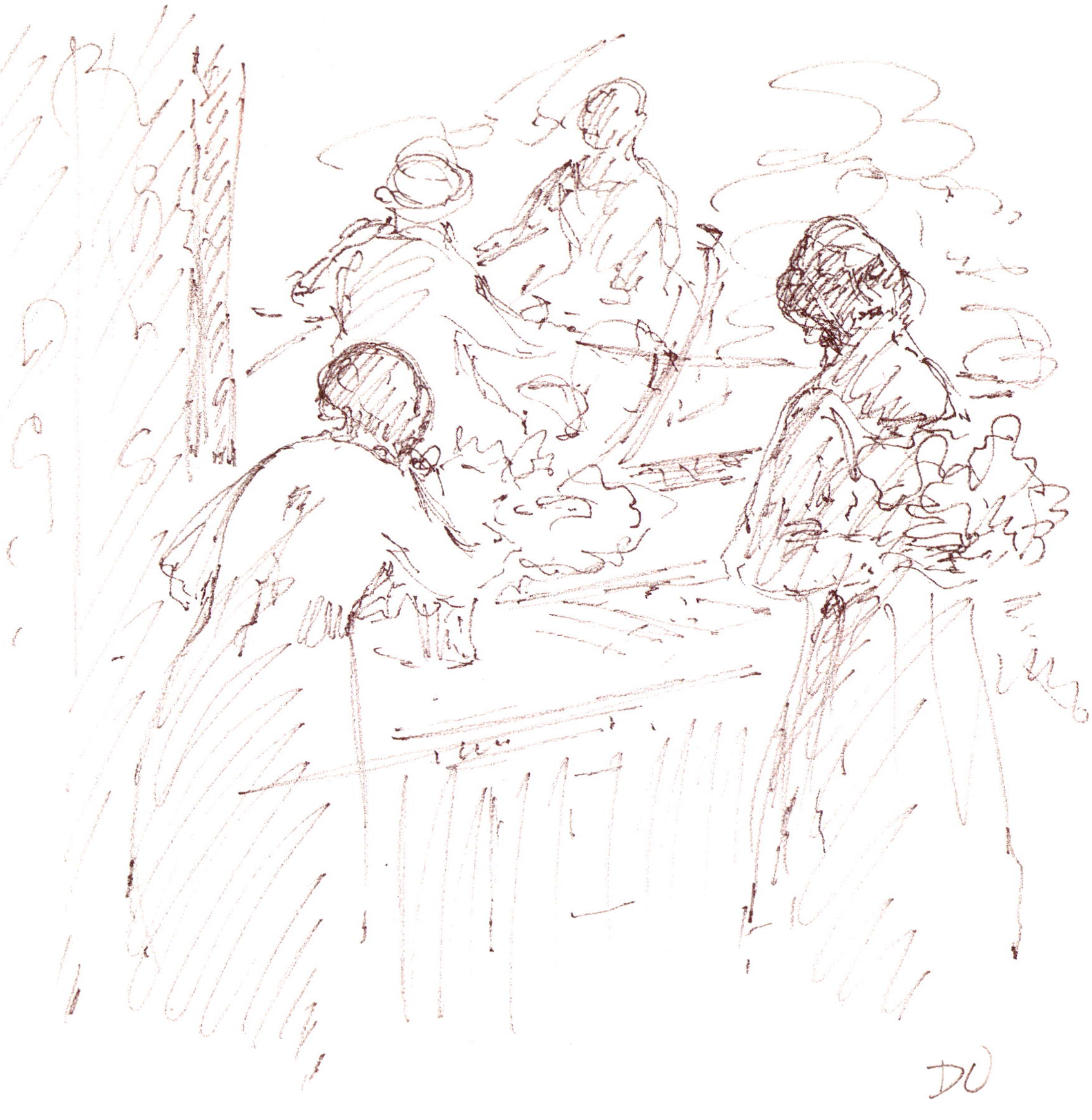
DO

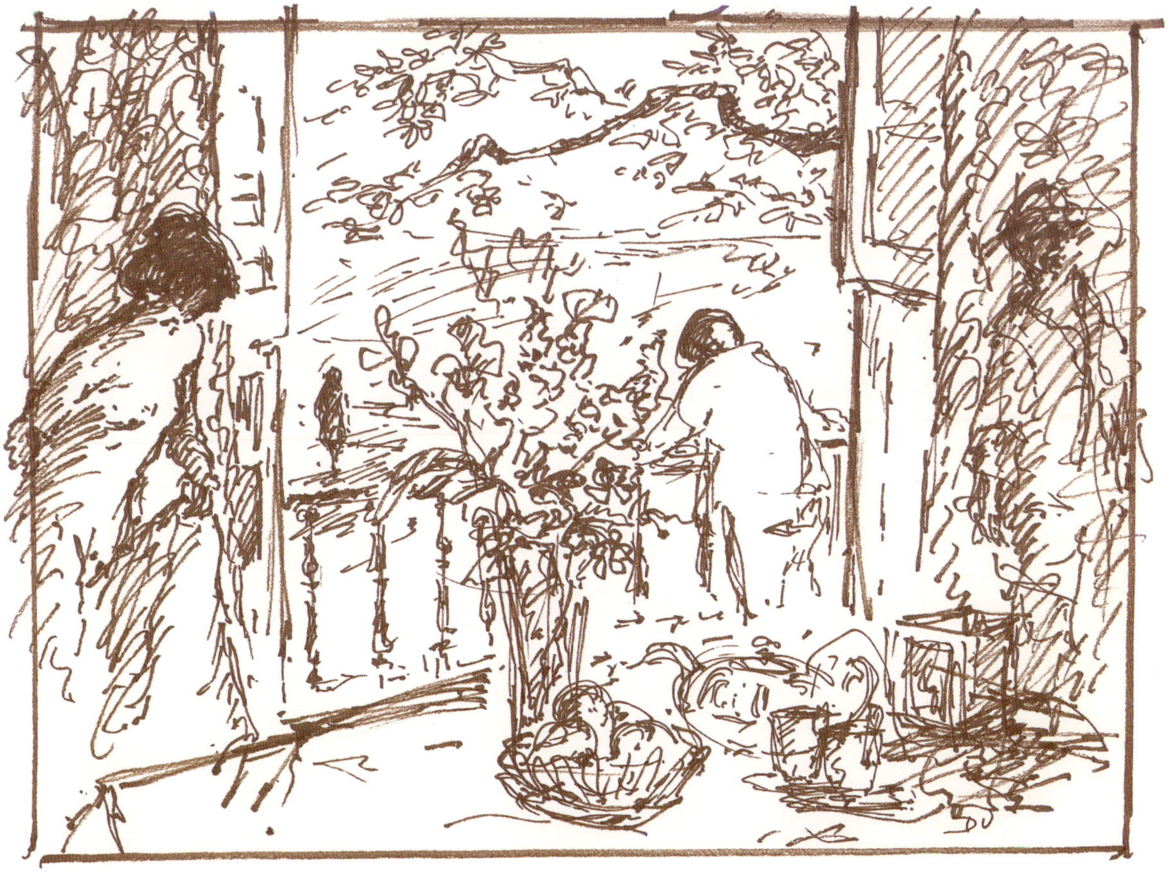

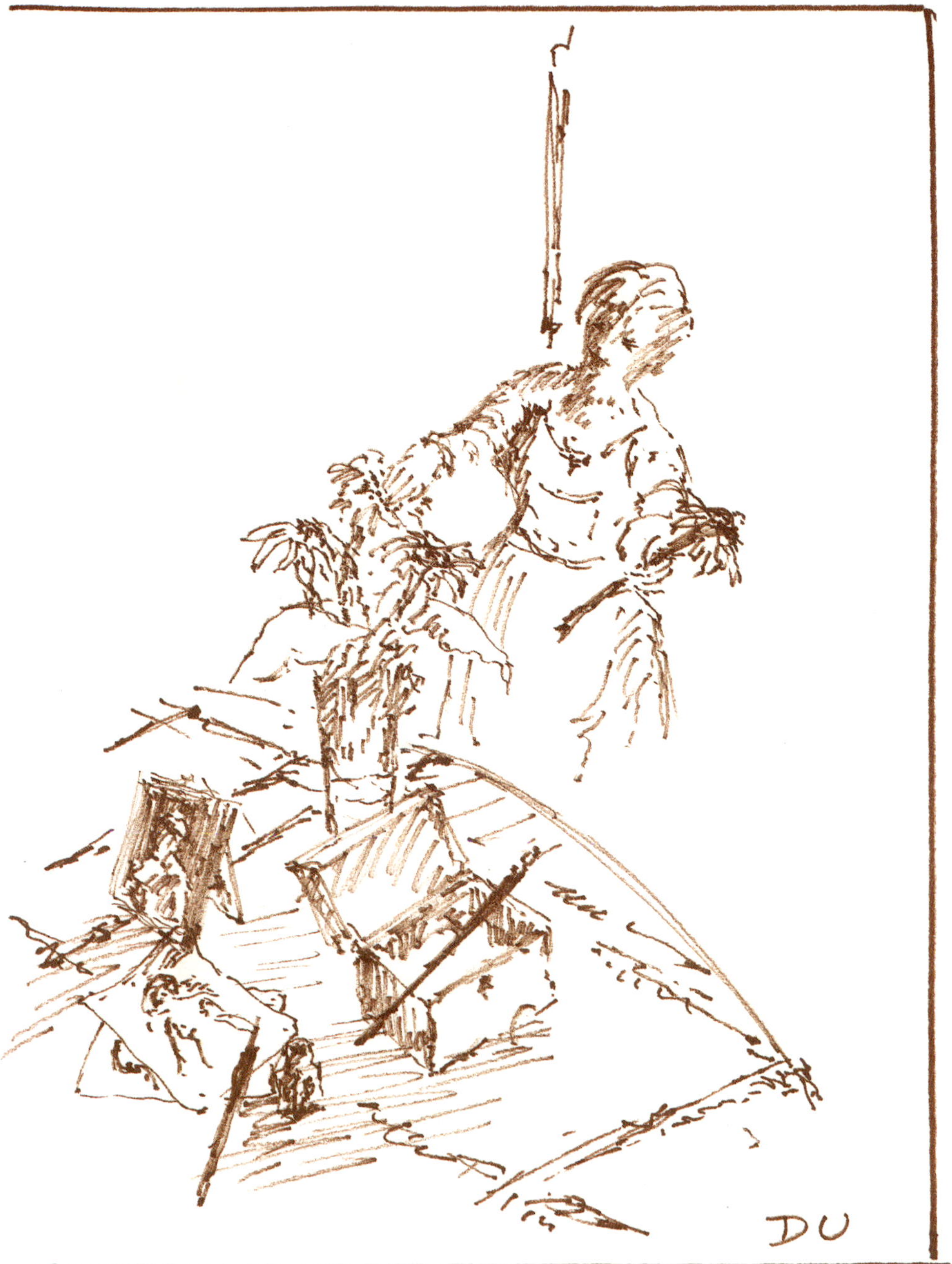
DU

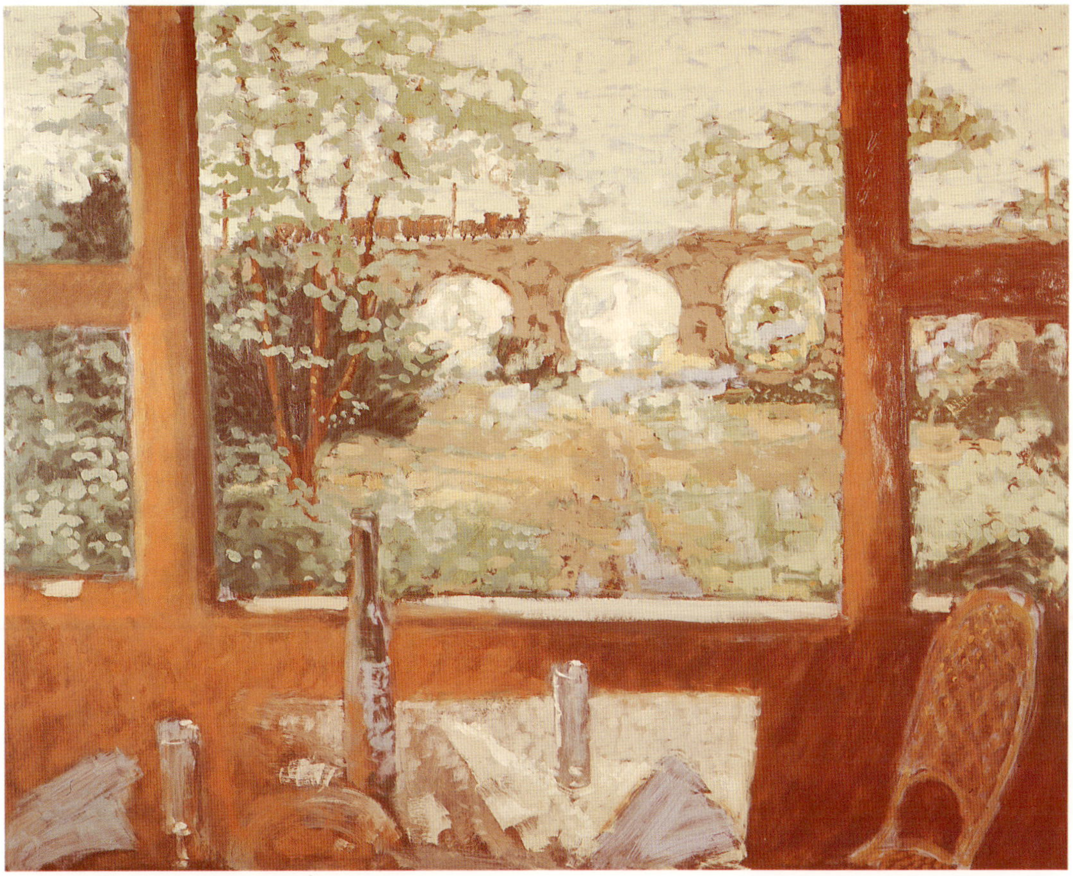

Part Eight - Parks

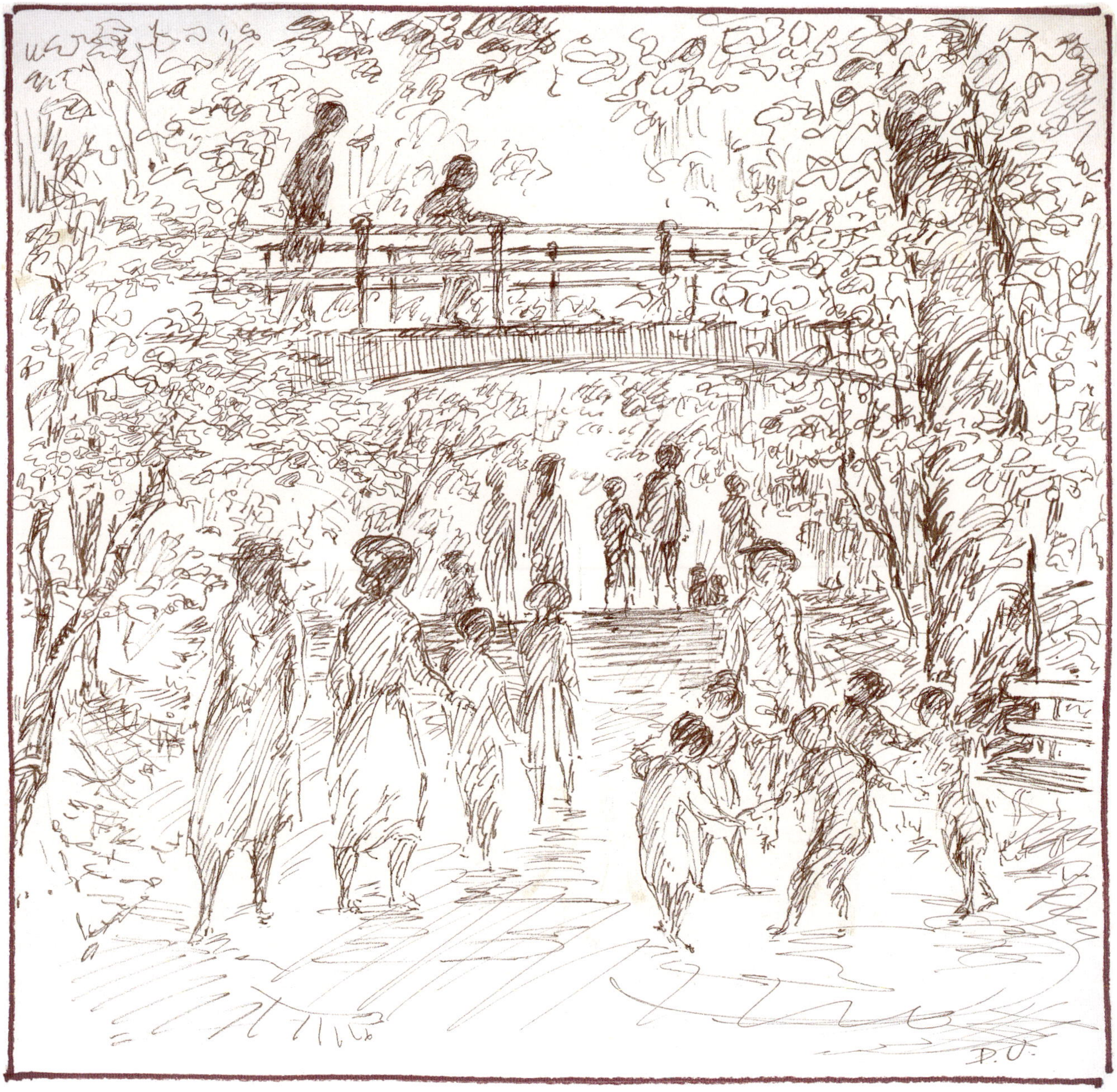

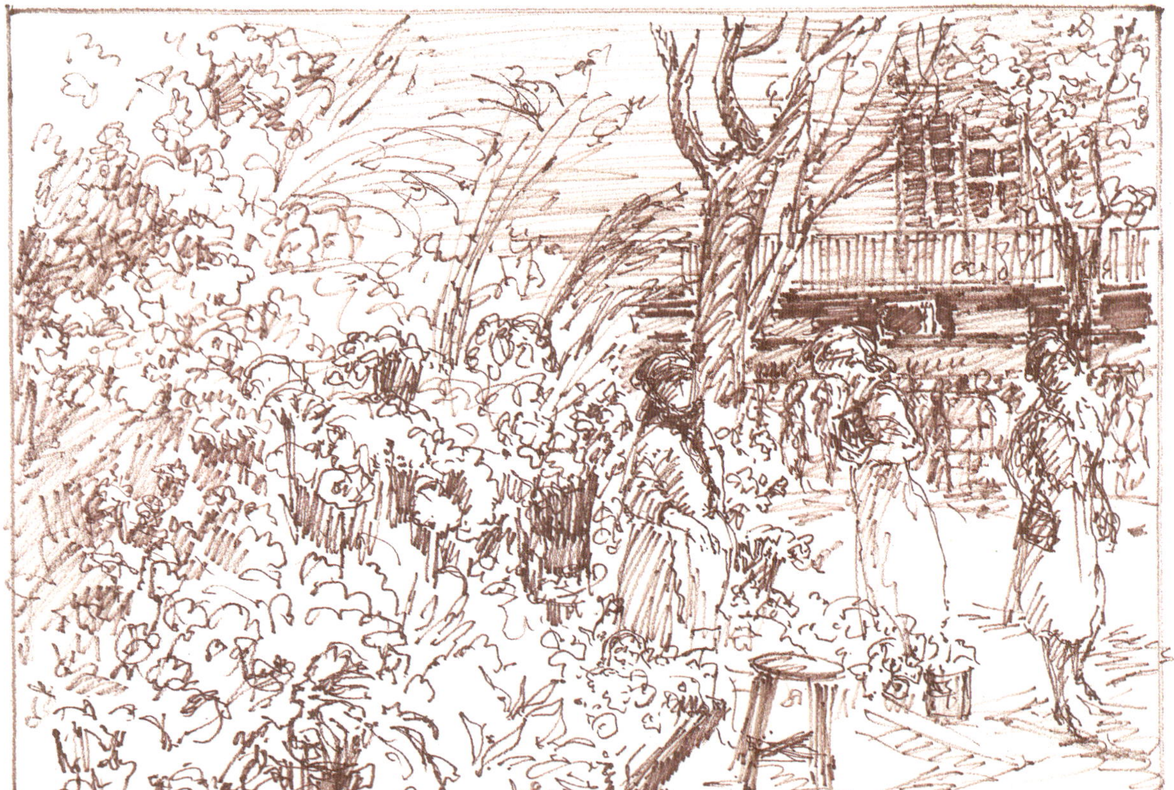

To be conscious of one's presence and talents shared with others and given to all - that's the artist's life.

Public parks have left many memories often called upon. The pleasures evident in the response of people who populate them on sunny days is what the pen seeks. The relaxed activities in contrast to children who push and pull from parents protecting hands on paths shaded by still shadows captivates the eye.

Each park wherever, possesses their own unique personality as my parks have theirs. Having enjoyed many beautiful parks, parts and moments of each seem ever on call when needed. Parks visited included ones in Kyoto, Vienna, Amsterdam, Paris, London, Helsinki, New York and Chicago. There has been no attempt in my drawings to identify them. Rather, they are subject notes expressing only the response to the quality remembered to be captured in line rather than in pigment.

It is the essence, the feeling felt in each park enjoyed that is important, to capture it the moment it surfaces from memory.

You have your park. Close your eyes and visualize it. What your mind's eye brings into focus is what impressed you most. Now draw a line around it. Once done, its presence will continue to bring pleasure. Ah! would everyone draw their line. What understanding and pleasure could be exchanged. Who could tell where it would lead.

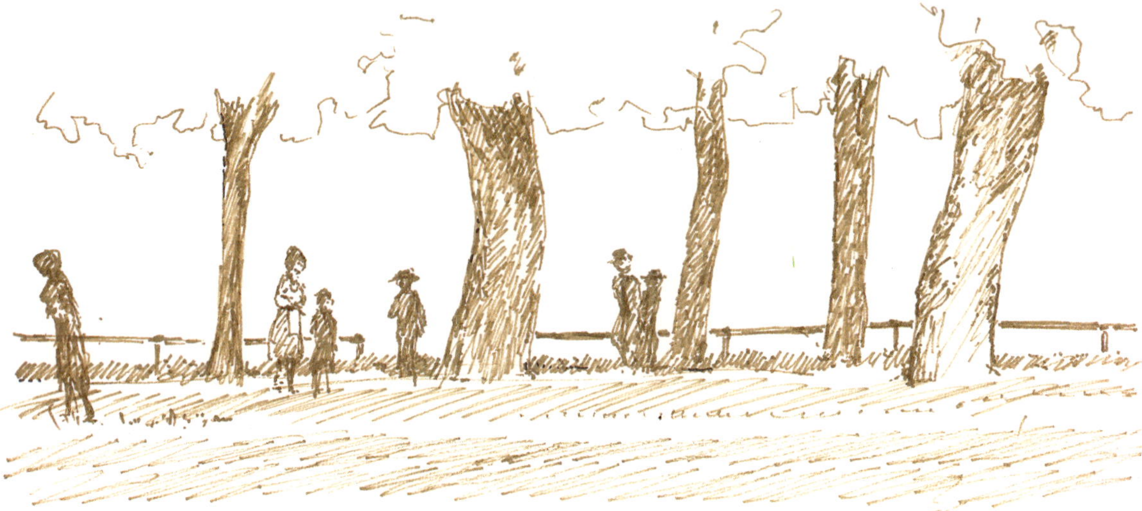

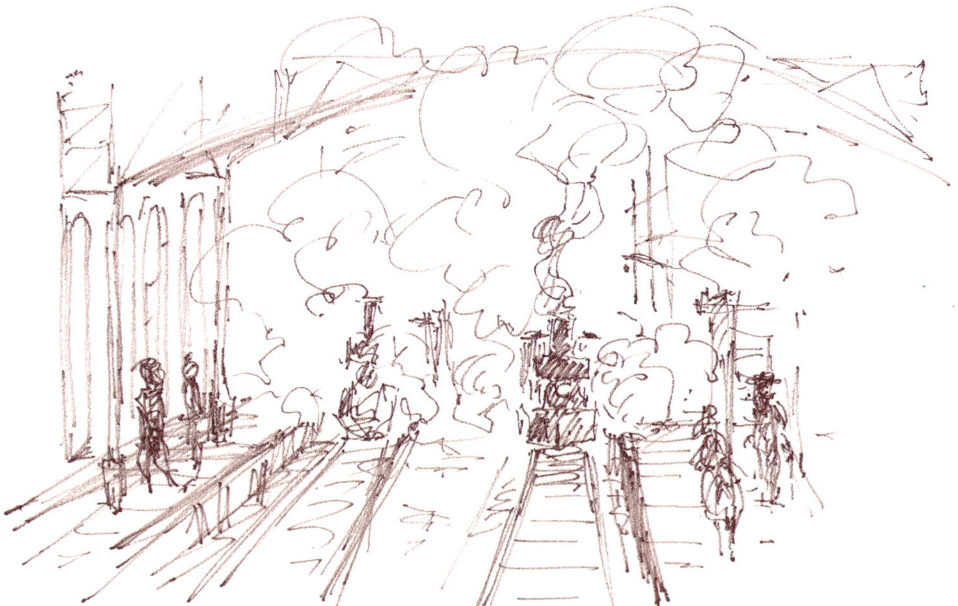

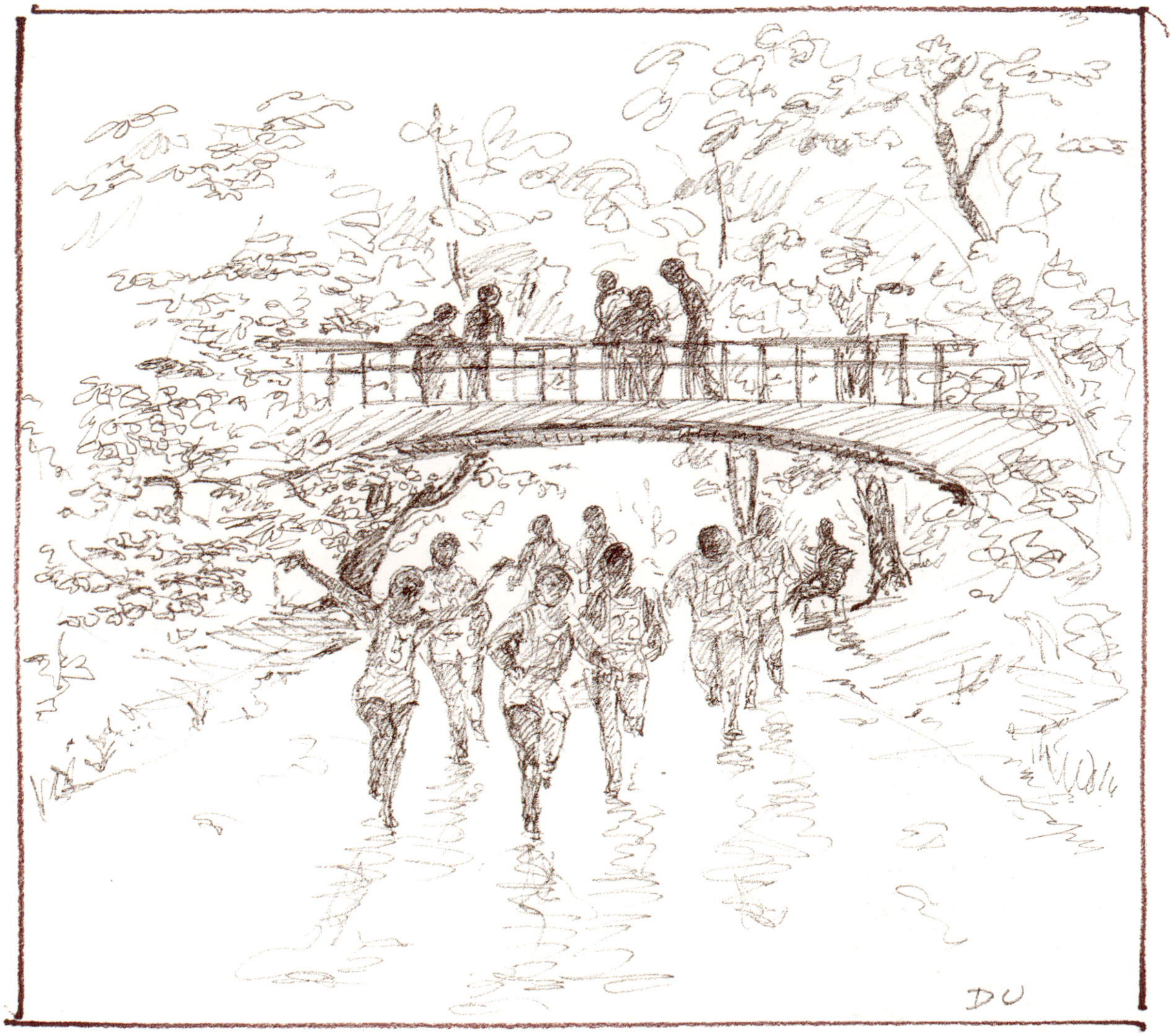
DU

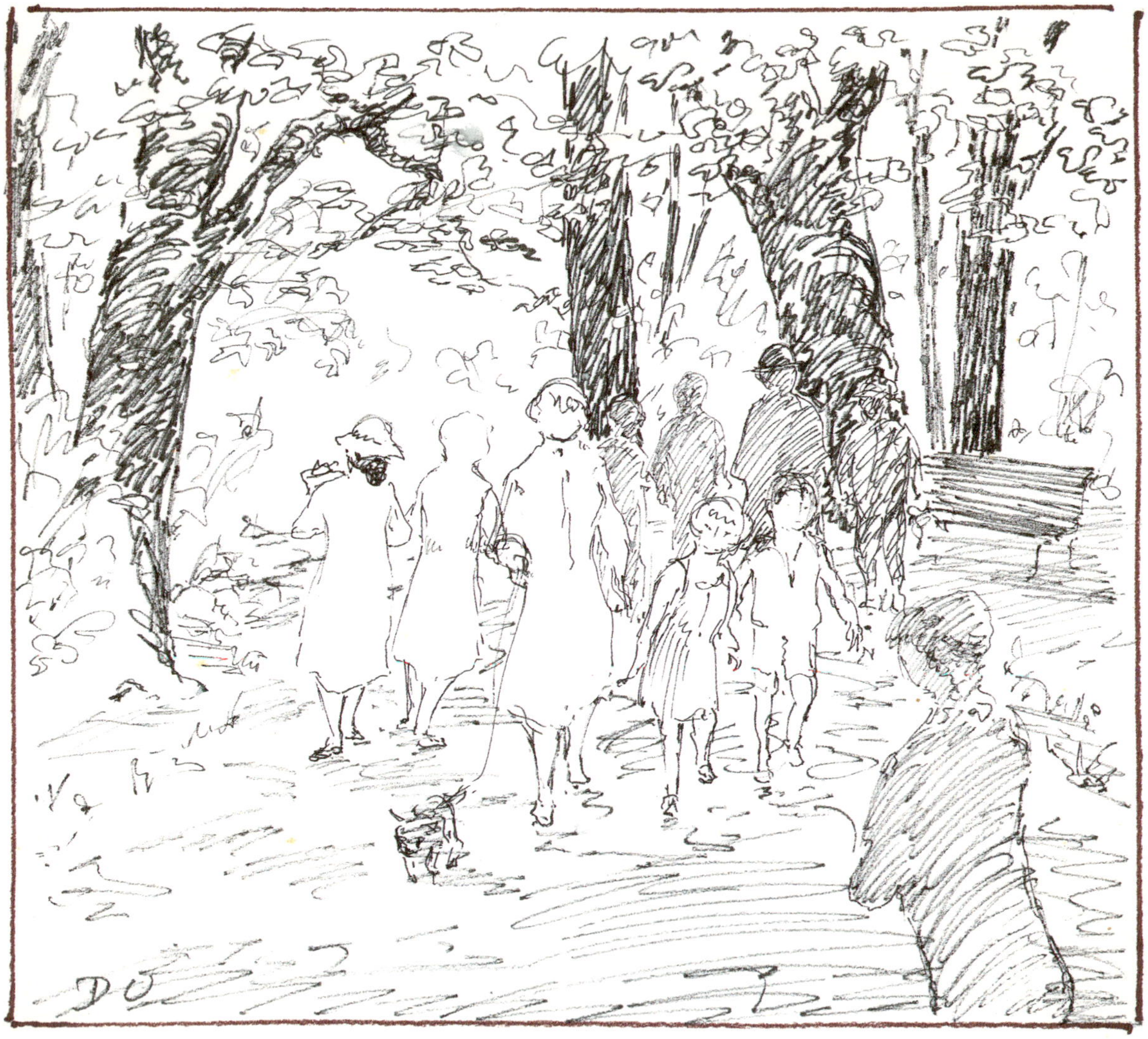

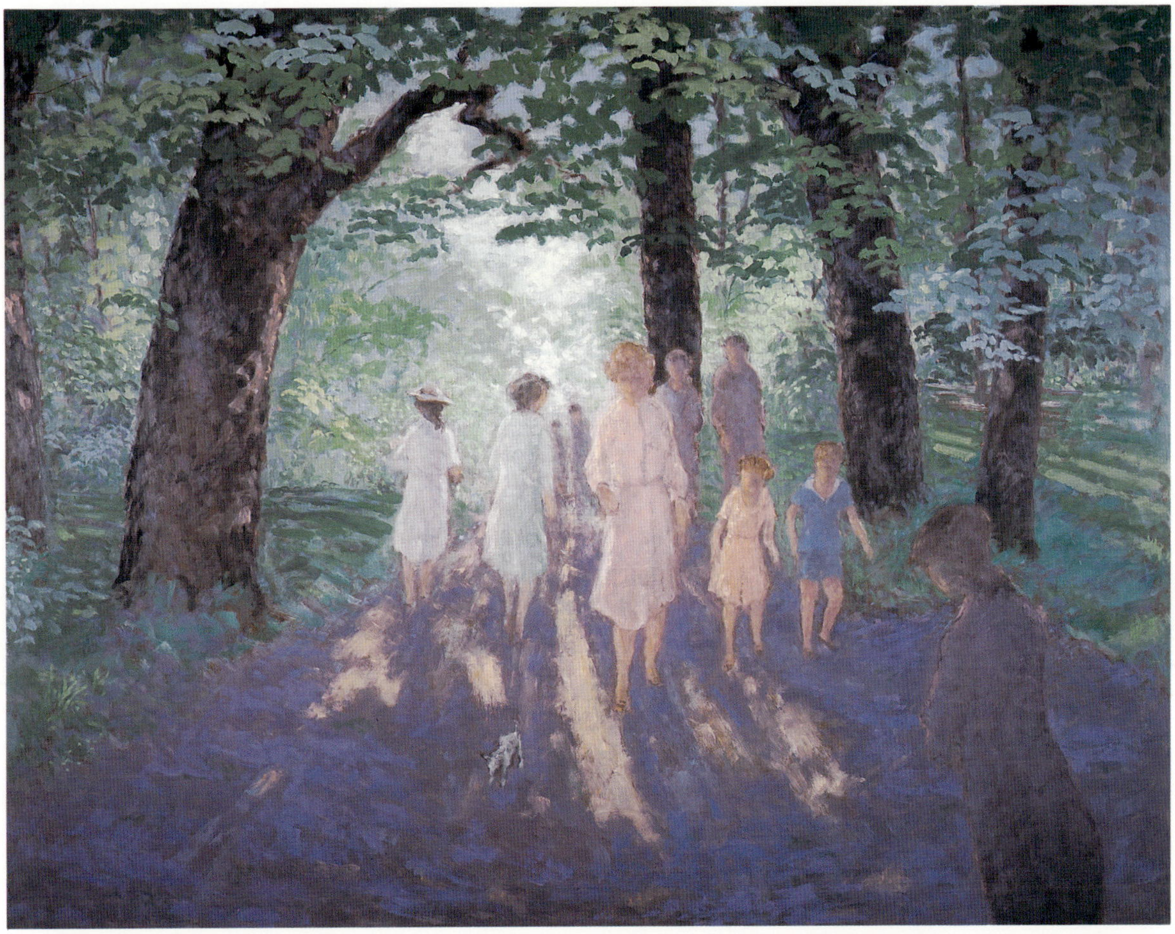

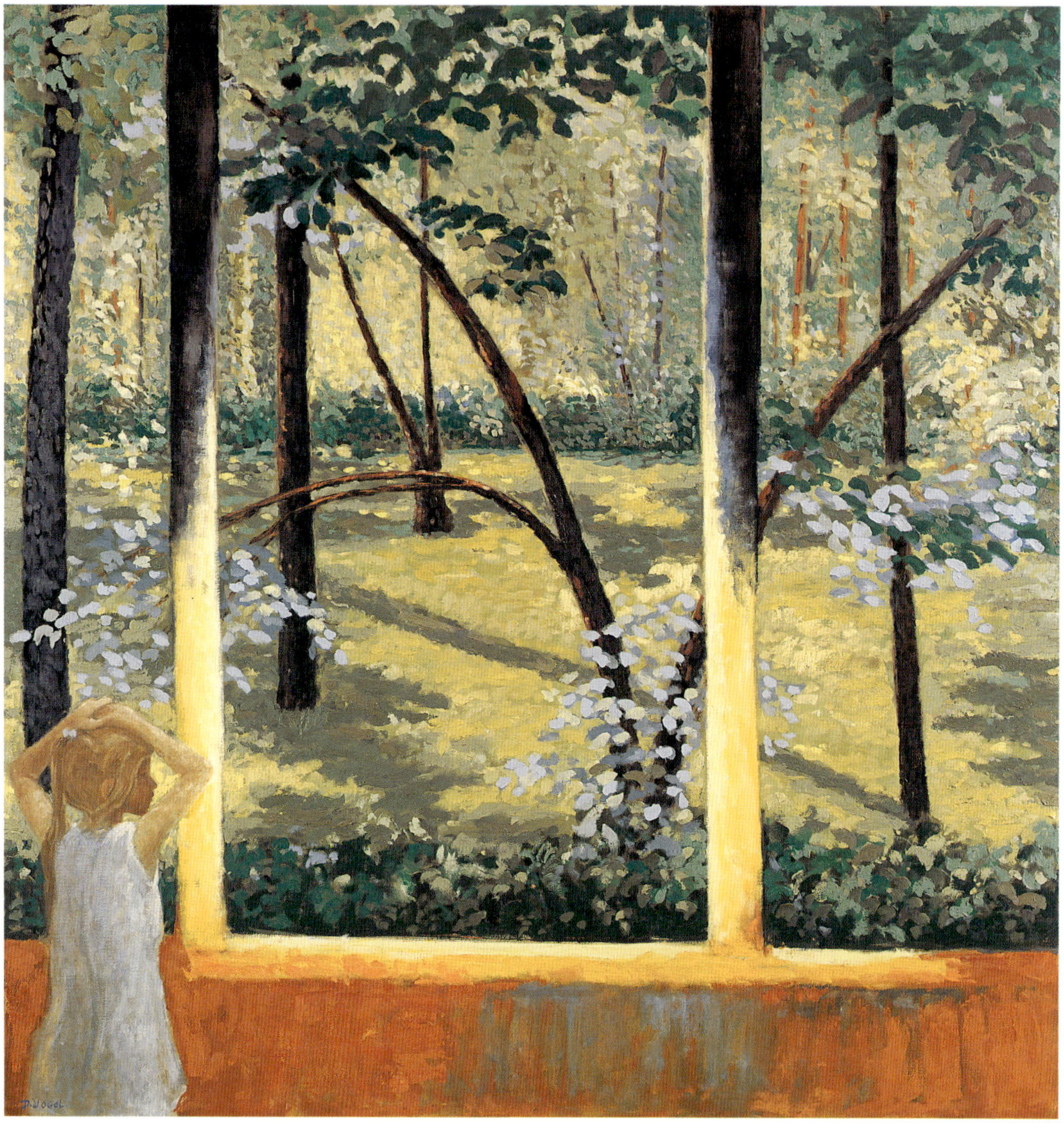
D.VOGEL

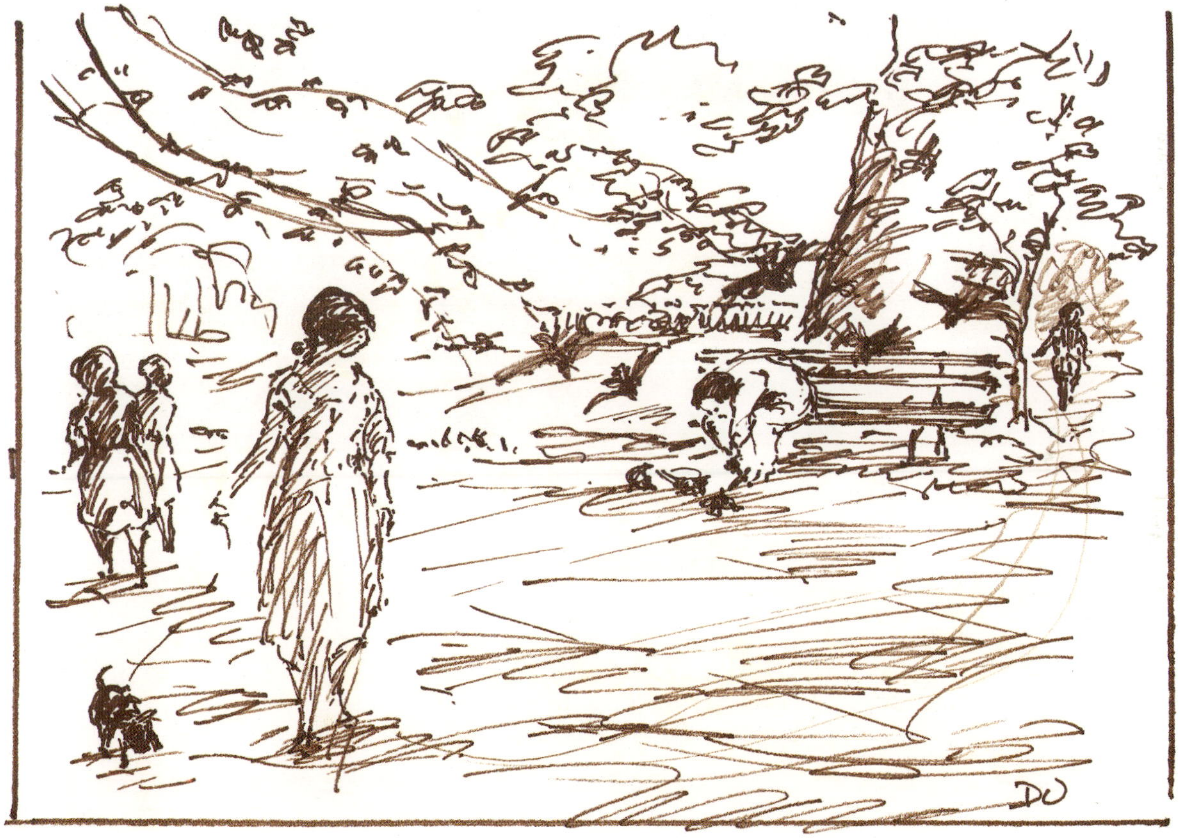
DU

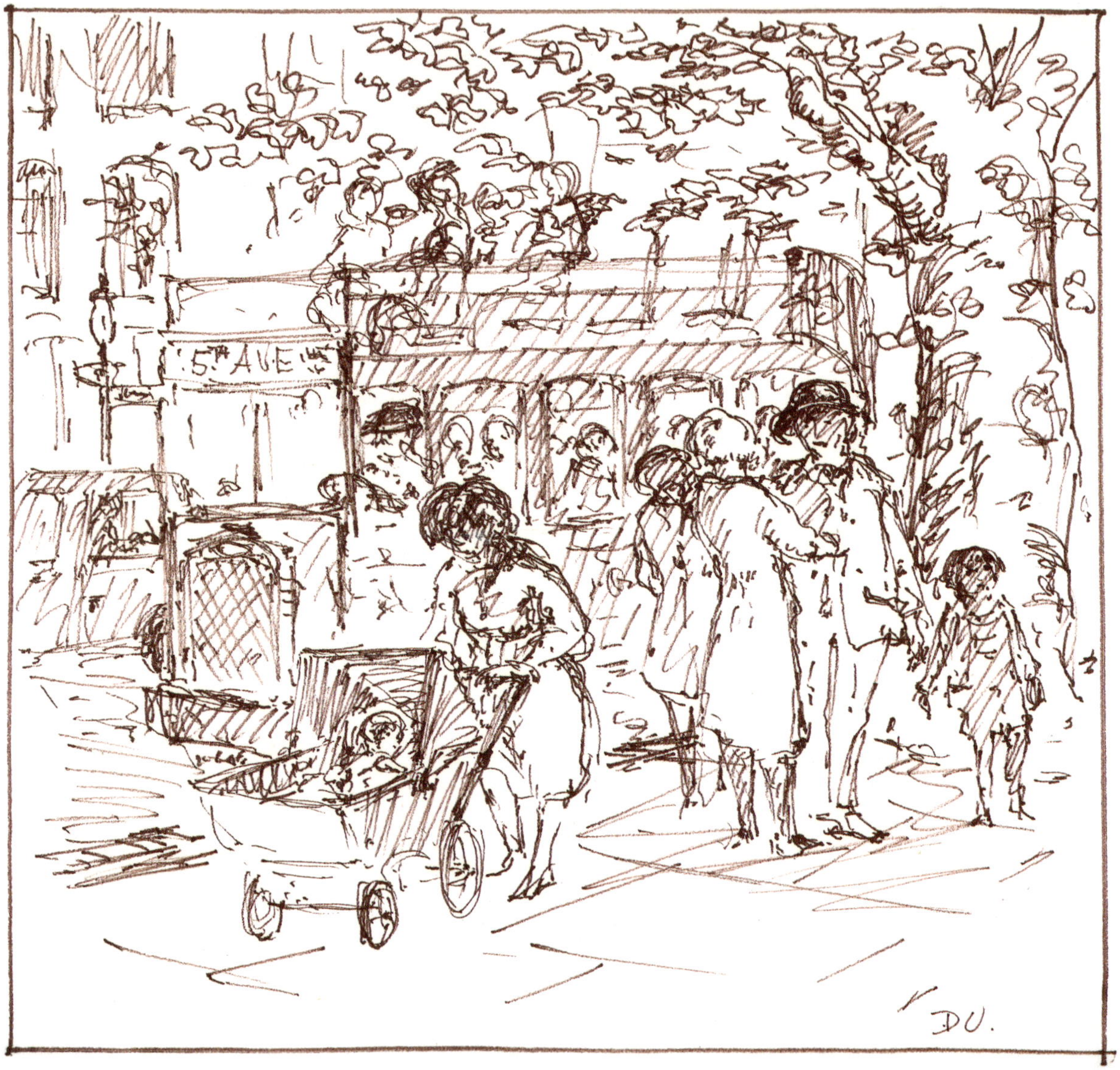
5TH AVE
DU.

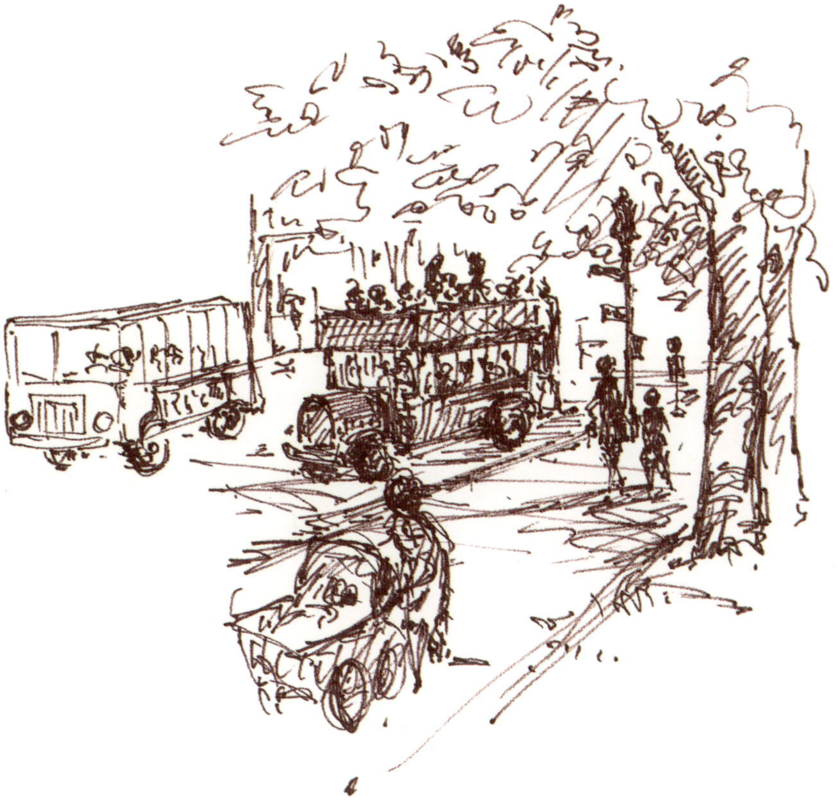

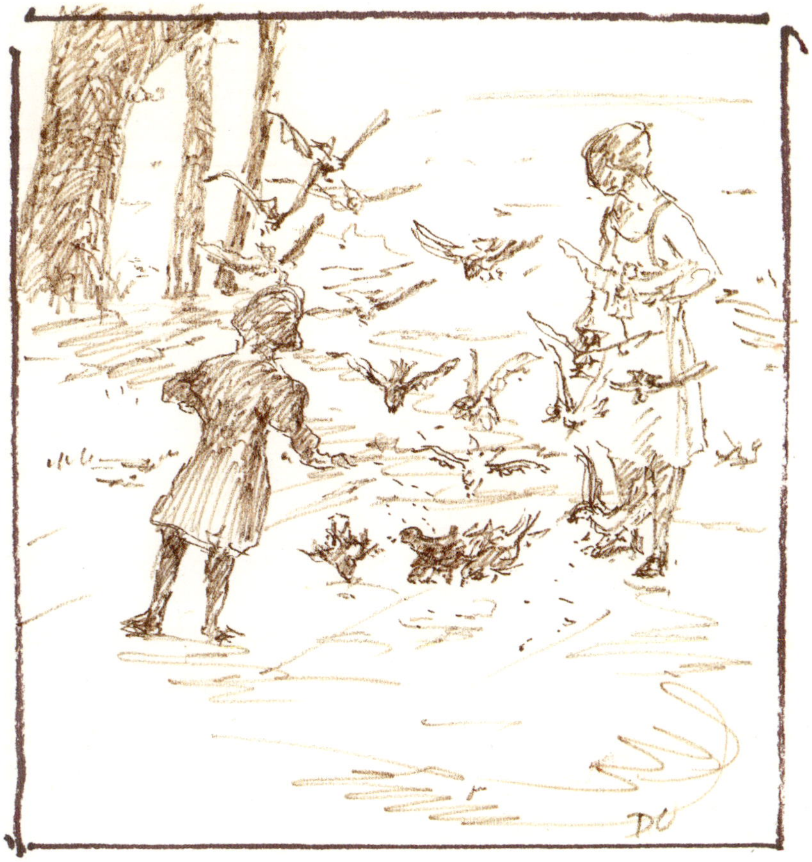
DU

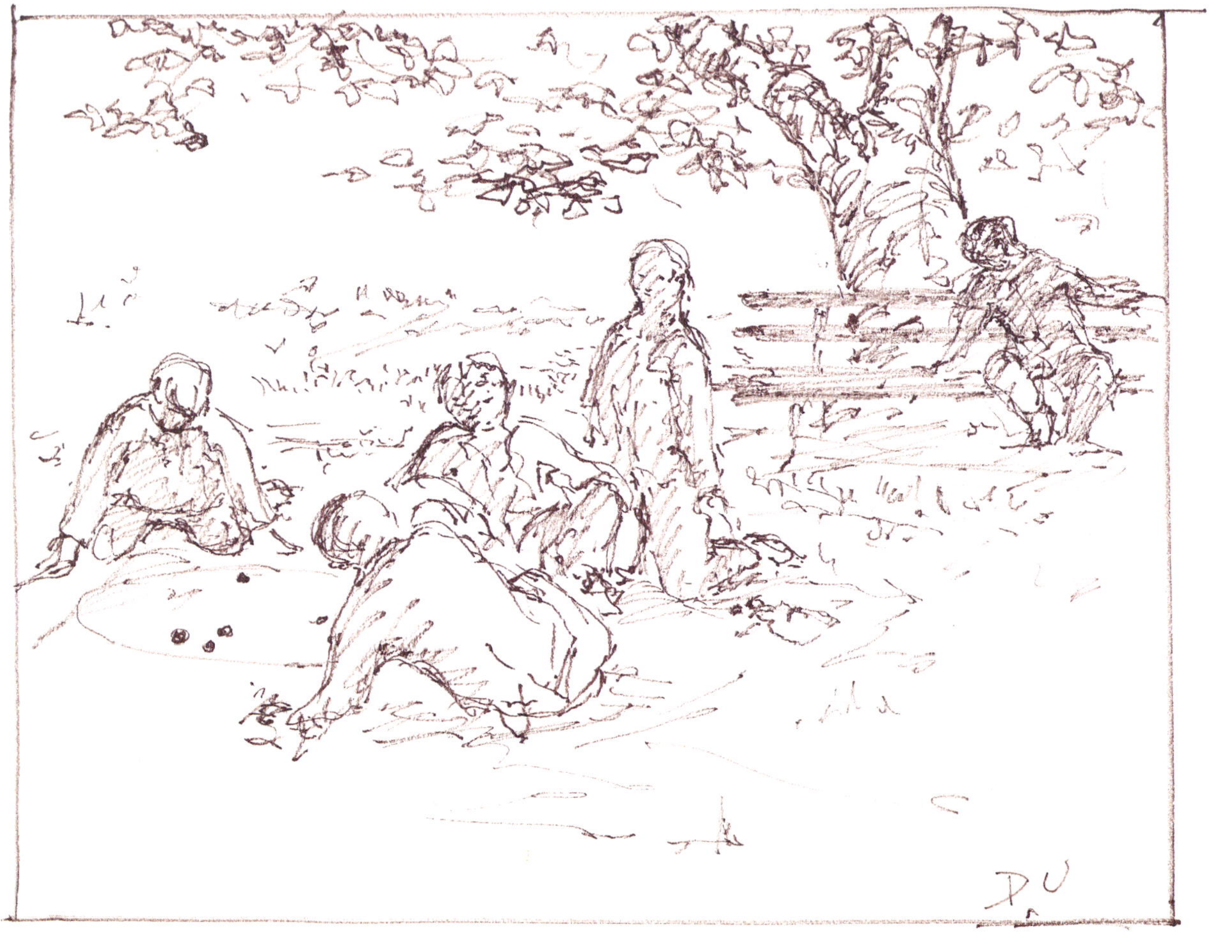

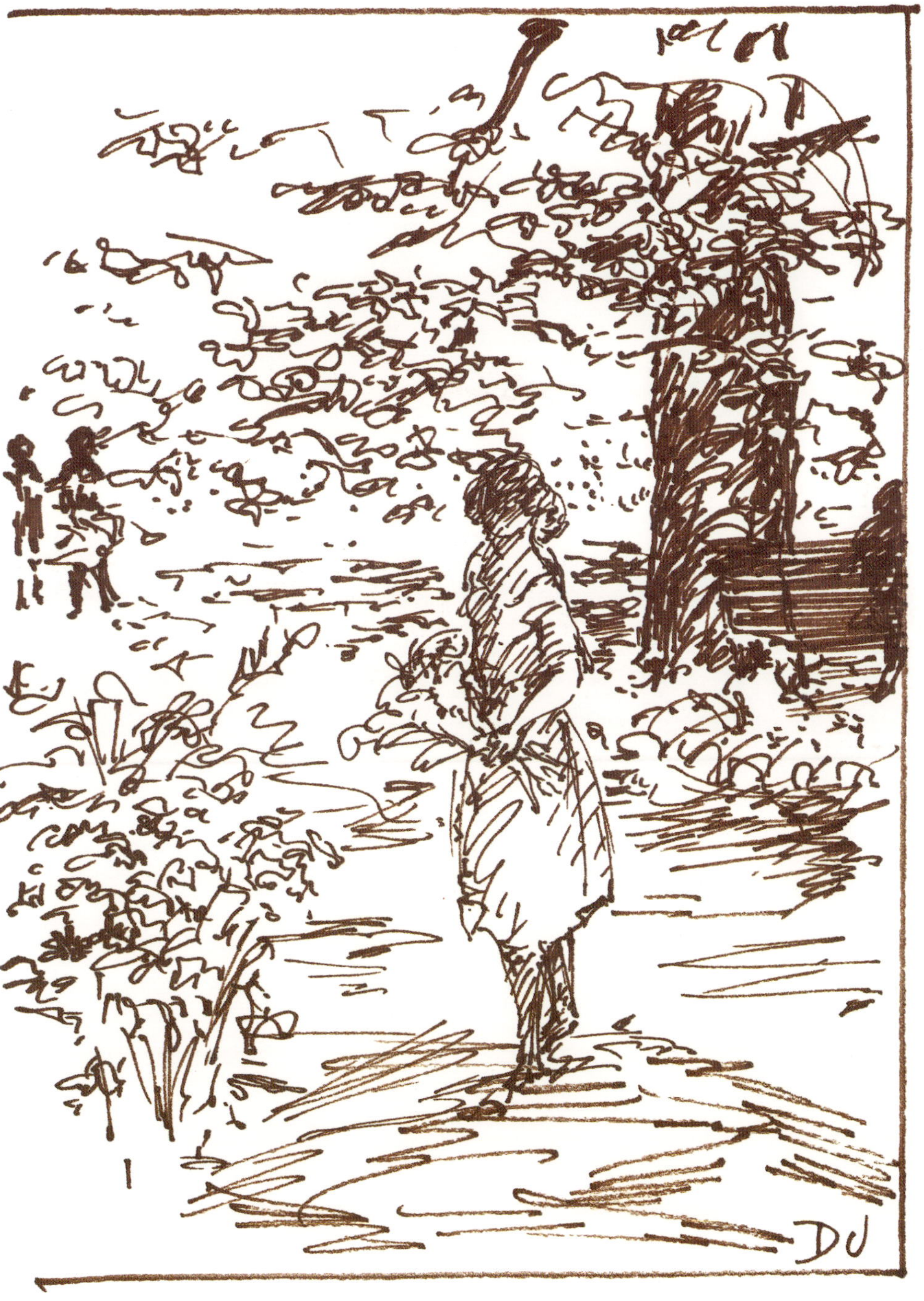

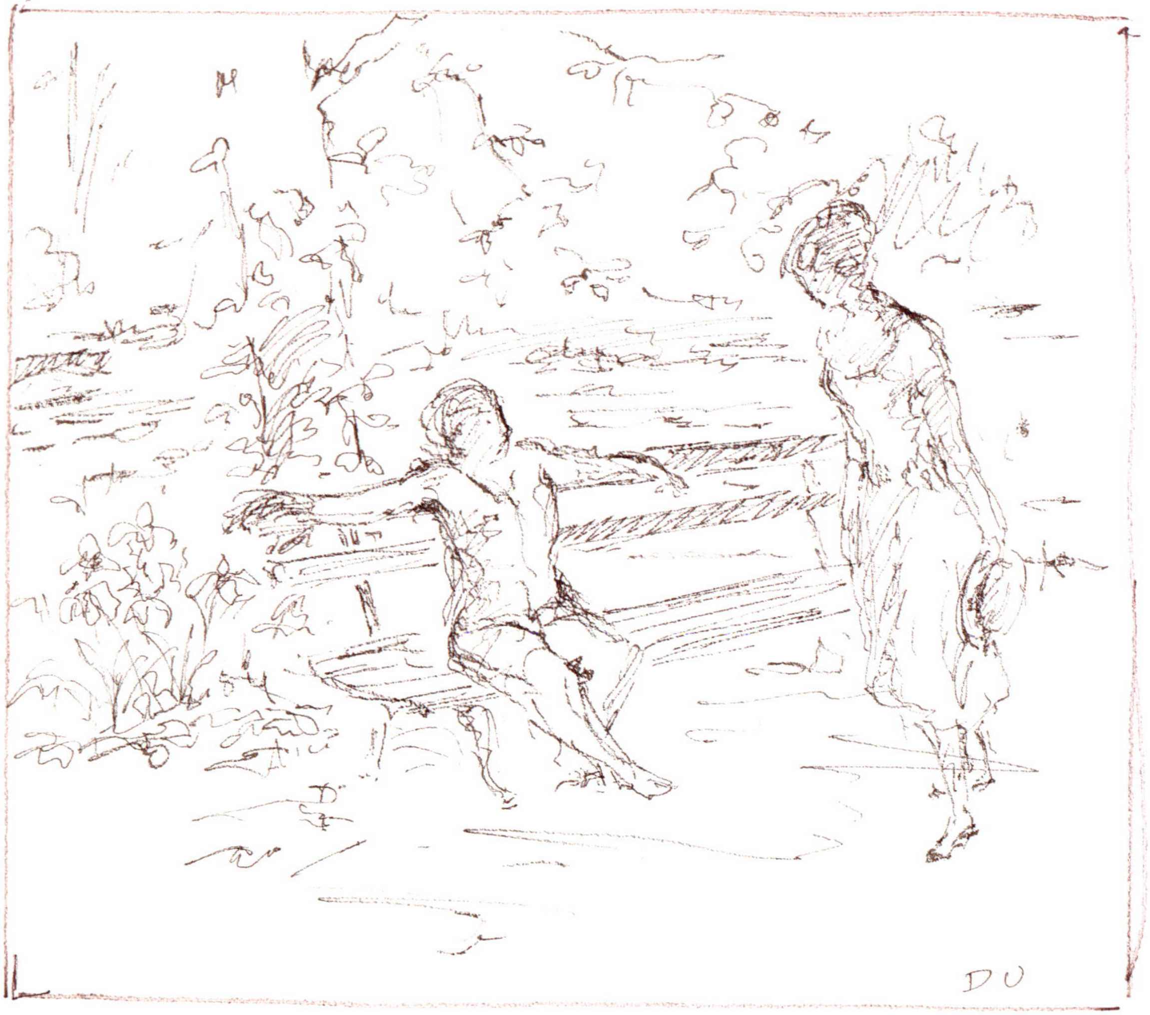
DU

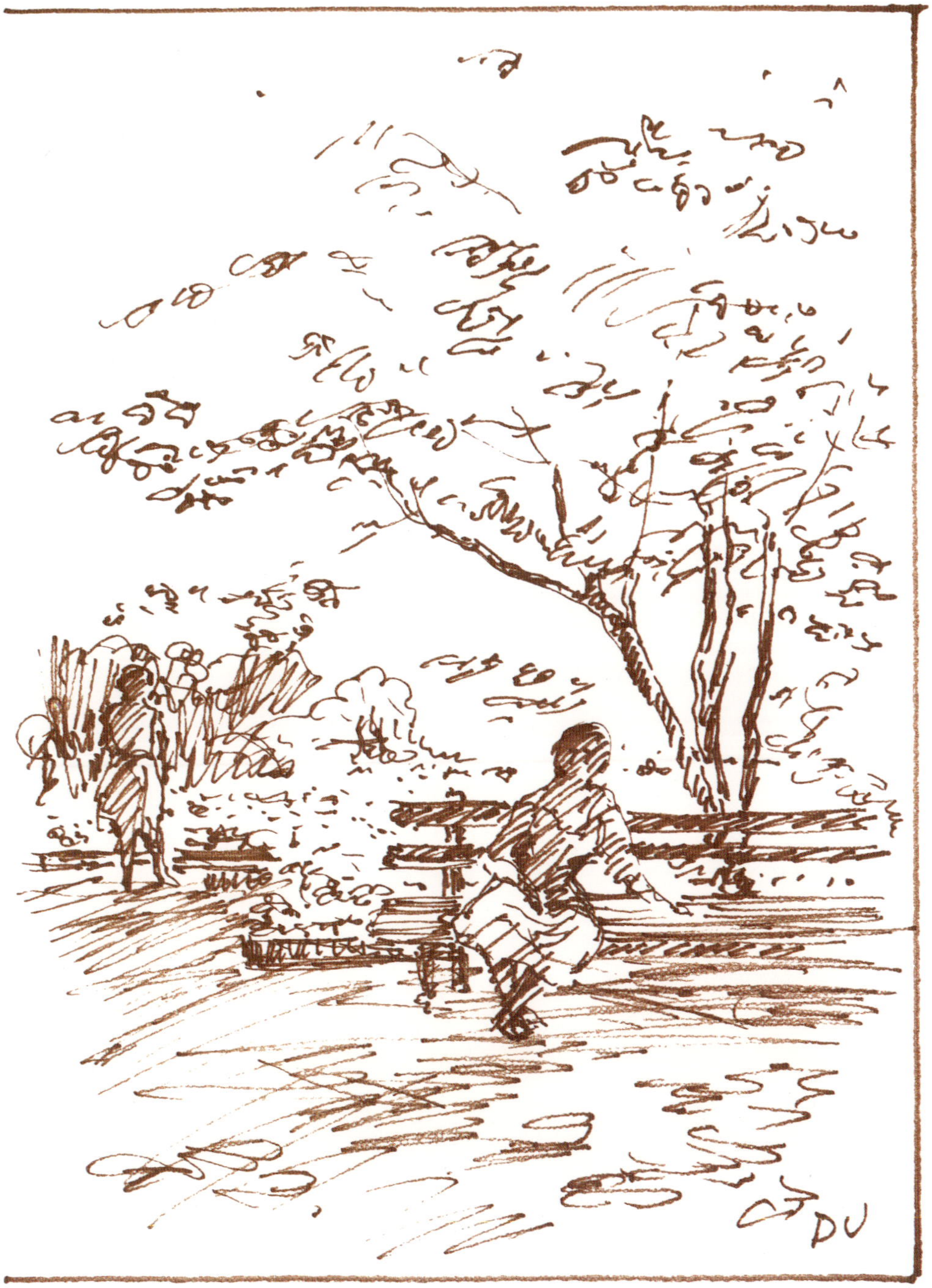
DV

Part Nine - Light and Air

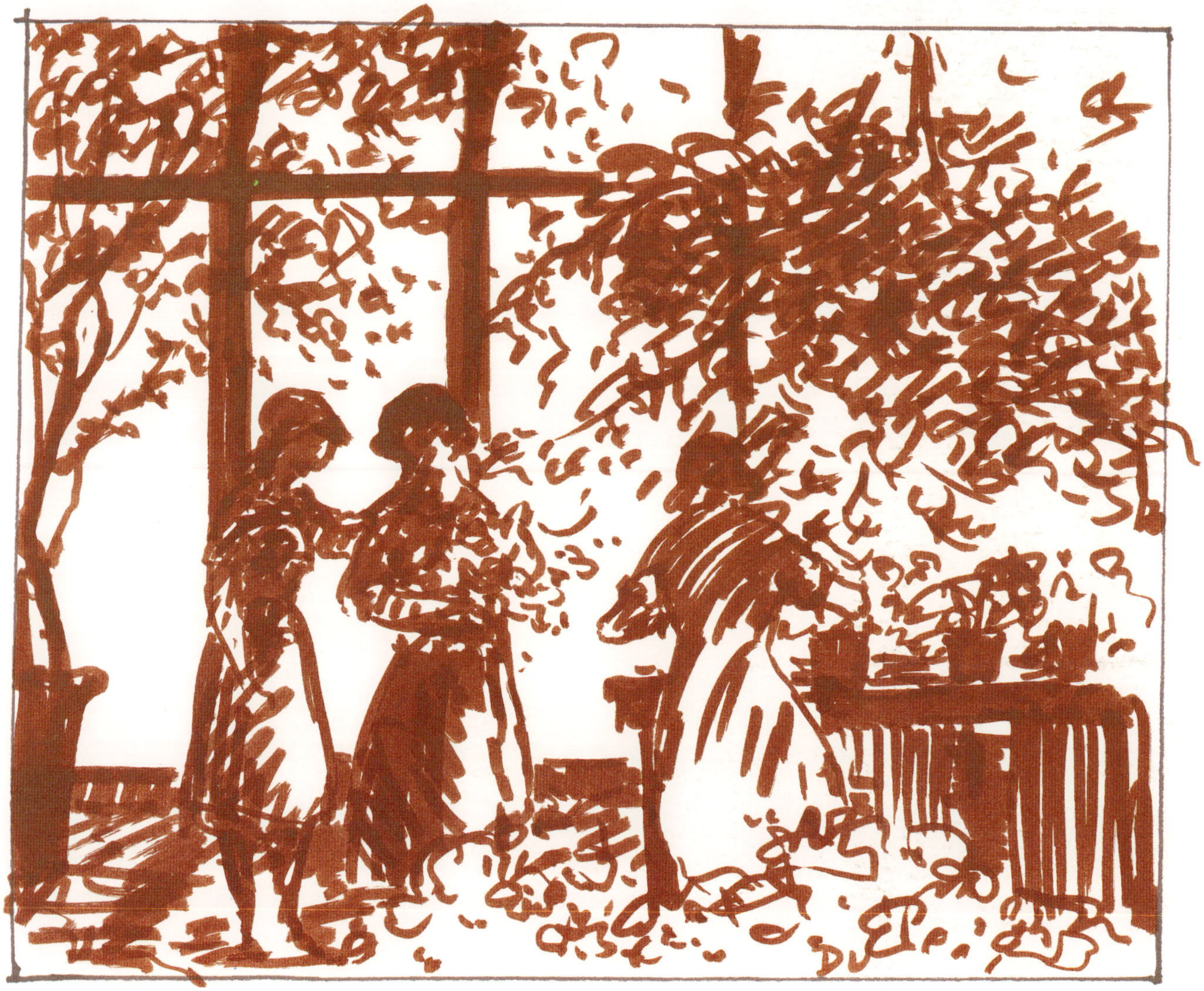

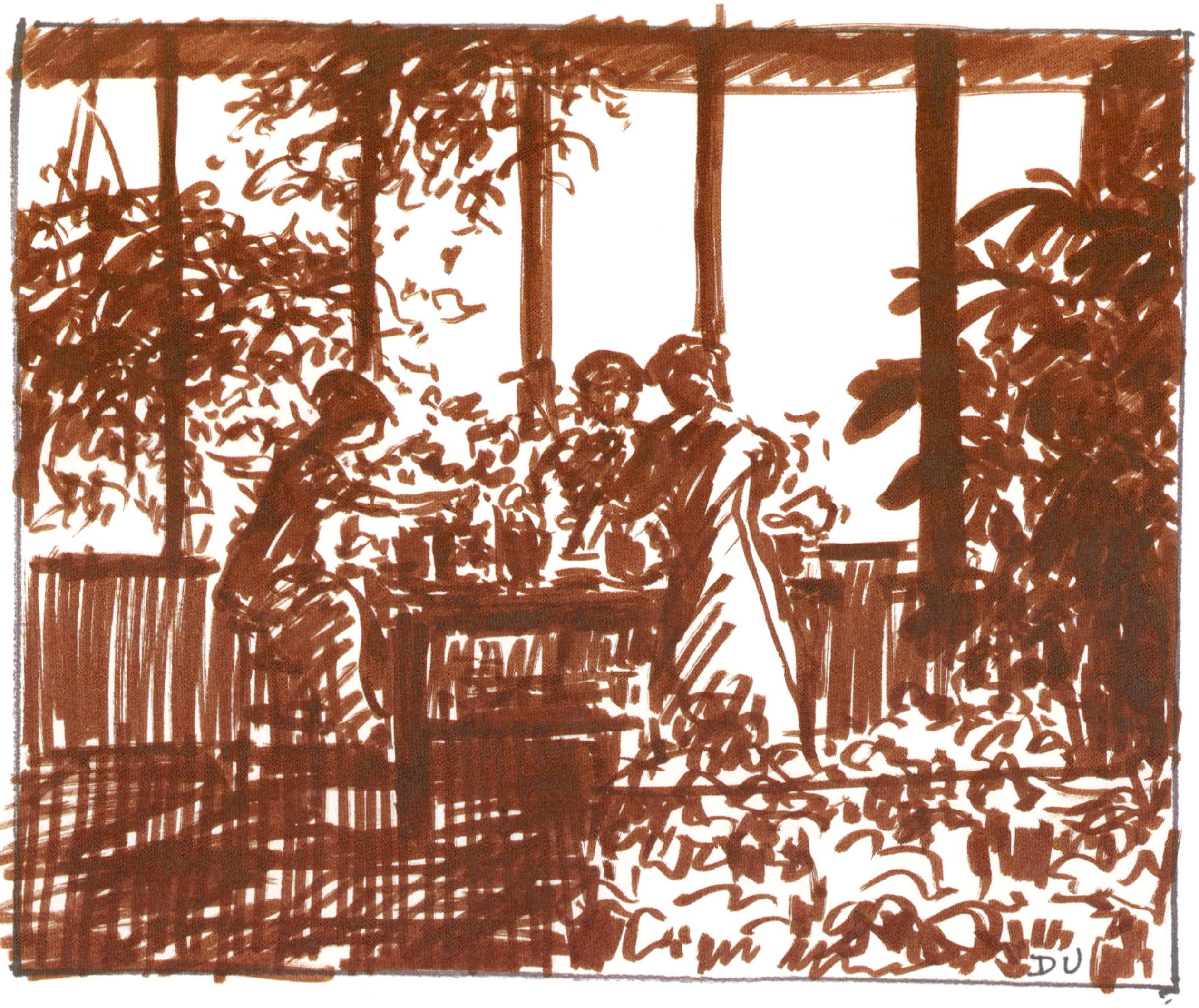
DU

I would not suggest to you how to live. My intent is only to share with you my expressions through my art.

Several years ago I wrote in a catalogue the following in attempting to express what I was seeking in my work. Always risky at best. However here it is. I would only add, in drawing as well,

Bright light
Diminished light
Bringing life to earth
Energy from heaven filtered
Through the dust of past artists

"Time, the most controlling measure of life, is marked by the presence and by the absence of light. Bright to dim, warm to cool, light gives even a sense of sound or silence, of fullness or of a void.

"These are the thoughts I seek to transform with paint, to translate into a personal poetry. And light, in its varying moods and facets is the real medium of my paintings. In each canvas a moment of light is caught and imprisoned, that its image in the eyes of others may lead to quiet moments of reflection, of tranquility and of serene warmth."

It is ever wondrous how bright a light can be expressed with a few strokes drawn with a brush. The varying density of light bringing with it a feeling of air suggesting time and mood becomes a conscious part of the simplest drawing.

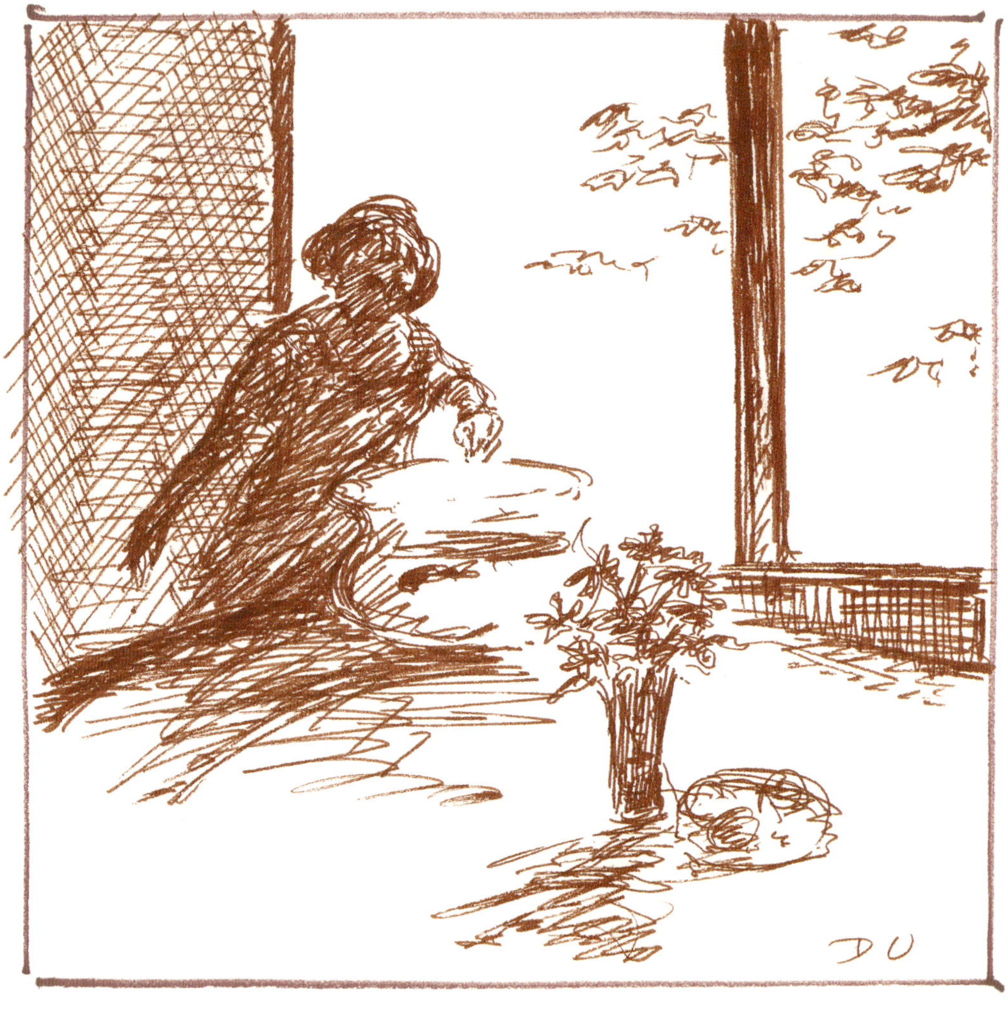
DU

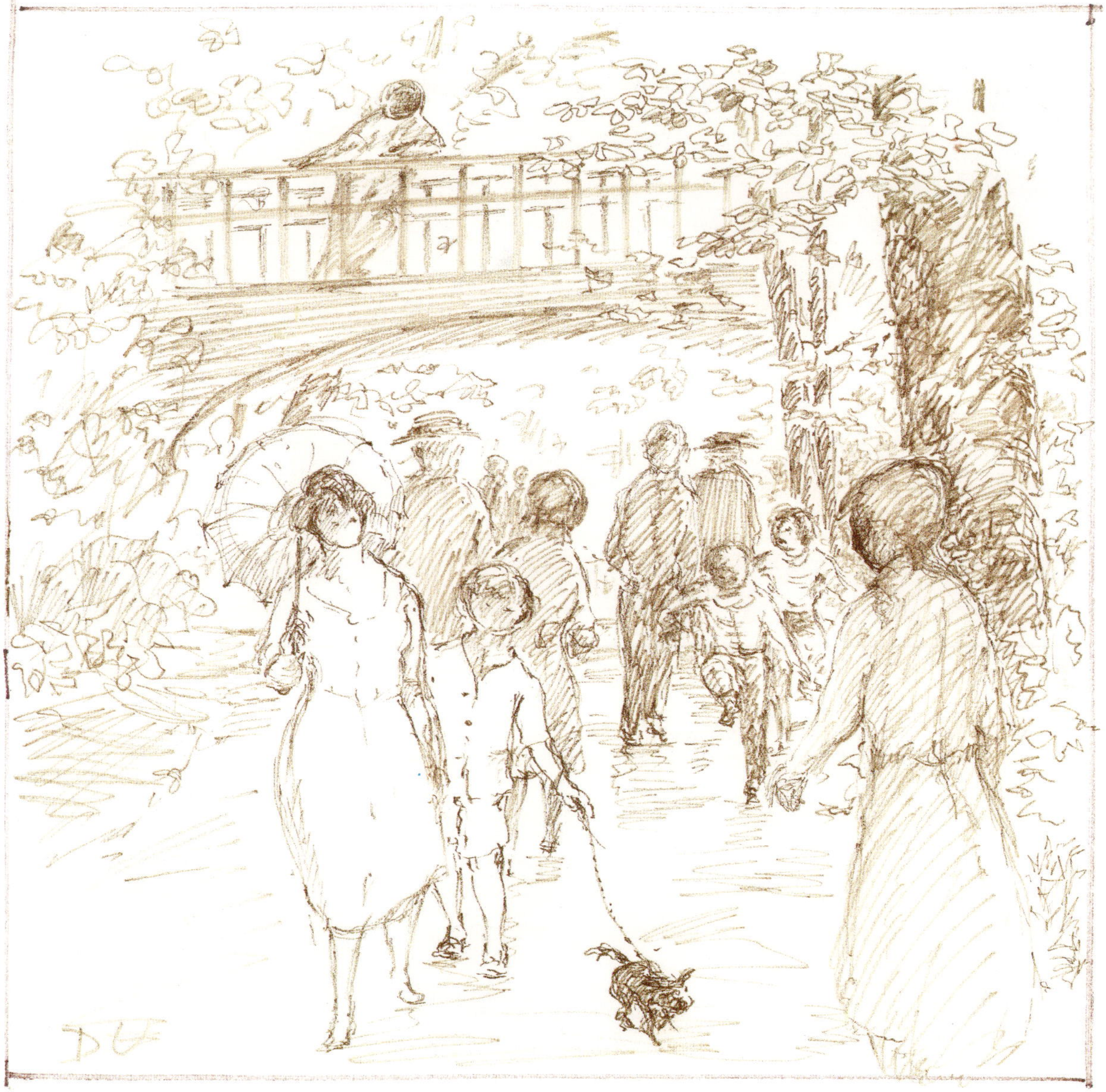

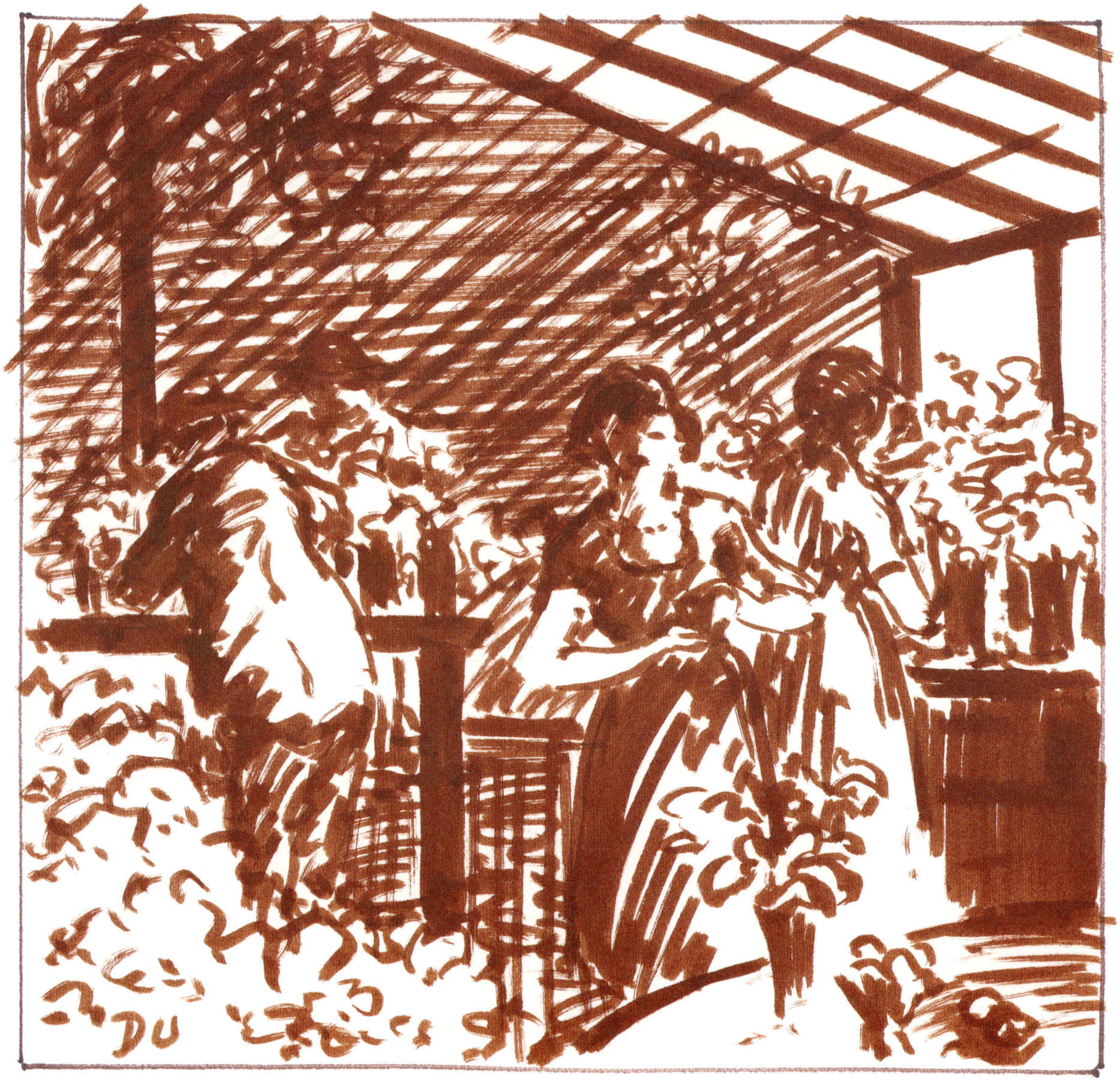

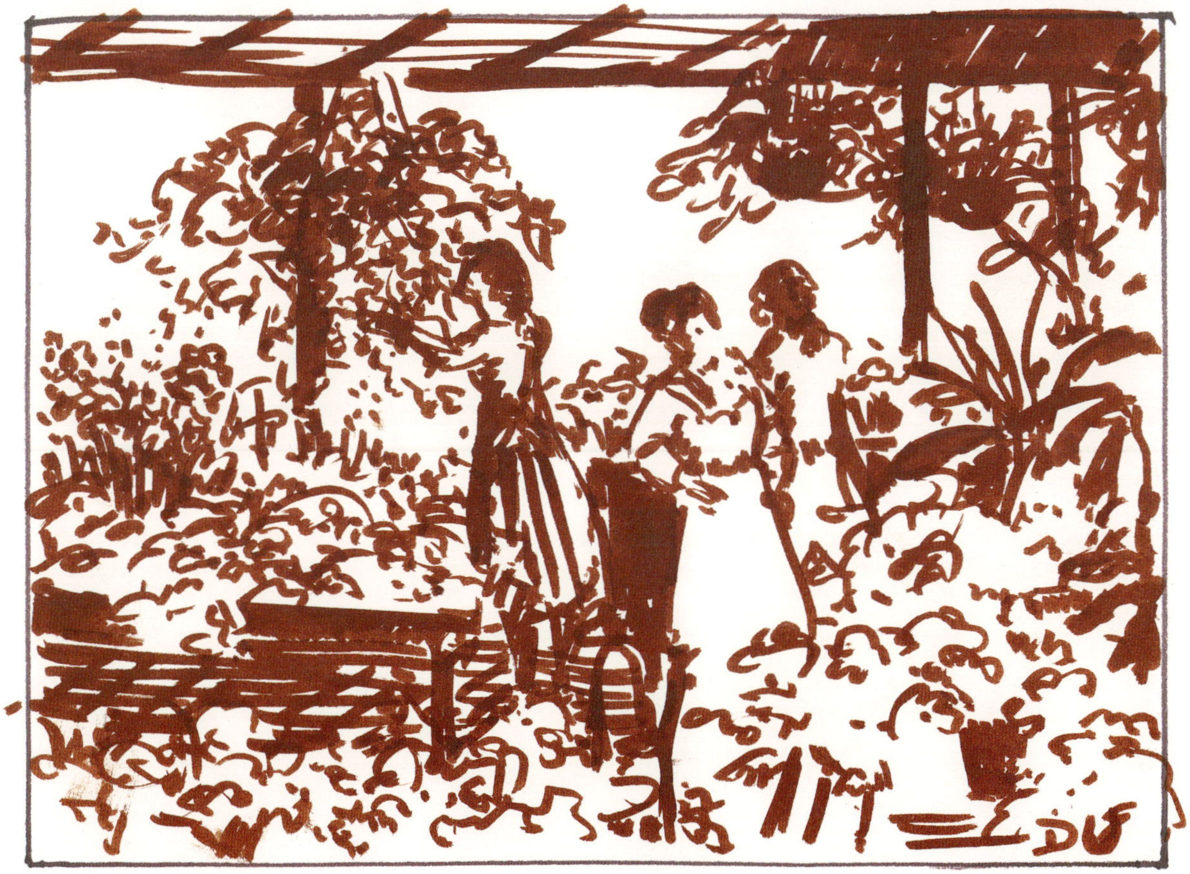
DW

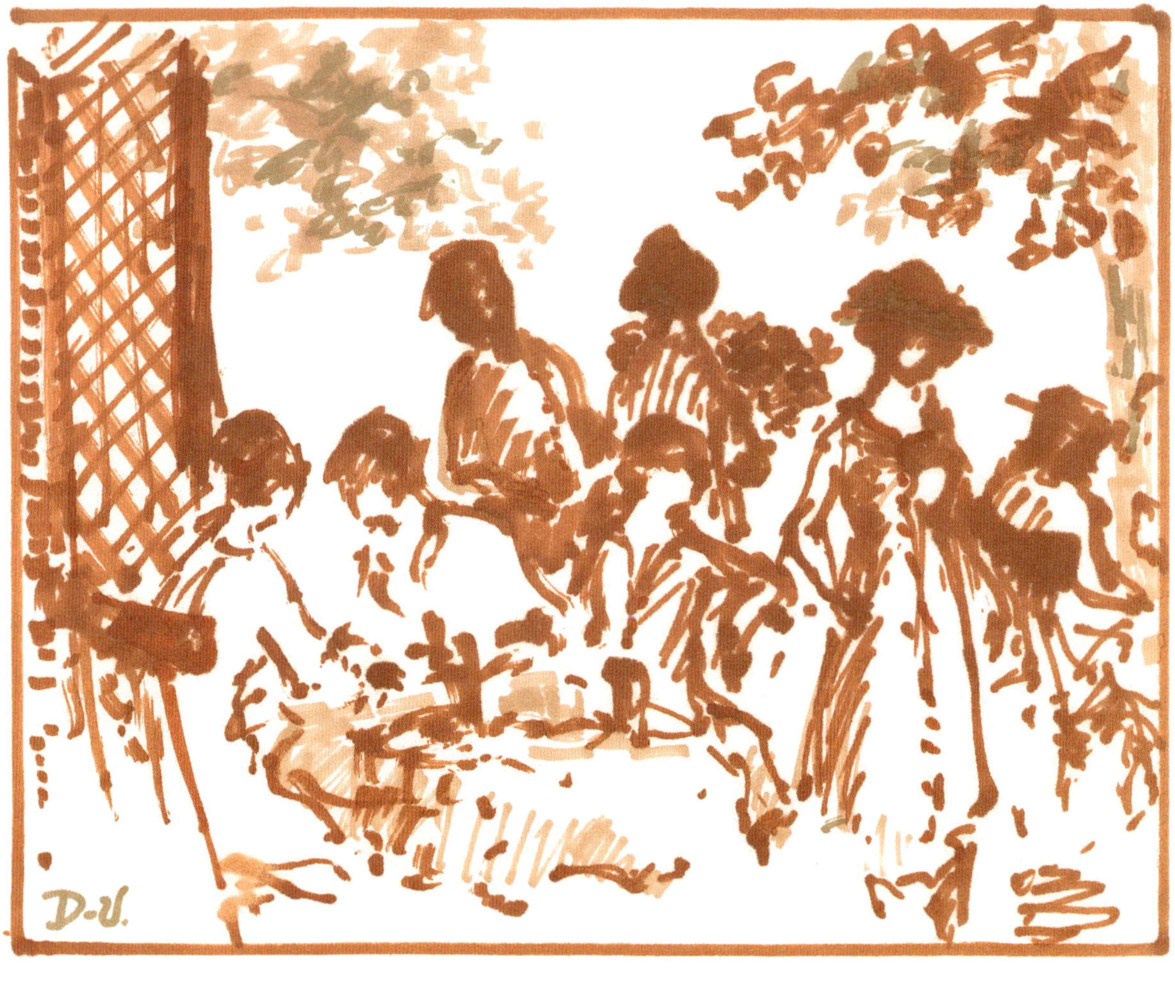
D-V.

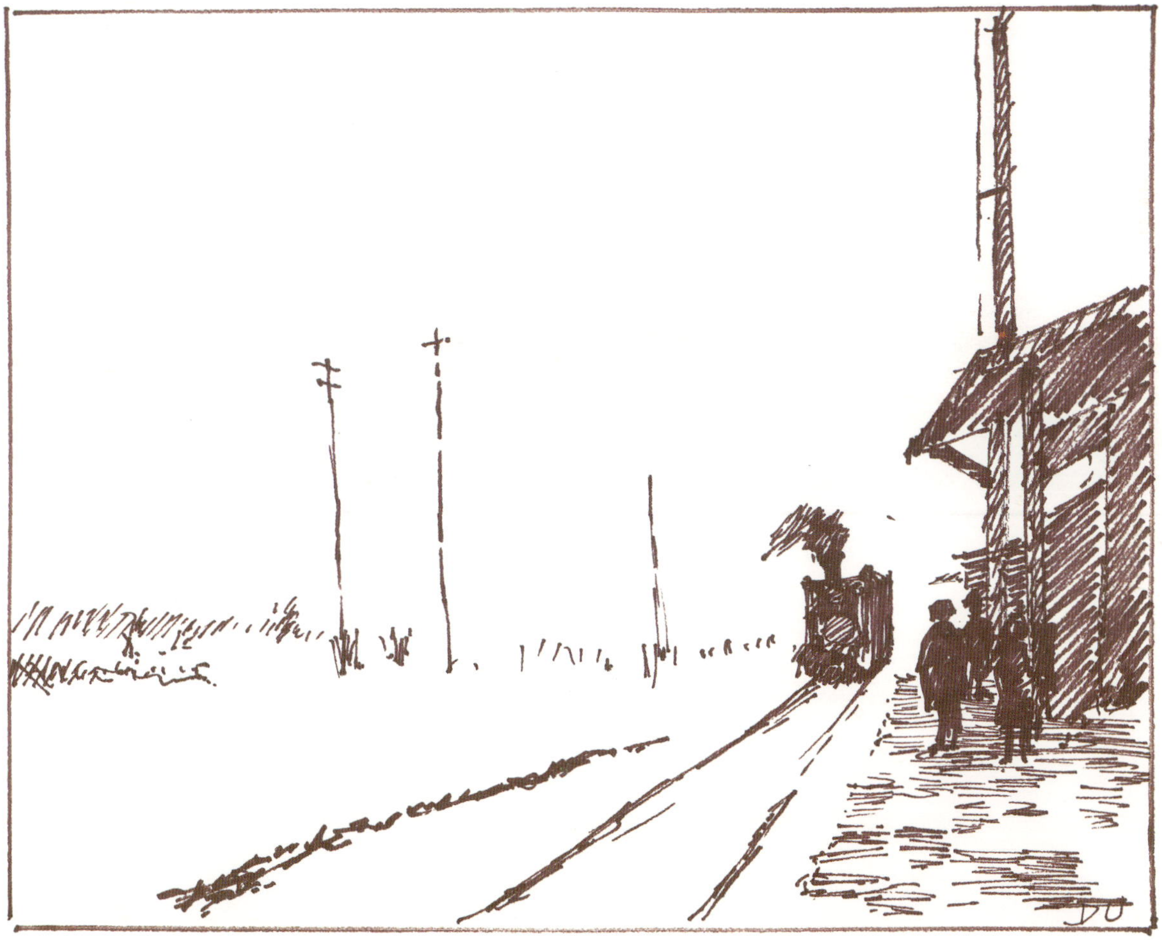

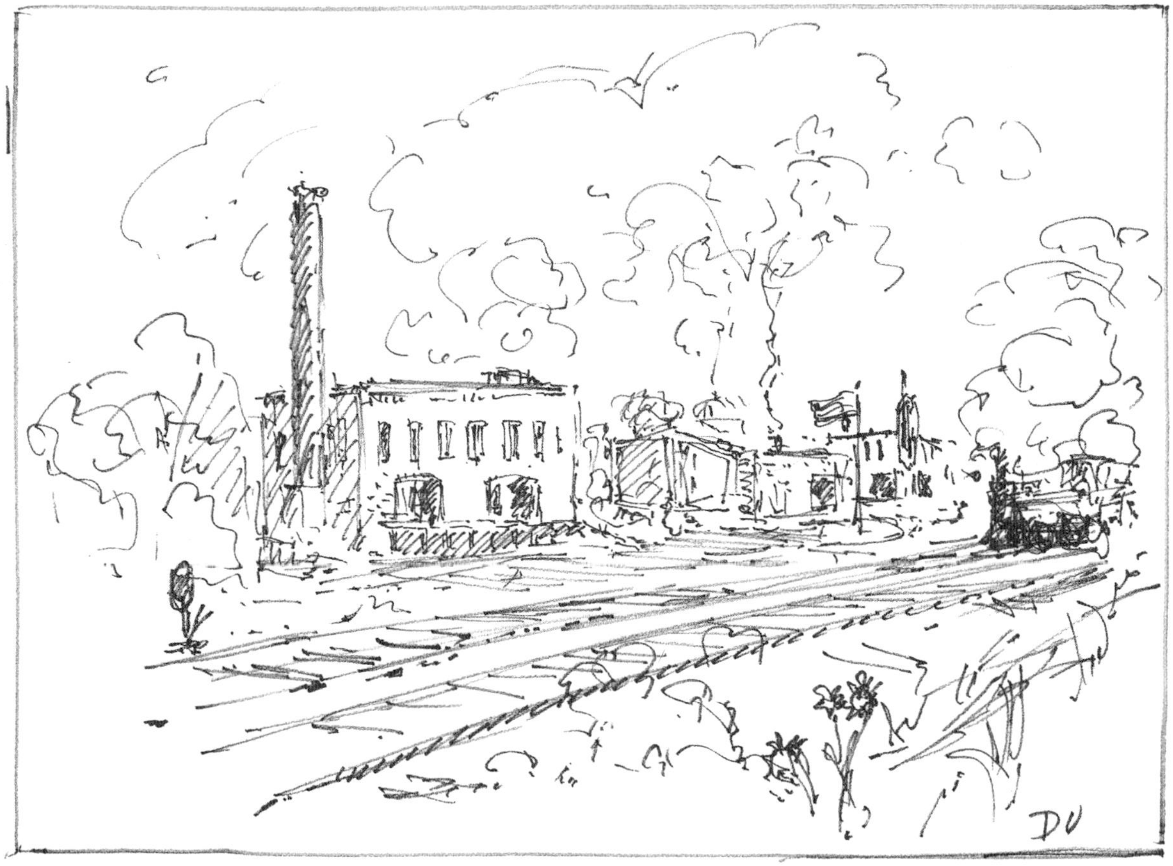
DV

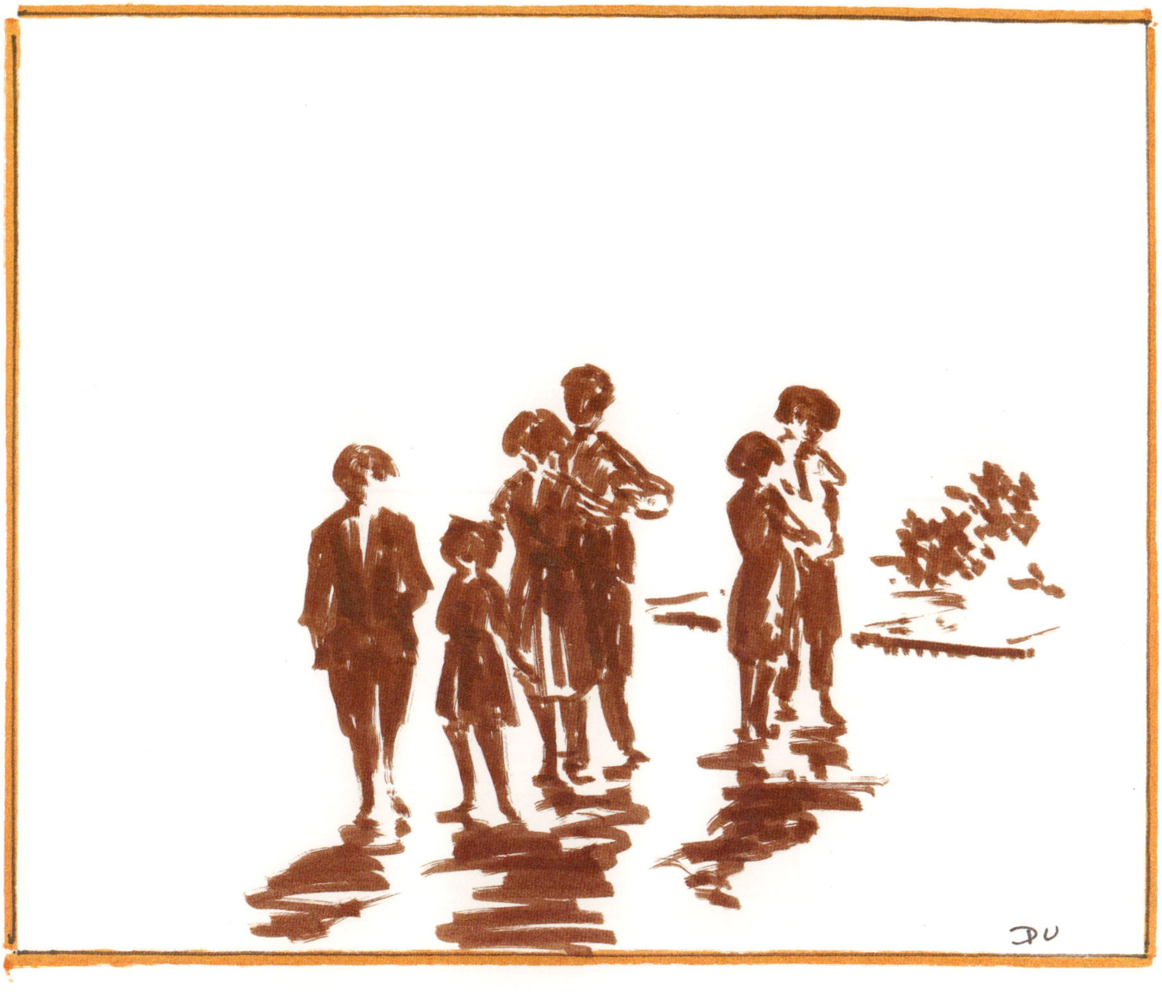

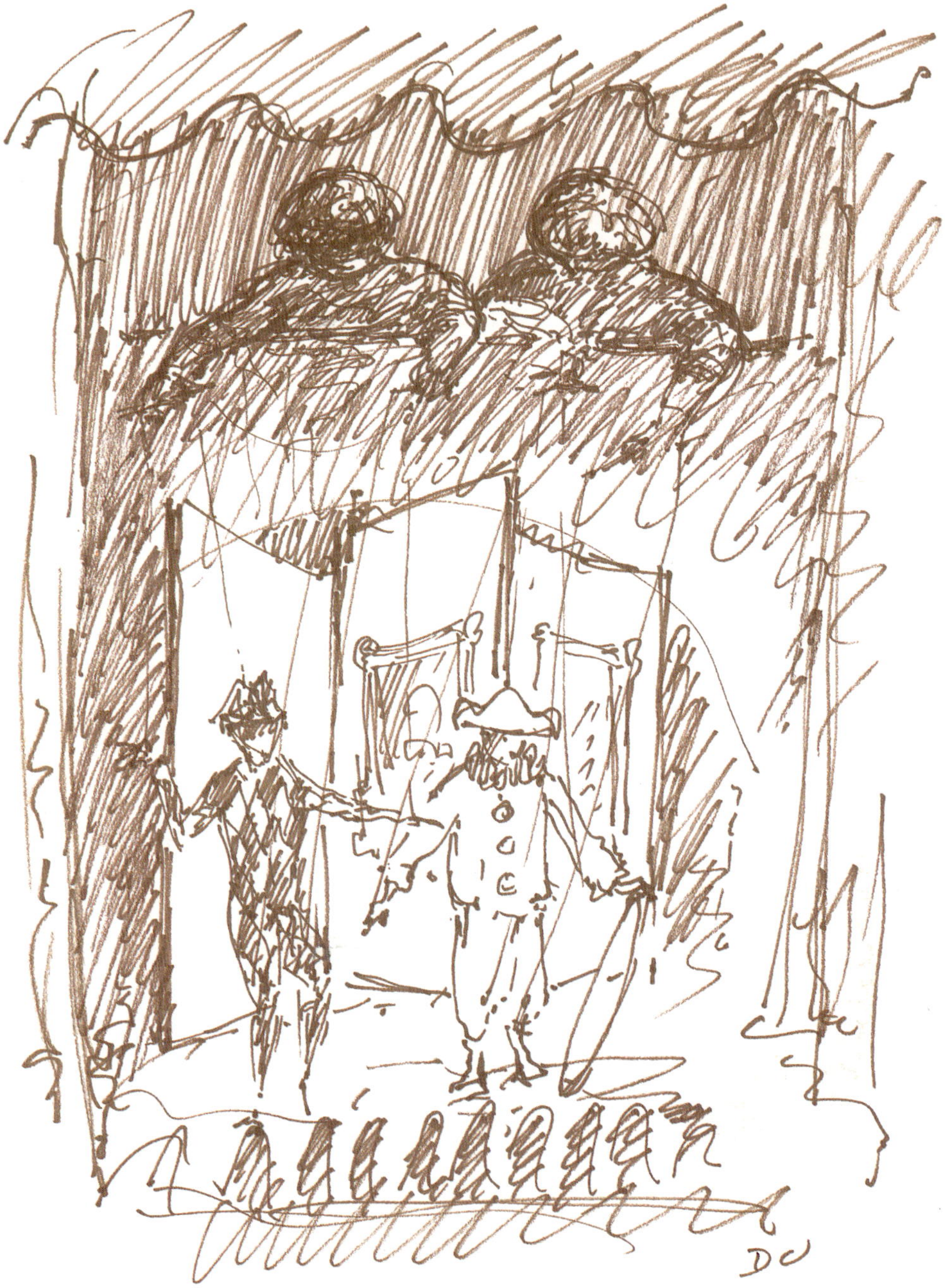

Conclusion

I hope you found in this volume some pleasure. Now that you have browsed through it, may I suggest that you revisit its pages from time to time. Do so to measure any difference in your response. As you study each drawing, you will see it and respond to it in different ways. The spirit of the drawing, as a whole, is most important. The quality of each line and its function are no less so. Give more than a few seconds to each drawing; learn to see, not merely look, and you will find the results rewarding.

These drawings and their resulting paintings are intended to introduce only one phase. They are totally honest, relaxed sketches, capturing fleeting thoughts. They are offered not as masterworks, but for the purpose of introducing you to what I hope will develop your interest to seek out and enjoy the drawings of the many great masters that await your attention.

There is much to be learned from children. The truest freedom of expression. They have no inhibitions or second thoughts to block their way. That is, not until a well-meaning adult rewards them. Once rewarded something begins to be lost. The freedom is compromised to the awards. Few seem able to survive or understand what has happened. This most likely happened to you. With this in mind it is the challenge presented here for you to recapture that freedom lost that offers so much pleasure.

Pick up a pencil, pen, or whatever, give thought of a favorite object or place and draw a line around it.

To hunger for collecting objects without discernment is like being obese—the adventure of taste is lost to the appetite.

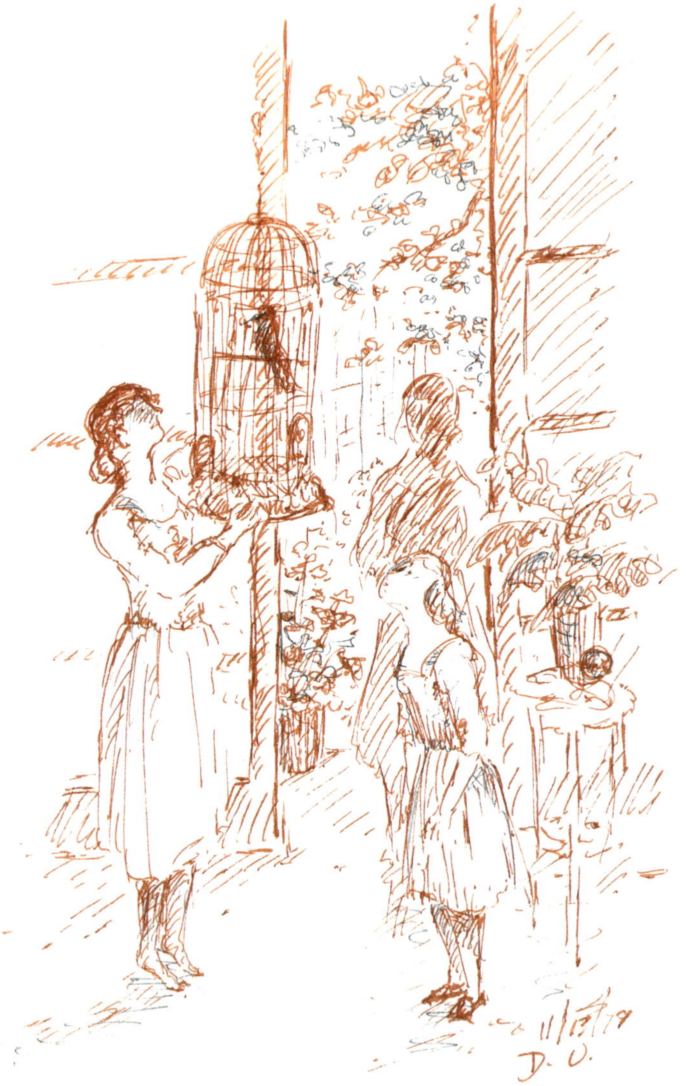

List of Illustrations

Paintings

Drawings

Page	Size in inches	Medium
cover	8 x 11 1/4	sepia on paper
2	10 3/8 x 11	sepia on ragboard
9	7 1/2 x 8 1/4	sepia on ragboard
10	11 7/8 x 13 1/8	sepia on ragboard
12	9 x 10	sepia on ragboard
14	8 1/4 x 9 3/4	sepia on ragboard
15	7 1/4 x 9	sepia on ragboard
17	8 1/4 x 11 1/8	sepia on paper
18	7 5/8 x 7 3/4	sepia on ragboard
19	7 1/2 x 8 1/2	sepia on ragboard
20	8 x 11 1/4	sepia on paper
21	11 1/4 x 8	sepia on paper
22	8 x 11 1/4	sepia on paper
23	11 1/4 x 8	sepia on paper
24	12 x 12	sepia on ragboard
26	9 1/2 x 7 7/8	sepia on ragboard
27	9 7/8 x 5 7/8	sepia on ragboard
28	8 5/8 x 12 1/8	sepia on ragboard
29 (top)	8 x 11 1/4	sepia on paper
29 (bottom)	8 x 11 1/4	sepia on paper
30	11 1/4 x 8	sepia on paper
31	9 1/2 x 10 3/8	sepia on ragboard
33	8 x 11 1/4	sepia on paper
34	10 1/8 x 10	sepia on ragboard
36	8 7/8 x 10	sepia on ragboard
37	9 x 11 7/8	sepia on paper
38	8 x 11 1/4	sepia on paper
39 (top)	7 1/8 x 7 1/4	sepia on ragboard
39 (bottom)	5 3/4 x 6 3/4	sepia on ragboard
40	11 x 8 1/2	sepia on ragboard
41	10 1/2 x 13 7/8	sepia on paper
42	8 x 9 1/2	sepia on paper
45	10 x 12 3/4	sepia on ragboard
47	7 x 8 1/4	sepia on paper
48	8 1/8 x 10	sepia on ragboard
49	8 x 11 1/4	sepia on paper
50	9 x 11 7/8	sepia on paper

Drawings (continued)

Page		Size in inches	Medium
52		$8^3/_4$ x $11^1/_4$	sepia on ragboard
53		$9^3/_4$ x $11^1/_4$	sepia on ragboard
54		8 x $11^1/_4$	sepia on paper
56		$8^7/_8$ x $12^7/_8$	sepia on ragboard
57		9 x $11^7/_8$	sepia on paper
58		8 x $11^1/_4$	sepia on paper
59		8 x $11^1/_4$	sepia on paper
60		$7^3/_4$ x $10^1/_2$	sepia on ragboard
61	(top)	$8^5/_8$ x $10^5/_8$ (verso p. 65)	sepia on ragboard
61	(bottom)	$9^1/_2$ x 13	sepia on ragboard
62		$8^1/_2$ x $11^1/_2$	sepia on ragboard
64		$10^1/_8$ x 12	sepia on ragboard
65		$8^5/_8$ x $10^5/_8$	sepia on ragboard
66		$11^1/_4$ x 8	sepia on paper
67		$9^1/_2$ x $11^3/_4$	sepia on ragboard
68		8 x $11^1/_4$	sepia on paper
69		$8^7/_8$ x $11^3/_8$	sepia on ragboard
70		$8^1/_4$ x 9	sepia on ragboard
71		8 x $11^1/_4$	sepia on paper
72		8 x $11^1/_4$	sepia on paper
74		8 x $11^1/_4$	sepia on paper
75		$9^1/_8$ x $12^1/_2$	sepia on ragboard
76		8 x $11^1/_4$	sepia on paper
78		8 x $11^1/_4$	sepia on paper
79		8 x $11^1/_4$	sepia on paper
81		8 x $11^1/_4$	sepia on paper
82		8 x $11^1/_4$	sepia on paper
84		8 x $11^1/_4$	sepia on paper
86		$8^3/_4$ x $11^5/_8$	sepia on chromecoat
87	(top)	$5^1/_4$ x 5	blue ink on chromecoat
87	(bottom)	$8^3/_4$ x $11^5/_8$	sepia on chromecoat
88		$10^7/_8$ x $10^7/_8$	sepia on ragboard
90	(top)	$10^1/_4$ x $12^7/_8$	sepia on ragboard
90	(bottom)	6 x $8^1/_2$	sepia on ragboard
91		8 x $11^1/_4$	sepia on paper
92		9 x $11^7/_8$	sepia on paper

Drawings (continued)

Page	Size in inches	Medium
94	$8^5/_8$ x 9	sepia on ragboard
95	$9^3/_4$ x $12^5/_8$	sepia on ragboard
97	9 x $8^7/_8$	sepia on ragboard
98	$10^1/_2$ x $13^3/_4$	sepia on paper
99	8 x $11^1/_4$	sepia on paper
100	$11^1/_4$ x 8	sepia on paper
101	8 x $11^1/_4$	sepia on paper
102	$11^1/_4$ x 8	sepia on paper
103	$11^3/_4$ x $11^1/_8$	sepia on ragboard
104	$11^1/_4$ x 8	sepia on paper
105	$11^1/_4$ x 8	sepia on paper
106	9 x $11^7/_8$	sepia on paper
107	$11^1/_4$ x 8	sepia on paper
108	$11^1/_4$ x 8	sepia on paper
109	$10^1/_2$ x $13^7/_8$	sepia on paper
111	8 x $11^1/_4$	sepia on paper
112	8 x $11^1/_4$	sepia on paper
114	$11^1/_4$ x 8	sepia on paper
116	8 x $11^1/_4$	sepia on paper
117	$11^1/_4$ x 8	sepia on paper
118	$11^1/_4$ x 8	sepia on paper
119	$11^1/_4$ x 8	sepia on paper
120	$7^3/_4$ x $9^3/_4$	sepia on ragboard
121 (top)	$7^7/_8$ x $9^3/_4$	sepia on ragboard
	(verso bottom p. 121)	
122	$11^1/_4$ x 8	sepia on paper
124	8 x $11^1/_4$	sepia on paper
125	$11^1/_4$ x 8	sepia on paper
127	8 x $11^1/_4$	sepia on paper
128	8 x $11^1/_4$	sepia on paper
129	$11^1/_4$ x 8	sepia on paper
130	$7^7/_8$ x $9^7/_8$	sepia on ragboard
131	$7^3/_4$ x $9^3/_4$	sepia on ragboard
133	$11^1/_4$ x 8	sepia on paper
134	8 x $11^1/_4$	sepia on paper
137	8 x $11^1/_4$	sepia on paper
138	$9^5/_8$ x 12	sepia on ragboard

Drawings (continued)

Page	Size in inches	Medium
139	$10^7/_8$ x 13	sepia on ragboard
140	$11^1/_4$ x 8	sepia on paper
141	$10^1/_4$ x $13^7/_8$	sepia on paper
142	$11^1/_4$ x 8	sepia on paper
143	$10^1/_8$ x $12^3/_8$	sepia on ragboard
144	$11^1/_4$ x 8	sepia on paper
145	8 x $11^1/_4$	sepia on paper
146	8 x $11^1/_4$	sepia on paper
148	$11^1/_4$ x 8	sepia on paper
149	$11^1/_4$ x 8	sepia on paper
150	10 x $8^3/_4$	sepia on ragboard
152	10 x $11^3/_4$	sepia on ragboard
153 (top)	$9^1/_4$ x $7^7/_8$	sepia on ragboard
153 (bottom)	8 x 11	sepia on ragboard
154	8 x $11^1/_4$	sepia on paper
156	$10^7/_8$ x 12	sepia on ragboard
157	12 x $10^1/_8$	sepia on ragboard
158	$11^1/_4$ x 8	sepia on paper
160	9 x $11^7/_8$	sepia on paper
161	$11^1/_4$ x 8	sepia on paper
162	8 x $11^1/_4$	sepia on paper
165	$7^1/_4$ x $6^3/_4$	sepia on ragboard
166	$11^1/_4$ x 8	black ink on paper
168	$10^1/_8$ x 11	sepia on ragboard
169	$8^1/_8$ x $14^1/_8$	sepia on ragboard
170	$7^1/_2$ x $7^1/_4$	sepia on ragboard
172	$8^5/_8$ x $12^1/_8$	sepia on ragboard
173	$11^7/_8$ x $9^3/_4$	sepia on ragboard
174	$8^5/_8$ x $12^1/_8$	sepia on ragboard
175	$8^1/_8$ x 10	sepia on ragboard
176	$8^3/_8$ x $10^1/_2$	sepia on ragboard
177	$7^3/_4$ x $9^1/_2$	sepia on ragboard
178	$9^3/_4$ x $13^1/_4$	sepia on ragboard
179	$10^1/_8$ x 9	sepia on ragboard
180	$11^1/_2$ x 8	black ink on paper
181	$11^1/_4$ x 8	sepia on paper
182	$8^1/_2$ x $6^1/_2$	sepia on ragboard

Drawings (continued)

Page	Size in inches	Medium
183	11 1/4 x 8	sepia on paper
185	11 1/4 x 8	sepia on paper
186	8 x 11 1/4	sepia on paper
188	8 x 11 1/4	sepia on paper
189	8 7/8 x 9 5/8	sepia on ragboard
192	8 7/8 x 9	sepia on ragboard
193	10 1/2 x 13 7/8	sepia on paper
194	11 1/4 x 8	sepia on paper
197	12 x 12	sepia on ragboard
198	10 x 13 1/8	sepia on ragboard
200 (top)	9 x 14 3/8	sepia on ragboard
200 (bottom)	8 3/8 x 11 1/8	sepia on ragboard
	(verso p. 222)	
201	10 1/8 x 11	sepia on ragboard
202	10 1/8 x 11	sepia on ragboard
205	8 x 11 1/4	sepia on paper
206	11 1/4 x 11 1/2	sepia on ragboard
	(verso top p. 207)	
207 (top)	11 1/4 x 11 1/2	sepia on ragboard
207 (bottom)	7 1/2 x 6 7/8	sepia on ragboard
208	8 1/4 x 10 1/4	sepia on ragboard
209	11 1/4 x 8	sepia on paper
210	10 x 11 1/8	sepia on ragboard
211	11 1/4 x 8	sepia on paper
213	10 1/8 x 11 7/8	sepia on ragboard
214	10 1/8 x 12	sepia on ragboard
216	7 1/2 x 7 1/2	sepia on ragboard
217	10 x 10	sepia on ragboard
218	9 7/8 x 10	sepia on ragboard
219	8 x 10 1/2	sepia on ragboard
220	8 3/4 x 10 1/2	sepia on ragboard
221	9 1/8 x 11 1/8	sepia on ragboard
222	8 3/8 x 11 1/8	sepia on ragboard
223	10 1/8 x 12	sepia on ragboard
224	11 1/4 x 8	sepia on paper
226	8 x 5 1/2	sepia on paper

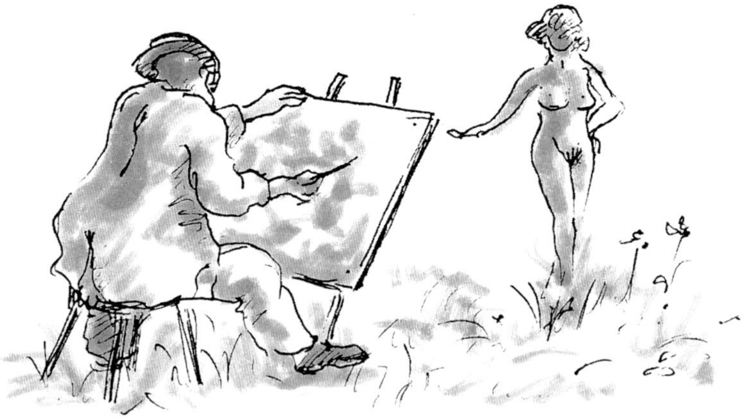

About the Painter - Author - Dealer

Donald Vogel has published several monographs and catalogues and co-authored, with his wife, two books for the Amon Carter Museum. He has also written his memoirs, Images; Charcoal and Cadmium Red, *which contains two short stories; and three mystery adventures:* Not for Revenge, King of the Hill, *and* The Transcendent Collector.

Vogel's painting has been well received. His work has been in many exhibitions and has earned national awards. His paintings now reside in collections in the United States, Canada, Mexico, South Africa, Italy, Germany, England, France and Japan.

He was born in Milwaukee, Wisconsin, in 1917. In 1942, after studying at the Art Institute of Chicago, Vogel moved to Dallas, Texas, where he became technical director for the Dallas Little Theater. He was an active painter at the time as well, exhibiting in museum shows and creating galleries for his work and the work of fellow artists.

Vogel established and built the first gallery of importance in the South and Southwest that dealt with major 20th century art — Valley House Gallery. He soon earned an international reputation as a knowledgeable and honest dealer. He has mounted many great exhibitions, and the gallery has become known to many as a second museum in Dallas.